FOREST COMMUNITY CONNECTIONS

Implications for Research, Management, and Governance

Edited By

ELLEN M. DONOGHUE

AND VICTORIA E. STURTEVANT

RESOURCES FOR THE FUTURE
WASHINGTON, DC, USA

An RFF Press book
Published by Resources for the Future
1616 P Street NW
Washington, DC 20036–1400
USA
www.rffpress.org

Library of Congress Cataloging-in-Publication Data

    Forest Community Connections: Implications for Research, Management, and Governance / edited by Ellen M. Donoghue and Victoria Sturtevant.
      p. cm.
    Includes bibliographical references and index.
    ISBN 978-1-933115-67-2 (pbk. : alk. paper) —
    ISBN 978-1-933115-68-9 (hardcover : alk. paper)
    1. Forest management—United States. 2. Community forestry—United States. 3. Forests and forestry, Cooperative—United States. I. Donoghue, Ellen M. (Ellen Mary) II. Sturtevant, Victoria Elmore, 1950-
    SD565.F539 2008
    333.75'150973—dc22
                                       2007050918

The paper in this book meets the guidelines for permanence and durability of the Committee on Production Guidelines for Book Longevity of the Council on Library Resources. This book was typeset by Andrea Reider. It was copyedited by Patti Miller. The cover was designed by Circle Graphics. Photo Credits: Background photo of the silhouetted sunset and forested ridges, Frank Vanni; man reaching down to harvest/ touch salal plants, Heidi Ballard; man standing next to small diameter log truck, Daniel Len; people standing in a stream, USDA Forest Service.

ISBN 978-1-933115-68-9 (cloth)   ISBN 978-1-933115-67-2 (paper)

About Resources for the Future *and* RFF Press

Resources for the Future (RFF) improves environmental and natural resource policymaking worldwide through independent social science research of the highest caliber. Founded in 1952, RFF pioneered the application of economics as a tool for developing more effective policy about the use and conservation of natural resources. Its scholars continue to employ social science methods to analyze critical issues concerning pollution control, energy policy, land and water use, hazardous waste, climate change, biodiversity, and the environmental challenges of developing countries.

RFF Press supports the mission of RFF by publishing book-length works that present a broad range of approaches to the study of natural resources and the environment. Its authors and editors include RFF staff, researchers from the larger academic and policy communities, and journalists. Audiences for publications by RFF Press include all of the participants in the policymaking process—scholars, the media, advocacy groups, NGOs, professionals in business and government, and the public.

Contents

PART III: COMMUNITIES AND FOREST GOVERNANCE

CONCLUSION

Contributors

Jennifer S. Arnold is a Ph.D. student in the School of Natural Resources and Environment at the University of Florida. Her research focuses on the social aspect of communally managed rangelands and use of participatory research to develop conservation and livelihood strategies that incorporate multicultural perspectives. Her work has been published in *Society and Natural Resources*, as well as other publications within the communities where she works.

Dennis R. Becker is assistant professor of environment and natural resource policy at the University of Minnesota. His research focuses on the evaluation and assessment of natural resource policies, in particular forest biomass utilization, national wildfire planning, and state-level environmental review. His book contributions include *People, Fire, and Forests: A Synthesis of Wildfire Social Science.*

Jill M. Belsky is director of the Bolle Center for People and Forests and professor of rural and environmental sociology at the University of Montana. Her research has focused on a variety of issues related to sustainable livelihoods and community-based forestry in western Montana and internationally, most recently in Bhutan. She has co-authored chapters in *Forest Communities, Community Forests* and *Qualitative Methods in Tourism Research.*

John C. Bliss is professor and Starker Chair in Private and Family Forestry at Oregon State University. His research explores the human and social dimensions of forest management, focusing on family forestry and forest-based rural development. John is co editor in chief of the journal *Small scale Forestry*. He has authored chapters in *Communities and Forests: Where People Meet the Land,*

Compatible Forest Management, and *Introduction to Forest Ecosystem Science and Management.*

Susan Charnley is a research social scientist and team leader in the Human and Natural Resource Interactions Program at the USDA Forest Service, Pacific Northwest Research Station, in Portland, Oregon. Her research focuses on community-based natural resource management, with an emphasis on communities and forest management in the western United States. Her publications have appeared in the journals *Conservation Biology, Forest Ecology and Management, Human Organization,* and the *Annual Review of Anthropology.*

Cecilia Danks is assistant professor at the Rubenstein School of Environment and Natural Resources at the University of Vermont. Her research focuses on public–private collaborations in community-based resource management that bridge sectors and scales to promote social and ecological sustainability. She also has contributed to socioeconomic monitoring, forest certification, and working forest issues. Her work has been published by the United Nations Food and Agricultural Organization, the IUCN, and the Ford Foundation.

Ellen M. Donoghue is a social scientist with the USDA Forest Service, Pacific Northwest Research Station. Her research focuses on the institutional dimensions of community and resource management agency interactions. Recent work includes understanding socioeconomic change in Pacific Northwest communities and the role of traditional ecological knowledge in collaborative resource management. In addition to journal articles and technical reports, she authored a chapter in *Compatible Forest Management.*

Maria E. Fernandez-Gimenez is assistant professor in the Department of Forest, Rangeland, and Watershed Stewardship at Colorado State University. Her research has focused on knowledge integration, ecological stewardship and monitoring, and social capital development in community-based natural resource management. Her work has been published in *Society and Natural Resources, Ecological Applications,* and *Environmental Conservation,* among other journals.

Richard Haynes is a program manager with the USDA Forest Service, Pacific Northwest Research Station, in Portland, Oregon, where he is responsible for social, utilization, and economics research. His own research involves both developing analytical methods for projecting market activity and using those methods in U.S. Forest Service planning and policy analysis. He was responsible for the Resources Planning Act Timber Assessments, serving as technical editor for five assessments.

Eric T. Jones is an environmental anthropologist at the Institute for Culture and Ecology. His research has looked at biodiversity conservation, participatory approaches to biological monitoring, ecosystem restoration of culturally important plant species, mushroom and truffle harvesting, and stewardship attitudes and practices by forest workers. His books include *Nontimber Forest Products in the United States.*

Linda E. Kruger is a social science team leader with the USDA Forest Service, Pacific Northwest Research Station, and affiliate faculty at both the University of Alaska Southeast, and at the Hatfield School of Public Administration, Portland State University. Her research interests include community vulnerability, resilience, and adaptive capacity. She served as a reviewer for *Natural Resources Canada*, the Northern Forestry Centre series of reports on vulnerability assessment of forest-based communities to climate change.

Kathryn A. Lynch is an environmental anthropologist and co-director of the Environmental Leadership Program at the University of Oregon. This interdisciplinary program is based on a service-learning model that engages students and community partners in collaborative learning. Her research has focused on community-based conservation, local knowledge, and biodiversity conservation in Ecuador, Peru, Indonesia, and the United States. Her publications include *Access, Labor, and Wild Floral Greens Management in Western Washington's Forests* and *Nontimber Forest Products and Biodiversity Management in the Pacific Northwest.*

Rhonda Mazza is a science writer and editor with the USDA Forest Service Pacific Northwest Research Station. She writes about research related to natural resource management and social issues related to society's uses of natural resources. Her previous books include *Compatible Forest Management.*

Margaret Ann Moote is coordinator of the social science and community outreach program at the Ecological Restoration Institute at Northern Arizona University. Her research has focused on collaborative forest restoration, multiparty monitoring, and institutional barriers to community-based conservation. She is co-author, with Hanna J. Cortner, of *The Politics of Ecosystem Management.*

Cassandra Moseley is the director of the Ecosystem Workforce Program (EWP) in the Institute for a Sustainable Environment at the University of Oregon. At EWP, she developed applied research and policy education programs, focused on community-based forestry, federal forest management, and the restoration workforce. She is co-editor of *People, Fire, and Forests: A Synthesis of Wildfire Social Science* and is co-author of *Collaborative Environmental Management: What Roles for Government?*

Mark Nechodom is a social scientist with the USDA, Forest Service Pacific Southwest Research Station. He is a visiting scholar and lecturer at the University of California, Davis, where he co-founded the land use and natural resources program. He served as the senior social scientist for the Lake Tahoe Assessment and the Sierra Nevada Framework. His research has focused on the institutional and policy dynamics of environmental decisionmaking and the use of life-cycle analysis in policy development.

Toddi A. Steelman is associate professor of environmental and natural resource policy within the Department of Forestry and Environmental Resources at North Carolina State University. Her research focuses on improving the governance of environmental and natural resources, with an emphasis on science, policy, and decisionmaking interactions. She is the co-author of *Collaborative Environmental Management: What Roles for Government?* and *Adaptive Governance: Integrating Science, Policy and Decision Making*, and numerous journal articles and book chapters.

Maria Stiefel was a science writer and editor with the USDA Forest Service, Pacific Northwest Research Station at the Sitka Wood Utilization Center, Alaska. Maria has a degree in history from the United States Military Academy at West Point and served five years as an active-duty military intelligence officer. She edited multiple reports and journal articles and was working on a national utilization strategy for woody biomass prior to her re-deployment to Iraq with the U.S. military.

Victoria E. Sturtevant is professor of sociology in the Department of Environmental Studies at Southern Oregon University. Her research has focused on forest communities in transition; collaborative stewardship, monitoring, and planning; and the social dimensions of wildfire. Her work has been supported by the Ford Foundation and by federal land management agencies and has been published in government technical reports, *Society and Natural Resources, Journal of Forestry*, and edited books.

Acknowledgments

This book represents a collective effort on the part of many people. We are grateful to our colleagues who gathered for a workshop in March 2005 to discuss the future of forest communities and management: Nils Christoffersen of Wallowa Resources, Lynn Jungwirth of the Watershed Research and Training Center, Tom Beckley of the University of New Brunswick, Margaret Shannon of the University of Vermont, and Penny Falknor, Bill Anthony, Dave Olson and Karin Whitehall of the USDA Forest Service, Region 6, and the chapter authors. The workshop launched two-years of discussions and writing that has culminated in this book. We thank the chapter authors for their commitment and willingness to share their considerable expertise.

Acknowledgments are due to several individuals and organizations. We thank Jamie Barbour of the Focused Science Delivery Program and Richard Haynes of the Human and Natural Resource Interactions Program, both part of USDA Forest Service's Pacific Northwest Research Station, for their intellectual support and funding of the workshop and book production. A host of other federal agencies, universities, and foundations have provided ongoing support for the authors' research. We are in debt to Rhonda Mazza for her outstanding editorial assistance and commitment to the objectives of the book. We appreciate the assistance in proofreading from Laura Beaton and Judy Mikowski. RFF Press made this book a reality. Don Reisman and his anonymous reviewers, provided expertise and criticism which improved the quality of this work.

Our fundamental thanks go to the communities and forest stewards who, over many years have generously shared their lives, ideas, and hopes. Finally and absolutely, we owe gratitude to our husbands, Ed Coulter and Alan Armstrong, for their tireless forbearance and support throughout this endeavor.

Introduction

1

Community and Forest Connections

Continuity and Change

VICTORIA E. STURTEVANT AND ELLEN M. DONOGHUE

In the far northeastern corner of Oregon, Wallowa County's forests, range, and prairie have provided livelihoods and identity for generations of residents. Fifty-eight percent of its 2 million acres are federally managed. When timber sales on the Wallowa-Whitman National Forest plummeted in 1994, all three mills in the county shut down, affecting more than 20% of the workforce (Christofferson 2005). Foreign competition and restructuring of the timber industry, along with continuing forest policy stalemate, kept all but one small, locally owned mill closed. Many young families left the area for jobs elsewhere, and residents who stayed supplemented resource-based incomes with jobs in town. As the traditional economy declined, so did civic capacity. Little League coaches were hard to find. The local hospital nearly went bankrupt as the number of patients who qualified for federal aid increased but federal reimbursements decreased. School enrollment dropped and along with it state funding, requiring the school district to reduce teaching staff and cut back to a four-day week.

Long-time Wallowa residents felt their way of life threatened by outsiders when in the late 1980s and 1990s environmental lawsuits and appeals were filed throughout the region, and the listing of the northern spotted owl and spring Chinook salmon under the Endangered Species Act halted most activity on federal land. In 1994, the Forest Service became the target for residents' fear and despair when three-fourths of the county voted against recognizing federal ownership of public land. The next year, the target shifted when two local environmentalists were hanged in effigy. Meanwhile, the land was showing signs of overuse and neglect—decades of overstory logging and fire suppression had left dense stands of small trees competing for water and nutrients and increasingly susceptible to insects and fire. Gradually, however, the community recognized that there was no going back and that collectively crafting a future was a better option. Potential listing of the endangered salmon runs provided the first opportunity and the Wallowa County/Nez Perce Tribe Salmon Habitat Recovery Plan involved farmers, ranchers, private forest owners, tribal officials, and Forest Service staff. Next came strategic economic development planning. Wallowa Resources was created as a nonprofit organization to build on these two processes and to create restoration-based forestry that could support the natural resource economy. A for-profit business consortium was formed to add value and find markets for the small-diameter logs generated by forest restoration and thinning projects.

Ten years later, Wallowa Resources continues to work with county government, private landowners, public managers, and environmental groups to fill the gaps left by departing industry, diminished public agencies, and divided communities. Early projects engaged citizens in the implementation and monitoring of forest and habitat restoration projects in order to build organizational credibility and train contractors. Its noxious weed eradication program—a collaborative effort with agencies, The Nature Conservancy, and residents and ranchers—monitors various methods of weed control and created an association through which ranchers can sell certified weed-free hay at a premium price. The Upper Joseph Creek Watershed Assessment, completed in 2003, surveyed 174,000 acres of mountainous forest and grasslands across a patchwork of private and federal public lands and became instrumental for Forest Service planners prioritizing projects. A Friday field school for local youth promotes a sense of place and stewardship and a summer field school brings university students to the area. Finally, in June 2004, the Forest Service offered a timber sale that wasn't appealed—the first in nearly a decade.

Nevertheless, larger economic and political forces continue to create challenges for this county 75 miles from the nearest Interstate. Its remote location and the transportation costs of raw materials and finished products are a handicap when competing against larger businesses in nearby counties. Growth in tourism, seasonal residents, and new residents (mostly urban retirees) has spurred the establishment of some new businesses. Enterprise, the county seat (population 2,000), now offers espresso, Mexican food, and micro-brews. Joseph (population 1,000) sports a main street adorned by bronze sculptures from local foundries, along with art galleries and cafes. Along with the place-based communities, Wallowa County consists of communities of interest, such as the Hells Canyon Preservation Council; indigenous communities, such as the Nez Perce tribe; communities of occupation, such as ranchers and artists; and temporal communities, such as oldtimers, newcomers, and visitors. Each contributes to continuity and change in the county, and each brings different understandings and expectations to projects connecting the health of the community to the integrity of the forest.

Wallowa County's story, with locally specific variations, is shared by many forest communities in the United States, especially those in the West surrounded by vast tracts of public land. Social and economic change have made forest communities increasingly difficult to define. They all are connected economically and culturally to forested landscapes, but that is where their similarities end. Timber extraction and dependency, two elements of past definitions (Freudenburg 1992), no longer are universal features. Remoteness, in the past a defining characteristic (England and Brown 2003), no longer applies, as technology and workforce mobility connect rural to urban places. Finally, forest communities no longer necessarily are small (Danks 2003), as timber mills increasingly are concentrated in county seats and cities located along major transportation corridors. The ability of communities to respond to change depends partly on the social, cultural, and economic conditions within the community and region. Some, like Wallowa County, draw on community resources to maintain traditional livelihoods while transitioning to tourism and forest amenity-based businesses. Communities with other natural resources may experience booms in employment from construction or oil and gas exploration. Communities with fewer natural amenities and low capacity to attract and retain businesses watch their young adults leave, taking with them a vital workforce and ties to family and community. Although each forest community has its own social and ecological context, interwoven through them all are the global and national forces of change and the degradation of ecosystems from intensive management, wildfire, invasive species, global warming, or flooding.

This book is about these changing forest communities: their response to altered forest policy and industries, their role in managing and restoring forests, and their engagement in new forms of forest governance. Communities' connections to forests are not simple and static but complex and evolving, presenting challenges to forest managers, communities, and researchers. The chapters in this book examine the factors that contribute to strong and resilient connections and those that undermine them; chapter authors explore a range of management issues, types of forest communities, and forest governance structures. This book also examines the still-developing science of forest communities: our ways of understanding and working with communities, our role in facilitating social learning and policymaking, and our contributions to community well-being and participation in forest management.

Social Forces of Change

Global timber markets and technology, sociodemographic transitions, shifting environmental values, and changing forest policy have transformed the nature of communities and their connections to forests. This introductory chapter describes these external forces, how they have changed the social dynamics of forest communities, and how these communities have forged new connections to one another and to their forests.

New Economies

For many generations the culture and economy of forest communities revolved around the timber industry, which offered prosperity in boom periods but poverty and unemployment during busts. Increasingly centralized and mobile capital has created a wood-products industry in which only companies able to respond to national and global trends survive. Jobs move to regions with available timber, capital moves to markets with the highest return, and machines replace people in both the woods and mills. Globalization has altered significantly the socioeconomic context for growing and manufacturing wood products. Companies recently have moved operations to temperate and subtropical regions of the Southern Hemisphere, where productive fiber farms—intensively cultivated, short-rotation tree plantations—and other advantages, such as more favorable tax and environmental regulations, provide a competitive edge (World Forestry Institute 2004). The low value of standing timber and the cost of forest restoration have driven timber companies to divest their U.S. holdings to real estate developers or Timber Investment Management Organizations (TIMOs) with short-term financial goals. For example, from 2002 to 2004, the Weyerhaeuser Company sold 250,000 acres of timberland in the Pacific Northwest, 174,000 acres in Tennessee, and 170,000 acres in the Carolinas. During this same period, Weyerhaeuser invested $1 billion in Uruguay to create pine and eucalyptus plantations and processing plants (Franklin and Johnson 2004). As forest industries disinvest from regions, timber on local, private forestlands loses its economic value, mills, and markets. Small, private forest landowners struggle to retain their land in the face of tax burdens, fragmentation among heirs, and competing land uses, such as residential development (Best and Wayburn 2001).

Forest policy also affects forest community economies, especially in the West. During the period 1987 to 2000, harvests on national forest land throughout the country fell from more than 12 billion board feet to 3.5 billion board feet (Arabas and Bowersox 2004). In the Forest Service's, U.S. Department of Agriculture, Region 6 in Oregon and Washington during that same period, the drop was even more precipitous, from 6 billion board feet to .5 billion board feet. During this period, 40% of mills closed and forest-related employment declined from 135,000 to 105,000 (Warren 1998). This downturn in employment had begun earlier in the decade due to restructuring and mechanization of the timber industry; one prediction estimated that even if timber production increased by 55% over the next 50 years, employment still would drop by 27% (GAO 1990).

Such changes are reflected in Figure 1-1, which shows that U.S. production of timber products largely has flattened out even though consumption is increasing. Case goods, such as furniture, that were a mainstay for some com-

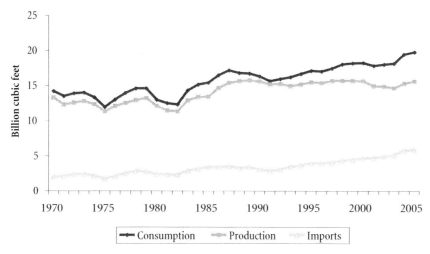

Figure 1-1. Trend in U.S. Timber Production, Consumption, and Imports, 1970–2005

munities in North Carolina, for example, are being replaced by imports from China and elsewhere. In the Pacific Northwest region, lumber production has stayed high, but the industry has shifted away from log exports and plywood production. New and expanded mills producing softwood and commodity-grade lumber are located along major transportation corridors, bypassing many forest communities.

Always a somewhat mobile work force, woods workers (e.g., loggers, tree planters, and harvesters of products such as mushrooms and decorative greens for floral arrangements) now travel long distances. Those who have lost their jobs in the woods or mills are difficult to track. For instance, qualitative studies of woods workers in northeastern California (Kusel et al. 2000) and Idaho (Carroll et al. 2000) found that most workers stay in their communities but retire or go to work for small logging outfits owned by independent contractors that offer irregular work, lower wages, and no benefits. A quantitative study in Oregon (Helvoigt et al. 2003) following a larger cohort of workers for a longer period (1988 to 1998) found that 42% stayed in the industry and had slightly higher wages, although not equal to the gains of other workers in the state; those who left the industry and community to work in the service, trade, or construction sectors lost earning power. This study used state records of those covered by unemployment insurance, and it is likely that the 28% no longer in that database still are working in the timber industry but irregularly.

The ability of forest communities to attract and sustain new economies—such as service, value-added manufacturing, and knowledge-based industries—depends upon access to aesthetic amenities, transportation, and communication. New residents drawn to forest communities' clean air and water, scenery, and recreational opportunities provide economic growth opportunities, new tax bases, and demand for services. Amenity-based population growth fuels economic development with new homes and businesses; real estate development can create, at least in the short run, more capital than wood products, as property values for developed land increase sharply, especially in proximity to metropolitan areas. For many families, the mailbox becomes a local source of income, as investment income, retirement benefits, or government payments increasingly account for much of the economy in many forest communities (Rasker 2001).

Research shows that inequality has risen in many of these communities. Between 1990 and 2000, among the 1,314 communities in the Northwest Forest Plan region of the Pacific Northwest, there was a statistically significant increase in income inequality for the 750 communities located within five miles of Forest Service and Bureau of Land Management lands (forest communities), but no significant change in income inequality for the 564 communities farther away (Donoghue and Sutton 2006). And, for both years, income inequality was statistically higher in the forest communities. On a smaller scale, a study found that in the Applegate Valley in Oregon (70% of which is managed by the federal government), the number of people living in mobile homes and in poverty was higher than in the surrounding, more urban areas, as was the number of people living in high-priced homes and with higher incomes for the period between 1980 and the early 1990s (Reid and Mattson 1993).

Other natural resource industries, such as ranching, mining, and fishing, add to the extractive economy of many forest communities but global competition, resource depletion, and new regulations endanger these industries. Isolated communities, in terms of geography or transportation, are the most dependent on natural resources with fewer opportunities for economic diversity or workforce training. Some leaders in these communities have sought other economic development options, such as prisons and natural gas exploration, while others lobby for a return to past levels of harvest in local national forests. Areas with depressed economies and low housing costs have become migration destinations for middle-income retirees and low-income people, causing increased social service needs and poverty in the community (Fitchen 1995; Charnley and Donoghue 2006).

Sociodemographic Trends

The rural population in most forested regions has grown rapidly; how people live on the land has changed as well. During the last three decades in nonmetropolitan areas, counties with more than 10% of their land in national forests grew significantly more than other counties: 19% between 1990 and 2000, mostly from net inmigration, compared to 13% for the nation as a whole (Johnson and Stewart 2007). Two land-use trends—the spread of urban and suburban places into forestlands (e.g., around Seattle, Denver, and Atlanta) and dispersed residential development in the hinterlands—present new issues for both communities and forests. Exurbanites began moving to rural areas during the back-to-land movement in the 1970s, but the pace and effect of migration on land use and communities have increased as self-employed professionals are able to maintain their urban connections with communication technology and improved transportation infrastructure. Baby boomers live and work year-round in lakeside cabins in the Midwest and mountain resorts in the West, African Americans are leaving northern cities to return to family forestland in the Black Belt of the South, and retirees are moving into forested hills outside of cities in the Southwest.

Urban flight and suburban sprawl have created an interface where new development encroaches on open spaces and forests—the wildland-urban interface (WUI). Some WUI areas occur where small towns or suburbia collide with forested or wild areas; some are more intermixed, with residences tucked into the forests on subdivided timber or ranch land. The WUI grew by 8.4 million homes during the 1990s, more than 60% of all new home construction during this period (USDA Forest Service 2007a,b.). These incursions create challenges for the management of both private and public forestlands and undermine the long-term integrity of the forest as large land holdings are fragmented and ownership changes frequently. Beginning in the 1990s, conversion of private forestland to development reached one million acres per year, a trend expected to continue (Stein et al. 2005). The East, which contains a higher proportion of private land, accounts for most of these acres; however, the private forests of the West, which often serve as a buffer between public lands and urban areas, are being diminished at a similar rate.

Another demographic trend is the increased immigration of Latinos and Asians to rural areas. New immigrants increasingly dominate the labor-intensive and skilled forest workforce: planting, thinning, and fire fighting. Other ethnic minorities, including Cambodians and Laotians, harvest nontimber forest products for commercial buyers or for cultural use. These "mobile" or "contingent" workers often are temporary employees of contractors, hired when needed and for whatever skills are in demand. They move with the seasonal work, but many are settled with their families in forest communities or nearby cities and some have become contractors themselves (Sarathy 2006). Racism and anti-immigration sentiment expressed in rural communities is fueled in part by fear that the growing underclass of migrant forestry workers will depress wages for long-term residents (Melton et al. 2007). Depending on the region, there can be social friction with other minority groups as well, such as Native Americans and African Americans, who have deep cultural links to tribal, family, or public forests.

These sociodemographic trends—growing population, expanding WUI, and increasing inmigration of exurbanites and ethnic minorities—create challenges not only for forest managers but for forest communities. Forest community residents integrate more with the urban economy as exurbanites maintain their previous connections and displaced natural-resource workers commute to jobs in urban places. Forestlands subdivided into gated communities provide havens for urban refugees and retirees but create new subcultures and undermine community cohesiveness (Krannich et al. 2006). As rural communities grow, new residents often are in the vanguard of local anti-growth politics, supporting zoning and protecting open space, including public forests. They give voice to some long-time residents' concerns regarding industrial-style forest management (Fortmann and Kusel 1990) but also "fence" private land, denying access for hunting, fishing, and gathering in areas that many residents and their families had considered community space (Brown 1995).

Increasing Environmentalism

Post-World War II economic growth and urbanization altered the lifestyles and values of much of the population and led to the "greening" of America. Increased affluence, cars, and highways took city dwellers to the nation's forests for fun and relaxation: camping, hiking, and skiing and, sometimes, the more traditional rural recreational pursuits of sport fishing and hunting. National forests, a primary source of non-consumptive, aesthetic, and recreational resources (Yaffee 1994), were showing the effects of decades of commodity-based resource production. Nationwide awareness and support for the protection of forest ecosystems grew with the political maturity of the environmental movement, whose media campaigns and organizational networks created citizen awareness and avenues for public involvement in forest planning. Modern environmentalism, built on a legacy begun in the late nineteenth century, emerged as a protest movement in the 1960s, matured into an institutionalized fixture in Washington, DC, in the 1970s and 1980s, and spread to watershed protection and other local groups in the 1990s.

   Environmental organizations offer a range of collective values concerning forest resources and ways of expressing them. Traditional conservation organizations such as the American Forestry Association (founded in 1875) sponsor the National Arbor Day Foundation and publish *American Forests*. The Sierra Club—founded in 1882 to "explore, enjoy, and preserve the Sierra Nevada and other scenic resources of the United States"—now boasts a membership of 1.3 million and describes itself as "the nation's leader in grassroots environmental litigation (Sierra Club 2007). More radical protest organizations such as Earth First!—founded in 1981 and known for "eco-sabotage" such as spiking old-growth trees—affirm the interconnection of all life and members' spiritual oneness with nature (Brulle 1996). The diversity of these organizations, their extensive networks, and variety of discourses have mobilized a broad public to challenge federal (and sometimes private) forest management policies and to press for new ones. Environmental groups have played a major role in the passage of significant legislation, particularly the Wilderness Act of 1964, the National Environmental Protection Act of 1969 (NEPA), and the Endangered Species Act of 1973. The last two mandated scientific analysis of environmental effects of planned action and public involvement and review. As scientific assessment took a central role in political debates and natural resource planning, traditional disciplines such as biology, geology, and chemistry were joined by new interdisciplinary fields such as landscape ecology and conservation biology that could address ecological systems at larger scales of analysis.

Forest Policy and Management

The Forest Service was created during the Progressive Era at the turn of the twentieth century to address concerns similar to those that drove the environmental movement of the 1960s and 1970s: economic change and crises, demographic growth and diversity, concern over resource destruction, and the call for a conservation strategy. The agency was established to protect forest lands through a system of reserves and regulations enforced by a bureaucracy of professionals and technically trained experts in silviculture. The first chief, Gifford Pinchot, managed according to the utilitarian philosophy he defined as "the greatest good, to the greatest number, for the longest time" (Pinchot 1947, 48). Scientific autonomy and expertise were intended to remove federal forest management from the political arena; the public interest was to be identified by expert calculation of material benefits and resource sustainability, not through public discourse (Cortner and Moote 1999). Efficiency, rationality, and sustainability—central tenets of Progressive Era forestry—are discernible in current federal land-management goals and strategies; however, public interests have shifted over the century and reshaped successive federal policy initiatives.

Stable Communities

After the Great Depression in the 1930s and continuing through the 1980s, forest management responded to the social goals of security and stability; a stable timber industry would lead to more livable and secure forest communities. Strategies such as "development sales," which entailed long-term contracts, and "sustained yield units," which directed timber from federal lands to local mills, were designed to encourage commitment to local communities, industry, and workers. Although mixed in their success, these efforts to link sustained yield and stable communities were seen as representing a "social contract" between the federal government and rural communities. For instance, the 1944 Sustained Yield Act was to "promote the stability of forest industries, of employment, of communities and of taxable forest wealth through continuous supplies of timber … for the purpose of maintaining the stability of such community or communities" (58 Stat. 132). The Forest Service would provide community stability by providing a predictable timber flow off federal land to stabilize the market; forest communities would provide a steady workforce and contribute wood products to build the country.

This perception of obligation to "dependent communities" was used by timber interests, their lobbyists, and sympathetic state and federal elected officials to justify unprecedented levels of harvesting after World War II. Not all agreed; some local communities and agency staff raised concerns about the effects of forest practices on valued species, habitat, and future employment, not only in the timber industry but also in recreation-based businesses such as wilderness and fishing guides. At the national level, growing demands for a diversity of forest uses and increasing skepticism concerning "sustainable management" forced a shift in policy.

Multiple Use

The Multiple-Use Sustained-Yield Act of 1960 directed that national forests be "administered for outdoor recreation, range, timber, watershed, and wildlife and fish purposes" and also the "establishment and maintenance of areas of wilderness." The act broadened the definition of sustained yield to include all renewable resources on national forestlands and dropped language linking sustained yield with community stability. Instead, resource productivity and market conditions would drive management and resources would be managed "so that they are utilized in the combination that will best meet the needs of the American people … without impairment of the productivity of the land" (P. L. 86-517, 16 USCS § 528-531). Although the goal was to provide land managers with mechanisms to resolve political disputes among competing user groups, the act lacked clarity and exacerbated the conflict among groups by pitting users against one another in a zero-sum battle (Cawley and Freemuth 1997). Forest managers frequently were put in the middle of this conflict, taking the role of "neutral arbiters" among interest groups and gauging their success at negotiating compromises by the range of discontents.

While user groups, including recreationalists, competed over access to valued resources and places, environmental groups protested the effects of intensified silvicultural practices and increased timber harvesting on public land. Congress responded with the Forest and Rangeland Renewable Resources Planning Act of 1974, which required management planning based on assessment of all renewable resources and appropriated funding for reforestation and other nonharvest treatments. This act was amended in 1976 by the National Forest Management Act for the Forest Service and the Federal Land Policy and Management Act for the Bureau of Land Management. These statutes directed the agencies to employ a sustained-yield, multiple-use approach to management; planning and decisionmaking were to be accountable, responsive, and predictable.

These acts, along with NEPA, broke apart the "iron triangle" of federal agencies, the timber industry, and congressional supporters by mandating public involvement in forest management planning and inviting outside scientific advice on assessments. Forestry no longer was the exclusive domain of scientifically trained professional foresters: wildlife biologists, fisheries biologists, soil scientists, geologists, and botanists were added to agency staff to complete ecological assessments. These agency "ologists," as well as interest-group scientists, brought new language and frameworks to the public debate over multiple use. Their data questioned the sustainability of timber flows off public lands and supported those who asserted that biological diversity and recreational values were being eclipsed by timber-production values.

The environmental legislation of the 1960s and 1970s expanded the ability of citizens and advocacy groups to use the judicial system as a tool for influencing federal agency decisions. By the 1980s, the Forest Service found most of its important decisions litigated in the federal courts (Keele et al. 2006) and the number of injunctions, protests, and appeals grew dramatically as controversies over national forests intensified between 1980 and 1992. For instance, the number of timber sales under review grew from 130 in 1991 (with 81 stayed, or prevented from moving forward) to 1,626 in 1992 (with 107 stayed) (Floyd 2004). A large majority of appeals were filed by environmental groups and individuals with environmental concerns; often the appellants lived some distance from where the projects were planned.

Critics of judicial challenges argue that they hinder land management decisionmaking processes; for instance, a Forest Service publication states that court decisions constrained professional expertise, effectiveness, and efficiency (USDA Forest Service 2002). Yet one Forest Service scientist argued that judiciary decisions filled the void created by a lack of legislative response to political and social gridlock (Swanson 2004); others, especially environmentalists, saw appeals and litigation as important tools for forcing agency accountability and catalyzing change (Vaughn and Cortner 2004). Forest community groups felt that battles in court moved decisionmaking too far from federal agency managers and scientists, with too little understanding of the effects of litigation on communities and the land (Cromley 2005).

Ecosystem Management and Healthy Forests

Debates over the future of forests reached a fevered pitch in the 1980s. In the Pacific Northwest, "old growth" forest became an environmental touchstone and its icon, the northern spotted owl (*Strix occidentalis caurina*), was federally listed as threatened in 1990. All over the country, the Endangered Species Act of 1973 ushered in a new era of protection of forest ecosystems

and management for species habitat. Multi-use, commodity-based management was replaced by ecosystem management, a new paradigm for forest management formulated by federal and state agencies and scientists and championed
by the Clinton administration.

Ecosystem management shifts protection of particular species to conservation of biological diversity in an entire watershed or forest ecosystem. It focuses
on multiple spatial scales and ownerships and requires integrated, landscape-
scale planning; it also considers site-specific management and the socioeconomic need for natural resource commodities. Adaptive management, an
iterative process of systematically varying forest management approaches, monitoring alternative outcomes, and adjusting course, is championed as a way to
address the complexity of ecosystems, learn from experiments and surprises,
and incorporate local knowledge and perspectives. Despite broad interest
in these new approaches, agencies and interest groups are unclear about the
implications for forest management, forest communities, and increasing consumer demand for timber. Much has been written about the promise of the
integrated, scientific approaches of ecosystem management and adaptive management; however, the same authors voice concern regarding unresolved para-
doxes, competing goals, and institutional barriers (Cortner and Moote 1999;
Stankey et al. 2003).

In the 2000s, a new political administration swung the pendulum of environmental and forest policy. In 2003, Congress passed the Healthy Forest
Restoration Act (HFRA) to legislate President Bush's Healthy Forests Initiative,
a response to a season of catastrophic wildfires in the West. This legislation further codified the goals of the National Fire Plan crafted in collaboration with
the Western Governors' Association, underscoring opportunities for local
collaborative planning and implementation of wildfire fuel-reduction projects.
Thinning forests densely stocked with small and dying trees would protect forest communities from the risk of unnaturally severe wildfires, insect outbreaks,
and disease, as well as provide jobs. In order to expedite hazardous fuels reduction, HFRA's regulatory reforms limited the use of environmental analysis,
administrative appeals, and litigation for designated WUI projects, striking at
the heart of mechanisms that had been effectively used by citizens and environmental groups for forest protection (Vaughn and Cortner 2004). Although
they acknowledge the importance of thinning in the interface, many environmentalists worry that the threat of wildfire is being used as an opportunity to
reframe forest policy and erode hard-earned regulatory safeguards.

Reduction in hazardous fuels and wildfire suppression have become federal
forest-management priorities. Fire suppression now accounts for 45% of Forest Service funding, up from 13% in the 1990s (McCarthy and Jenkins 2007).
Currently, 75% to 80% of timber leaving national forest lands comes from fuels
reduction, habitat improvement, and ecological restoration projects (Timko,
cited by Bosworth and Brown 2007). Forest restoration projects—including not

only thinning, prescribed burning, and revegetation, but a host of activities to restore habitat, reduce invasive species, restore recreation damage, and return stand structure, prairies, and savannas—are recognized as necessary to address degraded ecosystems, but they lack a powerful, well-organized constituency like that of the timber industry. Local-level constituencies for fuels treatment and restoration are emerging, however, as new forest community residents recognize their wildfire risk and woods workers seek new employment opportunities.

Sustainability, albeit without clear policy definitions and directives, continues to be a strong guiding principle of federal land management. Currently, the Forest Service participates in the Montreal Process, an international effort of 12 member countries that emerged from the 1992 Earth Summit. The goal is a common set of criteria and indicators for sustainable forest management to be applied at the national level to all forests of a country, across all types of land ownership. By endorsing these criteria and indicators, each participating country articulates a commitment to work toward sustainable management of its forests. Since 1994, the Forest Service partnered with forest community groups to advance understanding of how national, regional, and local efforts to develop sustainability criteria and indicators can be linked (Leahy and Gray 2004).

Forest Communities: Change, Endurance, Conflict, and Collaboration

Forest community transformations are driven by many "engines of social change" (Force et al. 2000), as the external social forces discussed above interact with local historical events, cultural legacies, political infrastructures, and social assets. Forest communities' dynamic social systems mediate these external forces and through social interaction create the meaning of community and place (Kaufman 1959; Wilkinson 1991). Webs of social relationships take shape around shared interests and common goals; increasingly, these social networks extend beyond forest communities, which are nested in larger ecological and social systems (Beckley 1998).

Shared interests do not depend on a shared place; communities of interest form around common beliefs or goals. For example, a multi-ethnic community of mushroom harvesters comes together from different localities for the harvest and joins advocacy groups, such as the Jefferson Center and Alliance of Forest Workers and Harvesters, to share harvest techniques, protect a common resource, and to negotiate with buyers. The distinction between community of interest and community of place—sometimes framed as "politics of interest" versus "politics of place"—has been used by forest managers and some community members to differentiate rights of access to natural resources. Yet, there are no entitlements attached to place; for instance, partial-year residents or frequent visitors hold attachment to place. In turn, some forest community residents are members of national communities of interest, such as the Wilderness Society and the Communities Committee. Communities of interest increasingly are important players in and beyond communities of place and can cooperate or compete in terms of strategies and goals regarding forest management. This book discusses forest communities of both place and interest, sometimes distinct, but often interwoven.

Change and Continuity

In forest communities, statues of lumberjacks and loggers as high school mascots still symbolize the connection between community identity and forests—an identity that roots long-time residents through good economic times and bad. But much has changed in these communities. Although the statues still stand, few mills remain and district ranger offices have been consolidated. Federal forest managers are less likely to have personal relationships with resource users; fewer participate in civic life. Local residents are more guarded in how they speak about forest resource use; loggers no longer proudly display symbols of their occupation.

In the West, traditional resource users, such as loggers, felt their way of life and community identity threatened by changes in federal forest policies that they believed privileged environmentalism. Some who felt powerless and alienated from federal forest managers found solidarity with the "Wise Use" movement, founded in 1988 to protect resource economies, assert private property rights, and fight the "locking up" of the forests. Local Wise Users resisted government regulations such as road closures with mounted posses. As in earlier sagebrush rebellions, dozens of "county supremacy" ordinances declared federal agency management of federal lands illegal and claimed the right to appropriate federal land. As a grassroots movement, Wise Use offered a voice for local community members who felt that their economic rights were being ignored and that their personal relations with federal agencies had been replaced by complex and bureaucratic processes. Bumper stickers asking "Are you an environmentalist or do you work for a living" spoke their frustration.

Wise Use was relatively short-lived as new residents and economic opportunities muted collective frustration and hostility toward government regulation; nevertheless, the social cleavages in rural timber and ranching communities had been exposed. Economic and cultural displacement of neighbors threatened not only the community, but the pastoral landscape, as landholders "cashed out" to real estate development. Some blamed the displacement on corporate timber practices and abandonment; others pointed to the political stalemate paralyzing public-resource management and reducing the authority of local land managers and the people most dependent on local forests.

By the late 1980s and 1990s, it became apparent to residents of communities in the West that adversarial advocacy tactics and more generalized conflict, simplified as "jobs vs. trees," were taking their toll on both the community and the forests. Leaders stepped up to call for a revitalized civic responsibility that embraced the broader community and their shared attachment to place. In Willapa Bay, Washington, leadership came from the timber industry, a minister, and a tribal leader; in Quincy, California, an unlikely combination included a county commissioner, a lawyer, and an environmental activist. They pulled together groups of residents who recognized that they were part of both the problem and the solution, such as those who joined together as the Applegate Partnership in Oregon and sported "No they" buttons. Seeking out former adversaries, including federal agency employees, residents in these communities worked to put aside differences and pool resources and knowledge for the sake of the community and forests. They drew on stocks of social capital—networks of mutual obligation and willingness to participate in community-wide efforts. They also found in their communities abundant human capital—training and experience in group dynamics, planning, and forestry. They created ad hoc groups, such as partnerships, bio-regional groups, and watershed councils. They found common ground in their desire to address the forest-policy gridlock and their recognition that the skills, expertise, and wisdom of local cultures remain critical assets for forest health and economic viability.

These partnerships, often called collaborative stewardship groups, have networked and grown across the landscape, primarily in western public-lands regions, but also in southern and northern communities with natural resource and land retention concerns. Some of these grassroots groups matured to community-based forestry organizations that collaborate regionally and nationally, participating in events such as Rural Voices for Conservation Coalition policy meetings and the National Network of Forest Practitioners' Week in Washington, DC. Other networks, such as the Forest Stewardship Council and Healthy Forests, Healthy Communities, which monitor third-party certification of sustainable forest practices and market sustainably produced wood products, are redefining valuation to reflect new forest principles.

Ethnically diverse and mobile forest workers and nontimber forest-product gatherers are creating parallel membership-based groups, sometimes networking with the community-based collaboratives. Peer-educational activities and multicultural, multilingual meetings to address diverse working peoples' concerns are organized by groups such as the Alliance of Forest Workers and Harvesters and the Jefferson Center in the Pacific Northwest. These organizations sponsor workforce assessments, testify to Congress, and lobby for changes in federal contracting and best-value mechanisms. They create community by identifying common threads through what might look like disparate interests. For example, herbicide spraying affects nontimber forest-product harvesters, basket makers, and the sprayers themselves. They share the tenet that the exploitation of workers and the exploitation of land are related and must be addressed together.

Decades of experimentation with community forestry in developing countries offer lessons on local empowerment, cultivation of local knowledge, equity, and new institutional arrangements for democratic decisionmaking. Some of this has informed approaches to community-based forestry in the United States that strive to integrate forest sustainability with community development. These new organizations and partnerships intend to represent communities but also work as intermediaries to access resources, information, and policymakers beyond communities. They seek the support of local and national environmental interests by deliberately supporting national environmental laws and engaging in multiparty monitoring. This model of collaborative stewardship, especially on federal lands, has not been fully embraced, however, either within or beyond communities. Federal policies encouraging collaborative stewardship still are finding their way to the ground and require new institutional arrangements and champions to build confidence and trust. It is not clear how enduring these new groups will be, given their sometimes precarious leadership and asset base, or whether they will serve as models for other communities, especially those struggling with multiple social and environmental issues.

One thing is clear: "Natural resource management that is linearly planned, externally controlled, and focused on a single interest is widely considered ineffective" (Guijt 2007, 3). Forest communities need the opportunity to act cohesively and coherently, to participate in decisions that directly affect them, and to engage in restoring the forests to which they are connected. As social scientists seeking to elucidate the consequences of the shift from single-interest-based forest management and external control of forest communities to collaborative stewardship and ecosystem management, we pose questions for exploration and identify methods of inquiry, many of which serve as the foci of the following chapters.

Forest Community Research

Just as the connections between forest and community have evolved, so has research about them. Tonnies' typology of *gemeinschaft* (community) and *gesellschaft* (society) (1887, 1957) often has been cited by social scientists mourning the "world lost"—homogeneous, cohesive rural communities rooted in place, shared past, and mutual obligation. Contemporary scholars understand that the typology of community and society (also known as the rural-urban continuum) no longer is appropriate for rural communities embedded in urban society. Nevertheless, those interested in resource sustainability are drawn to forest communities' connections to place and their ability to create local norms and decisionmaking processes that counter individualist, materialist market structures, and bureaucracies (Agrawal and Gibson 2001). Some scholars focus on the role of community as providing mediating institutions, defined by some as "social moorings that stand between the individual and the abstract institutions of the state and multinational corporations" (Lee and Field 2005, 2). Communities also mediate between society and forests. In the past, they have provided the practical knowledge, workforce, and infrastructure needed for managing and conserving forest ecosystems; social scientists study potential roles for the future.

Social science long has sought to understand the consequences of changes in timber economies and forest policy on individual access to and benefit from forest lands—how they contribute to the quality of life of families and the well-being of forest communities. Research builds on the legacy established by the Kaufmans' 1946 documentation of a forest town in transition, tracing the social effects of booms and busts in the industry and critically evaluating the link between timber output and community well-being (Kaufman and Kaufman 1946). Researchers differ in their definitions, methods, and findings about forest community transitions, but most agree that quality of life and social capital are important to consider but difficult to measure.

Researchers have assessed the changes in natural resource-based communities brought by changing policies and markets, focusing on poverty, disaffection, and social dislocation. Others highlight the innovative institutional arrangements and wealth of new assets brought by the increased connection of rural communities to urban society. Although the focus of much research is the individual worker, researchers continue to work at understanding emergent community dynamics and transitions. Some researchers depend on attitude surveys, others use secondary socioeconomic and demographic data at various levels of analysis, and still others interview or participate in daily life to discover informants' understandings. Although a theoretical perspective or research question can dictate methodology, many scientists attempt an integrative, multi-method approach.

Developing consensus among scientists, as well as with communities and other interested parties, about definitions and indicators of community and forest sustainability is one way to resolve differences in findings and implications. Another is to integrate multiple ways of knowing, including community-based or participatory research methods. Research on forest communities is important for those who act upon communities—including policymakers, nonprofit, and for-profit organizations—and also for those who act in communities. Social scientists study, and sometimes contribute to, community-based inquiry regarding local socioeconomic and ecological systems. They are interested in how the research process builds bridges among stakeholders and local organizations and institutions and how the outcomes integrate local and scientific knowledge and enhance forest stewardship and forest planning. Community outreach and educational workshops in forest restoration and wildfire mitigation are means of diffusing innovation and social acceptance of forest management, two areas of social science interest and applied research.

Social scientists are interested in power: how it is distributed within communities and how communities are embedded in dynamic hierarchies of power. Power arrangements inevitably determine the signature that our culture writes upon our landscapes. Social science studies how institutional arrangements and governance processes—land tenure, timber markets and federal agencies, and sovereign relations—determine access to forest assets and provide legitimacy to cultural practices and knowledge. Social science seeks to document the contribution of economic and cultural diversity to community and ecosystem resilience and the barriers to expression of diversity when the lack of power mutes groups. Finally, power differences within the institutions of both scientists and forest managers influence which methods or perspectives are used in problem framing and solution building. Social scientists increasingly have been interested in the role of institutions for power concentration and devolution—how bureaucratic policies and capacities structure, discourage, or invite participation in forest management.

What's Next?

The following chapters address specific connections among social forces, forest policy, forest communities, and forest ecosystems. They explore how social science is being used to define and assess community–forest relationships, how forest management issues shape communities and home communities, in turn, affect forest management, and how community access to forests is determined by governance structures and emerging institutional arrangements in communities.

In Part I, Understanding Forest Communities, three chapters reflect on the state of the art of conceptual and methodological approaches of forest community research. Social science has had to develop new ways of assessing forest communities and producing findings useful to interests as diverse as local civic leaders and national policy formulators. In Chapter 2, we discuss forest community social assessments as recent additions to large-scale ecosystem management, often in response to heightened public environmental concerns. Charnley continues the discussion of the assessment of community–forest connections in Chapter 3, presenting possible scenarios for socioeconomic monitoring, a range of methods and models, and potential applications to community development and forest management. In Chapter 4, Arnold and Fernandez-Gimenez describe participatory research that develops partnerships between researchers and community members, incorporating a diversity of stakeholder perspectives and knowledge and increasing the local relevance of natural resource studies.

Part II, Communities in the Context of Emerging and Persistent Forest Management Issues, addresses five key forest-management topics from the perspective of communities. Specific forest uses and issues—such as recreation, nontimber forest products, wood utilization, scenic amenities, wildfire, demographic changes, woods workers, and forest restoration—are emerging as specialized social science topics with their own bodies of literature and research agendas. Although some topics have long histories in social science research, the chapters in this section cover contemporary issues less well studied, such as ethnicity, forest workers and harvesters, and forest-restoration economies. In Chapter 5, Nechodom, Becker, and Haynes discuss the connection between forest restoration, community capacity, and economic markets, a new twist on classic research connecting timber flows and community stability. The importance of fire as a disturbance in the forest has been recognized by forest ecologists, but cooperation from communities will be necessary to reintroduce fire on the landscape. In Chapter 6, Steelman discusses how new federal wildfire policy goals are being adopted and integrated by communities to reduce their long-term wildfire risk. The increasing number of people moving into forested areas is the topic of Chapter 7, in which Kruger, Mazza, and Stiefel describe the challenges and opportunities for communities and forest managers created by amenity migration and recreation. Jones and Lynch, in Chapter 8, present an entirely different set of opportunities and challenges for integrating commercial nontimber forest product harvesters into forest communities and forest management. Harvesters often do other work in the woods or experience similar exploitation as members of a contingent and mobile workforce. In Chapter 9, Moseley describes the workforce component of forest restoration and institutional barriers to improving the quality of working conditions and economic compensation.

Part III, Communities and Forest Governance, examines enduring and emerging institutional arrangements for forest management. The roles of communities in forest governance are considered from the perspective of family, corporate, community, and public forest ownerships. Danks, in Chapter 10, catalogues the various roles organizations and community groups have played in bridging communities and managers in community-based forest management. Bliss, in Chapter 11, explores ways of better linking the family forestry community in ongoing, community-based forestry strategies. Owners of family forests are a type of forest community; they share mutual values and interests in forest stewardship. In Chapter 12, Belsky clarifies the various forms of "community forestry" that exist in the United States and discusses the implications of timber industry land divestiture on communities and ecosystems. Many of the groups discussed in these chapters gained organizational experience and legitimacy through their efforts in collaborative resource management. Moote, in Chapter 13, explores the challenges and opportunities of collaborative stewardship after more than a decade of experimentation in the United States.

In the Conclusion, we take stock of the knowledge presented in the chapters and examine several factors that influence how communities interact with forests and engage in forest management. We discuss how understanding and strengthening the connections between communities and forests are critical to achieving sustainable forest management.

References

Agrawal, A., and C. C. Gibson. 2001. *Communities and the Environment.* New Brunswick, NJ: Rutgers University Press.

Arabas, K., and J. Bowersox. 2004. Introduction: Natural and Human History of Pacific Northwest Forests. In *Forest Futures: Science, Politics, and Policy for the Next Century,* edited by K. Arabas and J. Bowersox. Lanham, MD: Rowman and Littlefield, xxiii–xlii.

Beckley, T.M. 1998. The Nestedness of Forest-Dependence: A Conceptual Framework and Empirical Exploration. *Society and Natural Resources* 11(2): 101–120.

Best, C., and L.A. Wayburn. 2001. *America's Private Forests: Status and Stewardship.* Washington, DC: Island Press.

Bosworth, D. and H. Brown. 2007. Investing in the Future: Ecological Restoration and the U.S. Forest Service. Journal of Forestry 105(4): 208–211. [??COULD OMIT IN TEXT PAGE 14, Timko, cited by]

Brown, B.A. 1995. *In Timber Country: Working People's Stories of Environmental Conflict and Urban Flight.* Philadelphia: Temple University Press.

Brulle, R.J. 1996. Environmental Discourse and Social Movement Organizations: A Historical and Rhetorical Perspective on the Development of U.S. Environmental Organizations. *Sociological Inquiry* 66: 58–63.

Carroll, M.S., K.A. Blatner, F.J. Alt, E.G. Schuster, and A.J. Findley. 2000. Adaptation Strategies of Displaced Idaho Woods Workers: Results of a Longitudinal Panel Study. *Society and Natural Resources* 13: 95–113.

Cawley, R.M., and J. Freemuth. 1997. A Critique of the Multiple Use Framework in Public Lands Decisionmaking. In *Western Public Lands and Environmental Politics,* edited by C. Davis. Boulder, CO: Westview Press, 32–44.

Charnley, S., and E. Donoghue. 2006. The Effects of the Northwest Forest Plan on Forest-based Communities. In *Socioeconomic Monitoring Results (vol. III): Rural Communities and Economies,* edited by S. Charnley. General Technical Report PNW-GTR-649. Portland, OR: U.S. Department of Agriculture, Forest Service, Pacific Northwest Research Station, 105–153.

Christoffersen, N. 2005. Wallowa Resources: Gaining Access to and Adding Value to Natural Resources on Public Lands. In *Natural Resources as Community Assets: Lessons From Two Continents,* edited by B. Child and M.W. Lyman. Washington, DC: Sand County Foundation and Aspen Institute, 149–175.

Cortner, H.J., and M.A. Moote. 1999. *The Politics of Ecosystem Management.* Washington, DC: Island Press.

Cromley, C.M. 2005. Community-based Forestry Goes to Washington. In *Adaptive Governance: Integrating Science, Policy and Decision Making,* edited by R.D. Brunner, T.A. Steelman, L. Coe-Juell, C.M. Cromley, C.M. Edwards, and D.W. Tucker. New York: Columbia University Press, 221–267.

Danks, C. M. 2003. Community-based Stewardship: Reinvesting in Public Forests and Forest Communities. In *Natural Assets: Democratizing Ownership of Nature,* edited by J. K. Blyce and B.G. Shelley. Washington, DC: Island Press, 243–260.

Donoghue, E.M., and N.L. Sutton. 2006. Socioeconomic Conditions and Trends for Communities in the Northwest Forest Plan Region, 1990 to 2000. In *Socioeconomic Monitoring Results (vol. III): Rural Communities and Economies,* edited by S. Charnley. General Technical Report PNW-GTR-649. Portland, OR: U.S. Department of Agriculture, Forest Service, Pacific Northwest Research Station, 7–36.

England, L. and R.B. Brown. 2003. Community and Resource Extraction in Rural America. IN Brown, D.L and L.E. Swanson. In *Challenges for Rural America in the Twenty-First Century*. University Park: Pennsylvania State University Press, 317-328.

Fitchen, J.M. 1995. Spatial Redistribution of Poverty Through Migration of Poor People to Depressed Rural Communities. *Rural Sociology* 60: 181–201.

Floyd, D.W. 2004. Managing Insurmountable Opportunities. *Journal of Forestry* 102: 8–9.

Force, J.E., G.E. Machlis, L. Zhang. 2000. The Engines of Change in Resource-Dependent Communities. *Forest Science* 46(3): 410-422.

Forest Ecosystem Management Assessment Team. 1993. Forest Ecosystem Management: An Ecological, Economic, and Social assessment. Portland, OR: U.S. Department of Agriculture, U.S. Department of Interior.

Fortmann, L., and J. Kusel. 1990. New Voices, Old Beliefs: Forest Environmentalism Among New and Long-standing Rural Residents. *Rural Sociology* 55: 214–232.

Franklin, J.F., and K.N. Johnson. 2004. Forests Face New Threat: Global Market Changes. *Issues in Science and Technology* 20: 41–48.

Freudenburg, W.R. 1992 Addictive Economies: Extractive Industries and Vulnerable Localities in a Changing World Economy. *Rural Sociology* 57(3):305-32.

General Accounting Office. 1990. Forest Service Timber Harvesting, Planning, Assistance Programs and Tax Provisions. Washington, DC: General Accounting Office.

Guijt, I. (ed.). 2007. *Negotiated Learning: Collaborative Monitoring in Forest Resource Management*. Washington, DC: Resources for the Future.

Helvoigt, T.L., D.M. Adams, and A.L. Ayre. 2003. Employment Transitions in Oregon's Wood Products Sector During the 1990s. *Journal of Forestry* 101: 42–46.

Johnson, K.M., and S.I. Stewart. 2007. Demographic Trends in National Forest, Recreational, Retirement, and Amenity Areas. In *Proceedings: National Workshop on Recreation Research and Management*, edited by L.E. Kruger, R. Mazza, and K. Lawrence. Portland, OR: U.S. Department of Agriculture, Forest Service, Pacific Northwest Research Station, 187–199.

Kaufman, H.F., and L.C. Kaufman. 1946. *Toward the Stabilization and Enrichment of a Forest Community: The Montana Study*. Missoula: University of Montana.

Kaufman, H. F. 1959. Community as an Interactional Field. *Social Forces* 38:8-17.

Keele, D.M., R.W. Malmsheimer, D.W. Floyd, and J.E. Perez. 2006. Forest Service Land Management Litigation 1989-2002. *Journal of Forestry* 104(4): 196–202.

Krannich, R.S., P. Petrzelka, and J.M. Brehm. 2006. Social Change and Well-being in Western Amenity-growth Communities. In *Population Change and Rural Society*, edited by W.A. Kandel and D.L. Brown. Dordrecht, The Netherlands: Springer, 311–332.

Kusel, J., S. Kocher, J. London, L. Buttolph, and E. Schuster. 2000. Effects of Displacement and Outsourcing on Woods Workers and their Families. *Society and Natural Resources* 13: 115–134.

Leahy, J., and G. Gray. 2004. Criteria and Indicators: Finding Meaning for Communities. *Communities and Forests* 8: 1–5.

Lee, R.G., and D.R. Field. 2005. Community Complexity: Postmodern Challenges to Forest and Natural Resources Management. In *Communities and Forests: Where People Meet the Land*, edited by R.G. Lee and D.R. Field. Corvallis: Oregon State University Press, 291–303.

Lichter, D.T. 1993. Migration, Population Redistribution, and the New Spatial Inequality. In *The Demography of Rural Life*, edited by D.L. Brown, D.R. Field, and J. Zuiches. University Park, PA: Northeast Regional Center for Rural Development, 19–46.

McCarthy, L.F., and D.H. Jenkins. 2007. Ecological Restoration: A Fitting Goal for America's National Forests. *Journal of Forestry* 105(4): 212–214.

Melton, M., M. DeBonis, and E. Krasilovsky. 2007. Maltreatment & Injustice: An Overview of the Plight of Latino Forest Workers in the Southeast. Forest Guild Research Paper. www.forestguild.org/latinoforestworkers.html (accessed August 28, 2007).

Pinchot, G. 1947. *Breaking New Ground*. New York: Harcourt, Brace and Company.

Rasker, R. 2001. Your Next Job Will Be in Services. Should You Be Worried? In *Across the Great Divide: Explorations in Collaborative Conservation and the American West*, edited by P. Brick, D. Snow, and S. Van de Wetering. Washington, DC: Island Press, 51–57.

Reid, R.L., and Mattson, M. 1993. *Demographics of Applegate Region*. Southern Oregon Regional Services Institute. Ashland, OR: Southern Oregon State College.

Sarathy, B. 2006. The Latinization of Forest Management Work in Southern Oregon: A Case from the Rogue Valley. *Journal of Forestry* 104: 359–365.

Sierra Club. 2007. Home page. http://www.sierraclub.org/environmentallaw (accessed July 12, 2007).

Stankey, G.H., B.T. Bormann, C. Ryan, B. Shindler, V. Sturtevant, R. Clark, and C. Philpot. 2003. Adaptive Management and the Northwest Forest Plan: Rhetoric and Reality. *Journal of Forestry* 101(1): 40–46.

Stein, S.M., R.E. McRoberts, R.J. Alig, M.D. Nelson, D.M. Theobald, M. Eley, M. Dechter, and M. Carr. 2005. Forests on the Edge: Housing Development on America's Private Forests. General Technical Report PNW-GTR-636. Portland, OR: U.S. Department of Agriculture Forest Service, Pacific Northwest Research Station.

Swanson, F. 2004. Roles of Scientists in Forestry Policy and Management: Views from the Pacific Northwest. In *Forest Futures: Science, Politics, and Policy for the Next Century*, edited by K. Arabas and J. Bowersox. Lanham, MD: Rowman and Littlefield, 112–126.

Tonnies, F. 1957. *Community and Society*. New York: Harper Torchbook.

U.S. Department of Agriculture (USDA) Forest Service. 2007. Fire and Aviation Management 2007 Fire Season Fact Sheet. Summer. Washington, DC: USDA Forest Service.

———. The Process Predicament: How Statutory, Regulatory, and Administrative Factors Affect National Forest Management. www.fs.fed.us/publications.html (accessed August 17, 2007).

Vaughn, J., and H.J. Cortner. 2004. Using Parallel Strategies to Promote Change: Forest Policymaking under George W. Bush. *Review of Policy Research* 21(6): 767–782.

Warren, D. 1998. Production, Prices, Employment, and Trade in Northwest Forest Industries, Second Quarter 1997. Resource Bulletin PNW-RB-228. Portland, OR: U.S. Department of Agriculture, Forest Service, Pacific Northwest Research Station.

Wilkinson, K.P. 1991. *The Community in Rural America*. New York: Greenwood Press.

World Forestry Center. 2004. Who Will Own the Forest? Globalization and Consolidation Effects on Forests. Portland, OR: World Forestry Center.

Yaffee, S.L. 1994. *The Wisdom of the Spotted Owl: Policy Lessons for a New Century*. Washington, DC: Island Press.

Part I
Understanding Forest Communities

2

Social Assessment of Forest Communities
For Whom and for What?

VICTORIA E. STURTEVANT AND ELLEN M. DONOGHUE

Growing public interest in the sustainability of forests and forest communities has policymakers, federal land managers, and scientists looking to assessments to understand the effects of forest management practices on forest health and community well-being. Large-scale ecosystem assessments have been used to build knowledge about a bioregion prior to anticipated change in policy and management or as part of monitoring the effectiveness of forest policy. Community assessments—the systematic appraisal of the quality of life of individuals and social and occupational groups within communities and their relation to natural resource management—have become an integral part of ecosystem assessments.

These science-based assessments are an important opportunity for scientists to produce, compile, analyze, and synthesize data to help answer questions formulated by politicians and other policymakers. Calling upon science to resolve contested public resource policy issues is relatively new, and inviting social scientists to contribute sociological analysis is even more novel. In this chapter, we reflect on the experience and challenges of conducting community assessments as part of large-scale ecosystem assessments. We examine the multiple and sometimes conflicting expectations on social scientists to inform forest policy, further social science research regarding forest communities, and contribute to communities' understanding of the connections among natural resources, economies, and social values.

Policy directives for large-scale ecosystem assessments often come from agency planning and management documents or legislative mandates; these directives are interpreted by interdisciplinary scientific teams and developed into research questions that guide assessment processes. Scientists participating in large-scale assessments face a number of constraints and issues related to time, budgets, and the scope of the project. And most large-scale assessments are influenced by the multiple, sometimes conflicting, agendas of agency, community, research, and political stakeholders. Stakeholders are motivated by various factors and have a range of expectations for the outcomes of large-scale assessments, such as to gain politically, to mitigate losses through policy change, to improve management of forest resources, and to protect traditional ways of life in forest communities. Amid the numerous and complex influences on, and uses of, large-scale assessments a, fundamental question emerges: For whom and for what[1] are assessments conducted?

We examine the contributions of social scientists to four large-scale ecosystem assessments: the Forest Ecosystem Management Assessment Team (FEMAT), the Sierra Nevada Ecosystem Project (SNEP), the Interior Columbia Basin Ecosystem Management Project (ICBEMP), and the Northwest Forest Plan monitoring project (NWFP). The constructs, indicators, and units of analyses developed in these assessments serve as methodological models, providing baseline measures for further community assessments and monitoring. Federal and state forest managers currently are using social assessments to explore the connections between communities and forest ecosystems, and community organizations are undertaking social assessments at multiple scales to understand and respond to external and internal forces of change.

We have found that some of the most compelling challenges facing assessment teams come from the interface of policy directives and scientific limitations. This chapter presents five key tensions associated with community assessments that are influenced by the political and scientific drivers of large-scale ecosystem assessments, clarifies why these tensions exist, discusses some implications of the tensions, and offers ways to begin to resolve them. We concentrate on community-level social assessments that have been integral parts of large-scale ecosystem assessment projects. Our objective is to increase understanding about whom and what forest community assessments serve.

Selected Assessments

Recently in the western United States, several interagency, multidisciplinary ecosystem assessments have been conducted in response to heightened social concerns and lawsuits and in anticipation of changes in resource management. The FEMAT (1993), SNEP (1996), ICBEMP (Quigley and Arbelbide 1997), and NWFP (Charnley 2006) assessments were conducted on vast bioregional scales, reflecting a shift over the decades by federal land managers away from commodity and single-species oriented resource management to ecosystem and landscape-level management. The assessments also reflected resource managers' and society's growing appreciation of the interconnectedness of human communities with natural resources and the importance of social factors in conflicts over forest management.

Each ecosystem assessment had one or more community assessment components (Charnley 2006; Doak and Kusel 1996; FEMAT 1993; Harris et al. 2000; Kusel 1996; McCool et al. 1997). Participating in these ecosystem assessments was a landmark for social scientists, and several aspects of their work were innovative from both research and policy perspectives. They faced multiple objectives that required development of new methodologies for assessing socioeconomic conditions and trends for hundreds of communities within a bioregion. Each team of researchers for the community assessments defined its mandate in similar but slightly different ways. For FEMAT, ICBEMP, and SNEP, each was to elucidate community dependency on, and expectations for, natural resources and assess the ability of communities to respond to changes in land management. They were to provide an understanding of the current, and possible future, social and economic conditions of a wide range of communities, particularly as they relate to resource management, and to inform policymakers and managers about the social consequences of their impending decisions. They were not social impact assessments primarily because proposed management actions upon which to assess the community-level effects were not developed in advance of the assessments. The NWFP monitoring project, in contrast, was an assessment of progress toward meeting the socioeconomic goals of the plan.

The ecosystem assessment of the spotted owl region (FEMAT) was initiated by President Clinton, who specified that social benefits, including recreation, aesthetics, and other values, be assessed, as well as the effects on local communities of proposed changes in forest management. In addition, the assessment was to identify policies that would ease the expected economic and cultural transitions. The community assessment team was to use existing studies and data (including public comments on federal management plans) as the basis for their analysis of how various management options might relate to social values and affect timber-dependent communities, variously defined. However, no systematic, comparative research previously had been conducted on communities in this region at such large scales, and no methodological protocols existed.

The assessments for the Interior Columbia Basin and Sierra Nevada followed on the heels of FEMAT, sharing similar mandates and some scientists. Like FEMAT, they were to inventory the outcomes of management on ecologic, economic, and social systems. Unlike FEMAT, they were to assess conditions and trends before creating potential management alternatives or scenarios. Although not explicitly policy analyses, ICBEMP delineated the effect of "ecosystem management" on the maintenance of rural communities and economies. SNEP assessed comprehensive data and suggested management scenarios that could maintain the sustainability of the ecosystem while providing resources to human communities. The NWFP social and economic monitoring project addressed several evaluation questions in the NWFP Record of Decision (USDA and USDI 1994) that asked whether local communities and economies were experiencing positive or negative changes as a result of federal forest management.

Policy Directives and Community Assessments

Policy directives, such as statutory mandates, executive orders, regulatory requirements, and court orders, instructed agencies to conduct ecosystem assessments. Policy directives associated with large-scale assessments typically have been a response to society's increasing discomfort with critical and complex forest management issues, coupled with a sense of urgency to increase knowledge and take appropriate action. For the most part, policy directives indicated where, when, and why assessments occur.

Policy directives, however, do not define all aspects of assessment projects. They tend to say very little about how to conduct an assessment. The "how" questions are left to assessment teams to define and answer. For example, in FEMAT and the NWFP, President Clinton asked scientists to protect the forests but consider human dimensions. The NWFP community assessment team developed specific monitoring questions, defined the community-level unit of analysis, and grappled with other conceptual and methodological issues that either were not evident in the policy directive (Record of Decision) or had to be extrapolated from it.

The logic of deferring scientific processes to the science assessment teams is evident. However, when there is little or no precedent for science at the scale and scope defined by the policy directives, assessment teams may have to deal with unanticipated methodological and design issues. Thus, while they collect, analyze, and report on data sets of unprecedented size and complexity, assessment teams simultaneously push the proverbial scientific envelope. Scientific innovation was evident in each of the four social assessments referenced in this chapter.

Policy directives do not always make the "for whom" question explicitly clear. Agency executives and resource managers are key audiences for assessments, but which managers? In the case of the NWFP assessment project, for example, the managers and agency executives of 1994 who agreed that monitoring work should be done were not the same managers 10 years later when the first phase of monitoring was completed. As the audience shifted, so too did the types of questions and resource management problems that had emerged.

The issue of assessments "for whom" is subtlety different for social assessment teams compared to ecosystem assessment teams, although this difference typically is not acknowledged at the level of policy directives. For example, for the biophysical components of the NWFP monitoring project, the audience primarily was managers and decisionmakers, not the owls, trees, or riparian species that were monitored. In the case of the social assessment component, the policy directive vaguely identified "communities" as the unit of analysis but did not indicate what role communities would play in the assessment process, apart from being the subjects of monitoring. Some of the social assessments referenced in this chapter involved local stakeholders to some degree, but the direction to do this did not come explicitly from policy directives.

We now turn to the specific challenges facing social scientists participating in the social assessments described above. These emerge from our experience as researchers directly or indirectly involved in all four efforts, interviews with principal investigators, and our reading of assessment reports and others' reflection on the processes and outcomes. We have categorized the issues into five tensions: defining community, developing constructs, linking forest management and community well-being, seeking credible methods, and working in a highly charged political environment. Our resolutions are directed toward future large-scale assessments, as well as other efforts at assessing forest–community connections.

#1: Delimiting and Defining Communities

Policy directives for large-scale social assessments tend to specify a focus on the "community" level without clearly indicating what that means. To translate directive into assessments, researchers first must define the community unit of analysis. The definition of community is important because it sets the stage for other methodological choices made throughout the assessment process. Discussions, lessons learned, and cautionary notes on defining units of analysis are commonplace in the literature (Doak and Kusel 1996; Blahna et al. 2003; Donoghue 2003). We do not present guidelines for defining community but illustrate how researchers address methodological challenges of defining the community level of analysis in the context of these large-scale assessments.

The scale of ecosystem assessments complicates the process for defining communities. Researchers must assign thousands, sometimes millions, of people to identifiable geographic places that they would call "their community." Researchers run the risk of ignoring sizeable populations or of aggregating populations to a scale that is not meaningful to local residents. A related issue is that policy directives often are interpreted to refer to communities of place rather than communities of interest, such as people who belong to a national environmental association, or mobile communities, such as migrant workers who follow the work in the woods. Specific attention to communities of interest has been missing from most large-scale community assessments. Defining the community further is complicated by the need of large-scale assessments to draw links across several scales of analysis, from the community down to the household level or up to the regional or ecosystem level. In SNEP and NWFP, researchers used one of the smallest units of geography available from the census. Because the units were contiguous across the entire landscape, they could be aggregated up to other scales, such as ecoregions, planning provinces, counties, and states.

Assuming an assessment team can delineate geographically the community, it then has to define the social construction of the community. This entails identifying the conditions, processes, and structures to be assessed and the indicators and measures that will reflect them. Decisions about using secondary or primary data are complicated by data availability and suitability. In NWFP, researchers developed an index of socioeconomic well-being that was a composite of six indicators from the census. Similarly, the SNEP assessment developed a measure of socioeconomic status based on secondary data but decided to use primary data collected through community workshops to develop a measure of community capacity. ICBEMP also used community workshops to develop measures for community resiliency because secondary data did not adequately speak to these complex dimensions of community life. Commonalities across geographic boundaries, data sources, and data availability can be elusive, limiting the ways that secondary data can be used to reflect sociological constructs, such as community resiliency or community well-being.

Depending on how assessment teams resolve the issues of spatially delimiting the community and developing suitable indicators and measures to define the community, assessment teams could come up with any number of communities in a region. The NWFP project identified 1,314 communities in the region but intentionally kept the delimitations small, allowing for further aggregating of communities, if necessary. The ICBEMP community assessment largely focused on census places; however, these did not represent the entire population of people living in rural localities. One problem with assessments defining communities in a variety of ways is that scientists often are encouraged to report findings in terms of numbers; that is, how many communities lost jobs, how many gained jobs, how many have low capacity, how many have high capacity? Often times these quantified results and labels (e.g., low, medium, and high resiliency) are derived at by examining how one community stands relative to the next. But if the communities were defined differently, the relative relationship may change. Thus, careful attention should be paid to the configuration of populations into communities, particularly in large-scale community assessments.

Resolution

Defining the community as the unit of analysis can be thought of as a two-part process that involves: 1) establishing boundaries; and 2) determining qualities, characteristics, or conditions of a community that will be assessed. This dual distinction should be explicit in methodological discussions of social science research at the small scale. For example, findings can be difficult to interpret when emphasis is placed on sociological structures and processes, such as community resiliency, without full explanation and consideration of the geographic areas within which those processes occur. Attention to the unit of analysis is important in social assessments to minimize confusion about whose socioeconomic conditions and processes and what causal relations are being assessed or monitored. Increased clarity in policy directives about what is meant by community not only will help the research process but also will clarify expectations and help minimize conflicting interpretations and uses of the results.

#2: Developing Constructs While Conducting Assessments

This tension addresses the opportunities and constraints associated with advancing science while conducting large-scale assessments. The focus here is on the development of sociological constructs and measures. Sociological constructs provide conceptual structure to research. In large-scale community assessments, where policy directives may be vague in their concern for forest communities, constructs help assessment teams focus on specific aspects of community life, such as well-being, socioeconomic status, community capacity, and community resiliency. Constructs also guide methodological choices, such as the development of indicators and measures that serve as proxies for specific dimensions of a construct. In each of the four large-scale community assessments, researchers created sociological constructs and measures to assess how changing natural-resource management decisions effected, or would effect, forest communities (Charnley 2006; Doak and Kusel 1996; FEMAT 1993; Harris et al. 2000).

"Community capacity" emerged as the core construct of FEMAT's community assessment, defined as the "ability of residents, and community institutions, organizations, and leadership—formal and informal—to meet local needs and expectations" (FEMAT 1993, *vii–51*). Some researchers from FEMAT further developed the construct of community capacity in SNEP (Doak and Kusel 1996), changing the definition only slightly, but developing new methods to operationalize the construct. For ICBEMP, the concept "resiliency" was examined at several scales in a variety of reports but with little clarification as to how it differed from capacity. "Resiliency" was defined similarly to "capacity" as: "a community's ability to respond and adapt to change in the most positive, constructive ways possible for helping mitigate the impacts of change on the community" (Harris et al. 2000, 7). Like capacity, "resiliency" was a response to the premise of traditional community stability research that even-flow forest resource outputs would maintain healthy communities. The NWFP team focused on a construct of community socioeconomic well-being and developed measures that had not been used in previous assessments.

The sociological constructs and measures used in the assessments did not evolve from a long history of validated and replicated social science research. The few sociological constructs related to communities and resource management that existed prior to these assessments (e.g., stability) did not reflect adequately contemporary views that the relationship between forest communities and forests were complex and dynamic. Thus, the constructs and measures used in assessments had to be innovative, some building on predecessors and others breaking new ground.

The constructs of community capacity and resiliency, by definition, directed researchers to examine a range of community attributes and processes, such as leadership, civic responsiveness, and physical capital. Yet, the need to compare results across hundreds of communities required researchers to coalesce measures into single numeric scores that would allow for rankings of communities. In FEMAT, components of community capacity were grouped. Economic diversity, for instance, was included in physical capital along with environmental capital, physical attractiveness, industrial parks, and other physical dimensions. This was similar to SNEP, where local experts considered the social, human, and physical capital of a community but assigned only a single capacity rating. The community expert workbook in ICBEMP allowed for discrete ratings on numerous variables that through factor analysis were developed into four components of resiliency. Unlike FEMAT and SNEP, ICBEMP reported the community resiliency index alongside the scores for the four components of the resiliency scale.

By collapsing community attributes and dynamics into a single score, the assessments risked assigning similar capacity or resiliency scores to communities quite different in their combination of physical assets or social capabilities, thereby masking the complex properties of the concepts capacity and resiliency.

Perhaps because large-scale assessments are infrequent, few attempts have replicated the methods used in recent community assessments and thereby further developed and validated the constructs. For instance, scientists have not clarified the differences between "capacity" and "resiliency" or how these differ from other concepts frequently used, such as "sustainability" and "adaptability." The nascent constructs developed during these assessments drove the methods, and ultimately the findings, of the community assessments. However, without additional validation and clarification of the constructs, some results of community assessments may be perceived as immature science.

Resolution

Scientific advancement may be an expected outcome of social assessments, given the unprecedented scale, heightened expectations, and resources and support that large-scale assessments tend to garner. Indeed, large-scale assessments provide unique opportunities for scientists to advance knowledge. Perhaps more could be done, however, to advance construct development and measurement outside of social assessments so that the results of large-scale assessments are not so dependent on how assessment teams overcame definitional and methodological challenges.

In particular, there is a need to clarify constructs that have similar definitions but different names and measurements, such as "community capacity" and "community resiliency." Studies designed specifically to validate and develop constructs and measures would contribute to assessment processes. Similarly, many methodological challenges associated with operationalizing constructs using secondary and geospatial data may be overcome in ways that have not been explored. Incorporating construct development into routine social science theory and research is one way to ensure that future large-scale social assessments rest on more solid foundations.

#3: Linking Forest Policy and Community Well-Being

The effects of forest policy on society and natural resources are complex and reciprocal, as difficult to predict during policy implementation as they are to unravel in hindsight. Policy directives that initiate social assessments may create unintended tensions over expectations and deliverables. This is because large-scale assessments emerge when issues are complex, critical, and often highly politically charged. Large-scale assessments come with underlying expectations on the part of managers and society at large that social science will help clarify the causal relations between forest policy and community well-being. What often transpires, however, is decisionmakers expect answers to questions for which state-of-the art science continues to debate or has not developed adequate means to answer or were beyond the funding and resources allocated to the assessment team.

As indicated, the four large-scale community assessments were directed to assess how changing natural-resource management decisions affected, or would affect, forest communities (Charnley 2006; Doak and Kusel 1996; FEMAT 1993; Harris et al. 2000). Most community assessments used constructs with broader inferences and applications, however, rather than focusing on narrow connections between forest management and community well-being, such as timber-based jobs. The use of capacity and resiliency constructs in FEMAT, SNEP, and ICBEMP reflected the state-of-the-art thinking on dynamics of community change but may not have addressed specific concerns of forest managers. Social scientists are interested in understanding the ability of communities to adapt to change broadly defined (e.g., changes in demographics, global markets), but forest managers tend to want to know how communities will respond to specific changes in timber harvests or other forest policy.

Social science has revealed that the drivers of change in forest communities are multidimensional, arising from a complex mix of internal and external factors, such as sociodemographic changes, labor-saving technology, and international markets. Although large-scale social assessments have contributed to this understanding, they have not, for the most part, been able to address causal links between forest policy and community change. For instance, NWFP decisionmakers found the social assessment results inconclusive because they did not demonstrate a definitive connection between community socioeconomic change and the plan.

Resolution

Social scientists generally have acknowledged that clarifying causal links between changes in federal land-management policy and community change is a daunting challenge; yet, researchers continue to explore ways to meet such objectives (Jackson et al. 2004). Large-scale assessments represent a unique opportunity for theory development because of the breadth and depth of the amassed community-level data. Involving community members and local managers more closely in the assessment process and choosing multi-method research designs may help assessment teams identify and address causal questions. More narrowly focused research questions that explore specific links between elements of community health and forest policy may help to incrementally build a broader understanding of causes and effects, particularly if examined in a multi-method approach. Temporal analyses also may reveal patterns and relations across socioeconomic indicators and policy elements that clarify causal links. Thus, even given the complex nature of human and natural resource interactions, there may be ways to address cause-and-effect questions through carefully thought-out research questions and approaches. However, these approaches may reduce the scale of analysis, involve stakeholders who tend to be outside large-scale assessment processes, and require time— all of which may be undesirable from the standpoint of an agency executive "owner" of an assessment project. By virtue of their scale, political and historical mandates, and inexplicit "ownership," assessment projects may have difficulties meeting expectations to link forest policy with changes in community well-being.

#4: Seeking Credible Methods

The methodological challenges facing researchers assessing communities are well known and often discussed. Articles and books provide menus of methods and indicators, recommending their suitability for various research applications. Once choices are made, however, their implications for findings seldom are examined, particularly in reports for managers or policymakers. Reflections on methods more often are discussed in book chapters or scientific papers separate from large-scale assessment and policy-driven processes. As a consequence, social scientists risk overstating scientific understanding of complex concepts, such as resiliency, and minimizing the uncertainty of predictions, such as designating communities at risk.

The quantitative nature of economic and demographic data is useful to decisionmakers and communities seeking to measure community effects of forest management or evaluate progress in mitigating these effects. Quantitative data can provide efficient and effective summaries of information, suggest causality and relationships among indicators, and provide credible, objective evaluation. Numbers also can hide value judgments made in their gathering and presentation, attributing meaning to summary measures that may not reflect reality. Quantitative measures standardize experiences and consequences but do not capture how different community members, subcultures, or occupational groups define these experiences and consequences. This often-discussed disconnect between objective and subjective measures is one of many challenges facing social scientists wishing to participate effectively in large-scale assessments. Others include the incongruity of aggregate measures and structural conditions; the substantive difference between community disruption and community resiliency; and the disparity between western science and experiential, traditional, and indigenous knowledge. Because these incongruities and disparities are treated comprehensively in methods texts and in articles more generally, only a few examples of the methodological dilemmas that continually emerge in forest community assessments are presented here.

Social indicators aggregate individual data, such as population. In ICBEMP, researchers selected a sample of communities with significant population change for in-depth analysis of the constellation of factors in their social change. Net migration masks counter-movements that can transform communities with no apparent population change, such as communities losing young families and gaining amenity migrants. Similarly, poverty rates may remain stable while different occupation groups are cycling in and out of poverty due to the seasonal nature of their jobs.

Policymakers and biophysical scientists involved in the assessments expected social scientists to draw from social-impact assessment methodology conventionally employed in environmental impact statements for new projects or resource development. Social impact indicators focus on rapid population change and social disruption, such as increased crime and delinquency, substance abuse, and marital dissolution. Although these measures are useful for objective assessments of change or comparisons of communities, they do not serve as good proxies for complex social processes, such as civic engagement, and organizational networks, which reduce or enhance the ability of a community to meet residents' needs, deal with loss of traditional resource-based employment or other changes, and take advantage of opportunities and direct their own futures.

The large-scale assessments discussed in this chapter employed secondary socioeconomic data, partly because of limited timeframes and budgets, but also to meet the western scientific presumption that quantitative analysis is more explanatory and credible. Experiential, traditional, and indigenous knowledge, often captured with ethnographic research and qualitative methods, is more contextual and often requires narrative forms of disseminating results rather than tables or charts. Although western science connotes "rigor," traditional knowledge offers new insights based on age-old understandings of ecological integrity and community sustainability. The literature calls for integration of these approaches (Jones and McLain 2003) but does not suggest how to reconcile epistemological differences, much less methods and ethics.

Resolution

The sudden methodological invitation to participate in large-scale assessments left social scientists little time to prepare a unified approach to meeting the policy goals for their respective social assessments. However, they may not be able to reach full consensus. Social impact assessment, a more mature applied social science, has not reached an agreed-upon set of concepts or definitive list of variables (Burdge 2004). Rather than contributing to a proliferation of concepts, we encourage social scientists to continue refining and advancing these existing constructs and indicators. Incorporating construct development into routine social science programs is one way to ensure that future community assessments rest on firmer conceptual and methodological foundations. Just as earlier studies of community stability were tied to larger theories of social change (Machlis and Force 1990), measures of community capacity and resiliency would benefit from theories of social agency, social capital, and community theory. Political ecology and anthropological theories of the symbolic meanings of risk are examples of frameworks that can provide qualitative and contextual dimensions.

Multiple methodological approaches and different indicators allow triangulation and opportunities to resolve differing findings. Data collection over extended periods of time (or replication of studies) will help define the period over which rates of change are to be measured. Effects on some institutions, such as markets, might be more rapid than on others, such as families. Research teams with different skills—quantitative, qualitative, analytical, and intuitive— constructively can address methodological tradeoffs; the challenge will be to put together functioning teams of social scientists with different perspectives to work cooperatively addressing the same research question and integrating different findings. Standardized methods for generating qualitative data across multiple case studies and complementing secondary data analyses with qualitative community case studies, as done in the NWFP assessment, are potential multi-methods approaches.

#5: Addressing Competing Stakeholders

Community assessment teams work in highly charged political arenas: "working within the science-policy interface is inherently an exercise in politics and is far different from the conduct of routine research" (Mills and Clark 2001, *190*). The political debate driving western social assessments often was framed simply as jobs vs. owls or salmon, but the conflicts were multifaceted and played out locally and nationally with competing interest groups, agency managers, judges, and policymakers.

The mandates for the assessments were made by the president (FEMAT, NWFP), Congress (SNEP), courts (FEMAT), and agencies (ICBEMP)—all accountable to numerous watchdogs. In FEMAT, for example, the courts had made it clear that the central goal was biological diversity. As the head of the FEMAT team put it, sustainability of timber production was in a "subordinate position" to threatened species; if there was any "slack" in the mandated outputs, it was timber yields (Thomas 2004, 5). Biophysical scientists had some directives regarding spotted owls: what risk was allowable, what percent was considered viable, and over what period of time. The parameters for social scientists were not as clear. President Clinton asked scientists to protect the forests but consider human dimensions. There were no boundaries of acceptable effects on communities, no explicit goals for communities, and social scientists were left to guess how their science would be interpreted by decisionmakers.

Because it was not explicit as to "for whom" the assessments were done, the "for what" was likely to raise issues among various stakeholders concerned more about the implications for policy than the validity of the science. Assessment of communities' current and desired conditions depended on highly contested definitions of forest resources and occupational and cultural identities. Defining low-capacity or low-resiliency communities as "at risk" may qualify them for outside assistance but also can demoralize and paralyze community members and chase away potential business investment. Community experts tasked with rating communities for FEMAT understandably did not want to give communities and their members' labels that could be perceived as pejorative; they recognized that some stakeholders could be harmed by ratings or interpretations by the social assessment itself.

Resolution

Large-scale ecosystem assessments, by virtue of their scale and high political profile, place scientists at the science–policy interface in roles they may not expect. Research scientists work within more established paradigms and in less contentious settings. Scientists working at the policy–science interface work in more unsettled situations with less clearly defined relationships among researchers, managers, and stakeholders. Continued dialogue about roles and expectations may help researchers as they move from more routine research to the science–policy interface.

The culture of assessment science is more adversarial and controversial than routine research. Stakeholders may pit "my science" against "your science" and disagree over criteria for validation, but they also can participate in civic science (Lee 1993) during which citizens share positions regarding ecological and socioeconomic conditions and assess progress toward reaching their goals. Public participation in the assessment process can offer public knowledge and understandings that improve science; it also can bridge the boundaries between different actors—scientists, managers, and competing interest groups. For instance, the SNEP assessment designed a diverse array of methods for encouraging dialogue between scientists and stakeholders that facilitated gathering and verifying data. The NWFP assessment used qualitative data from interviews with community members and agency officials to complement community-level and regional analyses based on secondary data.

Conclusion

Large-scale community assessments create unique challenges for, and expectations on, social assessment teams, such as the large scale of the assessment and the lack of methodological blueprints. But perhaps more daunting is the uncertainty about "for whom" and "for what" the assessments are completed: for politicians who face constituent demands for sustainable forest management yet also for forest products and amenities; for forest managers and planners who must respond to court mandates and congressional expectations for new models of forest management; for community members who seek to reconnect to forest assets; for citizens who challenge traditional industrial forest management; or for fellow scientists who seek to further research. Scientists enter into demanding and ground-breaking assessment processes, often with restricted time and funding and with few answers to these fundamental questions. And, they are challenged to define their work so that it will be relevant to specific audiences.

Many factors influence the design and implementation of large-scale community assessments. Assessment teams develop and operate under explicit and implicit assumptions about communities, forest management, policy, and other factors. For instance, it is assumed that assessments benefit communities; communities are involved in assessments; researchers are sensitive to nuances in data and will be objective; indicators are reliable and valid across communities; community boundaries and characteristics are definable; communities are nested within other social scales; and forest management decisionmakers are committed to using assessment results to improve relations with, and futures for, forest communities. How these assumptions are addressed influences the design and outcomes of assessments.

The scale of assessments poses considerable methodological challenges to community assessment teams, including delimiting the community and developing appropriate indicators and measures of socioeconomic conditions and processes. Although scientific understanding of the complex factors influencing community change continues to advance, social scientists debate the definitions and measures for key constructs, such as community capacity and resiliency. Thus, out of necessity, critical scientific advancements are occurring concurrent with large-scale assessments. Any one of these factors—community definition, construct use and indicators and measures, political and management expectations—is enough to challenge more routine science. Large-scale social assessments have to deal with a host of factors and interactions of factors at scales previously untested and amplify the methodological issues often faced by social assessments at more manageable scales.

Also, the political and management drivers of assessments create other types of tensions, including lack of clearly defined research questions arising from policy directives, the existence of diverse stakeholders with interests in the assessment processes and outcomes, and expectations that assessments will clarify cause-and-effect relationships between policy and communities. Without clear expectations, the science of assessments can become mired in a web of normative disputes and issues of accountability. If the questions are not clear, how can scientists, decisionmakers, and the public determine the validity of the results?

Large-scale community assessments are resource intensive, all-encompassing, time-consuming processes that have the potential to influence resource management and community development. The idea of "assessing the assessments" initially seems absurd. And yet the lack of clarity in the policy directives, the use of unvalidated science at extraordinary scales, and the lack of defined ownership in processes and outcomes raises concern that assessments have unspecific purposes and uses. Greater transparency and interaction among stakeholders during assessment design likely will help clarify the issues surrounding for "who" and "what" community assessments serve. Although agencies may be the "owners" of the assessments, other stakeholders, particularly community leaders, may benefit from having more ownership in the process and results. Some methodological challenges, however, such as the development of constructs, indicators, and measures, may warrant specific attention as part of more routine science to build up the foundation from which they may serve future assessments and research. We discuss these tensions and challenges out of respect for those scientists who have been in the trenches of large-scale assessments. Our hope is to raise awareness and discussion of these issues so that in the future assessment teams are better prepared, not only armed with methodological processes and constructs, but asking the right questions, such as "for whom are these assessments" and "for what reason"?

We expect these tensions will appear in some form at other scales and time-frames; for instance, for agency social scientists tasked with assessing communities on their forests, academics seeking to analyze the connection between forest management and social change, or communities undertaking self-assessment. Definitions, delineations, constructs, and methods for gathering data will be constrained by data availability, and preliminary work is required to get the questions right. What are the goals of the community assessment—or for the community itself—and what are the anticipated obstacles for achieving these goals? Who are the stakeholders, what are their expectations of scientists, and what do they stand to gain or lose from the assessment? Assessments assemble existing knowledge to inform judgment regarding potential outcomes of policy, management, or social change. Scientists also must create new methods and findings that can be continually tested and validated by further research.

Note

1. The timeless questions "for whom and for what" posed by Clawson (1975) about forests and forest policy are relevant today for resource managers and social scientists interested in assessing the connections between communities and forests.

References

Beckley, T., J. Parkins, and R. Stedman. 2002. Indicators of Forest-dependent Community Sustainability: The Evolution of the Research. *The Forestry Chronicle* 78(5): 626–636.

Blahna, D.J., E. Carr, and P. Jakes. 2003. Using Social Community as a Measurement Unit in Conservation Planning and Ecosystem Management. In *Understanding Community-forest Relations,* edited by L. Kruger. General Technical Report PNW-GTR 566. Portland, OR: U.S. Department of Agriculture, Forest Service, Pacific Northwest Research Station, 59–80.

Burdge, R.J. 2004. *The Concepts, Process and Methods of Social Impact Assessment.* Middleton, WI: Social Ecology Press.

Charnley, S. (tech. coord.) 2006. *Northwest Forest Plan—The First 10 years (1994–2003): Socioeconomic Monitoring Results.* General Technical Report PNW-GTR 649. Portland, OR: U.S. Department of Agriculture, Forest Service, Pacific Northwest Research Station.

Clawson, M. 1975. *Forests for Whom and for What?* Washington, DC: Resources for the Future.

Doak, S., and J. Kusel. 1996. Well-being in Forest-dependent Communities, Part II: A Social Assessment Focus. In *Sierra Nevada Ecosystem Project: Final Report to Congress (vol. II): Assessments and Scientific Basis for Management Options.* Davis, CA: University of California, Centers for Water and Wildland Resources, 375–400.

Donoghue, E.M. 2003. *Delimiting Communities in the Pacific Northwest.* General Technical Report PNW-GTR-570. Portland, OR: U.S. Department of Agriculture, Forest Service, Pacific Northwest Research Station.

Field, D.R., and W. R. Burch. 1988. *Rural Sociology and the Environment.* New York: Greenwood Press.

Forest Ecosystem Management Assessment Team. 1993. Forest Ecosystem Management: An Ecological, Economic, and Social assessment. Portland, OR: U.S. Department of Agriculture, U.S. Department of Interior.

Fortmann, L.P., J. Kusel, and S.K. Fairfax. 1989. Community Stability: The Foresters' Figleaf. In *Community Stability in Forest-based Communities,* edited by D. LeMaster and J. Beuter. Beaverton, OR: Timber Press, 44–50.

Harris, C., W. McLaughlin, G. Brown, and D.R. Becker. 2000. *Rural Communities in the Inland Northwest: An Assessment of Small Rural Communities in the Interior and Upper Columbia River Basins.* General Technical Report PNW-GTR-477. Portland, OR: U.S. Department of Agriculture, Forest Service, Pacific Northwest Research Station, and USDI Bureau of Land Management.

Jackson, J.E., R.G. Lee, and P. Sommers. 2004. Monitoring the Community Impacts of the Northwest Forest Plan: An Alternative to Social Indicators. *Society and Natural Resources* 17: 223–233.

Jones, E.T., and R.J. McLain. 2003. The Importance of an Integrated Research Approach. In *Understanding Community-Forest Relations,* edited by L. Kruger. General Technical Report PNW-GTR-566. Portland, OR: U.S. Department of Agriculture, Forest Service, Pacific Northwest Research Station, 43–57.

Kaufman, H.F, and L.C. Kaufman. 1946. *Toward the Stabilization and Enrichment of a Forest Community: The Montana Study.* Missoula: University of Montana.

Kusel, J. 1996. Well-being in Forest-dependent Communities, Part I: A New Approach. In *Sierra Nevada Ecosystem Project: Final Report to Congress (vol. II): Assessments and Scientific Basis for Management Options.* Davis, CA: University of California, Centers for Water and Wildland Resources, 361–373.

———. 2001. Assessing Well-being in Forest-dependent Communities. In *Understanding Community-based Forest Ecosystem Management,* edited by G. J. Gray, M. J. Enzer, and J. Kusel. Binghamton, NY: Food Products Press, 359–384.

Kusel, J., and L.P. Fortmann. 1991. *Well-being in Forest-dependent Communities (vol. I).* Sacramento, CA: California Department of Forest and Rangeland Assessment Program.

Lee, K. 1993. *Compass and Gyroscope.* Washington, DC: Island Press.

Machlis, G.E., and J.E. Force. 1990. Community Stability and Timber-Dependent Communities: Future Research. In *Community and Forestry: Continuities in the Sociology of Natural Resources,* edited by W. Burch, Jr., D. Field, and R. Lee. Boulder, CO: Westview Press, 259–276.

McCool, S.F., J.A. Burchfield, and S.D. Allen. 1997. Social Assessment. In *An Assessment of Ecosystem Components in the Interior Columbia Basin and Portions of the Klamath and Great Basins (vol. 4),* edited by T.M. Quigley and S.J. Arbelbide. General Technical Report PNW-GTR-405. Portland, OR: U.S. Department of Agriculture, Forest Service, Pacific Northwest Research Station, 1873–2012.

Mills, T.J, and R.N Clark. 2001. Roles of Research Scientists in Natural Resource Decision-making. *Forest Ecology and Management* 153: 189–198.

Quigley, T.M., and S.J. Arbelbide (eds.). 1997. *An Assessment of Ecosystem Components in the Interior Columbia Basin and Portions of the Klamath and Great Basins* (Vol. 4).

General Technical Report PNW-GTR-405. Portland, OR: U.S. Department of Agriculture, Forest Service, Pacific Northwest Research Station.

Quigley, T.M., R.T. Graham, and R.W. Haynes. 1999. Interior Columbia Basin Ecosystem Management Project Case Study. In *Bioregional Assessments: Science at the Crossroads of Management and Policy*, edited by K. N. Johnson, F. Swanson, M. Herring, and S. Greene. Washington, DC: Island Press, 271–287.

Sierra Nevada Ecosystem Project (SNEP). 1996. *SNEP Final Report to Congress: Assessments and Scientific Basis for Management Options (vol. II)*. Davis, CA: University of California, Centers for Water and Wildland Resources.

Thomas, J.W. 2004. Sustainability of the Northwest Forest Plan: Still to be Tested. In *Forest Futures: Science, Politics, and Policy for the Next Century*, edited by K. Arabas and J. Bowersox. Lanham, MD: Rowman and Littlefield, 3–22.

3

Socioeconomic Monitoring and Forest Management

SUSAN CHARNLEY

Forests do not exist in isolation from human communities; people are a part of forest ecosystems. Thus, it is necessary to understand interactions between social and ecological systems to achieve sustainable forest management goals. Socioeconomic monitoring—the systematic observation and measurement of a set of social and economic indicators over time to obtain information about their status and trends—is one way of increasing understanding of these interactions. In the context of forest management, this is done by documenting changing social and economic conditions over time and providing insight into how these changes are linked to changes in forest management policy and forest conditions. Although socioeconomic monitoring is a key element of a "learning approach" to sustainable natural resource management that expands understanding of interactions between people and the environment (Keen and Mahanty 2006), to date socioeconomic monitoring often has not been integrated into forest management in the United States. The same is true of watershed management (Morton and Padgitt 2005) and ecosystem management more broadly (Busch and Trexler 2003b).

This chapter examines why socioeconomic monitoring for forest management has not advanced further and suggests ways to overcome some of the barriers to designing effective socioeconomic monitoring programs and integrating the results into forest management. Some of the constraints to socioeconomic monitoring—such as the failure of forest management agencies to implement adaptive management and limited budgets to support it—will be difficult to overcome. Others—such as views that it is unimportant, too difficult, unscientific, and will not yield information that can be used for management decisionmaking—can be addressed. I suggest ways of doing so through better program design and application of results, drawing on the example of the Northwest Forest Plan socioeconomic monitoring program in the discussion. I argue that careful construction of socioeconomic monitoring questions up front and a focus on monitoring indicators of the links between forest management and socioeconomic well-being that managers have the power to influence will improve program design. Engaging with managers to demonstrate how monitoring results can be integrated into planning and implementation; communicating results in easily understandable formats; explaining the scientific rigor of monitoring methods used; establishing benchmarks and thresholds for social and economic indicators; matching the scale at which monitoring takes place to the scale at which decisionmaking occurs; and better integrating research with monitoring will make it easier to apply socioeconomic monitoring results in forest management decisionmaking.

My focus is on socioeconomic monitoring for forest management in the United States, consistent with the geographic focus of this book, and on monitoring initiated by agencies and organizations that manage forests on public lands, rather than on monitoring initiated by communities, tribes, private forest owners, or other stakeholders, because this is the arena in which most socioeconomic monitoring for forest management takes place. Although I discuss monitoring in the context of forest management, the chapter is relevant for socioeconomic monitoring in a variety of natural resource management and conservation settings.

Socioeconomic Monitoring and Forest Management in the United States: The Current State of the Field

Scientists who write about ecosystem monitoring have observed that it is uncommon, although it is touted as an integral part of the adaptive natural resource management process (Fig. 3.1) and as necessary for providing information about whether resource management and conservation strategies are working (Busch and Trexler 2003a; Green et al. 2005; Kremen et al. 1994; Noon et al. 1999). Most of the literature on environmental monitoring pertains to air and water quality or focuses on individual plant and animal species. Few examples of ecosystem-scale monitoring programs for land management exist, and there is little evidence that monitoring information has helped inform natural resource management decisions and policy or avert environmental crises (Noon 2003). Socioeconomic monitoring for ecosystem management is even less common;[1] and monitoring associated with conservation projects also typically has focused on quantitative biological variables rather than on social and economic variables (Stem et al. 2005).

The current state of the field of socioeconomic monitoring for forest management can be summarized as follows:

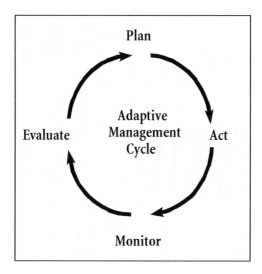

Figure 3-1. The Adaptive Management Process

- Ample literature identifies social and economic indicators that potentially can be monitored at the community, regional, and national scales. But there is little literature that demonstrates actual use of such indicators on the ground in monitoring programs, reports monitoring results, or that demonstrates how the results of socioeconomic monitoring have been used for forest management.
- Most of the socioeconomic monitoring that has occurred relies on quantitative social and economic indicators that can be tracked using secondary data sources or surveys. There are few examples that demonstrate the use of qualitative methods and data in socioeconomic monitoring.
- Although socioeconomic monitoring is on the rise, most examples of socioeconomic monitoring associated with forest management at the community scale consist of newly established programs or pilot studies. There are few examples of long-term socioeconomic monitoring programs for forest management.
- There are several excellent "how to" guides for conducting socioeconomic monitoring. But few examples demonstrate how such guides have been used to develop and implement socioeconomic monitoring programs.
- There is little evidence that socioeconomic monitoring has led to improved forest management policies and practices that have better outcomes for communities and increase the community benefits associated with forest management.

I illustrate these points by providing a brief overview of the existing literature on socioeconomic monitoring for forest management in the United States that

reflects the current state of the field. I organize this literature into five categories: state-of-the-environment monitoring, social and economic indicator
frameworks, forest certification monitoring, monitoring to support forest management on public lands, and participatory monitoring.

State-of-the-Environment Monitoring

Monitoring is not always associated with specific interventions; sometimes it
is used to track the status of key variables of interest in a country or region
(Stem et al. 2005). This type of monitoring can be referred to as "state-of-the-
environment" monitoring. An example is the Montreal Process Working Group
on Criteria and Indicators for the Conservation and Sustainable Management
of Temperate and Boreal Forests, begun in 1994 (The Montreal Process 2006).
This international monitoring effort, in which the United States participates,
takes place at the national scale to evaluate a country's progress toward sustainable forest management. Progress is evaluated using seven criteria and 67 indicators identified by the working group (see USDA FS 2004).[2] Two of the criteria
(and 39 associated indicators) pertain to socioeconomics: 1) maintenance and
enhancement of long-term multiple socioeconomic benefits to meet the needs
of society; and 2) legal, institutional, and economic frameworks for forest conservation and sustainable management.

   State-of-the-environment monitoring provides information about status
and trends in social and ecological conditions relating to forest sustainability.
It may reveal some effects associated with high-level policy, but it does not
demonstrate causality (Stem et al. 2005). Instead, it serves as a communication
tool that may trigger action by the public or policymakers. There have been
some attempts to use the Montreal Process criteria and indicators for monitoring sustainable forest management at the state and community scales. Oregon
was the first state to use the Montreal Process to assess forest sustainability at
the state level; the results are found in Oregon Department of Forestry (2000).
Sustainable Measures, Inc., and American Forests (2003) created a toolkit that
can help forest-based communities assess the ecological, economic, and social
aspects of forest resources locally using the Montreal Process Criteria and Indicators. The toolkit includes three case studies of communities that have tried
it and the lessons they learned.

   In 1999, the Forest Service began a pilot study called the Local Unit Criteria and Indicators Development (LUCID) test to assess the feasibility of monitoring ecosystem sustainability at the national forest scale (Wright et al. 2002).
The study focused on developing a set of criteria and indicators for monitoring sustainability on and around six pilot national forests, including the sustainability of socioeconomic systems, in support of adaptive ecosystem
management and forest planning. The result was a monitoring framework
containing a core suite of criteria and indicators for sustainability monitor-

ing. The framework is a resource that can be used to guide social and economic sustainability monitoring in forest communities (see Wright et al. 2002, Appendix 10).

Social and Economic Indicator Frameworks

The sustainability monitoring programs described above produced frameworks of indicators that are relevant for socioeconomic monitoring in the context of forest management. Other frameworks of social and economic indicators that can be used for monitoring sustainability and well-being in natural resource-based communities also have been developed (e.g., Beckley and Burkosky 1999; Hart 1999; Parkins et al. 2001; Seesholtz et al. 2004). This work typically identifies a set of socioeconomic indicators that can be used in monitoring but stops short of applying them in monitoring programs and reporting monitoring results that are useful for ecosystem management. Consequently, although indicator frameworks provide guidance for what to monitor, they do not provide guidance for how to monitor or demonstrate how socioeconomic monitoring results have been applied in the forest management context.

Other researchers have used social and economic indicators in conducting broad-scale assessments in support of forest planning and for social impact assessments associated with proposed forest management actions. There are several excellent examples of social assessments that demonstrate the use of such indicators in assessing social and economic conditions and trends and community well-being, resiliency, and capacity (e.g., Christensen et al. 2000; Doak and Kusel 1996; FEMAT 1993; Harris et al. 2000; Haynes and Horne 1997; McCool et al. 1997; Struglia et al. 2001). Similarly, the social impact assessment literature identifies social and economic indicators that can be used for assessing baseline conditions in an area and predicting how they may be affected by proposed interventions (e.g., Burdge 2004; ICPGSIA 2003; USDA FS 1988). Although the indicators used in such assessments were not developed within a monitoring framework, they do provide a frame of reference for building a set of indicators to use in socioeconomic monitoring programs and often contain baseline information against which to monitor.

Forest Certification Monitoring

Forest certification is a market-driven strategy for promoting sustainable forestry practices. Certification sets standards of operation for the forest industry that encourage ecologically sound, socially responsible, and economically beneficial forestry practices. Entities desiring certification must comply with a set of standards established by a forest certification system, such as that developed by the Forest Stewardship Council (FSC) or the Sustainable Forestry Initiative (SFI). The FSC has 10 principles and 56 associated criteria that are used to evaluate candidates. About half of the principles include socioeconomic standards and two of the ten do so explicitly: 1) conducting forest management in a way that enhances or maintains the long-term socioeconomic well-being of forest workers and local communities; and 2) recognizing and respecting the rights of indigenous peoples to own, use, and manage their lands and resources (FSC 2004). In contrast, the SFI assumes that social and economic issues will be addressed by U.S. laws and regulations and that the market is the best mechanism for addressing economic viability (Danks 2004).

Private organizations that have been accredited by the FSC or the SFI serve as certifying bodies and conduct assessments (or audits) of entities seeking certification to determine if the candidate produces wood and wood products in a manner that complies with the certification standards. Once a forest or a company is certified, monitoring is necessary to ensure that the certified entity continues to comply with the certification standards. Monitoring also may be required as part of a certified entity's forest management plan to document the social and ecological effects of harvesting and other operations. Despite the need and requirements, to date socioeconomic monitoring for forest certification has been limited, inconsistent, and produced little data (Danks 2004). Reasons for this include the difficulty of making the principles operational and evaluating them.

Monitoring for Forest Management on Public Lands

Most public forestlands in the United States are managed by the Forest Service. The National Forest Management Act (1976) requires the Forest Service to monitor forest plans to ensure that management systems do not impair the productivity of the land.[3] In the 1990s, the agency elevated the importance of monitoring by holding monitoring workshops; developing a national monitoring and evaluation strategy and a framework for inventory and monitoring; writing guidance on monitoring; establishing an Inventory and Monitoring Institute; and forming working groups to better implement monitoring and evaluation associated with forest plans (Powell 2004). The 2004 National Forest System Land Management Planning Rule states that a forest plan must describe the plan monitoring program, taking into account key social, economic, and ecological performance measures that are relevant to the plan area. The purpose of monitoring is to determine if a forest plan is achieving its multiple-use objectives and maintaining or progressing toward its desired conditions and objectives (USDA FS 2005a).

Although the importance of adaptive management and the need for monitoring to support it are now widely recognized within the Forest Service, to date most monitoring conducted by the agency still consists of implementation monitoring—which focuses on whether a management policy, program, or project was implemented the way it was supposed to be—rather than on effectiveness monitoring, which assesses whether a policy, program, or project is achieving its intended goals and objectives. Moreover, socioeconomic monitoring has received little attention by the agency. Exceptions are the LUCID project discussed above, the Northwest Forest Plan socioeconomic monitoring program (Charnley 2006), monitoring associated with the Forest Service stewardship contracting program[4] (Pinchot Institute for Conservation 2005), and the Collaborative Forest Restoration Program monitoring[5] (CFRP 2005b).

Other social monitoring relating to federal forest management in the United States focuses on human uses of public lands, especially visitation and recreation (e.g., the Forest Service National Visitor Use Monitoring Program, NVUM 2005), and on public attitudes, beliefs, and values about forest management (e.g., The National Survey on Recreation and the Environment, Shields et al. 2002). These programs are designed to produce monitoring data that are useful at the regional and national scales; they are less valid at the community and individual national forest scales.

Participatory Monitoring

Participatory monitoring associated with forest management, such as multiparty monitoring[6] and community-based monitoring,[7] occurs when community members or groups of interested stakeholders organize to monitor forest resources or forest management activities and their social or ecological effects (e.g., Bliss et al. 2001; CFRP 2005b; Lynch et al. 2004). The participatory approach to monitoring can be used in any of the kinds of monitoring programs described above. There are several examples of participatory monitoring relating to forest management in the United States.

Some community-based organizations have taken the initiative to conduct monitoring that evaluates the links between management actions on nearby federal forests and socioeconomic trends in their communities and counties. For example, the Watershed Research and Training Center in Trinity County, California, has monitored several community and county-scale socioeconomic indicators, as well as timber harvest levels, timber values, mill closures, and related employment associated with public and private lands in the county (Danks et al. 2002; Wilson 2003). The Northeast Oregon Community Assessment Workgroup monitored social and economic conditions and trends in three northeastern Oregon counties and restoration and stewardship contracting projects in national forests in the Blue Mountains (Wallowa Resources et al. 2004). These types of monitoring programs help communities, agencies, and others understand the social and economic effects of forest management practices.

In the Southwest, stakeholder groups have become involved in monitoring collaborative forest restoration projects in national forests. They are determining how well the projects are achieving their social and ecological goals and if restoration forestry techniques and plans need to be altered to improve results

(CFRP 2005a). Another example of participatory monitoring comes from Lynch et al. (2004), who describe nontimber forest product harvesters monitoring the amount and distribution of nontimber forest product species on federal forest lands and harvester impacts on them.

Several organizations have developed handbooks to guide the participatory monitoring process. The Forest Service, in collaboration with several partner organizations, has produced a series of handbooks that guide participants through the process of gathering and evaluating social and ecological monitoring data associated with forest restoration projects (USDA FS 2005b). Moseley and Wilson (2002) provide a guidebook for developing multi-party monitoring programs that focus on activities relating to forest management on public lands and community forestry—specifically, forest restoration and maintenance projects, the use of by-products from forest restoration projects, and grants and other investments. Pilz et al. (2006) have written a guide for multi-party biological monitoring for forest management. Another handbook focuses on participatory monitoring for community forestry projects (Davis-Case 1998). More broadly, some handbooks are designed to help communities monitor the results of rural community development projects and conservation efforts and community sustainability (e.g., Margoluis and Salafsky 1998; NCRCRD 1999).

Why Has Socioeconomic Monitoring for Forest Management Not Advanced Further?

There are several possible explanations for why the field of socioeconomic monitoring for forest management has not advanced further. Monitoring in general in the context of forest management often is viewed as one component of the adaptive management process. Adaptive management is an approach to managing ecosystems in which management actions are implemented and their effects monitored and learned from so that future management actions can be improved (Bormann et al. 1999; USDA FS 2005a). However, adaptive management is not well established as an approach to forest management. Despite the rhetoric around the concept, it rarely has been implemented on the ground (Bormann et al. 2007; Stankey et al. 2003) and has been much more influential as an idea than as a way of undertaking conservation (Lee 1999). If adaptive management is not implemented, monitoring as one component of the adaptive management process is not likely to be systematically implemented either.

If monitoring is conducted, it could reveal that forest management strategies are not succeeding in meeting their goals. Governments and organizations that do not like the information they get from monitoring might then "shoot the messenger." Terborgh and Davenport (2002) make this point in the context of monitoring the status of protected areas in developing countries. There, governments may be reluctant to cooperate with monitoring organizations because doing so could reveal threats to these areas, such as widespread illegal logging, which, if publicized, could make them look bad; it is not safe to fail (Borgerhoff Mulder and Coppolillo 2005). To the extent that monitoring associated with forest management does occur, ecological monitoring is conducted more frequently than socioeconomic monitoring. One explanation for this imbalance could be that forest management in the United States typically takes place within defined geographical areas where people do not reside (e.g., forests located on public or private industrial lands). Thus, monitoring the biophysical components of the ecosystem may appear more relevant. If socioeconomic monitoring does occur, it often focuses on human activities within the forest, such as extraction, visitation, recreation, and resource use, to understand how these uses affect biophysical resources. This type of monitoring falls short, however, because forest management also affects socioeconomic conditions in forest communities and socioeconomic conditions in forest communities affect forest management on public and private lands. Monitoring these relations is as important as monitoring the direct effects of human use on forest ecosystems.

Another explanation for the imbalance between biophysical and socioeconomic monitoring may be that socioeconomic goals and objectives have not been incorporated into forest management plans and policies; therefore, socioeconomic monitoring to evaluate the effectiveness of these plans and policies is not called for. Since the late 1980s, a large literature has developed debating the merits of incorporating social-justice and economic-development objectives into natural resource management and conservation policies and projects (see Brandon et al. 1998; Brechin et al. 2003; McShane and Wells 2004; Terborgh et al. 2002). Although many people assert that effective conservation strategies are contingent upon including such objectives, others argue that these strategies cannot be expected to deliver on both environmental conservation and socioeconomic goals and that these should be pursued independently.

Even if socioeconomic objectives are incorporated into forest management policies and plans (which usually they are), monitoring progress toward meeting these objectives may not be a priority. Monitoring is expensive. Funding frequently is inadequate to support good monitoring programs, so they often are not implemented fully (Noon 2003). Spending limited funds on project implementation may be a higher priority than monitoring (Tolle et al. 1999). And it can take a long time for the social effects of a policy or project to be realized. This means long-term monitoring is necessary to see results, increasing the cost (Trexler and Busch 2003). In a climate of scarce resources, agencies and organizations only may monitor the things they consider essential or that they are legally required to. Even when socioeconomic monitoring is required legally, it may not be done due to a lack of funds or other priorities. The distribution of funding also reflects agency biases about which forest management questions are most compelling, which rarely are the socioeconomic ones. For example, only $1.6 million of the $50.2 million spent on Northwest

Forest Plan monitoring between 1994 and 2005 went toward socioeconomic work (Bormann et al. 2007). Over half of the money went to monitoring the northern spotted owl (*Strix occidentalis caurina*), listed as threatened under the Endangered Species Act.

Without legal or regulatory requirements, forest management agencies and organizations may only invest in monitoring if they believe it is in their interest to do so. In this case, socioeconomic monitoring only may occur if decisionmakers believe that the health of forest ecosystems depends on the health of associated socioeconomic systems or that their ability to achieve the ecological goals associated with forest management will be compromised if socioeconomic goals are not realized too. Although community-based groups may place a higher priority on socioeconomic monitoring, locally driven monitoring efforts depend on the presence of people who have the interest, capacity, and resources to initiate it. Such community-based groups are not widespread.

The underemphasis on socioeconomic monitoring also may be explained by a shortage of knowledge, experience, and models for how to go about it. Monitoring methods in general have not been perfected yet (Terborgh and Davenport 2002), and socioeconomic monitoring methods are no exception. Monitoring is a difficult and complex process, and in the absence of models, accepted methods, and protocols, it is necessary to invest a great deal of time in developing and testing approaches. Particularly at the community scale, socioeconomic monitoring is not a well-developed science. The difficulty of figuring out how to do it can be a disincentive. It is easier to monitor things for which protocols exist and that people have experience with and know how to monitor. Nevertheless, there is a growing body of work to draw on in developing methods and protocols for socioeconomic monitoring and forest management at the community scale, which will help overcome this barrier.

Finally, forest management agencies and conservation organizations may believe that socioeconomic monitoring will not yield information that is useful for decisionmaking. Theory about the links between forest management and socioeconomic conditions in forest communities is still poorly developed. If socioeconomic monitoring is not perceived as useful and its ability to inform decisionmaking related to forest management is poorly understood, why invest in it? Monitoring can be a meaningless exercise if it does not have clear ties to the forest management process and agencies and organizations in a position to fund it may not see these ties.

Ways Forward

Some barriers to socioeconomic monitoring—such as a failure of forest management agencies and organizations to implement adaptive management and the lack of funding to support monitoring—may be difficult to overcome. Other barriers may stem from unfamiliarity with it on the part of decisionmakers working for forest management agencies and organizations—who rarely are trained in the social sciences. I discuss barriers associated with the use of socioeconomic monitoring information below by offering suggestions for making it more relevant to forest management through better program design and better application of results. I use the case of socioeconomic monitoring associated with the Northwest Forest Plan to illustrate some of my points (see Charnley 2006).

The Northwest Forest Plan is a broad-scale ecosystem-management plan adopted in 1994 that applies to 22 million acres of Forest Service- and Bureau of Land Management-managed land in the Pacific Northwest. It aims to balance the need for protecting older forest habitat and endangered species with the need to maximize economic and social benefits from forests to help maintain community stability and assist with economic development and diversification in communities affected by cutbacks in federal timber harvesting (USDA and USDI 1994). The plan required a monitoring program to track progress in meeting these goals, which led to establishment of the Northwest Forest Plan socioeconomic monitoring program in the late 1990s.

Program Design

The first step in designing a socioeconomic monitoring program is to identify the monitoring questions. Although this appears straightforward, identifying the right monitoring questions can be difficult. Monitoring questions should be designed to address the priority information needs of forest managers and to be durable, so that the monitoring results—which may not be produced for several years—still will be relevant. Including clients of the monitoring information (forest managers, community members, and other stakeholder groups) and scientists in the process of formulating monitoring questions will help ensure that they are relevant to those who have an interest in the monitoring program and that they produce useful information when answered. In the Northwest Forest Plan case, the questions posed for monitoring in 1994 were not always precise, easily answerable, or relevant for subsequent decisionmaking needs. This shortcoming was addressed through a new process implemented in 2006 to define core questions for long-term monitoring by holding a series of workshops in which participating stakeholders identified and ranked priority monitoring questions.

As noted earlier in this chapter, most of the socioeconomic monitoring that has occurred relies on quantitative social and economic indicators that can be tracked using secondary data sources or surveys. Forest management agencies and organizations often perceive monitoring based on quantitative social and economic indicator data from existing, secondary sources as being adequate and reliable. However, there are limitations to relying on such data alone, as Force and Machlis (1997) and Jackson et al. (2004) point out. Monitoring that tracks existing quantitative data from secondary sources can reveal change in select social and economic indicators and provide a general picture of the social and economic context in which forest management takes place. Data gathered for other purposes, however, may not answer the monitoring questions. Furthermore, the scale at which the data were collected may not be the scale needed; they do not reveal what the change reflected by the indicators looks like on the ground and how people experience it, and they do not reveal how social and economic change might be linked to forest management actions. Effective socioeconomic monitoring for forest management generally requires a methodological approach that combines gathering quantitative data from existing, secondary sources with primary data collection in communities (both quantitative and qualitative). This approach was used for the Northwest Forest Plan socioeconomic monitoring program, with positive results.

Finally, it is important in program design to focus monitoring on the things that link forests and communities that forest managers have some ability to influence. If forest managers cannot take actions that will influence social and economic monitoring trends or increase the effectiveness of forest management policy and plans, the monitoring information cannot be used for adaptive management. Northwest Forest Plan socioeconomic monitoring did this by focusing monitoring on those things associated with forest management that had been identified through previous research as contributing to community well-being. For example, a reliable supply of wood produced from federal forestlands is important because it is needed to support community investments in processing technologies and businesses that utilize wood in manufacturing value-added products. Contracting jobs in forest restoration provide employment opportunities to local residents and contribute to ecosystem management goals in forests. Maintaining agency field offices in rural communities provides local jobs, enhances collaborative relationships between agencies and communities, and keeps agency employees (who often contribute significantly to community capacity) in communities. And, agency community economic assistance programs can make a significant contribution to economic development in rural communities. Thus, the Northwest Forest Plan monitoring program monitored the volume of timber offered for sale from federal forest lands, agency procurement contracting, agency employment and number of field offices, and community economic assistance. These all are things that forest managers have the ability to influence. Focusing monitoring in this way gives forest managers information about trends in the socioeconomic benefits that forests provide to communities and whether these benefits are increasing, declining, or remaining steady. They can use this information to determine if management action is needed.

Communicating Monitoring Information

Once socioeconomic monitoring has been completed, how can the information best be communicated and integrated into forest management decisionmaking? The adaptive forest management cycle has four steps: plan, act, monitor, and evaluate. Social scientists involved in monitoring and evaluation should not disengage from this process once monitoring and evaluation are complete. Instead, they should be actively involved in integrating monitoring and evaluation results back into planning and implementation. Direct interaction with decisionmakers to explain the monitoring results, their implications, and potential management responses to observed changes is critical.

Monitoring information also needs to be communicated in a format that is accessible to forest managers and other decisionmakers. Quantitative data that are presented in charts, tables, and graphs communicate information quickly and easily. Spatial data presented in maps also are easy to communicate and can be integrated with biophysical data. Qualitative monitoring information is more difficult to communicate, as it generally requires a lot of writing, which can result in long reports. To the extent possible, qualitative monitoring data should be presented concisely and simply. The use of figures and tables goes a long way in communicating monitoring results to managers and decisionmakers.

Establishing Benchmarks and Thresholds

Forest managers may not know when to use the results from socioeconomic monitoring because socioeconomic monitoring indicators typically lack benchmarks and thresholds. A benchmark is the value of an indicator that represents the desired condition one is trying to achieve through a management action (Bormann et al. 1999). It may be expressed as a bounded range of variability that is desirable or as a specific value. A threshold is a region of change in the value of an indicator that represents a trigger point beyond which it is unacceptable to go. One characteristic of effectiveness monitoring is that there are benchmarks associated with the monitoring indicators that set the standard for measuring progress toward achieving management goals and evaluating success. Threshold values also should be identified that indicate when a management intervention is needed. Thresholds and benchmarks provide mechanisms for linking monitoring to adaptive management by indicating when managers should intervene and change course or when management practices are working.

It can be difficult to establish benchmarks and thresholds for socioeconomic indicators. At what point is a socioeconomic condition unacceptable, warranting action by decisionmakers? And who defines the benchmarks and thresholds, thereby determining what constitutes acceptable or unacceptable socioeconomic conditions in communities? The Northwest Forest Plan Record of Decision stated, "Because of the complexity of the relationships and the number of factors involved … it is not possible to set specific or definite thresholds or values that would cause a reevaluation of the goals and overall strategy of these standards and guidelines" (USDA and USDI 1994, E-9). Although it is difficult to establish benchmarks and thresholds for socioeconomic indicators, failing to do so may leave managers not knowing when to act.

Experts in monitoring emphasize the importance of establishing quantifiable expectations regarding the goals of natural resource management policies and actions so that managers will know if management plans are producing the desired results. More effort should be made to identify concrete social and economic goals and expectations relating to forest management that are explicitly stated in qualitative or quantitative terms. Quantitative expectations, benchmarks, and thresholds run the risk of being arbitrary; and qualitative expectations, benchmarks, and thresholds can be imprecise and subjective. Nevertheless, developing standards against which to monitor when designing socioeconomic monitoring programs will make monitoring information more useful. One way of doing this would be through a multi-party process in which a cross-section of stakeholders collaborates to develop such standards, thereby making them meaningful to the specific monitoring context. These standards will help managers gauge when to act in response to monitoring trends.

Scale

Forest management policy and plans generally are created at large scales but are implemented locally and have local effects. Community-scale monitoring is needed to document these effects and assess effectiveness. The challenge lies in aggregating community-scale monitoring results so that they can be used to make meaningful statements for informing broad-scale policy formulation and planning. Adding to this difficulty is the fact that places and communities differ and the answer to the monitoring questions may be: "It depends." One can look to communities for patterns and commonalities upon which to base generalizations, but the significant findings may be rooted in variation; for example, in understanding why a forest management policy has different effects in different communities. Community-scale monitoring results that cannot be generalized to support broad-scale ecosystem management and that do not imply a one-size-fits-all solution, however, may not be useful for decisionmaking at the ecosystem scale.

Thus, it is important to identify the appropriate scale at which monitoring results can inform decisionmaking. Monitoring a sample of communities across a broad geographic area may make it possible to identify key patterns, themes, and insights that can improve our understanding of how the relationship between forest management and community well-being varies across geographic areas and community types. This can help guide broad-scale forest management but may be most useful for local-level decisionmaking. Alternatively, broad-scale monitoring using secondary data may indicate red flags in certain places where more in-depth, community-scale investigation and primary data gathering can be focused to identify causes and locally specific solutions. Monitoring approaches will need to be adapted as needed to support decisionmaking locally or across a large region.

Integrating Research with Monitoring

Finally, socioeconomic monitoring information may be difficult to apply to forest management because it is difficult to identify and measure cause-and-effect relationships between forest management actions and socioeconomic change in communities. Decisionmakers may not know if a forest management policy or practice is the cause of an observed social or economic trend, if other variables are the cause, or how forest management combines with other influencing factors to affect social and economic conditions and trends in a place. This uncertainty makes it difficult to identify what actions they can take to produce more favorable results.

One solution is to better integrate research with monitoring. Monitoring is the repeated observation and measurement of indicators over time to assess change. By itself, it does not fully reveal the causes of change, identify links between management actions and monitoring trends, or indicate what actions will alter undesirable trends. Such understandings emerge from a strong foundation of research. Thus, "monitoring and research exist within a positive feedback loop in which descriptive monitoring analyses generate hypotheses that catalyze research inquiry directed at causation and vice versa" (Busch and Trexler 2003a, 4). Existing social science research findings relating to forests and communities should be used to inform the development of monitoring questions and indicators and to build hypotheses about cause-and-effect relationships that can be tested through monitoring and research. Monitoring results, in turn, should inform new research agendas that address management needs and help decisionmakers understand what actions they can take to contribute to positive socioeconomic conditions and trends in forest communities. Understanding what community benefits are produced from forests and forest management policies can be sufficient to identify important variables to monitor, even if it is unclear to what extent producing these benefits—versus other variables—is affecting community well-being.

Conclusion

I have argued in this chapter that socioeconomic monitoring can contribute much to forest management, but there is work to do to improve its application and relevance. Biophysical monitoring information alone is insufficient for assessing ecosystem health and the effectiveness of forest management and conservation interventions; social, political, economic, and cultural monitoring information also is needed (Stem et al. 2005). Socioeconomic monitoring is a critical component of the adaptive management process, providing a mechanism for obtaining information about the results of resource management actions that managers can use to develop future management policies and practices. It provides information about the current state of, and long-term changes in, social and economic conditions in communities, counties, and wider geographic regions. It illuminates the links between these conditions and forest management. Socioeconomic monitoring also makes it possible to evaluate how well natural resource management agencies and conservation organizations are meeting their social and economic goals. Monitoring makes it possible to assess the strategies developed to achieve these goals, to determine if they are being implemented effectively, and potentially how to improve them. It also helps generate hypotheses regarding the causes of undesirable trends that can be tested through research and used to develop solutions.

Socioeconomic monitoring produces information that can help forest managers enhance the social and economic benefits that forests and forest management provide to communities and regions. It is also a process that can build relationships and knowledge among the people involved, especially when undertaken by a mixed group of stakeholders. As such, socioeconomic monitoring creates an opportunity for forest managers and community members to develop deeper understandings and stronger relationships. This can lead to collaborative forest stewardship activities in which community members and forest managers pool resources and work together to address forest management problems. Indeed, healthy forest communities can be an asset to managers in achieving their forest management goals. Therefore, it is in the interest of forest management agencies and organizations to conduct socioeconomic monitoring that will help them enhance their ability to contribute to socioeconomic well-being in forest communities through their management actions.

A major contribution to the field now would be for those who are engaged in socioeconomic monitoring to document their methods, demonstrating how they have applied social and economic indicators in the monitoring process, and to show how their monitoring results have been used to improve both forest management and forest-related benefits to communities, with case examples. Demonstrating how socioeconomic monitoring can make a difference on the ground to both community well-being and the ecological health of forests will help make it a priority for investment by natural resource managers and will move the field forward.

Notes

1. One example unrelated to forestry is the global socioeconomic monitoring initiative for coastal zone management (Bunce and Pomeroy 2003; Bunce et al. 2000).

2. The Montreal Process defines criteria as conditions or processes by which sustainable forest management may be assessed; indicators are variables relating to an aspect of a criterion that can be described and measured.

3. A forest plan is a document or set of documents that integrates and displays information relevant to the management of a national forest.

4. The fiscal year 1999 Omnibus Appropriations Act authorized the Forest Service to implement a pilot stewardship contracting program to test innovative ways of conducting ecological restoration work. Stewardship contracts are designed to achieve land-management goals in the national forests while providing social and economic benefits to local communities. Subsequent appropriations bills have expanded Forest Service and Bureau of Land Management authorities to conduct stewardship contracting. Monitoring and evaluation of the stewardship contracting projects are required.

5. This monitoring program was established as a result of the Community Forest Restoration Act of 2000, which created a Cooperative Forest Restoration Program in New Mexico that includes project monitoring as a requirement.

6. Multi-party monitoring consists of monitoring by a mixed group of people who are affiliated with local communities; local, regional, or national interest groups; and public agencies (CFRP 2005a).

7. Community-based monitoring refers to monitoring activities designed to produce information on social and ecological factors affecting a community that is needed or desired by the community and in which members of the community participate (Bliss et al. 2001).

Acknowledgments

I would like to thank Dennis Becker, Ellen Donoghue, Anne Moote, Douglas Powell, and Vicky Sturtevant for their extremely helpful review of and comments on earlier drafts of this chapter. Participants in the communities and forests workshop also provided valuable feedback and discussion that helped advance my thinking on socioeconomic monitoring and improve the chapter. I am also grateful to Rhonda Mazza for her editorial assistance.

References

Beckley, T.M., and T.M. Burkosky. 1999. *Social Indicator Approaches to Assessing and Monitoring Forest Community Sustainability.* Northern Forestry Centre Information Report NOR-X-360. Edmonton, Alberta: Canadian Forest Service, Northern Forestry Centre.

Bliss, J., G. Aplet, C. Hartzell, P. Harwood, P. Jahnige, D. Kittredge, S. Lewandowski, and M.L. Soscia. 2001. Community-based Ecosystem Monitoring. In *Understanding Community-based Forest Ecosystem Management*, edited by G.J. Gray, M.J. Enzer, and J. Kusel. Binghamton, NY: Food Products Press, 143–167.

Borgerhoff Mulder, M., and P. Coppolillo. 2005. *Conservation: Linking Ecology, Economics, and Culture.* Princeton, NJ: Princeton University Press.

Bormann, B.T., R.W. Haynes, and J.R. Martin. 2007. Adaptive Management of Forest Ecosystems: Did Some Rubber Hit the Road? *BioScience* 57(2): 186–191.

Bormann, B.T., J.R. Martin, F.H. Wagner, G.W. Wood, J. Alegria, P.G. Cunningham, M.H. Brookes, P. Friesema, J. Berg, and J.R. Henshaw. 1999. Adaptive Management. In *Ecological Stewardship: A Common Reference for Ecosystem Management* (Vol. III), edited by W.T. Sexton, A.J. Malk, R.C. Szaro, and N.C. Johnson. Oxford: Elsevier Science Ltd., 505–534.

Brandon, K., K.H. Redford, and S.E. Sanderson. 1998. *Parks in Peril: People, Politics, and Protected Areas.* Washington, DC: The Nature Conservancy and Island Press.

Brechin, S.R., P.R. Wilshusen, C.L. Fortwangler, and P.C. West. 2003. *Contested Nature: Promoting International Biodiversity with Social Justice in the Twenty-first Century.* Albany, NY: State University of New York Press.

Bunce, L., and R. Pomeroy. 2003. *Socioeconomic Monitoring Guidelines for Coastal Managers in Southeast Asia.* Townsville, Australia: World Commission on Protected Areas and Australian Institute of Marine Science.

Bunce, L., P. Townsley, R. Pomeroy, and R. Pollnac. 2000. *Socioeconomic Manual for Coral Reef Management.* Townsville, Australia: Australian Institute of Marine Science.

Burdge, R. J. 2004. *A Community Guide to Social Impact Assessment.* Middleton, WI: Social Ecology Press.

Busch, D.E., and J.C. Trexler. 2003a. The Importance of Monitoring in Regional Ecosystem Initiatives. In *Monitoring Ecosystems: Interdisciplinary Approaches for Evaluating Ecoregional Initiatives,* edited by D.E. Busch and J.C. Trexler. Washington, DC: Island Press, 1–23.

———. eds. 2003b. *Monitoring Ecosystems: Interdisciplinary Approaches for Evaluating Ecoregional Initiatives.* Washington, DC: Island Press.

Charnley, S. (tech. coord.). 2006. *Northwest Forest Plan—The First 10 Years (1994-2003): Socioeconomic Monitoring Results.* Six Volumes. General Technical Report PNW-GTR-649. Portland, OR: U.S. Department of Agriculture, Forest Service, Pacific Northwest Research Station.

Christensen, H.H., W.J. McGinnis, T.L. Raettig, and E.M. Donoghue. 2000. *Atlas of Human Adaptation to Environmental Change, Challenge, and Opportunity: Northern California, Western Oregon, and Western Washington.* General Technical Report PNW-GTR-478. Portland, OR: U.S. Department of Agriculture, Forest Service, Pacific Northwest Research Station.

Collaborative Forest Restoration Program (CFRP). 2005a. *What is Multiparty Monitoring? Handbook 1, The Multiparty Monitoring Handbook Series.* Flagstaff, AZ: Ecological Restoration Institute.

———. 2005b. *Monitoring Social and Economic Effects of Forest Restoration. Handbook 5, The Multiparty Monitoring Handbook Series.* Flagstaff, AZ: Ecological Restoration Institute.

Danks, C. 2004. Socioeconomic Monitoring in Forest Certification in the U.S. Paper Presented at the Monitoring Science and Technology Symposium, September 20–24, Denver, CO.

Danks, C., L.J. Wilson, and L. Jungwirth. 2002. *Community-based Socioeconomic Assessment and Monitoring of Activities Related to National Forest Management, Parts 1 and 2.* Hayfork, CA: The Watershed Research and Training Center.

Davis-Case, D. 1998. Community Forestry: Participatory Assessment, Monitoring and Evaluation. *Community Forestry Note No. 2.* Rome, Italy: Food and Agriculture Organization of the United Nations.

Doak, S., and J. Kusel. 1996. Well-being in Forest-dependent Communities. Part 2: A Social Assessment. In *Sierra Nevada Ecosystem Project: Final Report to Congress: Assessments and Scientific Basis for Management Options* (vol. 2). Davis, CA: University of California, Center for Water and Wildland Resources, 375–402.

Force, J.E., and G.E. Machlis. 1997. The Human Ecosystem Part II: Social Indicators in Ecosystem Management. *Society and Natural Resources* 10: 369–382.

Forest Ecosystem Management Assessment Team (FEMAT). 1993. *Forest Ecosystem Management: An Ecological, Economic, and Social Assessment.* Portland, OR: U.S. Department of Agriculture, U.S. Department of the Interior [and others].

Forest Stewardship Council (FSC). 2004. *FSC Principles and Criteria for Forest Stewardship.* Report No. FSC-STD-01-001. Washington, DC: Forest Stewardship Council.

Green, R.E., A. Balmford, P.R. Crane, G.M. Mace, J.D. Reynolds, and R.K. Turner. 2005. A Framework for Improved Monitoring of Biodiversity: Responses to the World Summit on Sustainable Development. *Conservation Biology* 19(1): 56–65.

Harris, C., W. McLaughlin, G. Brown, and D.R. Becker. 2000. *Rural Communities in the Inland Northwest: An Assessment of Small Rural Communities in the Interior and Upper Columbia River Basins.* General Technical Report PNW-GTR-477. Portland, OR: U.S. Department of Agriculture, Forest Service, Pacific Northwest Research Station.

Hart, M. 1999. *Guide to Sustainable Community Indicators.* West Hartford, CT: Sustainable Measures.

Haynes, R.W., and A.L. Horne. 1997. Economic Assessment of the Basin. In *An Assessment of Ecosystem Components in the Interior Columbia Basin and Portions of the Klamath and Great Basins:* (Vol. IV), edited by T. M. Quigley and S. J. Arbelbide. General Technical Report PNW-GTR-405. Portland, OR: U.S. Department of Agriculture, Forest Service, Pacific Northwest Research Station, 1715–1869.

Interorganizational Committee on Principles and Guidelines for Social Impact Assessment (ICPGSIA). 2003. U.S. Principles and Guidelines for Social Impact Assessment. *Impact Assessment and Project Appraisal* 21(3): 223–270.

Jackson, J.E., R.G. Lee, and P. Sommers. 2004. Monitoring the Community Impacts of the Northwest Forest Plan: An Alternative to Social Indicators. *Society and Natural Resources* 17: 223–233.

Keen, M., and S. Mahanty. 2006. Learning in Sustainable Natural Resource Management: Challenges and Opportunities in the Pacific. *Society and Natural Resources* 19: 497–513.

Kremen, C., A.M. Merenlender, and D.D. Murphy. 1994. Ecological Monitoring: A Vital Need for Integrated Conservation and Development Programs in the Tropics. *Conservation Biology* 8(2): 388–397.

Lee, K.N. 1999. Appraising Adaptive Management. *Conservation Ecology* 3(2): 3.

Lynch, K.A., E.T. Jones, and R.J. McLain. 2004. *Nontimber Forest Product Inventorying and Monitoring in the United States: Rationale and Recommendations for a Participatory Approach.* National Commission on Science for Sustainable Forestry. http://ifcae.org/projects/ncssf1/ (accessed February 25, 2007).

Margoluis, R., and N. Salafsky. 1998. *Measures of Success: Designing, Managing, and Monitoring Conservation and Development Projects.* Washington, DC: Island Press.

McCool, S.F., J.A. Burchfield, and S.D. Allen. 1997. Social Assessment. In *An Assessment of Ecosystem Components in the Interior Columbia Basin and Portions of the Klamath and Great Basins: Volume IV*, edited by T. M. Quigley and S. J. Arbelbide. General Technical Report PNW-GTR-405. Portland, OR: U.S. Department of Agriculture, Forest Service, Pacific Northwest Research Station, 1871–2009.

McShane, T.O., and M.P. Wells. 2004. *Getting Biodiversity Projects to Work. Towards More Effective Conservation and Development.* New York: Columbia University Press.

Morton, L.W., and S. Padgitt. 2005. Selecting Socio-economic Metrics for Watershed Management. *Environmental Monitoring and Assessment* 103: 83–98.

Moseley, C., and L.J. Wilson. 2002. *Multiparty Monitoring for Sustainable Natural Resource Management.* Eugene, OR: Ecosystem Workforce Program, University of Oregon.

National Visitor Use Monitoring Program (NVUM). 2005. http://www.fs.fed.us/recreation/programs/nvum (accessed March 15, 2006).

Noon, B.R. 2003. Conceptual Issues in Monitoring Ecological Resources. In *Monitoring Ecosystems: Interdisciplinary Approaches for Evaluating Ecoregional Initiatives*, edited by D.E. Busch and J.C. Trexler. Washington, DC: Island Press, 27–71.

Noon, B.R., T.A. Spies, and M.G. Raphael. 1999. Conceptual Basis for Designing an Effectiveness Monitoring Program. In *The Strategy and Design of the Effectiveness Monitoring Program for the Northwest Forest Plan*, edited by B.S. Mulder, B.R. Noon, T.A. Spies, M.G. Raphael, C.J. Palmer, A.R. Olsen, G.H. Reeves, and H.H. Welsh. General Technical Report PNW-GTR-437. Portland, OR: U.S. Department of Agriculture, Forest Service, Pacific Northwest Research Station, 21–48.

North Central Regional Center for Rural Development (NCRCRD). 1999. *Measuring Community Success and Sustainability: An Interactive Workbook.* Ames, IA: North Central Regional Center for Rural Development, Iowa State University.

Oregon Department of Forestry. 2000. Oregon's First Approximation Report for Forest Sustainability. Salem, OR: Oregon Dept. of Forestry.

Parkins, J.R., R.C. Stedman, and J. Varghese. 2001. Moving Towards Local-level Indicators of Sustainability in Forest-based Communities: A Mixed-method Approach. *Social Indicators Research* 56: 43–72.

Pilz, D., H. Ballard, and E.T. Jones. 2006. *Broadening Participation in Biological Monitoring: Handbook for Scientists and Managers.* General Technical Report PNW-GTR-680. Portland, OR: U.S. Department of Agriculture, Forest Service, Pacific Northwest Research Station.

Pinchot Institute for Conservation. 2005. *Final Report of the National Monitoring and Evaluation Team of the USDA Forest Service Stewardship Contracting Pilot Program.* Washington, DC: The Pinchot Institute for Conservation.

Powell, D.S. 2004. Chronology of Monitoring and Evaluation Events. Internal Report. Washington, DC: U.S. Department of Agriculture, Forest Service.

Seesholtz, D., J. Russell, and D. Wickwar. 2004. Social and Economic Profile Technical Guide. Draft. Washington, DC: U.S. Department of Agriculture, Forest Service, Inventory and Monitoring Institute.

Shields, D.J., I.M. Martin, W.E. Martin, and M.A. Haefele. 2002. *Survey Results of the American Public's Values, Objectives, Beliefs, and Attitudes Regarding the Forest and Grasslands: A Technical Document Supporting the 2000 USDA Forest Service RPA Assessment.* General Technical Report RMRS-GTR-95. Fort Collins, CO: U.S. Department of Agriculture, Forest Service, Rocky Mountain Research Station.

Stankey, G.H., B.T. Bormann, C. Ryan, B. Shindler, V. Sturtevant, R.N. Clark, and C. Philpot. 2003. Adaptive Management and the Northwest Forest Plan: Rhetoric and Reality. *Journal of Forestry* 101(1): 40–46.

Stem, C., R. Margoluis, N. Salafsky, and M. Brown. 2005. Monitoring and Evaluation in Conservation: A Review of Trends and Approaches. *Conservation Biology* 19(2): 295–309.

Struglia, R., P.L. Winter, and A. Meyer. 2001. *Southern California Socioeconomic Assessment: Sociodemographic Conditions, Projections, and Quality of Life Indices.* Riverside, CA: U.S. Department of Agriculture, Forest Service, Pacific Southwest Research Station.

Sustainable Measures, Inc., and American Forests. 2003. Forest Sustainability Indicator Tools for Communities. http://communitiescommittee.org/fsitool/index.html (accessed March 7, 2006).

Terborgh, J., and L. Davenport. 2002. Monitoring Protected Areas. In *Making Parks Work: Strategies for Preserving Tropical Nature,* edited by J. Terborgh, C. van Schaik, L. Davenport, and M. Rao. Washington, DC: Island Press, 395–408.

Terborgh, J., C. van Schaik, L. Davenport, and M. Rao. 2002. *Making Parks Work: Strategies for Preserving Tropical Nature.* Washington, DC: Island Press.

The Montreal Process. 2006. www.mpci.org/home_e.html (accessed April 4, 2006).

Tolle, T., D.S. Powell, R. Breckenridge, L. Cone, R. Keller, J. Kershner, K.S. Smith, G.J. White, and G.L. Williams. 1999. Managing the Monitoring and Evaluation Process. In *Ecological Stewardship: A Common Reference for Ecosystem Management (Vol. III),* edited by W. T. Sexton, A. J. Malk, R. C. Szaro, and N. C. Johnson. Oxford: Elsevier Science Ltd., 585–602.

Trexler, J.C., and D.E. Busch. 2003. Monitoring, Assessment, and Ecoregional Initiatives: A Synthesis. In *Monitoring Ecosystems: Interdisciplinary Approaches for Evaluating Ecoregional Initiatives,* edited by D.E. Busch and J. C. Trexler. Washington, DC: Island Press, 405–424.

U.S. Department of Agriculture, Forest Service (USDA FS). 1988. Forest Service Handbook 1909. Washington, DC: USDA FS.

———. 2004. National Report on Sustainable Forests—2003. Washington, DC: USDA FS.

_____. 2005a. National Forest System Land Management Planning. 36 CFR Part 219. *Federal Register* 70(3): 1023–1061.

_____. 2005b. Southwestern Region State and Private Forestry—Collaborative Forest Restoration Program. www.fs.fed.us/r3/spf/cfrp/monitoring/ (accessed March 7, 2006).

U.S. Department of Agriculture, Forest Service, and U.S. Department of the Interior, Bureau of Land Management (USDA and USDI). 1994. Record of decision for amendments to Forest Service and Bureau of Land Management planning documents within the range of the northern spotted owl. Washington D.C.: USDA-Forest Service and USDI-Bureau of Land Management.

Wallowa Resources, Oregon State University, Grande Ronde Model Watershed Program, and Malheur, Umatilla, and Wallowa-Whitman National Forests. 2004. *Social and Economic Monitoring in the Blue Mountains: Grant, Union and Wallowa Counties as Case Studies.* Enterprise, OR: Wallowa Resources.

Wilson, L.J. 2003. *Change in Timber-dependent Communities: A Comparison of Communities with Mill Closures to those Without.* Hayfork, CA: Watershed Research and Training Center.

Wright, P.A., G. Alward, T. Hoekstra, B. Tegler, and M. Turner. 2002. *Monitoring for Forest Management Unit Scale Sustainability: The Local Unit Criteria and Indicators Development (LUCID) Test, Technical Edition.* Fort Collins, CO: U.S. Department of Agriculture, Forest Service, Inventory and Monitoring Institute.

4
Engaging Communities Through Participatory Research

JENNIFER S. ARNOLD AND
MARIA E. FERNANDEZ-GIMENEZ

Communities long have been of interest to researchers and natural resource managers because implementation of management concepts ultimately depends on acceptance, adoption, and adaptation by people, many of them living in forest communities. Further, researchers and land managers value community studies that provide insight into the economic, social, and cultural dimensions of land use and forest management. Collaboration with communities that live or work close to the land also may allow for a deeper understanding of the resource and its importance to a diversity of stakeholders. However, many researchers, especially those in the natural sciences who have been trained to maintain "scientific objectivity," struggle with how to involve communities in the research process without compromising the validity of their findings.

Anthropologists, sociologists, and other social scientists have met this challenge by developing research methodologies that allow for, and even encourage, partnerships between researchers and community members, while maintaining high standards of validity and scientific rigor (Society for Applied Anthropology 1983). However, such community-based research methods remain poorly understood and underused within most natural resource disciplines. In this chapter, we present participatory research as a method and a philosophy of engaging community participants in research, emphasizing the potential of this process to transform relationships among community members, researchers, and the forests they live in and study. Because there are many more skeptics than practitioners of participatory research in natural resource disciplines, we focus on ethical issues and clarify methodological differences between conventional "objective" research and participatory research. In our discussion, we highlight the unique sources of validity that participatory research offers, which suggest the untapped potential of this approach in natural resource management. We foresee that the expanded use of participatory research will increase the local relevance of natural resource science, better incorporate a diversity of stakeholder perspectives and knowledge, and ultimately lead to a deeper understanding of forest ecosystems and the human communities that live and work in them.

In our discussion we draw directly from our own experiences as participatory researchers, as well as the broader literature on participatory research. The four cases discussed in this chapter include two related projects conducted with members of the Tohono O'odham Nation in Southern Arizona: a participatory rangeland planning project and a participatory rangeland curriculum project (Arnold 2004; Arnold and Fernandez-Gimenez 2007; Hays 2004; Hays, Fernandez-Gimenez, and the Sif Oidak Livestock Committee 2005). Both projects directly addressed expressed community needs while including research components that engaged community members as co-researchers. A third case involved our work with a collaborative group in northwest Colorado, where we helped build community capacity for adaptive management and monitoring while studying the collaborative process (Bishop 2005). The fourth case involved research with members of the Alaska Beluga Whale Committee on that group's use and integration of traditional ecological knowledge and science (Fernandez-Gimenez, Huntington, and Frost 2006).

What is Participatory Research?

In its simplest form, participatory research requires that people who have a direct interest in the outcome of a research project participate in the research process. More specifically, participatory research can be described as a continuum of participant involvement, with functional participation at one extreme and empowering participation at the other (Johnson et al. 2001). Functional participation enlists local people to assist in data collection or analysis without participating in the development of research goals or methods. At the other end of the spectrum, empowering participation describes a power-sharing relationship between scientists and local people acting as co-researchers, who share decisionmaking authority throughout the research process, from posing research questions, developing methods, and collecting and analyzing data, to interpreting findings for local application. The concept of empowering participation, although difficult to achieve in its purest form, represents the core philosophy of participatory research (Reason and Bradbury 2001). Inherent in this approach is the belief that every individual has the capacity and the right to engage in critical dialogue and action about his or her situation in life (Freire 1970) and that conclusions reached through group learning demonstrate unique validity as a result of the synthesis of knowledge from a diversity of participants (Hall 2001; Lather 1986; Reason and Bradbury 2001). Although empowering participatory research is not appropriate to address all types of research questions, it is particularly well-suited to address the human dimensions of natural resource management and the local application of ecological theories to on-the-ground management.

Applications of Participatory Research

In the United States, participatory research has a long history in the applied social science fields, such as education and public health. Its application in the natural resource disciplines has been limited, however, with few researchers utilizing participatory methods until recently. Internationally, participatory research methods have been used widely in agriculture and natural resource management. They developed among international development organizations over several decades as part of a growing commitment to decentralization and democracy (Chambers 1994). From early projects that focused on small-scale farm improvements in Africa, Asia, and Latin America (Amanor 1993; Horton 1984), the use of participatory research has evolved to address more sophisticated research questions, such as participatory evaluation of adaptive management in Australia, Britain, and the United States (Everett 2001; Ison and Russell 1999; Pound et al. 2003; Pretty and Frank 2000;). Other studies from various contexts also have found participatory methods useful to examine the social dynamics operating within collaborative management partnerships (Ballard 2004; Chuenpagdee, Fraga, and Euan-Avila 2004; Everett 2001; Van Riper 2003). These studies have found that participatory processes facilitate communication and trust among diverse stakeholders, resulting in an increased understanding of the resource and increased capacity for effective and lasting management partnerships (Chuenpagdee, Fraga, and Euan-Avila 2004; Everett 2001). Although few published studies in the United States have followed an empowering participation model, those that have done so (e.g., Ballard 2004; Everett 2001; Van Riper 2003) offer insight into the potential to apply this approach more widely to forest management and research in the United States.

Common to most of these projects is the intent to devolve decisionmaking power from government and research organizations back to resource users and local community members. Unfortunately, some researchers champion participatory methods but employ only limited forms of functional participation, usually soliciting local knowledge as a data source for conventional analysis (Payton et al. 2003; Zanetell and Knuth 2002). This type of participation does not engage community members in the problem-solving process or prepare participants to confront problems beyond the bounds of a particular research project. Recently, critics have pointed out the dangers of publicly supporting participatory and democratic processes while following an extractive, expert-dominated research and development model (Cooke and Kothari 2001; Goebel 1998; Quaghebeur, Masschelein, and Nguyen 2004). Despite these challenges, we believe that empowering, participatory research has transformative potential when applied thoughtfully in appropriate settings. To advance the practice of participatory research in U.S forest communities, in the following sections we discuss key ethical and methodological considerations in planning and carrying out participatory research in natural resource settings.

Ethical and Methodological Considerations

Because many researchers in natural resource fields have not conducted research in a participatory setting and the role of the researcher in this setting is quite different from conventional research settings, it is useful to take a closer look at the researcher's role and power-sharing relationship with community members. This rebalancing of roles is the source of potential ethical and methodological dilemmas for conventionally trained researchers; however, the power-sharing role of the researcher also is a unique strength of participatory research. Throughout these sections, we draw on our own experiences as researchers working with communities of natural resource users. We also draw on the lessons learned by scientists and community members in other applied settings where participatory research is well established.

Role of the Researcher

" 'Nature' is something [scientists] watch and they're not part of it—like they're going to the movies. Researchers don't view themselves as being part of this thing in front of them. They are a part of it. When they see themselves as a part of it and not separate from it … there are gains on both sides." —Native member, Alaska Beluga Whale Committee, interviewed as part of a research project on the integration of science and local knowledge in co-management.

In this quotation, a community member laments that few researchers reflect on or value their roles in the communities where they work or study. From her perspective, everyone benefits when scientists participate in village life, recognize the effects of their actions both as researchers and fellow humans, and come to understand the intertwined fates of resources, communities, and researchers. One goal of participatory research is for researchers to better understand and respond to the social and cultural contexts of their investigations, which happens most profoundly when researchers become members (if only temporary ones) of the community they are studying.

A participatory approach to research means that the researcher's role must shift from that of an objective collector and analyzer of data to that of a facilitator of cooperative learning focused on applied problem-solving (Ison and Russell 1999). In the eyes of many historically marginalized communities, this shift is long overdue (Davis and Reid 1999; Schell and Tarbell 1998). Many rural communities and indigenous groups see research as an intrusive and threatening activity, based on their experience with research that extracted and exploited local knowledge (Horner and Ostermeier 2004). In response, some communities have developed research protocols that spell out community expectations of research projects and researcher responsibilities (Akwesasne Task Force on the Environment 1996; Alaska Native Knowledge Network 1993), whereas others simply close the door to researchers altogether (Horner and Ostermeier 2004). As a result, participatory research may be the only viable research approach with some communities.

Because researchers and community members invest significant time in dialogue during the early stages of project initiation, it is possible to identify goals and responsibilities that meet the interests of each of the parties involved. The time invested in this initial stage is critical to building the trust and interest that provide momentum to carry both researchers and community members along the sometimes bumpy road of participatory research. These early stages of elaborating roles, responsibilities, and expectations for both researchers and local participants lay the groundwork for trust, scientific rigor, and ethical behavior.

Cultivating Personal and Professional Relationships

As researchers become more closely involved in community life and develop relationships with community members, they must clarify for themselves and for community members the boundaries and expectations associated with overlapping personal and professional relationships. For example, can the depth of a researcher's participation in a community ultimately threaten the accuracy of data, as personal relationships form between the researcher and community members? Some researchers may perceive that close relationships with community participants lead to personal bias in data collection and interpretation, whereas others feel that such relationships enable greater cross-cultural understanding and a more intimate view of the social interactions within the community. Conventional research approaches require that personal bias be eliminated to the extent possible, whereas the participatory approach suggests that personal bias or identity and relationships with community participants cannot and should not be eliminated but discussed and challenged alongside data interpretations (Denzin and Lincoln 2000).

Similarly, questions may arise about which researcher interactions and communications with community members are personal and confidential and which may be treated as data. When a researcher is a participant in community life, it may be difficult for the researcher, and for others, to know when she is acting in the role of researcher and when she is not. A researcher using participant observation, for example, is always observing, if not immediately and overtly recording, patterns of community life and interactions. The more the researcher is taken for granted by others as a participant and immerses herself in the experience of participation, the richer the potential data. To translate these experiences into dense, useful, and reliable data, the participant observer must document them meticulously and apply critical self-reflection to her analysis. Ethically, the researcher is obligated to clarify and come to an agreement with community members about which interactions may be recorded as data and which are "off the record."

The most informal and personal comment from a growing friendship between a researcher and a community member can help the researcher understand the complex social histories and interpersonal politics operating "behind the scenes" of a community project, but if outside the agreed-upon format for data collection, this information must be excluded from formal data analysis. To introduce such new information, the researcher in her role as group facilitator can tactfully, without referring to the original context, raise related issues or dig deeper into topics otherwise "too obvious" for discussion. Within these participatory group discussions, which are usually part of the negotiated format for data collection, conversations can be recorded and analyzed as part of the agreed-upon data set. The researcher also can raise issues from casual conversation within other agreed-upon formats for data collection, such as interviews, surveys, or other methods designed according to particular research goals. In this way, personal relationships may contribute indirectly to the research process without compromising the trust and confidentiality agreements between researchers and community members.

Developing Goals and Methods in Partnership with Community Members

After a meeting to discuss the potential for a participatory research project with a newly formed collaborative group in a public land-dominated county, a soft-spoken rancher approached us with his ball cap in his hand and asked with a puzzled expression, "I don't understand how this works. By participating in our group, aren't you going to change the thing you are studying?" As the rancher quickly identified, our proposed approach was at odds with conventional research, which seeks to control observer bias and influence on the research subject. Yet the strength of an open-ended and flexible approach is that local partners help guide researchers to the appropriate questions and methods to suit the interests and constraints of their communities. When community participants are involved in formulating research goals and questions, participants begin to take greater interest and ownership in the project. The community meeting described above was the start of a participatory research project that focused eventually on assisting the new group to explore the potential for adaptive management and multi-party monitoring as part of a large-scale resource management planning effort.

The research topic grew out of the group's early discussions, while the research process helped the group better understand the potential benefits and challenges of adaptive management and gave them practical experience with designing and carrying out a multi-party monitoring project. Because of the direct relevance of the research question to the group's needs and interests, the workshops and interviews conducted as part of the research attracted an array of participants and broad-based support among representatives of traditionally adversarial interest groups. The activities that formed part of the research protocol led to greater understanding and respect among participants for the knowledge and values held by different members of the group. The final research results had implications both for the local group and for agency policy on adaptive management. In this case, rather than taking pains to avoid influencing their research subjects, the researchers used the research process as an educational and capacity-building opportunity for the group that was the "subject" of the research.

Interpreting Findings

"I've never heard about this research before, and I don't agree with it. You can't use theories to explain O'odham ways."—Community research participant commenting during a meeting to discuss preliminary research design as part of the Tohono O'odham participatory curriculum development project.

Community comments, such as these by a Tohono O'odham elder in our participatory curriculum development project, reflect the resentment built up after more than a century of researcher-controlled publications explaining intimate cultural matters such as religious beliefs, family interactions, and community struggles against dominating external political structures (Davis and Reid 1999; Simpson and Driben 2000; Tuhiwai Smith 1999). Participatory research seeks to redress past exploitation by empowering local people to tell their own stories and author their own interpretations to present to the public in partnership with researchers. Critical to this process is the art of dialogue and a willingness on the part of all participants to negotiate meaning (Wallerstein 1999). Often group discussions are at the heart of the co-learning process. Instead of adopting a hypothesis and testing a single theory against the data collected, grounded theory can be used to build theory from the data in an ongoing, iterative process (Bernard 2002; Strauss and Corbin 1998). In our participatory research project with the Tohono O'odham that focused on natural resources curriculum development, we searched for existing theories from the literature that resembled the community interactions and social dynamics important to rangeland management, and we introduced some of these in participatory discussions of data interpretation. Ultimately, we adopted the social capital framework set forth by Woolcock (1998) to help interpret patterns of inter- and intra-community cooperation related to natural resource management (Arnold 2004; Arnold and Fernandez-Gimenez 2007). Although one project participant objected to this use of "outsider theory" to interpret local social relationships, other participants, including local elders, found that it resonated with concepts central to O'odham *himdag* or way of life.

Presentation of Research: How to Handle Unflattering Findings

The problem of unflattering findings presents both an ethical dilemma and a challenge to the scientific validity of the research. On one hand, an explicit goal of participatory research is to provide benefits to the participating individuals, groups, and communities. At the very least, the research should not harm the group being studied. On the other hand, it would be a breach of professional ethics and scientific validity to ignore or fail to disclose unflattering research results. Such situations must be handled with care and sensitivity. Nondisclosure of findings that do not influence overall conclusions may be acceptable, especially when it does not involve overlooking illegal or unethical behavior and revealing these findings would damage the group's capacity in some way (Brugge and Kole 2003; Minkler 2004).

The potential for unflattering findings points to the importance of having clear and mutually agreed-upon participatory research protocols at the outset that specify the responsibilities of the researchers and community participants and the extent and limits of community influence over published results (Minkler 2004). It also highlights the importance of an ongoing discussion of research findings and interpretations among researchers and community research partners. These discussions and invitations to review draft manuscripts provide groups the opportunity to correct factual errors, dispute interpretations, and clarify statements that may have been taken out of context, leading to erroneous inferences. The process of presenting and discussing preliminary findings with community groups can be extremely valuable both to the researchers' understanding of these groups and to the groups' own self-understanding. These discussions often lead to new insights, additional supporting data, or important exceptions and discrepancies. In several cases, some of our findings could have been viewed in a negative light, but our community research partners affirmed our interpretations and elaborated on their significance from the community perspective. In other instances, group members agreed with our overall interpretation but objected to specific language used to describe their case, which they felt was unnecessarily negative. In this situation, it was easy to accommodate the group's concerns while meeting our standards of accuracy and validity.

Validity in Participatory Research

"Some of the older books [from] the older writers that came out here [to the reservation were based on] one man's interpretation of what this one individual said to him. A lot of it was good, but at the same time, a lot of it didn't sound right. But with this project here, you've got all these groups of people that actually were together and worked together on this thing. It was more than just one person, so it's not just one individual interpretation."—Community research participant interviewed at the close of the Tohono O'odham participatory curriculum development project.

As this quotation demonstrates, validity in participatory research is tied strongly to who is invited to participate and how they are able to contribute (Berardi 2002; Reason and Bradbury 2001). Researchers have the responsibility to reach out to seemingly uninterested individuals and create a comfortable space for knowledge sharing and group learning in order to discover the insights that each person brings to the discussion (Fischer 2000; Nieto 2000). This can be especially challenging in communities that are suspicious of or intimidated by researchers, but these challenges often can be overcome with respect, patience, and a generous dose of humor.

Central to participatory research is the commitment to critical reflection. Describing one's identity in connection to the topic of study allows researchers to express frankly the cultural and ideological beliefs that they bring to a study and challenge those same beliefs and assumptions against the empirical data collected and discussed with other participants (Bryndon-Miller 2001; Seidman 1998). Dialogue and discussion among diverse participants are the means to exchange knowledge, negotiate shared meanings, and build theories shaped by the contributions of local people and events. Construct validity is a measure of internal validity that is assessed by documenting the adoption, rejection, and adaptation of working theories to find those that are best suited to explain local phenomena (Denzin and Lincoln 2000). For example, the researcher and community partners may trace participant contributions and reflect on the evolution of ideas that resulted from participant interactions, constructively learning from group successes and mistakes.

Triangulation and member checking, both common elements in social science research, are also powerful tools to assess the internal validity of participatory research. Triangulation is the comparison of data collected from different sources and by different methods to challenge or accumulate evidence in support of specific interpretations (Bernard 2002). Triangulation in participatory research goes beyond comparing interview transcripts against meeting notes to looking closely at the diversity of participants involved and the diversity of settings where participants interact, with the knowledge that a particular setting might put some participants at ease while causing others to be reserved. Member checking refers to the review of research findings and interpretations by research participants (Bernard 2002). Member checking in participatory research extends beyond consulting a handful of participants at the close of a project to engaging a diverse group of individuals in the process of analysis, theory building, and public presentation.

Catalytic validity is a measure of validity unique to participatory research. It is based on evidence that as a consequence of participation, the research process led to personal insights and innovative action beyond the scope of the original project (Denzin and Lincoln 2000; Lather 1986). Catalytic validity especially is relevant when one research goal is to increase the capacity of participants to seek their own solutions to local problems. In our experience using participatory research to develop and evaluate a rangeland curriculum, local participants took what we helped start to the next level. Public interest in natural resources education grew as a result of our participatory project, and this interest blossomed into public support for establishing a locally based, natural resources degree program at the Tohono O'odham Community College.

Recognizing that local participation was the only way to incorporate local culture and elders' knowledge into the program, the college institutionalized participatory methods within their natural resources program to establish the program's mission statement and continue development of specific classes (Arnold 2004; Arnold and Fernandez-Gimenez 2007). Catalytic validity is a direct measure of the transformative nature of participatory research. In the context of participatory research, advocating change or initiating action does not weaken the study's validity. Rather, when participants put the knowledge or awareness that they gained from the research project to work in their own lives, the accuracy of the knowledge is tested quickly in real-world situations.

Practical Considerations for Working with Communities and Community Groups

Who Initiates Research? How Much Time Is Needed?

"And you're an outside person who came in and did it. And hopefully in the future we will have people from within that will have that drive to do [research]. If not, it's always going to be someone else coming in to do it. But I guess as a matter of getting people interested, wanting to make a difference, [it worked out]."—Community research participant interviewed at the close of the Tohono O'odham participatory curriculum development project.

Can participatory research that is initiated by a researcher from outside the community be considered "community-based?" The spectrum of researcher and community collaboration is broad. It includes everything from research initiated by an outside researcher utilizing functional participation of community groups, to research initiated by community groups that contract with outside researchers to fulfill their own research priorities, to research partnerships in which communities work hand-in-hand with researchers to develop their own capacity to implement all phases of research. In natural resource management, instances where the community group designs and conducts the research are relatively rare and occur primarily in the context of ecological monitoring projects (Schell and Tarbell 1998). With participatory research projects, effective and balanced researcher–community partnerships are most likely to occur when some community members have had experience with higher education or when researchers have had personal life experiences that allow them to identify closely with community members (Sixsmith, Boneham, and Goldring 2003).

In our experience, the most successful and rewarding participatory research projects are those that emerge from an existing relationship between researchers and communities, a situation that enables research priorities to develop comfortably from expressed community needs. These relationships take time to develop and to flourish and must be maintained and strengthened over months or years (Ahmed et al. 2004; Israel et al. 1998; Sixsmith, Boneham, and Goldring 2003). It is often a challenge for researchers, and for community groups, to invest the necessary time to build relationships and get to know one another prior to launching a research project (Wallerstein 1999). Most funding sources do not provide support for the cultivation and groundwork that underlie successful participatory research. This means that researchers and community groups interested in this type of partnership must be creative in establishing institutional relationships that support continued commitment of time and resources. It is not unusual to come to the close of a particular research effort and feel as though the researcher–community relationship is just beginning to reach its potential.

In our participatory research project on the Tohono O'odham Nation, we worked with nine O'odham villages to facilitate a community-based range-management planning process (Hays et al. 2005). In the course of the planning process, it became clear that there was no good information on how livestock grazing affects the plant communities that comprise most of the 500,000 acres of rangeland used by these communities and, thus, no scientific basis for management recommendations. We documented local knowledge of livestock foraging patterns and perceptions of sites at risk for accelerated degradation, but we also discovered that local livestock owners did not have a clear understanding of the effects of grazing on perennial grasses in the area. Federal agencies (the Bureau of Indian Affairs and the Natural Resources Conservation Service) assumed that the arid shrubland would respond to grazing in the same way as desert grasslands in the southeastern part of the reservation, but this assumption was untested. This led to a research project that assessed the effects of historical grazing pressure on the density of perennial forage grasses in the area. Results showed that livestock probably have little effect on these grasses and suggested that palatable shrubs compose a more important part of livestock diets in this area, leading to the implication that management of shrubs would be a more appropriate focus for improved resource management.

The educational and technical assistance we provided helped us learn about the communities and vice versa. The time commitment necessary to establish relationships with community members was supported within the institutional framework of Cooperative Extension and made possible through the personal dedication of graduate students who regularly participated in meetings and attended community events (Arnold and Fernandez-Gimenez 2007; Hays et al. 2005). The research project grew out of our discussions and interactions with community members, and research questions were developed jointly to address local needs while enabling us, as researchers, to explore questions with theoretical and practical implications beyond the context of a specific group.

Community Gatekeepers and Community Guides

In participatory research with communities, key individuals often serve as "gatekeepers" or "guides." The term "gatekeeper" implies a function of regulating the researcher's access to community members, sometimes creating a barrier to effective participation, whereas a "guide" more often serves as a facilitator of the participatory process, linking the researcher with key community members and helping to interpret the community context. In some cases, the same individual may serve both to regulate and facilitate access. Once a researcher establishes a relationship with the community group, the intermediary role no longer may be needed, whereas other times the guide or gatekeeper continues to play a key role throughout the project. When the researcher's culture or language differs from that of community members or when there is historic suspicion of, or animosity toward, researchers or outsiders generally, the role of guide is critical. When working with diverse communities, multiple guides are important to involve distinct subgroups. Ideally, the individual who serves as a guide is highly respected within the community and is someone able and willing to communicate honestly with researchers about sensitive issues.

We encountered multiple layers of gatekeepers and guides in our rangeland planning project with nine villages of the Tohono O'odham Nation. One individual, a leader within the group, served as our initial bridge to community members and an ongoing guide, encouraging community members to participate in the project, while relaying concerns and questions back to the researchers when community members were uncomfortable stating them directly. As interest grew among the members of the group, representatives from the nine villages served as intermediaries between the planning group and their communities. Village representatives assumed direct responsibility for gaining community approval for our research and planning project and for keeping villagers informed of project activities, but in so doing, they limited our direct interaction with villagers. We considered the possibility that participation could have been enhanced if we were given the chance to meet with villagers directly. During a reflective stage of the Tohono O'odham curriculum project, several participants commented that it would be difficult for us as outsiders to interact directly with villagers to discuss rangeland management—that even community members involved in the project found this difficult to do with other community members. In our case, it seemed that representative participation was the only option. Ultimately, the village representatives had greater ownership in the project and developed a deeper understanding of it because they took responsibility for explaining and discussing it with their communities.

Divided Communities and Divisive Issues

The very definition of "community" is a subject of academic debate (Agrawal and Gibson 2001). As Russell and Harshbarger (2003) point out, we should not assume that community members are interested in empowering other members through research or action. When the participatory research approach is inclusive and seeks to redress past imbalances in power, it is not surprising that some community members are threatened and may oppose the project altogether. How community is defined and the degree to which it is inclusive and representative of potential research partners can affect participatory research in several ways.

Where change is a desired result of participatory research, it is important that the community research partners are representative of the broader community the research seeks to benefit. Failure to recognize and incorporate key stakeholders can threaten the success and validity of research, just as it has undermined conservation and development initiatives in the past (Russell and Harshbarger 2003). The number and diversity of community-research participants is a practical aspect of the participatory research process, but it is also data that should be collected, analyzed, and presented alongside primary findings addressing central research questions.

One way to counter potential problems is to convene a research committee or working group that solicits participation from a wide array of community members and groups to give structure to the participatory research process (Agency for Healthcare Research and Quality 2003). We took this approach in our participatory curriculum project on the Tohono O'odham Nation. By actively and continuously inviting a broad range of participants to contribute to the curriculum and the associated research, we were successful in incorporating and addressing the interests of many different community groups. Nevertheless, despite significant effort spent in outreach activities, participation was not balanced geographically to represent all areas of the reservation, and community members who were not employed by the tribal government or other agencies did not commit as much time to the project as participants who were professionally or politically involved. However, through analysis of participant contributions, we found that elder community members, who may have attended only one or two meetings, still made significant contributions to the research findings since the sincerity and thoughtfulness of an individual's comments often were more important than the number of meetings he or she attended.

Although these participatory strategies can be successful in many community settings, when the focal issue for research and action is one that deeply divides the community and when there is not an ongoing, collaborative attempt to manage the conflict constructively, participatory research may not be appropriate or effective (Minkler 2004).

Sharing Funds, Results, and Credit

"I don't know about the research. I would have to ask, how far is it going to go? Is it going to end here? Or is it going to get published, sold or whatever? If it's going to be something else, then that has to be discussed. [People have] to be aware of that. And I'm sure you're going to get comments." —Community research participant interviewed at the conclusion of the Tohono O'odham participatory curriculum development project.

If community groups are to be true research partners and contribute their time and efforts to the research project, it is only fair that they are compensated and that they receive formal credit for their contributions. Like many of the issues addressed here, it is important to have open and early discussions with prospective research partners about these important issues. Sometimes compensation can take the form of payment to community researchers or to community organizations. Often it takes less tangible forms, such as educational workshops, technical assistance, or other forms of community capacity building. We have found that well-intentioned efforts to share grant funds with community partners can go awry if the community group is not able to serve as its own fiscal agent and the funds must be channeled through another organization that does not share the group's understanding of or commitment to the research project.

Returning the results of the research to the community is an essential part of the participatory research process and ideally happens at various stages of the research as part of an interactive process, rather than just at the end as a final report. In our Tohono O'odham project, we sent out periodic mailings and scheduled presentations to update current and potential research participants and to increase public awareness of the project. We also created brochures and articles for local newspapers. In addition, we provided community members and local libraries with copies of published results.

When the community genuinely has engaged in the research process, whether in functional or empowering mode, their contributions should be acknowledged. We generally discuss at the outset of the participatory project how we expect authorship to be shared with the community group, and, generally, the group reviews and is an author on posters, presentations, and nontechnical publications. We also have invited key community researchers to participate as authors in our scholarly publications if they have the time and interest to participate in a dialogue about the interpretation and presentation of results and to review and comment on draft manuscripts. We have found working with community researchers on scholarly papers to be an interesting and rewarding process. In some cases, our community co-authors have been very effective in disseminating the research products to policymakers or resource managers, both within and outside their communities.

The Transformative Potential of Participatory Research

Although community-based participatory research requires significant investments of time and energy to achieve true collaboration, the benefits, such as increased trust among participants, improved understanding of diverse perspectives through knowledge sharing, and increased local capacity to initiate and continue innovation, can lead to profound individual, community, institutional, and even societal transformations.

For an individual, involvement in participatory research can lead to a better understanding of the diversity of perspectives surrounding an issue. After a participatory research discussion, participants often express personal accomplishment and increased awareness. Community members often convey increased confidence from interacting as intellectual peers with academic researchers, while researchers are intellectually charged and humbled as a result of the insights offered by local people (Nussbaum et al. 2004). These are the emotions of collaborative learning, and it is this shared experience that forges relationships among vastly different individuals, leading to increased social capital for continued collaboration. Although participatory research is not immune to insensitivity, misunderstandings, and potentially hurtful effects on participants, it is the responsibility of researchers to facilitate mutual respect, open lines of communication, and mitigate conflict to the extent possible.

For a community, the process of working together to accomplish a shared goal brings people together to discuss their interests and concerns. This has the potential to build trust and the relationships needed to move forward in collaborative partnerships for effective and fair resource management. Prior to a participatory research project, individuals with shared interests in resource management may not even be aware of the others' existence, but after the project, most have a clear understanding of the other individuals, their organizations, and interests in the resource, an awareness that lays the foundation for future collaboration (Arnold 2004; Arnold and Fernandez-Gimenez 2007; Chuenpagdee, Fraga, and Euan-Avila 2004; Everett 2001).

When individuals take part in participatory research as representatives of larger organizations, such as universities, government agencies, or local community groups, trust gained among participants can translate into increased trust in the organizations and institutions represented. For example, many participants feel validated that their concerns warrant significant time contributions from academic professionals, and such interactions lead to positive opinions of the professionals involved and their sponsoring university or agency. This is especially significant given the lingering suspicion and resentment in many communities toward researchers due to past extractive studies.

The process of publishing and distributing participatory research findings can have positive societal effects. As more researchers become involved in participatory research and results from these studies are presented in mainstream venues, the breadth of "researchable" topics is expanded and notions about whose knowledge is valuable in addressing those topics through the research process are transformed.

Implications for Researchers, Communities, and Institutions

Participatory research has important implications for researchers and communities. It can enrich our understanding of the interactions between human communities and their environment while building community capacity and fostering personal, community, and institutional transformations. Although participatory research holds promise, it is important to acknowledge that this approach is not always appropriate or feasible. When the researcher has tightly focused research goals with minimal flexibility in defining research questions or methodology, there is little room for participatory research. When the time needed to build trust and maintain relationships between researchers and community partners is not available, it is difficult to carry out truly participatory research, and superficial efforts risk failure. When a community or community group is deeply divided on an issue closely related to the research, it may be difficult to gain participation of key community members or groups, and the legitimacy of the research may be undermined. Finally, the sensitivity of the research theme may lead the community to reject the prospect of research altogether.

For researchers, engaging in participatory research can be exciting, rewarding, and also risky. The initial time investment in building relationships and sharing power over research questions, methods, and interpretation can mean that research takes much longer to reach fruition. There is a greater likelihood of uncompleted projects, and the research products may be more difficult to publish in high-status scientific outlets. However, benefits are evident when community members and researchers are able to ask novel research questions and forge new understandings beyond what either could accomplish alone.

There also are risks to investing time and effort in participatory research for community groups, including the possibility that the results will not prove as useful as expected. Perhaps the greatest challenge to community groups is the willingness to approach the research from an open, critical, and self-reflective stance, understanding that the research may yield findings that challenge the group's self-image or the image that it hopes to project to the public, funders, or policymakers. Because a major source of validity in participatory research is the process of critical self-reflection and dialogue, communities and researchers who are unwilling to engage in this process should consider carefully whether participatory research is the appropriate approach for them.

It also is worthwhile to reemphasize the importance of establishing clear protocols for the participatory research process from the outset. The joint discussion and negotiation of these protocols is an important step in building trust and can expose potential problem areas early on. Discussions of the research protocols and relationships between outside and community researcher partners should continue throughout the project to be sure that all partners understand and are in accordance with the research process. In some cases, it may be helpful to formalize the research relationship through a memorandum of understanding among the partner organizations.

Participatory research also has implications for institutions. As support for higher education wanes in many state legislatures, to say nothing of declining federal funding, it is crucial that the public have a personal relationship with their university and value its activities—research as well as education. What better way to build such relationships with the university's constituencies than to forge together a research agenda to meet their needs? Universities, particularly land-grant institutions, would do well to recognize the long-term benefits to their own sustainability of fostering and rewarding genuine participatory research with their constituents' communities. The Agricultural Experiment Stations, associated with land-grant institutions and originally created to support "mission-oriented" research directly benefiting the ranchers, farmers, and natural resource users of their respective states, offer substantial opportunities to support long-term research partnerships between universities and communities. This type of institutional framework could provide funding and logistical support for the community outreach necessary to build researcher–community relationships before the research goals and methodologies needed to apply for funding are developed.

For academic and agency researchers, many of the barriers to participatory research are institutional. Conventional research funding may be appropriate when there is an existing research partnership that has generated questions and methods, but these funding sources do not support the establishment of new partnerships and exploratory discussions through which researchers and community groups jointly identify a research agenda. There are exceptions, of course, to this rule, primarily in the arena of large, nongovernmental donor organizations such as the Ford and Kellogg Foundations. Ford's Community Forestry Fellowship program provides support for graduate students to live in resource-based communities to build relationships and identify research projects that meet community needs. This program is positioned to foster institutional transformation by changing the way that natural resource scholars are trained to conduct research with forest and rangeland communities. There is a need for more such open-ended funding sources to help bring communities and researchers together to fashion collaborative and participatory research projects.

In the natural resource disciplines, the qualitative social science research methods often most appropriate for participatory research still are poorly understood, and the venues for publishing such research are fewer and lower in status than mainstream natural resource or social science journals. Many scientific peers still define the researcher's role as objective and value-neutral and question the validity of findings in which an explicit intent of the research is to effect change among research participants. It can be challenging to explain the value and validity of participatory research in this intellectual culture. If universities and government research agencies were to evaluate the effects of service and outreach activities on their constituencies, they would recognize the multiple benefits conferred by participatory research and could begin to create incentives for scientists to engage with communities for knowledge generation, knowledge transfer, and local capacity building.

Conclusion

Participatory research is an approach for conducting research with communities that can play a unique role in deepening our understanding of the human dimensions of natural resource management. It is not without methodological, ethical, and practical challenges for researchers and community partners. At its best, participatory research promotes critical self-analysis leading to an improved understanding of the social, cultural, and economic dimensions of resource use and improved community capacity to confront local resource concerns beyond the scope of a single research project. Participatory research also can build trust and open lines of communication among individual participants and participating organizations, which ultimately can increase the potential for effective and equitable resource management. Participatory research is not appropriate for all research questions or settings, and institutional incentives for engaging in participatory research remain weak in natural resource fields. Where time is available and both researchers and community partners are willing and able to engage in authentic dialogue that reveals and questions the assumptions of all participants in the research process, participatory research can be transformative for individuals, communities, and institutions.

Note

1. O'odham word meaning "Anglo," from the word "American."

References

Agency for Healthcare Research and Quality. 2003. *Community-based Participatory Research: Assessing the Evidence.* Evidence report/technology assessment Number 99. Rockville, MD: Agency for Healthcare Research and Quality.

Agrawal, A., and C.C. Gibson. 2001. *Communities and the Environment.* New Brunswick, NJ: Rutgers University Press.

Ahmed, S.M., B. Beck, C.A. Maurana, and G. Newton. 2004. Overcoming Barriers to Effective Community-based Participatory Research in US Medical Schools. *Education for Health* 17(2): 141–151.

Akwesasne Task Force on the Environment. 1996. *Protocol for Review of Environmental and Scientific Research Proposals.* http://www.northnet.org/atfe/webdocs/atfe_protocol.pdf (accessed October 18, 2007).

Alaska Native Knowledge Network. 1993. *Alaska Federation of Natives: Guidelines for Research.* http://www.ankn.uaf.edu/afnguide.html (accessed October 18, 2007).

Amanor, K. 1993. Understanding Farmers' Knowledge: Introduction. In *Cultivating Knowledge: Genetic Diversity, Farmer Experimentation and Crop Research,* edited by W. de Boef, K. Amanor, K. Wellard and A. Bebbington. London: Intermediate Technology Publications, 1–13.

Arnold, J.S. 2004. What is the Value of Participation? Building Social Capital to Support Sustainable Management of Tohono O'odham Rangelands. MS thesis, School of Natural Resources, University of Arizona, Tucson, AZ.

Arnold, J.S., and M. Fernandez-Gimenez. 2007. Building Social Capital Through Participatory Research: An Analysis of Collaboration on Tohono O'odham Tribal Rangelands in Arizona. *Society & Natural Resources* 20: 481–495.

Ballard, H.L. 2004. Impacts of Harvesting Salal (*Gaultheria shallon*) on the Olympic Peninsula, Washington: Harvester Knowledge, Science, and Participation. PhD dissertation, Environmental Science, Policy and Management, University of California, Berkeley, CA.

Berardi, G. 2002. Commentary on the Challenge to Change: Participatory Research and Professional Realities. *Society & Natural Resources* 15: 847–852.

Bernard, R. 2002. *Research Methods in Anthropology: Qualitative and Quantitative Approaches.* Walnut Creek, CA: Alta Mira Press.

Bishop, D. 2005. Collaborative Adaptive Management and Participatory Monitoring: Case Studies of the Northwest Colorado Stewardship. MS thesis, Colorado State University, CO.

Bliss, J., and A.J. Martin. 1989. Identifying NIPF Management Motivations with Qualitative Methods. *Forest Science* 35(2): 601–622.

Brugge, D., and A. Kole. 2003. A Case Study of Community-based Participatory Research Ethics: The Healthy Public Housing Initiative. *Science and Engineering Ethics* 9(4): 485–501.

Bryndon-Miller, M. 2001. Education, Research, and Action: Theory and Methods of Participatory Action Research. In *From Subjects to Subjectivities: A Handbook of Interpretive and Participatory Methods*, edited by D. L. Tolman and M. Bryndon-Miller. New York: New York University Press, 76–94.

Chambers, R. 1994. Participatory Rural Appraisal (PRA): Challenges, Potentials and Paradigms. *World Development* 22(10): 1437–1454.

Chuenpagdee, R., J. Fraga, and J.I. Euan-Avila. 2004. Progressing toward Co-management Through Participatory Research. *Society & Natural Resources* 17: 147–161.

Cooke, B., and U. Kothari. 2001. *Participation: The New Tyranny*. New York: Zed Books.

Davis, S.M., and R. Reid. 1999. Practicing Participatory Research in American Indian Communities. *American Journal of Clinical Nutrition* 69(suppl): 755S–759S.

Denzin, N.K., and Y.S. Lincoln, (eds.). 2000. *The Handbook of Qualitative Research*. Thousand Oaks, CA: Sage Publications.

Everett, Y. 2001. Participatory Research for Adaptive Ecosystem Management: A Case of Nontimber Forest Products. In *Understanding Community-based Forest Ecosystem Management*, edited by G.J. Gray, M. J. Enzer, and J. Kusel. Binghamton, NY: Food Products Press, 335–357.

Fernandez-Gimenez, M. E., H.P. Huntington, and K.J. Frost. 2006. Integration or Cooptation? Traditional Knowledge and Science in the Alaska Beluga Whale Committee. *Environmental Conservation* 33(4): 306–315.

Fischer, F. 2000. *Citizens, Experts, and the Environment: The Politics of Local Knowledge*. Durham, NC: Duke University Press.

Freire, P. 1970. *Pedagogy of the Oppressed*. New York: Continuum.

Goebel, A. 1998. Process, Perception and Power: Notes from 'Participatory' Research in a Zimbabwean Resettlement Area. *Development and Change* 29: 277–305.

Gray, G.J., M.J. Enzer, and J. Kusel. 2001. *Understanding Community-based Forest Ecosystem Management*. Binghamton, NY: Food Products Press.

Hall, B.L. 2001. I Wish This Were a Poem of Practices of Participatory Research. In *Handbook of Action Research*, edited by P. Reason and H. Bradbury. Thousand Oaks, CA: Sage Publications, 171–178.

Hays, J.U. 2004. Perennial Grass Abundance and Livestock Management in the Arid Rangelands of the Sif Oidak Dist, Tohono O'odham Nation. MS thesis, School of Natural Resources, University of Arizona, Tucson, AZ.

Hays, J.U., M.E. Fernandez-Gimenez, and the Sif Oidak Livestock Committee. 2005. Community-based Rangeland Planning on the Tohono O'odham Nation. *Rangelands* 27: 15–19.

Horner, L.A., and D.M. Ostermeier. 2004. Assessing Capacity for Collaboration and Sustainable Forestry in a Western Tennessee Community. Paper read at 10th International Symposium on Society and Resource Management, June 2–6, Keystone, CO.

Horton, D.E. 1984. *Social Scientists in Agricultural Research: Lessons from the Mantaro Valley Project, Peru*. Ottawa, Canada: International Development Research Centre.

Ison, R., and D. Russell. 1999. *Agriculture Extension and Rural Development: Breaking Out of Traditions*. Cambridge, UK: Cambridge University Press.

Israel, B.A., A.J. Schulz, E.A. Parker, and A.B. Becker. 1998. Review of Community-based Research: Assessing Partnership Approaches to Improve Public Health. *Annual Review of Public Health* 19: 173–202.

Johnson, N., H.M. Ravnborg, O. Westermann, and K. Probst. 2001. User Participation in Watershed Management and Research. *Water Policy* 3: 507–520.

Lather, P. 1986. Issues of Validity in Openly Ideological Research: Between a Rock and a Soft Place. *Interchange* 17(4): 63–84.

Minkler, M. 2004. Ethical Challenges for the "Outside" Researcher in Community-based Participatory Research. *Health Education and Behavior* 31(6): 687–697.

Nieto, S. 2000. *Affirming Diversity: The Sociopolitical Context of Multi-cultural Education.* New York: Addison Wesley Longman.

Nussbaum, R.H., P.P. Hoover, C.M. Grossman, and F.D. Nussbaum. 2004. Community-based Participatory Health Survey of Hanford, WA, Downwinders: A Model for Citizen Empowerment. *Society & Natural Resources* 17: 547–559.

Payton, R.W., J.J.F. Barr, A. Martin, P. Sillitoe, J.F. Deckers, J.W. Gowing, N. Hatibue, S.B. Naseem, M. Tenywa, and M.I. Zuberi. 2003. Contrasting Approaches to Integrating Indigenous Knowledge about Soils and Scientific Soil Survey in East Africa and Bangladesh. *Geoderma* 111: 355–386.

Pound, B., S. Snapp, C. McDougall, and A. Braun, eds. 2003. *Managing Natural Resources for Sustainable Livelihoods: Uniting Science and Participation.* Sterling, VA: Earthscan Publications.

Pretty, J., and B.R. Frank. 2000. Participation and Social Capital Formation in Natural Resource Management: Achievements and Lessons. Paper read at International Landcare Conference, March 3, Melbourne, Australia.

Quaghebeur, K., J. Masschelein, and H.H. Nguyen. 2004. Paradox of Participation: Giving or Taking Part. *Journal of Community and Applied Social Psychology* 14: 154–165.

Reason, P., and H. Bradbury (eds.). 2001. *Handbook of Action Research.* Thousand Oaks, CA: Sage Publications.

Russell, D., and C. Harshbarger. 2003. *Groundwork for Community-based Conservation: Strategies for Social Research.* Walnut Creek, CA: Altamira Press.

Schell, L.M., and A.M. Tarbell. 1998. A Partnership Study of PCSs and the Health of Mohawk Youth: Lessons from Our Past and Guidelines for Our Future. *Environmental Health Perspectives Supplements* 106: 833–840.

Seidman, I. 1998. *Interviewing as Qualitative Research: A Guide for Researchers in Education and the Social Sciences.* New York: Teachers College Press.

Simpson, L.R., and P. Driben. 2000. From Expert to Acolyte: Learning to Understand the Environment from an Anishinaabe Point of View. *American Indian Culture and Research Journal* 24(3): 1–19.

Sixsmith, J., M. Boneham, and J.E. Goldring. 2003. Accessing the Community: Gaining Insider Perspectives from the Outside. *Qualitative Health Research* 13: 578–589.

Smith, S., D.G. Willms, and N.A. Johnson. 1997. *Nurtured by Knowledge: Learning to Do Participatory Research.* Ottawa, Canada: International Development Research Centre.

Society for Applied Anthropology. 1983. Ethical and Professional Responsibilities. http://www.sfaa.net/sfaaethic.html (accessed February 1, 2006).

Strauss, A., and J. Corbin. 1998. *Basics of Qualitative Research.* Thousand Oaks, CA: Sage Publications.

Tuhiwai Smith, L. 1999. *Decolonizing Methodologies: Research and Indigenous People.* London: Zed Books, Ltd.

Van Riper, L. 2003. Can Agency-led Initiatives Conform to Collaborative Principles? Evaluating and Reshaping an Interagency Program through Participatory Research. PhD dissertation, University of Montana, Missoula, MT.

Wallerstein, N. 1999. Power Between Evaluator and Community: Research Relationships within New Mexico's Healthier Communities. *Social Science Medicine* 49: 39–53.

Woolcock, M. 1998. Social Capital and Economic Development: Toward a Theoretical Synthesis and Policy Framework. *Theory and Society* 27: 151–208.

Zanetell, B., and B.A. Knuth. 2002. Knowledge Partnerships: Rapid Rural Appraisal's Role in Catalyzing Community-based Management in Venezuela. *Society and Natural Resources* 15: 805–825.

Part II

Communities in the Context of Emerging and Persistent Forest Management Issues

5

Evolving Interdependencies of Community and Forest Health

Mark Nechodom, Dennis R. Becker, and Richard Haynes

The demand for public goods from our nation's forests has grown with population and income and, with it, the complexity of managing forest resources and the number of connections between forests and surrounding communities. The evolution of the public's demand over the past 60 years has shifted from goods chiefly tied to logging and manufacturing of lumber and panel products to a wider range of products and services. Communities acting as agents in forest restoration on public timberlands increasingly are vital to the enhancement of wildlife habitat, watershed protection, and recreational opportunities. Communities also are vital to reducing the risks of wildfire to human populations.

This chapter explores the role that forest communities and the wood-products industries located within those communities, play in the restoration and management of forest ecosystems in the West. This rapidly evolving role is driven by perceptions that an unacceptable amount of public forests have become unhealthy due to an abundance of dense stands of small-diameter trees resulting from decades of wildfire suppression (Schmidt et al. 2002). These overly dense stands are described as being outside their historic range of ecologic variability and as vulnerable to large-scale insect infestations and the occurrence of catastrophic wildfire. Actions intended to lessen the risk of catastrophic wildfire are attempts to restore forests to a more healthy condition.

There are several key drivers of change in forest management associated with forest restoration. Together they illuminate choices for the future of public forests, as well as the role of communities in public forest management. First, there are concerns that the increasing risk of catastrophic wildfires threatens public safety, as well as the sustainability of forested ecosystems (Covington 2003). Second, there is the paradox inherent in forest-restoration strategies that by returning to a healthy state of fire-adapted ecosystems, at some point fire will need to be reintroduced into those ecosystems. To do so without losing key ecosystem functions and causing dramatic loss of life and property will require substantial investment in the removal of over-abundant small trees and brush. To date, this material has had minimal economic value and has been largely incapable of offsetting the high cost of fuels treatment. Third, whether focused on the wildland-urban interface or remote forested regions, the scale of proposed forest thinning to remove accumulated fuels is quite significant. Approximately 126 million acres of public forestlands across the country are at high risk of losing key ecosystem components to wildfire unless forest fuels can be reduced significantly (USDA Forest Service 2000). The Government Accountability Office estimates that 39 million acres in the western United States require some form of thinning (GAO 1999). Of that, the Forest Service estimates that 9.5 million acres of public forests and 5.1 million acres of private forests could be thinned taking into consideration exclusions for wilderness and other sensitive areas (Skog et al. 2006). Fourth, when one considers harvesting costs ranging from $250 to $800, or even $5,000, per acre (Fight and Barbour 2005; USDA Forest Service 2002) it is hard to imagine that the American public would be willing to pay outright for fuel-reduction treatments across a meaningful portion of the millions of acres at risk. When the high costs of production and the generally lower finished product values are combined, the utilization of small-diameter trees from fuel-reduction treatments is not financially viable at a significant scale under current market conditions in most locations.

Forest-restoration strategies involving mechanical thinning, prescribed fire, and eradication of invasive and exotic plant populations will involve complex interactions of communities and forest industries. Forest communities possessing the human capital and knowledge to facilitate these activities are critical both for defining and establishing acceptable management actions and for developing partnerships to implement mutually agreeable projects. A viable forest-products manufacturing sector that can utilize material being thinned in various restoration efforts is critical since product recovery can help to offset the high cost of treatment. At the same time, growing urban populations in the West, attracted by a variety of lifestyles and amenity values, are encroaching upon forests. New residents and their expectations for various ecosystem attributes add complexity to an already difficult challenge.

We argue in this chapter that land mangers will find themselves depending more on communities as goals for public forest management more frequently involve forest-health restoration and hazardous-fuel management. This involves engaging community capacities in forest restoration, enabling institutions to facilitate restoration activities, and developing the industrial infrastructure to utilize a range of materials removed as part of restoration practices. Embedded in this proposition is the recognition that older variations of timber dependency will be more multidirectional in the new millennium. Land managers increasingly will rely on forest communities and related industries in pursuit of desired outcomes at the landscape scale.

Forest Restoration and Community Opportunities

A number of indicators suggest that public forest management is shifting away from an industrial model of timber extraction toward the explicit enhancement of ecosystem services. This shift is predicated on a desire to produce the benefits of healthy forests for individual and social welfare. Ecosystem services provided by healthy forests include wildlife habitat, air and water quality, public safety, and fire-resilient ecosystems. For the arguments we advance in this chapter, we adopt the more constrained definition of ecosystem services advanced by Boyd and Banzhaf (2006), which narrows the range of ecosystem services to "those components of nature directly enjoyed, consumed or used to yield human well-being." This definition distinguishes ecosystem services from the broader array of ecosystem functions that are necessary precursors or conditions to the production of ecosystem services that are directly enjoyed, consumed, or used by humans.

This emerging shift in public forest management can be witnessed in keystone federal forestry policies and statutes enacted in recent decades (USDA Forest Service 1993; Vig and Kraft 2006). Most recent among them are the Healthy Forest Restoration Act of 2003 (P.L. 108–148) and the National Fire Plan adopted in 2000. At the core of the Healthy Forest Restoration Act is an explicit emphasis on restoring forested ecosystems through community wildfire planning, market research and enhancement for fuel-reduction byproducts, and through revised forest planning procedures. The objective of the National Fire Plan, which permeates nearly every aspect of federal forest management today, is to guide agency responses to severe wildfire by increasing coordination of firefighter resources, biomass utilization incentives, and community assistance grants. Funding appropriated pursuant to the Healthy Forest Restoration Act and the National Fire Plan increasingly supports the bulk of timber management activities in the western United States, which is tied integrally to forest-restoration objectives. Although the means may vary, and not all policies focus on enhancement of ecosystem services, the emerging goal of forest management in this decade appears rooted in forest health and the benefits provided by restoration.

The salience of an ecological approach is reinforced in the media with dramatic images of wildfires burning through communities, informing public debate about the ecological condition of public lands. These images also have substantially altered the political landscape of forest policy. It increasingly is clear that without some form of active intervention, a great number of areas risk severely damaging key ecosystem functions that will take decades to recover. Interventions are likely to include a combination of prescribed, controlled fire and mechanical thinning that will be necessary before wildland fire can be reintroduced safely into the environment. The removal of these accumulated fuels provides an opportunity for forest communities, especially those communities previously dependent upon timber from public lands (Becker and Viers 2007). Residents in these communities possess a variety of skills and can assist with prescribed burning, harvesting, and wood-products manufacturing necessary to thin forests. Based on this recognition, greater emphasis is being placed on building and sustaining community capacities to utilize fuel-reduction byproducts to recoup the high costs of removal (GAO 2005).[1] However, without adequate markets to absorb the generally low-value biomass, the cost to supplement restoration activities remains politically untenable considering the scale of proposed restoration. At the same time, there is only a limited appreciation of the scale of the problem (Haynes 2003). For example, in 2000 the softwood lumber industry in the interior West consumed 830 million cubic feet of logs to produce nearly 5.8 billion board feet of lumber and 485 million cubic feet of residues. Assuming the need to thin 1 million acres per year (and that an average of 1,000 cubic feet will be removed from each acre), we will need to find uses and markets for 1 billion cubic feet per year. This would require a doubling of the processing capacity in the interior West alone. It is unclear how private capital could be attracted to invest at this scale. And without adequate markets or comparable public payments to offset cost differentials, there is little incentive for communities or related forest industries to participate.

Contributing to the problem was industry restructuring during the 1990s, as the wood-products industry evolved into a highly efficient but less product-diverse industry with a focus on lumber production primarily for domestic markets and on using timber from private timberlands (Barbour et al. 2003; Haynes 2003; and Haynes and Fight 2004). It is an integrated industry that uses both logs and residues (45% of each log ends up as mill residues). New and surviving mills are located along main transportation corridors in proximity to the private lands where timber is procured. Some rural areas, though forest-based, have little local forest-products manufacturing infrastructure. Harvested logs are shipped to manufacturing centers farther away, resulting in lower stumpage prices than in the past and employment reduction despite of relatively high harvest levels.

There are two components to this new wood-products industry. Along the West Coast, it focuses on 14–20 inch (35.6–50.8 cm) logs and there is little capacity to handle logs over 24 inches (61 cm) in diameter. The other component is an evolving small-log industry located throughout the West using logs between 4.5 and 10 inches (11.4– 25.4 cm) in diameter at the small end. The recent changes in the forest-products industry have left many wondering if local industry infrastructure can be maintained or reestablished where it has closed. Table 5-1 illustrates how much wood is needed to sustain four typical types of mills. It also shows the residue generation from the mills available for residue-based manufacturing or power generation. In western Washington and northern Oregon, the pulp and paper industry is supported almost entirely from these residues. In the interior West, these residue-based industries are less available, meaning that forest operations will depend on the extent that the sawlog components of stands can be sold; disposing of chips is costly. Public land managers are challenged to sustain forest operations that can provide sufficient log flows, as illustrated in Table 5.1, so that returns on investments will be attractive

Table 5-1. Wood Requirements for Different Size Sawmills

	Units of measure	Micro sawmill	Small sawmill	Medium sawmill	Large sawmill
Production per shift	Thousand board feet, lumber scale	5.0	50.0	150.0	400.0
Annual production[a]	Million board feet, lumber scale	1.25	12.5	37.5	100.0
Chip, sawdust production[b]	Million cubic feet	0.07	0.70	2.10	5.60
Annual log requirement (2 board feet overrun)[c]	Million board feet, log scale	0.625	6.250	18.75	50.0
Annual log requirement (4 board feet overrun)[d]	Million cubic feet	0.156	1.56	4.67	12.5
Log truckloads per year[e]		130	1,302	3,906	10,417
Chip vans per year[f]		55	549	1,648	4,394
Direct jobs created[g]		5.7	57.5	172.5	460.0

[a] Computed assuming 250 operating days for one shift.

[b] Computed as 45 percent of log input volume (in cubic feet).

[c] Computed assuming an overrun of 2 board feet (there are 2 board feet of lumber scale for every board foot of log scale scribner).

[d] Computed assuming 4 board feet (log scale) per cubic foot.

[e] Computed assuming 1,200 cubic feet of logs per truckload.

[f] Computed assuming 16 units per truckload (2.5 cubic feet of pulp chips per cubic foot of solid wood).

[g] Computed using a factor of 9.2 direct jobs per million board feet of timber harvested (Washington and Oregon).

to private investors. They also are challenged to find ways to engage community capacities to mobilize private industry. Communities, for their part, are
challenged to identify ways to engage in forest-restoration opportunities that
minimize the barriers to utilization.

Utilization Options and the "Commodification of Waste"

The fundamental shift currently under way in federal forest policy and management emphasizes the production of ecosystem services. Provision of these
services in western forests often requires active management, including removal
of substantial amounts of biomass. Biomass and small-diameter timber then
become byproducts, or even waste products, associated with the production of
healthy forests. Assuming that direct public payments are likely to be insufficient to offset restoration costs, we are left with three fairly distinct options.
The first involves the development of new high-value products from small-
diameter trees of mixed species, including using a substantial portion of currently noncommercial species. The second option involves a substantial
reduction in the cost of fuels treatments, including new harvesting techniques
and a likely increase in the use of prescribed fire. The third option involves
increasing revenues to land managers by capturing some of the values of
ecosystem services resulting from restoration activities and the protection and
enhancement of those services.

The first option, new high-value products, is being pursued by way of significant federal investment in research and demonstration projects. The Biomass
Research and Development Act of 2000 (Title III of the Agricultural Risk Protection Act of 2000, P.L. 106–224) authorized up to $219 million for fiscal years
2002 through 2015 to coordinate and accelerate biobased products and bioen-
ergy research and development. An additional $160 million were authorized by
the Energy Policy Act of 2005 (P.L. 109–58) for biomass utilization research and
biorefinery construction. More than $36 million were awarded to community
organizations and businesses through Forest Service community assistance programs in fiscal years 2001 through 2003 (Becker et al. in prep), and federal agencies made an additional $54 million available for utilization, product
development, and marketing in fiscal years 2004 and 2005 (GAO 2006). Numerous other research and agency budgets, not to mention state university programs, are dedicated to the development of new products from small-diameter
trees. Progress has been made (LeVan-Green and Livingston 2001), but increasing the value of material previously of limited or no value alone will not offset
the cost of utilization, especially when new products must compete with established ones in the marketplace.

The second option for reducing harvesting costs will be difficult given the
highly refined nature of commercial logging enterprises. Equipment increasingly is more efficient, but the costs of operation and maintenance also are
increasing, as are equipment purchase prices. Small-diameter trees also have

higher per-unit harvesting, handling, and processing costs than larger, more valuable trees (Fight and Barbour 2005). Combined, these costs can reduce market competitiveness, which in turn reduces revenue to loggers and producers who already are constrained by small profit margins. Moreover, depending on the density of harvest sites and the distance to manufacturing facilities, transportation costs may account for 40% or more of total costs (Han et al. 2004). Local manufacturing capacity to utilize the material from forest thinnings, as well as the sheer volume of trees removed, will have the greatest effect on the reduction of harvest costs (Kluender et al. 1998; Shaffer 1989; Spelter and Alderman 2003). But these cost reductions will need to balance long-term forest health with the economic realities of harvest intensity and tree size.

The third option involves increasing the returns to land management by capturing some of the value of ecosystem services. Payments for ecosystem services—calculated as avoided costs of watershed restoration after wildfires and fire suppression, and lost timber and recreation revenues—have been identified as a source to help offset the costs of restoration. Transfer of these payments could be used to leverage private investment and provide incentives for management and collaboration that would benefit communities in proximity to forests. This is, however, the most problematic option because many of the benefits derived by society from forest ecosystems have been defined broadly as public goods (e.g., air and water quality) and, consequently, are free for general use. There are many problems to overcome. As Boyd and Banzhaf (2005, 3) point out, "[b]ecause most ecosystem services are public goods, markets are not available to provide clear units of account." The need for the valuation of these public goods and their enhancement only recently has become evident because of societie's perceptions of their relative scarcity (underpinned by substantial improvements in our knowledge of ecosystem functions). A recent National Research Council synthesis of the problem points out that the need for ecosystem enhancements have become "unavoidable" partly because of the increasing cost to public health and well-being by doing nothing. "It may be costly to protect, conserve, and restore ... ecosystems, and the costs are borne by giving up benefits in other parts of the economy, now or in the future" (NRC 2004, *22*).

Despite the problematic nature of payments for ecosystem services, advocates often cite the benefits that public forests provide to communities. Without the ability to value benefits like production of clean air and water, critical habitat for fish and wildlife, and community protection, it is difficult to describe quantitatively the tradeoff of benefits from forest restoration against the costs. For example, the inability to trade among public goods limits our ability to compare the benefits of fuels reduction against the avoided costs of wildfire suppression or ecological degradation. As demonstrated by the effect of severe wildfires, some costs are more easily calculated (e.g., lost timber revenues), while others are more obscure (e.g., increased particulates in the atmosphere contributing to respiratory illness, lost value of fish habitat or soil productivity, or lost carbon sequestration). Our ability to develop integrative plans for forest restoration that also benefit human communities remains constrained without markets or policy mechanisms that aid in the estimation of benefits, or, as Quinn and Quinn (2001) point out, a means of comparing values so that trade-offs can be understood better.

The Community Connection

Common to these three options is the recognition that a great deal of biomass will need to be removed to provide clean air and water, wildlife habitat, and community protection from catastrophic wildfires. In some places, markets may develop for biomass products from small-diameter trees, where revenues can be used to help offset the high costs of treatment. In these cases, forest restoration may become a sustainable economic activity. This, as previously suggested, presents an opportunity for communities but only to the extent that the private sector is able to benefit. Here, any policy aimed at reducing the density of trees subsequently will require partnering with those businesses and community stakeholders having the capacity to plan for, finance, and utilize the resulting material.

This premise provided the framework of the Healthy Forest Restoration Act. It authorized the exclusion of certain fuel-reduction projects from comprehensive environmental review to reduce public-sector overhead and expedite removal of small-diameter trees and brush. The act also encouraged collaboration between federal agencies and local communities in the preparation of community-based fuels treatment plans. Federal research funds were authorized in the hopes that markets would be developed to offset costs. The act made it clear that private industry and communities have a role to play. What is less clear is the extent to which federal resources will be appropriated to facilitate participation of communities and industry in reducing fire risks and enhancing ecosystem services. Still missing is a clear strategy for creating market institutions and processes that take into account the monetary values of restoration and the externalities of catastrophic wildfire. As a result, a viable biomass utilization industry has yet to materialize.

Historically, there has been a reluctance on the part of the federal government to finance private-sector development like that discussed here, but history also is replete with congressional and agency efforts to benefit the public good. The nexus between forest restoration and vital communities matters because communities are necessary to the delivery of the ecosystem benefits of public forest management. The history of the evolution of forest policy offers insight into the delivery of these public benefits.

Evolution of Land Management and Communities

The federal government's role in the evolution of forest and conservation policy in the United States is well documented (Hays 1987; Ruth 2000; Steen 1976).

Key to that role has been a long-standing tenet that forest regulation designed to produce an even flow of timber will best benefit neighboring communities where processing facilities are located and where woods and manufacturing workers live (SAF 1989). This tenet was formed by observing the timber boom-and-bust cycles in the Lake States, the southern Appalachians, and in the mid-South that often left distressed or abandoned communities. As the wood-products industry shifted west in the 1920s, this belief came to dominate public-forestry policy discussions, which lasted until the early 1950s, when employment declines were observed in spite of stable or rising harvests.

The evolution of forest management practices changed dramatically in the decades following World War I (Hays 1959; Kaufmann 1967; Lustig 1982). During this period, fire suppression became an important component of the new "scientific management" paradigm based partly on technological innovations of the day and a belief that forestry experts could manipulate forests for specific outcomes (Pyne 1981). After World War II, the public forests came under heavy pressure to produce timber for home construction in the 1950s, which was accompanied by a growing demand for recreation opportunities and "amenity" properties (Dana and Fairfax 1980). In addition, a vertically integrated forest industry evolved, with extensive privately owned timberlands as companies attempted to maintain timber supplies. Statutes such as the National Environmental Policy Act of 1969, the Clean Air Act of 1970, and the Endangered Species Act of 1973 collectively represented an emerging social consensus about the need for better environmental quality and accountability (Cubbage et al. 1993). The present-day desire to value ecosystem services reflects that social consensus, while the intent to manipulate the environment to accomplish desired outcomes reflects an earlier manifestation of active forest management.

Sustained Yield and Community Stability

An alliance among the forest-products industry, communities, and counties emerged in the 1930s that advocated maintaining or increasing federal timber harvests to benefit the economic and social well-being of neighboring communities. This alliance was rooted in the ways that sustained-yield policies evolved, with a deliberate focus on community economies and social well-being. Two framing concepts are key to this historical evolution. The first is based in nineteenth century silviculture and an early twentieth century understanding of ecosystem development. The second concept is rooted in the progressive conservationists' conviction that scientific management could bring about an accommodation between the concentration and accumulation of wealth on the one hand and broader social equity on the other (Hays 1959; Lustig 1982). The implications of this framing influence how forest management is conducted today and how public benefits are derived from forest restoration.

The silvicultural view fundamentally was informed by Fredrick Clements's notion of "climax stages" in ecosystems (Clements 1916; Worster 1977), where forests reach a stage in their natural cycles of development in which they no longer are productive. In 1905, when Gifford Pinchot assumed administrative control over the national forests, forest management doctrine was based in nineteenth century German forestry, under which harvest should not exceed growth (Pinchot 1915). Following an extensive assay of their conditions, Pinchot declared many of the forests to be "biological deserts," due to their apparent lack of regeneration (Clary, 1986; Pinchot 1947; Steen 1976). Achieving sustained-yield, in which harvest equals growth, would require intensive management to "restart" growth cycles that could support productive forests and, therefore, production forestry. In some instances, achieving sustained yield would require a well-planned and controlled liquidation of timber stands that were beyond rotation age, a formula proposed in 1922 by forester E.J. Hanzlik (Parry et al. 1983).

Pinchot further directed that timber sales from national forests would be guided by two principles. First, sales would be regulated to provide a steady supply of timber products, which would give stability to the industry as a whole. Second, preference in stumpage sales would be given to local communities to ensure the "welfare of the public ... and promote the upbuilding of the country" (USDA Forest Service 1908; see also Pinchot 1947). Integrating industry health and public welfare was manifested in the long-term social goal of community stability. The result was that public timber lands would be managed so that a continuous supply of forest products would be available to local wood-products industries in such a way as to maximize employment within resource limitations, costs of production, and market availability. Forest policy would then be pursued to ensure equitable distribution of the resulting benefits among those immediately dependent upon the resources (Kaufman and Kaufman 1946; Pinchot 1947).

One can see in these developments a foreshadowing of the provisions of the "sustained-yield units" created under the National Industrial Recovery Act of 1933 (Sched. C, Art VIII, NIRA, 1933) and the Multiple-Use Sustained-Yield Act of 1944 (P.L. 78–273, 16 U.S.C. § 583, 583a-583i), which were to help stabilize communities affected by the boom-and-bust cycles of the lumber market. In particular, the Multiple-Use Sustained-Yield Act was passed "to promote the stability of forest industries, of employment, of communities, and of taxable forest wealth, through continuous supplies of timber." But by the late 1920s, the economics of scale in the timber industry already had begun to shift from smaller mills supplying local markets to larger operators participating in national and global markets. The ensuing Depression sent many smaller producers into bankruptcy and forest communities into a tailspin, revealing how Pinchot's policies of sustained-yield forestry were not sustaining communities (Parry et al. 1983; see also Prudham 1998).

The broad goals of marrying public forest management to community stability were pursued even as lawmakers voiced concerns that programs would create an unhealthy dependence on federal resources that eventually would render the goals ineffective and non-competitive (Richardson and Mason 1983). The National Forest Management Act of 1976 (P.L. 94-588, 16 U.S.C. §§ 1600-1614) directed Forest Service managers to consider the effect of federal actions on forest communities when developing plans. The act also required the Forest Service to identify timber-dependent communities, giving rise to a class of communities, primary in the West, where at least 10% of employment was involved in timber processing. The Cooperative Forestry Assistance Act of 1978 (P.L. 95–313) consolidated a range of legislative initiatives focused on fire protection, technical assistance to private landowners, public and private forest health, new technologies and markets for wood utilization, and urban forestry. Forging a new direction, the act authorized the secretary of agriculture to provide financial, technical, and educational assistance to state foresters and cooperative-extension directors, which in turn enabled them to provide assistance to private-forest landowners to promote sustainable forestry and community development. The additional Economic Action and Rural Development Program authorities of 1990 created even more explicit goals of economic-revitalization assistance to forest communities (16 U.S.C. §§ 2101-2114, P.L. 95–313 as amended in 1990; 7 U.S.C. 6601 note, P.L. 101–624, Subtitle G of title XXIII).

Historically, substantive efforts to support forest communities have been reactions to major disruptions like the Great Depression of the 1930s, the whiplash of post–World War II economic booms, and the dizzying changes in timber-harvest policies in the Pacific Northwest and California in the last decade of the twentieth century. This raises some fundamental questions: Why presently is there an apparent resistance to codification in federal law of the relationship between the vitality and success of forest communities and the achievement of emerging forest ecosystem sustainability goals? Previous policy frameworks do not support the accomplishment of these goals. Moreover, the policies that have been developed to address forest health issues largely have gone unfunded. And why are there not federal and state mandates and ongoing institutional support for the relationship between public forest management and the economic and social viability of proximate communities?

To answer these questions, one must consider the historical connections between agency management, community economic development, and the interpretation of legislative intent. On the one hand, the long history of commercial timber production from public lands had the effect of creating secondary economic benefits and investment opportunities in forest communities. This created expectations that the connection between harvesting trees on federal land and investment in private-sector processing infrastructure were closely, often necessarily, related; and, in fact, they were. On the other hand, this encouraged those who interpreted the legislative intent of the statutes outlined above to argue liberally that federal laws designed to facilitate development of community capacity and investment in the wood-products industry also, by extension, constituted a mandate to federal agencies to direct resources explicitly to the maintenance and enhancement of community economic stability. In other words, what began as a complementary "trickle down" effect of public timber production became codified, in the eyes of some, as an obligation.

Forest Service officials often took pride in the "nonmarket" benefits associated with a well-functioning timber economy, such as social welfare, increased infrastructure, and secondary and tertiary industry development. But when the sale of federal timber began to plummet in the early 1980s, other sources of timber were not substituted easily. Many have argued that the Forest Service was derelict in meeting its statutory mandates to support community development and economic stability, but a strict interpretation of the statutes does not reveal a legal obligation. Although arguments for sustaining communities with federal timber have relied on a moral imperative, they have not withstood the scrutiny of the courts. The "dependency" relationship between communities and federal timber evolved through legitimate social needs but the legal foundations of such always have been tenuous.

Forest Restoration Needs and Community Responses

We can see notions of forest health dependence embedded in the contemporary faith in the eventual development of a small-diameter wood-products utilization industry whose revenues are to be part and parcel of the forest-restoration economy. The essential issue is how to govern the collective actions of the forest-products industry, land owners, communities, and public agencies who share in forest management and its outcomes. The public's changing appreciation of the array of services and public benefits provided by forests[2] challenges the traditional approaches to governance. These have relied on a mix of formal planning processes by land management agencies, market-based solutions to valuation questions, and regulations (mostly at the state level) that influence both the design and application of forest management practices. Throughout the West, as through much of the developed world, there are attempts to supplement market-determined actions with processes that try to find equilibrium among environmental protection, employment that contributes to economic prosperity, public access, and social justice.

Already there are forest communities mobilizing to develop wildfire protection plans. Some are working with regional economic development organizations and financial institutions to bring together capital for investment in local biomass industry infrastructure. In other cases, forest communities are focusing on building trust among stakeholders and community residents to find collaborative solutions to local problems or to prioritize areas most in need of restoration. Still other community groups volunteer their time and expertise to conduct biological inventories and complete the planning required for state and federal project approval, compensating for the lack of agency capacity to prepare fuel-reduction projects. All are examples of community action made possible by residents bringing together a combination of past experiences, common values, and skills. In short, human and social capital is filling a policy void (Becker 1975; Putnam et al. 1993; Wilkinson 1991; Zekeri et al. 1994).

A second driver of community mobilization is the opportunity to capitalize on favorable policies or program objectives (Tilly 1971). The Healthy Forest Restoration Act authorized funding for efforts to develop Community Wildfire Protection Plans, which, when completed, will be eligible for federal funding for fuel treatments and local capacity-building. In some instances, community organizations are working closely with local businesses to apply for enterprise development funds (e.g., low-interest loans, grants, and small-business assistance loans) to facilitate the purchase of equipment or to secure government contracts to harvest and utilize small trees. Collaborative partnerships are working with federal and state granting agencies to fund community and industry capacity-building that expands the ability to utilize restoration byproducts and the development of related enterprises. Two examples from the Southwest include the Four Corners Sustainable Forests Partnership (FCSFP) and the Collaborative Forest Restoration Program (CFRP). The federally funded FCSFP began in 1997 as a four-state effort in Arizona, New Mexico, Colorado, and Utah to reduce wildfire risks by investing in projects to affect fuels reduction through community development. The CFRP was established as a pilot program in New Mexico through the Community Forest Restoration Act of 2000 (Title VI, P.L. 106–393). It received $5 million annually from fiscal years 2001 to 2006 to provide cost-share grants for forest–restoration planning, treatment, and wood utilization. Both encourage collaboration with stakeholders and reinvestment in community capacity, much in the way that collaborative approaches were used in the Northwest Forest Plan (Donoghue et al. 2006).

The federal government in recent years also has sought to facilitate expansion of wood-utilization enterprises via revised contracting authorities. The Forest Service and Bureau of Land Management received new authority to implement stewardship contracting and agreements in Section 323 of the 2003 Appropriations Act (P.L. 108–7), which authorizes the pooling of restoration-related activities and trading of goods for services. Some activities, such as site preparation, tree planting, pre-commercial thinning, and trail and campground maintenance, have declined as agency budgets have been reduced (Moseley 2006). Stewardship contracting allows for multi-year contracts selected on a "best-value" basis whereby contractors and community groups work in collaboration with federal agencies to achieve a broad range of activities that improve land conditions. Stewardship contracting provides a means for agencies to contribute to the development of forest communities and restore and maintain ecosystems, while providing for a continuing source of local income and employment.

Community responses to perceived policy voids and their attempts to capitalize on policy opportunities tend to focus on local action. However, communities also are mobilizing to affect forest policy at the state and national levels. With increasing frequency, community forestry groups lobby Congress and agency officials to increase budget allocations for fuel treatments. Others seek more favorable state policies to facilitate economic development zone designation or changes in building codes or public procurement requirements to accommodate greater wood utilization. Finally, many communities support state mandates such as Renewable Portfolio Standards, which would encourage the use of biomass from forest restoration treatments to generate renewable power.

Significant economic barriers remain despite these myriad efforts. In many parts of the West, high transport costs and low marginal values for products derived from forest thinnings will require public investment of a magnitude not previously seen in order to make a restoration economy viable. State and federal governments have been reluctant to shoulder the associated financial burden, despite arguments for the public benefits that may be achieved. In the absence of market-based institutions for public forest management, public policy and related government investment are surrogates for market price signals. Crafting public policy with deliberate investment in certain sectors helps in establishing either fungibility among disparate values or trade-offs among goods and services. The deliberate engagement of consumers, producers, and beneficiaries in the transition to a restoration economy would clarify values that are not easily monetized or subject to market trading. As Cortner and Moote observe:

> Markets are themselves political institutions, and the availability of goods and services and the prices at which those goods and services are bought and sold are heavily influenced by government policy. Consequently, changes in government policy can create an institutional climate in which market forces are used to reinforce ecosystem management goals and reward the private sector for producing ecosystem benefits and pursuing long-term ecological sustainability (1999, *122*).

Forest restoration through active management must be economically viable. Reducing harvesting and processing costs or increasing the value of products cannot be accomplished without some form of market intervention. Market-based approaches to meeting the challenges we have described will require lasting institutional arrangements that accommodate the needs of a broad range of stakeholders.

Conclusion

In the past century, we have seen the evolution of a class of forest communities often characterized as "timber dependent." Now, we see the emergence of a more dynamic and encompassing relationship between communities and forests that can be called "forest health dependent." Many in these communities will have jobs directly related to hazardous fuel treatments, fire suppression, and processing of the biomass removed. Naturally in many communities there will be a range of opinion about how to manage risks or to capitalize on development opportunities. Where consensus does emerge around desired restoration objectives, economic barriers are likely, in many cases, to continue to impede progress.

Friederici (2003) notes that successful forest restoration at a meaningful scale will need to benefit and sustain the social and economic fabric of human communities. Although it is possible that the current trajectory of forest health could leave future generations with compromised abilities to sustain key ecosystem functions on public lands, there are clear opportunities to employ community capacities to enhance ecosystems. Under current market conditions, there are relatively few opportunities to realize net positive value by harvesting small trees without explicit government and policy intervention. The protection and enhancement of ecosystem services will rely on the participation, skills, and investment of forest communities and private industry. Without the engagement of the skills and capacities found in forest communities, forest restoration is unlikely to be sustainable.

For decades, communities in the West have depended on public lands for their economic and social well-being. But land management agencies now increasingly are dependent upon the capacities of forest communities to achieve broader ecosystem objectives. These objectives are ineluctably tied to public demands for wildlife habitat, clean air and water, enhanced recreation opportunities, and the protection of life and property from catastrophic wildfire. The challenge is to get the connections right among communities, governance, and the ecosystem benefits derived from forest restoration.

Notes

1. Memorandum of Understanding on Policy Principles for Woody Biomass Utilization for Restoration and Fuel Treatments on Forests, Woodlands, and Rangelands. Signed June 18, 2003, by the U.S. Department of Agriculture, U.S. Department of Energy, and U.S. Department of the Interior. http://www.fs.fed.us/forestmanagement/Woody-BiomassUtilization/documents/BiomassMOU_060303_final_web.pdf.

2. In the United States, retaining some forestlands in public ownership (71% is private and 29% is public), has been one attempt to impose a broader set of management goals than what might be expected from just market actions.

References

Barbour, R.J., D.D. Marshall, and E.C. Lowell. 2003. Managing for Wood Quality. In *Compatible Forest Management*, edited by R.A. Monserud, R.W. Haynes, and A.C. Johnson. Dordrecht, The Netherlands: Kluwer Academic Publishers, 299–336.

Becker, G.S. 1975. Human Capital: A Theoretical and Empirical Analysis. *The Journal of Political Economy* 70: 9–49.

Becker, D.R., and J. Viers. 2007. Matching the Utilization of Forest Fuel Reduction By-products to Community Development Opportunities. In *People, Fire, and Forests*, edited by T. Daniel, C. Raish, M.S. Carroll, and C. Mosely. Corvallis, OR: Oregon State University Press, 157-170.

Becker, D.R., M. Nechodom, A. Barnett, T. Mason, E. Lowell, D. Graham, and J. Shelly. In prep. USDA Forest Service Efforts to Develop Biomass Utilization Capacity in the Western U.S. Using Community Assistance Programs. Manuscript accepted for publication in the *Journal of Forestry*.

Boyd, J., and H.S. Banzhaf. 2005. Ecosystem Services and Government Accountability: The Need for a New Way of Judging Nature's Value. *Resources* 158: 16–19.

Boyd, J., and S. Banzhaf. 2006. What Are Ecosystem Services? The Need for Standardized Environmental Accounting Units. Discussion paper 06-02. Washington, DC: Resources for the Future.

Clary, D.A. 1986. *Timber and the Forest Service.* Lawrence, KS: University Press of Kansas.

Clements, F.E. 1916. *Plant Succession: An Analysis of the Development of Vegetation.* Carnegie Institute of Washington Publication, No. 242. Washington, DC: Carnegie Institution.

Cortner, H.J., and M.A. Moote. 1999. *The Politics of Ecosystem Management.* Washington, DC: Island Press.

Covington, W.W. 2003. Restoring Ecosystem Health in Frequent-fire Forests of the American West. *Ecological Restoration* 21(1): 7–11.

Cubbage, F.W., J. O'Laughlin, and C.S. Bullock, III. 1993. *Forest Resource Policy.* New York: John Wiley & Sons, Inc.

Dana, S.T., and S.K. Fairfax. 1980. *Forest and Range Policy: Its Development in the United States* (2nd ed.). San Francisco: McGraw-Hill.

Donoghue, E.M., C. Stuart, and S. Charnley. 2006. *Socioeconomic Monitoring Results.* Volume IV: Collaboration. PNW-GTR-649. Portland, OR: U.S. Department of Agriculture, Forest Service, Pacific Northwest Research Station.

Fight, R.D., and R.J. Barbour. 2005. *Financial Analysis of Fuel Treatments.* General Technical Report PNW-GTR-662. Portland, OR: U.S. Department of Agriculture, Forest Service, Pacific Northwest Research Station.

Friederici, P. (ed.). 2003. *Ecological Restoration of Southwestern Ponderosa Pine Forests.* Washington, DC: Island Press.

General Accounting Office (GAO). 1999. *Western National Forests: A Cohesive Strategy is Needed to Address Catastrophic Wildfire Threats.* Report to the Subcommittee on Forests and Forest Health of the House Committee on Resources. GAO/RCED-99-65. Washington, DC: General Accounting Office.

Government Accountability Office (GAO). 2005. *Natural Resources: Federal Agencies Are Engaged in Various Efforts to Promote the Utilization of Woody Biomass, but Significant Obstacles to its Use Remain.* Report to the House Committee on Resources. GAO-05-373. Washington, DC: General Accountability Office.

———. 2006. *Wood Utilization: Federal Research and Product Development Activities, Support, and Technology Transfer.* Report to the House Committee on Agriculture, Nutrition and Forestry. GAO-06-624. Washington, DC: Government Accountability Office.

Han, H.S., H.W. Lee, and L.R. Johnson. 2004. Economic Feasibility of an Integrated Harvesting System for Small-diameter Trees in Southwest Idaho. *Forest Products Journal* 54(2): 21–27.

Haynes, R.W. (ed.). 2003. *An Analysis of the Timber Situation in the United States: 1952–2050.* General Technical Report PNW-GTR-560. Portland, OR: U.S. Department of Agriculture, Forest Service, Pacific Northwest Research Station.

Haynes, R.W., and R.D. Fight. 2004. Reconsidering Price Projections for Selected Grades of Douglas-fir, Coast Hem-fir, Inland Hem-fir, and Ponderosa Pine Lumber. Research Note. PNW-RN-561. Portland, OR: U.S. Department of Agriculture, Forest Service, Pacific Northwest Research Station.

Hays, S.P. 1959. *Conservation and the Gospel of Efficiency: The Progressive Conservation Movement, 1890–1920.* Cambridge, MA: Harvard University Press.

———. 1987. *Beauty, Health, and Permanence: Environmental Politics in the United States, 1955–1985.* New York: Cambridge University Press.

Kaufman, H. 1967. *The Forest Ranger: A Study in Administrative Behavior.* Baltimore, MD: Johns Hopkins University Press.

Kaufman, H.F., and L.C. Kaufman. 1946. Toward the Stabilization and Enrichment of a Forest Community: The Montana Study. In *Community and Forestry: Contributions in the Sociology of Natural Resources,* edited by R.G. Lee, D.R. Field, and W.R. Burch. Boulder, CO: Westview Press, 27–39.

Kluender, R., D. Lortz, W. McCoy, B. Stokes, and J. Klepac. 1998. Removal Intensity and Tree Size Effects on Harvesting Cost and Profitability. *Forest Products Journal* 48(1): 54–59.

Lee, K. 1993. *Compass and Gyroscope: Integrating Science and Politics for the Environment.* Washington, DC: Island Press.

LeVan-Green, S.L., and J. Livingston. 2001. Exploring the Uses for Small-diameter Trees. *Forest Product Journal* 51(9): 10–21.

Lustig, R.J. 1982. *Corporate Liberalism: The Origins of Modern American Political Theory, 1890–1920.* Berkeley, CA: University of California Press.

Moseley, C. 2006. *Procurement Contracting in the Affected Counties in the Northwest Forest Plan: 12 Years of Change.* PNW-GTR-661. Portland, OR: U.S. Department of Agriculture, Forest Service, Pacific Northwest Research Station.

National Research Council (NRC). 2004. *Valuing Ecosystem Services: Towards Better Environmental Decision-making.* Washington, DC: National Academy of Sciences.

Parry, B.T., H.J. Vaux, and N. Dennis. 1983. Changing Conceptions of Sustained-yield on the National Forests. *Journal of Forestry* 81(3): 14–41.

Pinchot, G. 1915. *A Primer of Forestry.* Farmers' bulletin 173, 358. Washington, DC: Government Printing Office.

———. 1947. *Breaking New Ground.* New York: Harcourt, Brace.

Prudham, W.S. 1998. Timber and Town: Post-war Federal Forest Policy, Industrial Organization, and Rural Change in Oregon's Illinois Valley. *Antipode* 30(2): 177–196.

Putnam, R.D., R. Leonardi, and R. Nanetti. 1993. *Making Democracy Work: Civic Traditions in Modern Italy.* Princeton, NJ: Princeton University Press.

Pyne, S.J. 1981. Fire Policy and Fire Research in the U.S. Forest Service. *Journal of Forest History* 25(2): 64–77.

Quinn, J.B., and J.F. Quinn. 2001. Forging Environmental Markets. Issues in Science and Technology. http://www.issues.org/16.3/quinn.htm (accessed June 23, 2006).

Richardson, E, and D.T. Mason. 1983. *Forestry Advocate.* Santa Cruz, CA: Forest History Society.

Ruth, L. 2000. Changing Course: Conservation and Controversy in the National Forests of the Sierra Nevada. In *A Vision for the U.S. Forest Service: Goals for Its Next Century,* edited by R.A. Sedjo. Washington, DC: Resources for the Future, 213–256.

Schmidt, K.M., J.P. Menakis, C.C. Hardy, W.J. Hann, and D.L. Bunnell. 2002. *Development of Coarse-scale Spatial Data for Wildland Fire and Fuel Management.* General Technical Report RMRS-GTR-87. Fort Collins, CO: U.S. Department of Agriculture, Forest Service, Rocky Mountain Research Station.

Shaffer, R. 1989. Location Theory and Community Economic Development. In *Community Economics: Economic Structure and Change in Smaller Communities,* edited by R. Shaffer. Ames, IA: Iowa State Press, 46–70.

Skog, K.E., R.J. Barbour, K.L. Abt, E.M. Bilek, F. Burch, R.D. Fight, R.J. Hugget, P.D. Miles, E.D. Reinhardt, and W.D. Sheppard. 2006. *Evaluation of Silvicultural Treatments and Biomass Use for Reducing Fire Hazard in Western States.* Research Paper FPL-RP-634. Madison, WI: U.S. Department of Agriculture, Forest Service, Forest Products Laboratory.

Society of American Foresters (SAF). 1989. *Report of the Society of American Foresters National Task Force on Community Stability.* SAF 89-06. Bethesda, MD: SAF.

Spelter, H., and M. Alderman. 2003. *Profile 2003: Softwood Sawmills in the United States and Canada.* Research paper FPL-RP-608. Madison, WI: U.S. Department of Agriculture, Forest Service, Forest Products Laboratory.

Steen, H.K. 1976. *The U.S. Forest Service: A History.* Seattle, WA: University of Washington Press.

Tilly, C. 1971. Do Communities Act? *Sociological Inquiry* 43: 209–240.

U.S. Department of Agriculture Forest Service. 1993. Principal Laws Relating to Forest Service Activities. USDA Agriculture Handbook #435. Washington, DC: U.S. Government Printing Office.

———. 2000. Protecting People and Sustaining Resources in Fire-adapted Ecosystems–A Cohesive Strategy, the Forest Service Management Response to the General Accounting Office Report, GAO/RCED-99-65. Washington, DC: Government Accountability Office.

———. 2002. Lake Tahoe Basin Management Unit: Fuels and Vegetation Management Review. USDA Forest Service, Region 5 Lake Tahoe Basin Management Unit. http://www.fs.fed.us/r5/ltbmu/fuels-review/ltbmu-fuels-review-final.pdf (accessed June 20, 2006).

Vig, N.J., and M.E. Kraft. 2006. *Environmental Policy: New Directions for the Twenty-first Century.* Washington, DC: CQ Press.

Wilkinson, K.P. 1991. *The Community in Rural America.* New York: Greenwood Press.

Worster, D. 1977. *Nature's Economy: A History of Ecological Ideas.* New York: Cambridge University Press.

Zekeri, A.A., K.P. Wilkinson, and C.R. Humphrey. 1994. Past Activeness, Solidarity, and Local Development Efforts. *Rural Sociology* 59(2): 216–235.

6

Communities and Wildfire Policy

Toddi A. Steelman

In 2000, federal wildfire policy shifted from a reactive approach dominated by wildfire suppression to a more proactive approach that aimed to reduce the long-term wildfire risk to communities and the environment (USDA and USDI 2000; WGA 2001). Since the 1990s, more people have settled in what is called the wildland urban interface (WUI)—the place where humans and forests meet. This expanding patchwork pattern of residential development has resulted in humans residing closer to the areas where wildfire occurs, so that human communities are a central concern in this new approach to wildfire management.

Every community in the WUI faces different challenges and possesses unique attributes to address their wildfire risk. A sustainable approach to mitigating the long-term wildfire risk at the community level would allow communities to craft their own distinctive responses to the risks they face. Initially, the new federal wildfire approach specified four broad goals that could be adopted and integrated by communities to achieve their desired wildfire response: 1) improving fire prevention and suppression; 2) reducing trees, shrubs, and other vegetative growth (known as "hazardous fuels") near communities; 3) restoring fire-adapted ecosystems; and 4) promoting economic opportunity and social capacity-building through community assistance. However, more recent policy directives and subsequent allocation of resources have narrowed the federal approach to focus on fire suppression and hazardous fuel reduction to the exclusion of the other goals. These changes call into question the long-term feasibility of a sustainable, community-based wildfire policy.

This chapter explores wildfire policy from the perspective of communities. It begins by examining important trends related to the changing nature of the wildfire problem, including shifting settlement patterns and past and current policy approaches that shape community responses to wildfire threats. The chapter then summarizes the limited empirical research about community response to wildfire threats. The chapter concludes with policy implications and suggestions for future work on communities and wildfire policy that could contribute to a more sustainable wildfire policy that reduces the long-term risk to communities.

Communities and the Wildland Urban Interface

Hundreds, if not thousands, of communities are at risk from wildfire throughout the United States (GAO 2001). The shift in community and residential patterns during the 1990s largely created the current WUI. Americans migrated to the West and South, and many settled in dispersed residential areas along the WUI. From 1990 to 2000, the number of houses in the WUI grew by 67.8% in the Rocky Mountains and by 29.4% in the South, while on the West Coast and in the North, the growth rate was lower at 17.7% and 12.7%, respectively (Stewart et al. 2005). States with the highest WUI rates of housing-unit increase include Nevada (59.5%), Arizona (31.9%), Utah (28.4%), Idaho (27.7%), and North Carolina (25%) (Stewart et al. 2005). These settlement patterns mean more people and property are at risk from wildfire.

The encroachment into the WUI is exacerbated by an increased risk of catastrophic fire due to prolonged drought, diseased forests, deleterious grazing and timber practices, and 100 years of fire suppression. The combination of these social and natural events has resulted in costly, catastrophic fires that impact communities in numerous ways. The 2000, 2002, and 2003 wildfire seasons burned 8.4, 6.9, and 6.7 million acres, respectively, resulting in enormous fire suppression costs and posing risks to hundreds of communities (NIFC 2005). Consider that in 2003, wildfires in Southern California destroyed 3,640 homes, killed 22 people, forced 40,000 people to evacuate, and cost more than $2.04 billion in insured losses (Ferguson 2003; ISO 2003).

Communities are diverse, complex social systems made up of individuals with different perspectives. Consequently, fire can have multiple effects on a community and these can vary across groups, over time, and geographically across communities (Carroll and Daniels 2003). Fire events can provide opportunities for, "restoration, rebuilding, and community fire planning … and develop the trust and shared understandings necessary for effective concerted action" (Carroll et al. 2005, *317*). As a galvanizing event, a fire can provide the opportunity to share food, living space, labor, money, fellowship, and other resources. But wildfires also can contribute to "fragmentation within and among the communities and between communities and outside agencies" (Carroll et al. 2005, *317*). As the threat and actual occurrence of wildfires in the WUI has grown and the number of people living in the WUI has increased, policy has changed to reflect the need to protect communities from these catastrophic events, and we are learning how communities react in the aftermath.

Wildfire Policy Changes 1905–2005

Catastrophic fires in the late 1800s and early 1900s resulted in a national policy that emphasized suppression. Historically, the United States removed local influence from the professionalized and depersonalized infrastructure of fighting and researching wildfire (Pyne 1997 [1982]). This legacy has resulted in organizational structures and practices that sometimes are incompatible with community concerns and a more sustainable wildfire approach.

The Forest Service was established in 1905 in part to address wildfire and the erosion, flooding, and water quality problems that followed fire. Wildfire suppression enabled the emergent Forest Service to demonstrate its authority and expertise to the nation, while also squeezing out the influence and traditional practices (such as prescribed fire, which was deemed reckless and immoral by the Forest Service) of Native Americans and frontier inhabitants—the communities of the day (Pyne 1997 [1982], *101–112*).

Historic philosophies about fire color contemporary possibilities in fire mitigation. Suppression is seen as the only realistic option in some places, whereas in others, prescribed fire, natural burning, and other measures are acceptable. The historic Forest Service conception of wildfire created a belief that fire could be controlled, thus giving way to policies based on suppression. But this is only one construct; different communities have understood fire in different ways. For instance, Native American communities celebrated the dual nature of creation and destruction of all forces, thereby embracing a notion of balance between these opposing forces (Kimmerer and Lake 2001). Consequently, prescribed fire was used by indigenous people throughout North America to shape the landscape and regenerate ecosystems. Appalachian hardwood forests were encouraged by indigenous burning that promoted resprouting after fire. Midwest tall-grass prairies were influenced heavily by Native American burning. Sugar pine in the Sierra Nevada was promoted by tribal groups through prescribed fire (Kimmerer and Lake 2001). In the early 1900s, Native Americans, as well as some timber owners, promoted the importance of fire use for their livelihoods (Pyne 1995).

In spite of the rich history associated with prescribed fire and natural burning, a suppression approach became the dominant focus within the Forest Service. The expertise of the agency was celebrated as the beliefs and practices of other communities were marginalized. The organizational infrastructure that accompanied suppression policy took years to evolve and resulted in a hierarchical, militaristic institution devoted to expert fire management. In 1908, Congress passed an appropriations bill that gave the Forest Service the ability to receive advance funds to fight fire in cases of emergency (Busenberg 2004). This off-budget, deficit-spending provision allowed the Forest Service to spend money in excess of its annual appropriation and to be reimbursed by Congress through an emergency supplemental appropriation. Expenditures could be held accountable only after the fact, providing little incentive to reign in resources, which led to an expansion of suppression efforts. The Weeks Act of 1911 established interstate compacts to support fire fighting and created a grant program to support fire patrol and fire suppression on private lands by state forestry agencies. The 1924 Clarke-McNary Act expanded the grant program to build the administrative infrastructure of the state forestry departments and disseminated federal standards for fire protection to the states (Davis 2004). In the 1930s and 1940s, suppression policy and infrastructure expanded. Readily available labor from the Civilian Conservation Corps and military equipment from World Wars I and II contributed to the creation of a paramilitary organization that sought to protect civilians from the danger of fire (Pyne 1995). After the end of the Korean War, additional military hardware was channeled to state fire cooperators through the federal excess-equipment program (Pyne 1995). Over the following 50 years, the Forest Service strengthened the federal–state wildfire fighting partnership, which emulated military efficiency. Nonetheless, despite of the enormous resources and infrastructure devoted to suppression efforts, the number and intensity of high-profile wildfires in the United States increased in the 1990s (Dombeck et al. 2004). Inadequacies of the suppression approach, including escalating damage to people, property and infrastructure; threats to citizen and firefighter safety; and injury to natural systems led to reconsideration of wildfire policy goals and purpose (Busenburg 2004).

New Goals—A New Approach

In response to the catastrophic wildfire season of 2000, the secretaries of the interior and agriculture submitted a report to then-President Bill Clinton making suggestions for reducing the effect of wildfires on human and ecological communities (USDA and USDI 2000). This new policy was a significant departure from the previous policy. These recommendations, along with funding from Congress, resulted in the National Fire Plan (NFP). In 2001, Congress directed the Departments of Interior and Agriculture to work with the Western Governors' Association to develop an implementation strategy for the NFP. The NFP and Western Governors' Association's 10-Year Comprehensive Strategy (WGA strategy) identifies four goals to reduce the risk of wildfire and to build collaboration among communities and all levels of government: 1) improving fire prevention and suppression; 2) reducing hazardous fuels; 3) restoring fire-adapted ecosystems; and 4) promoting community assistance, which entails creating economic incentives and industries to reduce fuels and restore ecosystems while building social capacity (WGA 2001, 2002). The WGA strategy recognizes the importance of fire suppression, especially near homes and communities, but moves away from a reactive stance. The four goals are "designed to foster a proactive, collaborative, and community-based approach to reducing wildland fires that works side-by-side with effective traditional approaches to fire suppression and fire-fighting readiness" (WGA 2001, 3). These new, national goals—formulated in part with input from community, local, state, and federal representatives—were meant to be implemented at "the local level in an ecologically, socially and economically appropriate manner" (WGA 2002, 6). Each goal was deemed equally important to a successful long-term strategy of mitigating wildfire risk (WGA 2002).

In 2002, another policy initiative was launched in response to that year's wildfire season. President George W. Bush announced the Healthy Forests Initiative (HFI), which emphasized the hazardous-fuel-reduction goals of the NFP. The HFI entailed administrative reforms to streamline and prioritize hazardous-fuel-reduction projects. The administrative reforms dealt predominantly with expediting hazardous-fuel-reduction projects through changes in the National Environmental Policy Act (NEPA) and the Endangered Species Act (ESA) (USDA et al. 2002). In November 2003, Congress passed the Healthy Forests Restoration Act (HFRA) in reaction to the catastrophic wildfires in Southern California, and this codified the NEPA and ESA reforms first articulated in the HFI administrative actions. HFRA allows the Forest Service and Bureau of Land Management to conduct hazardous-fuel-reduction projects on up to 20 million acres of federal land (P.L. 108–148). Priority areas for fuel-reduction projects include the WUI, which can be defined by the communities at risk. The law recommends $760 million in annual funding for hazardous-fuel-reduction projects and directs agencies to spend half of congressional appropriations each year in the WUI. One of the most debated provisions of HFRA amended the NEPA to give the agencies an expedited review processes (cf 16 USC 6512 Sec. 102-108). More than 200 environmental groups opposed the HFRA because of the restrictions placed on NEPA and ESA procedures that altered their ability to appeal and litigate perceived problematic management plans (Berman 2003). Nonetheless, at the time of its passage HFRA had wide bipartisan support in Congress, as well as support among many community-based forestry activists.

As this brief history makes clear, in a relatively short time period the federal wildfire approach has been mandated to change from a top-down, militaristic-inspired suppression policy to a more collaborative and community-oriented approach with multiple goals. With an existing organizational infrastructure heavily invested in suppression practices, change has not been without its challenges. As the federal approach changed, communities sought to influence the direction of the new policy, and the new policy has shaped how communities can respond to their wildfire threats.

Community Influence on Policy

Although the new approach heralds from the federal government, the NFP, the
WGA strategy, HFI, and HFRA did not originate solely through a top-down
process. Leadership within and among communities tends to be diffuse, and
the principal organized presence of communities in the wildfire arena has been
through community-based forestry groups. Working from the grassroots since
the late 1990s, community-based forestry groups have been a vocal and active
participant in fostering change in national forest policy, including wildfire policy (Kusel 2003). They participate and seek influence because they are the most
economically and ecologically dependent on the resources in question. For
community-based forestry practitioners and activists in the western United
States, healthy forests mean managing and restoring ecosystems so they are less
prone to catastrophic wildfire, restore ecosystem functions, and capture the
economic benefits from ecosystem restoration and hazardous-fuel reduction.

During the 1990s, a group of representatives from community-based forestry
and watershed groups devised a set of principles and worked for legislative
change to support their vision (Cromley 2005; Gray et al. 2001). Their self-iden-
tified goals—stewardship, investment, process, and monitoring—reflect substantive as well as social needs to effect meaningful change (Gray et al. 2001).
Stewardship emphasizes a commitment to the health of land. Investment
addresses the resource needs of communities to enable them to "restore and
maintain healthy ecosystems and develop lasting stewardship between ecosystem and communities" (Gray et al. 2001, 22). Process is important because
community-based advocates want open, democratic processes that enable the
empowerment of communities. Monitoring involves gathering and sharing
"information in ways that build trust, promote learning, and ensure accountability, including taking immediate corrective measures to inform future actions"
(Gray et al. 2001, 22). These goals have led community-based forestry practitioners to work with Congress and other policy professionals to seek adequate
appropriations and funding, revise contracting and procurement practices, and
promote collaboration with communities to allow greater flexibility in management of federal lands for better stewardship (Cromley 2005). This advocacy
agenda coincided with the wildfire events of 2000, 2002, and 2003, which created
a window for policy change. As such, the ideas promoted by these community-
based advocates were incorporated, at least partially, into the major legislative
efforts that emerged in response to the catastrophic wildfire seasons.

One example of community influence on the new wildfire approach is the
inclusion of a local-benefit criterion when awarding contracts for hazardous-
fuel-reduction projects. Historically, the Forest Service and other natural
resource agencies considered economic opportunities for businesses and people in rural communities as part of their decisionmaking criteria for federal
projects and awards (Waggener 1977). These projects often were associated with

timber work, but the decline in timber harvesting on federal land reduced the number of work contracts awarded in many rural communities. When the NFP was crafted, community-based forestry organizations requested that Congress consider economic development opportunities when awarding contracts for hazardous-fuel-reduction projects. This local-benefit criterion made funding available to reduce hazardous fuels on public lands, while providing economic benefits to rural communities and workers. Moseley and Toth (2004) found, on average, that local contractors in Oregon and Washington captured more contracts funded through the NFP than other non-NFP contracts.

This example illustrates the interdependence of economic and ecological health from the perspective of community-based forestry practitioners. This interdependence extends to the overall principles that community-based forestry groups promote in forest policy. For the most part, community-based forestry groups have been successful in getting their goals—stewardship, investment, process, and monitoring—integrated into elements of the NFP, the WGA strategy, HFI, and HFRA. However, these groups have experienced less success in seeing these victories implemented on the ground (Cromley 2005).

Policy Influence at the Community Level

Communities are influenced by the NFP, the WGA strategy, HFI, and HFRA predominantly through the funding and programs that are available to them via federal and state agencies. For instance, federal and state agencies have discretion in how NFP money is requested and allocated to different priority programs in different states. These state-level programs roughly correspond to the goals laid out in the WGA strategy.

Communities can undertake many different activities to reduce their risk from natural disasters, including wildfire, and these can be categorized as either structural or social measures (Cigler 1988). Structural responses to wildfire disasters focus on concrete aspects of response, such as building materials that can withstand fire, vegetation management programs, building codes, land-use regulations, insurance, evacuation plans, and warning systems for predicting and tracking fires to assist in evacuation. Social responses entail decisionmaking, collaboration, organization, education, management, and planning techniques that help communities assess, choose, implement, and support structural responses. The two categories are not necessarily mutually exclusive but distinguish between more- and less-tangible actions. The goals of the NFP, the WGA strategy, HFI, and HFRA include fire prevention and suppression, hazardous-fuel reduction, ecosystem restoration and community assistance. For the most part, these are tangible, structural actions. The WGA strategy intended collaborative, community-based processes to emphasize the importance of social responses to accompany these structural activities.

The new federal approach includes specific policies that provide additional financial and organizational incentives to communities. Communities may use resources obtained through the NFP, HFI, or HFRA to respond to the threats they face, or they may draw upon their own resources. Most NFP, HFI, and HFRA funding goes to fire prevention and suppression and the reduction of hazardous fuels. A statewide study of community response to wildfire threats in Arizona, Colorado, and New Mexico found that comparatively smaller amounts of funding go to restoring fire-adapted ecosystems and providing community assistance (Steelman et al. 2004a). Consequently, one of the effects of the NFP, HFI, and HFRA on communities has been to prioritize fire prevention and suppression and hazardous-fuel reduction over ecosystem restoration and community assistance.

Hazardous-Fuel Reduction and Community Efforts

Communities have different perceptions about wildfire and the types of solutions that are acceptable for their specific locales. The HFI and HFRA emphasize hazardous-fuel reduction, and funding available through the NFP and HFRA has enticed communities to address this particular threat. Consequently, much more is known about community perceptions, attitudes, and behaviors related to hazardous-fuel reduction than to ecosystem restoration or community assistance.

Research has sought to understand individual and community perceptions of different hazardous-fuel treatments on public and private lands, how public education encourages homeowner support, and how agencies should interact with communities and the public. Two themes that play throughout the hazardous-fuel-reduction research is the importance of trust between government agencies and the publics with which they need to work (Manfredo et al. 1990; Vogt et al. 2005; Winter et al. 2004) and the need to appreciate the contextual variation from community to community and, potentially, from person to person (Nelson et al. 2005). In other words, government managers are more likely to be successful in their hazardous-fuel-reduction efforts if they consider contextual features that appeal to homeowners, rather than forcing one model on them (Nelson et al. 2005; Shindler et al. 2002), and focus on building and maintaining trust in citizen–agency interactions (Winter et al. 2004).

Different communities are concerned about different social, economic, and ecological values associated with hazardous-fuel-reduction efforts near their communities. Communities also have different levels of knowledge and experience that influence their thinking about wildfire management options (Vogt 2003). For instance, residents near California's Sequoia National Park were more worried about smoke effects from prescribed fire on public lands than property loss (Winter et al. 2002). A history of life and property losses related to prescribed fire in Michigan's lower peninsula led those communities to be more circumspect of prescribed fire (Winter and Fried 2000). Individuals in Oregon's Blue Mountains, where logging is more widespread and supports many local economies, raised concerns about burning trees that could be harvested commercially and so favored mechanical thinning over prescribed fire (Shindler and Reed 1996). Urban residents in Utah were less aware of wildfire and thus less informed about fuel-management options than rural communities in Arizona, Colorado, and Oregon (Brunson and Shindler 2004). Grazing as a fuel-management technique was more acceptable in the Arizona and Colorado communities where livestock are more prevalent. The concerns of each community reflect the diversity of experience, skill, and knowledge in each environment.

Individuals within communities also value their own personal landscapes differently. Place attachment is partially a function of aesthetics, and these considerations are important to residents who also might want to reduce their threat from wildfire. Consider for instance that homeowners in Florida and Minnesota prefer "natural" landscapes, which include vegetated views, wildlife, recreation, quiet, solitude, and privacy (Nelson et al. 2003). Although homeowners recognize the risk posed by wildfire, they differ in their perceptions of what constitutes an effective prevention measure and the actions they will take to reduce risk. Reducing hazardous fuel around private homes or creating defensible space, therefore, depends on property-owner perceptions and an evaluation of trade-offs among uncertain and potentially conflicting values (Daniel et al. 2003). Property owners are reluctant to support uniform hazard-reduction treatments, like large fuel breaks, which do not consider aesthetic or other values (Daniel et al. 2003). Not taking any action to reduce hazardous fuels is an appealing option for some given these considerations. Nelson et al. observe, "Some very knowledgeable people understand the risk of wildland fire and purposefully decide not to alter their landscape to reduce their risk" (2003, *61*).

Clearly communities approach the challenge of wildfire with multifaceted concerns, and these complexities are mirrored in the research on hazardous-fuel-reduction at the community level. Since most of the research on structural community responses to wildfire threats focuses on hazardous-fuel reduction, little is known about ecosystem restoration efforts or attempts to build sustainable economic enterprises to support ecosystem restoration or hazardous-fuel-reduction industries, which are equally important components in a long-term strategy to reduce threats of wildfires in communities. In addition to the research on hazardous-fuel reduction, there also is work on the social responses associated with the new wildfire policy.

Collaboration and Community Capacity

Collaboration is mentioned explicitly in the NFP, the WGA strategy, and HFRA as a key component to engender success in mitigating the risk of wildfire. Social responses, including collaborative activities, are important for helping support and integrate various structural responses to wildfire, such as fire suppression, hazardous-fuel reduction, ecosystem restoration, and community assistance (Jakes et al. 2003; Kruger et al. 2003; Steelman and Kunkel 2004). Also, collaborative planning in HFRA was strategically intended to get parties involved in planning and to take ownership of forest management, such as hazardous-fuel reduction.

In communities, working relationships or networks between public agencies and private landowners enable information to flow in numerous venues, such as homeowner associations, parent–teacher associations, and stakeholder groups. Active and open communication facilitates numerous purposes in wildfire response, from the creation of defensible space to the implementation of new ecosystem-restoration industries. Collaboration through task forces, working groups, advisory councils, partnerships, committees, and teams are some of the ways people organize to share information, educate others, and coordinate responses among the many stakeholders relevant to their particular concerns. Some collaborative groups work to achieve one goal, like the Lawrence County Fire Advisory Board in Spearfish, South Dakota, which focuses solely on improving fire prevention and suppression (Hudson et al. 2003). Other groups, like the Orleans–Somes Bar Fire Safe Council in California, work simultaneously to reduce hazardous fuels, restore fire-adapted ecosystems, and improve fire prevention through the reintroduction of natural fire regimes (Sturtevant et al. 2005). Wallowa Resources in Oregon endeavors to restore the land while finding economic opportunity for current and future generations of rural people (Sturtevant et al. 2005). The Ruidoso Wildland Urban Interface Group provides a forum for local, state, and federal stakeholders to share information about hazardous-fuel-reduction activities (Steelman and Kunkel 2003b; Sturtevant et al. 2005).

Communities with the networks, leadership, and ability to mobilize resources (social capital); knowledge and skills (human capital); heritage and experience with fire; knowledge of the locality; and attachment to place (cultural capital) make a difference in the ability to carry out successful fire-management planning and implementation (Kruger et al. 2003). These different types of capital fortify a community's capacity to engage in effective fire-mitigation programs because responses are designed for specific audiences and take into account the history and current conditions of the community (Kruger et al. 2003).

The importance of collaboration also is built into the HFRA, through the urging of the Western Governors' Association and community-based forestry groups. A centerpiece of the HFI and HFRA is the community wildfire protection plan (CWPP). To receive funding from HFRA, a community must have a CWPP, which brings together residents; property owners; local, state, and federal agencies; and others to create and prioritize a vision for addressing hazardous fuel treatments in the WUI. Although past collaborative efforts have given communities a say in public-land management plans, CWPPs are meant to provide communities with a leadership role in drawing the WUI boundaries and identifying the areas for priority hazardous-fuel treatment (Newman 2004). Different groups or individuals take the lead in different communities. Local government and fire departments, state foresters, private-property owners, and others have spearheaded efforts to reduce fuel on public lands, while also addressing the interjurisdictional challenges of working concurrently on private lands (Cope 2004; Jungwirth 2004; Lewis and Hubbard 2004).

Despite the acknowledged importance of collaboration and community-based focus, problems with collaboration, in conjunction with underinvestment in community capacity-building, have been identified as a shortcoming in the current implementation of the new wildfire policy (WGA 2004). Observers of the policy cite systematic challenges at the local, state, and federal levels (Daly 2004; Gregory 2005; WGA 2004). Some of these problems are due partly to a shortage of technical resources to conduct CWPPs and engage in collaborative practices, such as multi-party monitoring and stewardship contracts, especially in lower resource areas (Daly 2004; Tucker 2005). Other problems arise out of agency inexperience with collaborative practices and resistance to changing old habits. For instance, agencies find it more convenient to collaborate with each other than to include nongovernmental people. The time investment in collaboration can be seen as inefficient when there is great pressure within state and federal agencies to demonstrate that they are treating the maximum number of acres of hazardous fuels (Gregory 2005). As this summary of research indicates, the work on the social responses associated with the new wildfire policy emphasizes the importance of collaboration and community capacity-building. However, carrying out these practices has been challenging, thereby jeopardizing the effect that the structural responses, such as hazardous-fuel reduction, could have in the longer term.

Sustainable Community Responses

Much of the work by social scientists on wildfire has focused on individual attitudes, behaviors, and perceptions about hazardous-fuel reduction and the importance of collaborative processes and community capacity. As such, there is little work that focuses on holistic responses by communities per se (Field and Jensen 2005). A small number of case studies of community responses to wildfire have been conducted (Steelman et al. 2004b; Steelman and Kunkel 2003a). These case studies reveal that few communities take a completely integrated approach in terms of pursuing fire suppression and prevention, reducing hazardous fuels, restoring fire-adapted ecosystems, and promoting community assistance. In other words, most communities pursue one or two

goals, depending on their individual priorities and the incentives provided by
state and federal programs; a minority pursue more holistic strategies.

Flagstaff, Arizona, has made progress toward all four goals in the new wildfire approach (Steelman and Kunkel 2003a; Sturtevant et al. 2005). Because
Flagstaff has integrated these goals into a cohesive action plan, the community
has a better chance of mitigating the threat of wildfire in the long term. The
structural responses crafted for each goal area appear to be accompanied by
strong social responses. For instance, Flagstaff improves fire prevention and
suppression through the Ponderosa Fire Advisory Council (PFAC), a 16-mem-
ber group that includes all fire agencies within the greater Flagstaff area, along
with Coconino County, Northern Arizona University, and the National Weather
Service. The PFAC meets once a month to discuss and act upon a variety of
wildfire issues. These include joint training sessions, public-education activities, hazard assessment and response needs, general information sharing, special activities and projects, development of standard operating procedures, and
purchase of specialized equipment. Although the principal mission is sharing
information, over time that has evolved to include coordination, response planning to emergencies, and resource sharing. The City of Flagstaff Fire Department has a special Fuel Management Division that engages in home
assessments and conducts its own hazardous-fuel-reduction programs. The
Fuel Management Officer and Assistant Fuel Management Officer create stewardship plans for defensible space at no cost to the homeowner and carry out
prescribed burning. The Greater Flagstaff Forest Partnership (GFFP) seeks to
restore fire-adapted ecosystems, while also developing ecologically sustainable
utilization industries tied to restoration projects. Working collaboratively with
environmentalists, scientists, the Forest Service, and other governmental organizations, the GFFP focuses on 100,000 acres of WUI surrounding Flagstaff and
uses restoration approaches involving mechanical thinning and prescribed fire.

The PFAC, City of Flagstaff Fire Department Fuel Management Division, and
the GFFP work individually to pursue their respective goals, but the overall effect
results in a more long-term, sustainable approach to wildfire. Fires are suppressed when necessary but efforts also are made to reduce hazardous fuels and
restore ecosystems to prevent future catastrophic fire. The development of community economic opportunities results in new industries that can support sustained hazardous-fuel-reduction activities and ecosystem-restoration services.
The ultimate goal is a self-supporting economy in harmony with the surrounding environment that reduces risk to human and ecological communities alike.

Flagstaff is an exceptional example. Other communities are most likely to
pursue only improvements in fire prevention and suppression and reductions
in hazardous fuels. Failure to develop industries that support hazardous-fuel
reduction or recognize the importance of restoring ecosystems means communities will depend on federal, state, or local assistance to continuously reduce
hazardous fuels or maintain the work already completed. Without an infra-

structure that can support a restoration economy, communities will remain at risk or dependent on an unsustainable flow of resources to mitigate their wildfire threat.

Implications

Despite existing efforts by federal, state, and local governments and communities, wildfire remains a high risk in many areas. It is not known if systematic progress is being made toward reducing the number of communities at risk. However, the conditions that contribute to the wildfire problem—human settlement in the WUI, drought, and dense, flammable vegetation on millions of acres of land—remain.

The adoption of the NFP, the WGA strategy, HFI, and HFRA broadened the approach to wildfire management to include hazardous-fuel reduction, ecosystem restoration, and community assistance to confront the problems facing human and ecological communities. The four goals were promoted by community-based forestry groups and many others to address the multiple facets of wildfire mitigation that are important at the community level. In the words of the Western Governors' Association, "This community-based approach to wildland fire issues combines cost-effective fire preparedness and suppression to protect communities and the environment with a proactive approach that recognizes fire as part of a healthy ecosystem" (2001, 2). To date, however, greater emphasis has been placed on hazardous-fuel reduction to the exclusion of the ecosystem-restoration and community-assistance goals (Daly 2004; WGA 2004). This has two effects. First, it limits the responses that communities can take. Second, it calls into question the ability to realize a long-term, sustainable response from the community level. Hazardous-fuel reduction is a necessary but insufficient solution to the wildfire problem. Without emphasis on ecosystem restoration, which reestablishes the natural role of fire on the land to result in more sustainable ecological conditions, and community assistance, which establishes local economic foundations for the continued removal of hazardous fuels and ecosystem-restoration practices, the federal government and Forest Service will continue to need to provide billions of dollars per year in perpetuity to address the wildfire problem. A sustainable solution must integrate the multiple goals intended in the NFP while giving communities the opportunity to shape these to their specific needs.

From a research standpoint, significantly less is known about ecosystem restoration or community assistance efforts, such as building capacity for small-diameter timber industries. Even less is known about how all four goals fit together at the community level, where they must be effectively integrated to achieve a long-term, sustainable solution. Researchers and practitioners could help promote ecosystem restoration or community assistance by learning more about the opportunities for and obstacles to achieving these goals at the community level. The experiences and lessons learned in places that have succeeded in engaging effective ecosystem restoration and community assistance projects need to be documented and shared widely.

Collaboration, communication, information sharing, and capacity building are at the heart of the community-based planning and implementation advocated by the WGA strategy and community-based forestry groups. Effective community responses to wildfire provide evidence of the importance of community capacity to facilitate and integrate comprehensive responses to wildfire threats. However, problems with collaboration in all facets of wildfire response indicate that this social resource perhaps is suffering from underinvestment and inattention. Researchers have a role to play in documenting cases of successful community approaches and the social responses that contribute to these successes. Likewise, researchers can play a role in highlighting areas where collaboration is problematic and empirically assess the obstacles. Much more could be known about which agencies in which regions do a better job of fostering collaboration within and among communities.

If the building blocks to a sustainable wildfire policy rest on the foundation of the four goals of fire suppression, hazardous-fuel reduction, ecosystem restoration, and community assistance, then the mortar that holds them together is the collaboration and communication that happens within and among communities and between communities and agencies. At present, the foundation is fragile, due to an overemphasis on fire suppression and hazardous-fuel reduction, and the mortar is weak, due an underappreciation of social resources. Researchers, practitioners, communities, and agency officials all have a responsibility to work through these challenges to cultivate a more sustainable, long-term wildfire policy that reduces the risk to communities.

Acknowledgments

The author would like to thank Caitlin Burke, Ellen Donoghue, Linda Kruger, Sarah McCaffrey, and Victoria Sturtevant for helpful comments on previous versions of this chapter. All errors remain the sole responsibility of the author.

References

Berman, Dan. 2003. Enviros Fight Traditional Allies on Healthy Forests Compromise. *Environment and Energy Daily* Oct. 16. http://www.eenews.net/EEDaily/2003/10/16/archive/4?terms=Enviros+Fight+Traditional+Allies+on+Healthy+Forests+Compromise (accessed August 21, 2005).

Brunson, M.W., and B.A. Shindler. 2004. Geographic Variation in Social Acceptability of Wildland Fuel Management in the Western United States. *Society and Natural Resources* 17: 661–678.

Busenberg, G. 2004. Wildfire Management in the United States: The Evolution of Policy Failure. *Review of Policy Research* 21(2): 145–156.

Carroll, M.S., and S. Daniels. 2003. Fire in Our Midst: A Look at Social Science Research Issues at the Community Level. In *Humans, Fires and Forests—Social Science Applied to Fire Management*, edited by H.J. Cortner, D.R. Field, P. Jakes, and J.D. Duthman. Workshop summary, Jan. 28–31, Tucson, AZ.

Carroll, M.S., P.J. Cohn, D.N. Seesholtz, and L.L. Higgins. 2005. Fire as a Galvanizing and Fragmenting Influence on Communities: The Case of the Rodeo–Chediski Fire. *Society and Natural Resources* 18: 301–320.

Cigler, B. 1988. Current Policy Issues in Mitigation. In *Managing Disaster, Strategies and Policy Perspectives*, edited by L.K. Comfort. Durham and London: Duke University Press, 39–52.

Cope, R. 2004. Community Wildfire Protection Plans from Four Angles. *Journal of Forestry* 102(6): 4–7.

Cromley, C. 2005. Community-based Forestry Goes to Washington. In *Adaptive Governance: Integrating Science, Policy and Decision Making*, edited by R.D. Brunner, T.A. Steelman, L. Coe-Juell, C.M. Cromley, C.M. Edwards, and D.W. Tucker. New York: Columbia University Press, 221–267.

Daly, C. 2004. Hearing Before the Subcommittee on Forestry, Conservation and Rural Revitalization of the Senate Committee on Agriculture, Nutrition, and Forestry, Hearings on the Implementation of the Healthy Forests Restoration Act. United States Senate 108th Congress, Second Session, June 24.

Daniel, Terry C., Ed Weidemann, and Dawn Hines. 2003. Assessing Public Tradeoffs Between Fire Hazard and Scenic Beauty in the Wildland–Urban Interface. In *Homeowners, Communities, and Wildfire: Science Findings from the National Fire Plan*, P. Jakes compiler, General Technical Report NC-231. St. Paul, MN: U.S. Department of Agriculture, Forest Service North Central Research Station, 36–44.

Davis, C. 2004. The West in Flames: The Intergovernmental Politics of Wildfire Suppression and Prevention. *Publius: The Journal of Federalism* 31(3): 97–110.

Dombeck, M.P., J.E. Williams, and C.A. Wood. 2004. Wildfire Policy and Public Lands: Integrating Scientific Understanding with Social Concerns across Landscapes. *Conservation Biology* 18(4): 883–889.

Ferguson, E. 2003. Congress Sends Forest Fire Bill to President. Gannett News Service, November 22.

Field, D.R., and D.A. Jensen. 2005. Humans, Fire and Forests: Expanding the Domain of Wildfire Research. *Society and Natural Resources* 18: 355–362.

General Accounting Office. 2001. The National Fire Plan: Federal Agencies Are Not Organized to Effectively and Efficiently Implement the Plan. Washington, DC: U.S. General Accounting Office.

Gray, G.J., M.J. Enzer, and J. Kusel. 2001. Understanding Community-based Forest Ecosystem Management: An Editorial Synthesis. In *Understanding Community-based Forest Ecosystem Management*, edited by G.J. Gray, M.J. Enzer, and J. Kusel. New York: Food Products Press, 1–25.

Gregory, L. 2005. Representative of the Wilderness Society Testimony before the Subcommittee on Forests and Forest Health, U.S. Department of Agriculture, of the House Committee on Resources. USFS and BLM Accomplishments on Healthy Forests Restoration Act. February 17.

Hudson, R.P. Jakes, E. Lang, and K. Nelson. 2003. Spearfish, South Dakota, and the Northern Black Hills: Steps to Improve Community Preparedness for Wildfire. USDA Forest Service, North Central Research Station. http://www.ncrs.fs.fed.us/ pubs/1834 (accessed August 21, 2005).

Insurance Services Office. 2003. Insurers to Pay California Policyholders $2.04 billion for Wildfire Losses, Estimates ISO's Property Claim Services Unit. http://www .iso.com/press_releases/2003/11_17_03.html (accessed July 13, 2005).

Jakes, P.J., K. Nelson, E. Lang, M. Monroe, S. Agrawal, L. Kruger, and V. Sturtevant. 2003. A Model for Improving Community Preparedness for Wildfire. In *Homeowners, Communities, and Wildfire: Science Findings from the National Fire Plan*, P. Jakes compiler, General Technical Report NC-231. St. Paul, MN: U.S. Department of Agriculture, Forest Service, North Central Research Station, 4–9.

Jungwirth, L. 2004. Community Wildfire Protection Plans from Four Angles. *Journal of Forestry* 102(6): 4–7.

Kimmerer, R.W., and F.K. Lake. 2001. The Role of Indigenous Burning in Land Management. *Journal of Forestry* 99(11): 36–41.

Kruger, L.E., S. Agrawal, M. Monroe, E. Lang, K. Nelson, P. Jakes, V. Sturtevant, S. McCaffrey, and Y. Everett. 2003. Keys to Community Preparedness for Wildfire. In *Homeowners, Communities, and Wildfire: Science Findings from the National Fire Plan*, P. Jakes compiler, General Technical Report NC-231. St. Paul, MN: U.S. Department of Agriculture, Forest Service, North Central Research Station, 10–17.

Kusel, J. 2003. Introduction. In *Forest Communities, Community Forests*, edited by J. Kusel and E. Adler. Lanham, MD: Rowman and Littlefield, xv–xxi.

Lewis, P., and J. Hubbard. 2004. Community Wildfire Protection Plans from Four Angles. *Journal of Forestry* 102(6): 4–7.

Manfredo, M.J., M. Fishbein, G.E. Hass, and A.E. Watson. 1990. Attitudes Toward Prescribed Fire Policies. *Journal of Forestry* 99(7): 19–23.

Moseley, C., and N.A. Toth. 2004. Fire Hazard Reduction and Economic Opportunity: How Are the Benefits of the National Fire Plan Distributed? *Society and Natural Resources* 17(8): 701–716.

National Interagency Fire Center (NIFC). 2005. Wildland Fire Statistics. In National Interagency Fire Center Fire Statistics. http://www.nifc.gov/stats/wildlandfirestats.html (accessed August 21, 2005).

Nelson, K.M., C. Monroe, and J. Fingerman Johnson. 2005. The Look of the Land: Homeowner Landscape Management and Wildfire Preparedness in Minnesota and Florida. *Society and Natural Resources* 18: 321–336.

Nelson, K.M., C. Monroe, J. Fingerman Johnson, and A.W. Bowers. 2003. Public Perceptions of Defensible Space and Landscape Value in Minnesota and Florida. In *Homeowners, Communities, and Wildfire: Science Findings from the National Fire Plan*, P. Jakes compiler, General Technical Report NC-231. St. Paul, MN: U.S. Department of Agriculture, Forest Service, North Central Research Station, 55–62.

Newman, C. 2004. Community Wildfire Protection Plans from Four Angles. *Journal of Forestry* 102(6): 4–7.

Pyne, S.J. 1997[1982]. *Fire in America: A Cultural History of Wildland and Rural Fire.* Seattle and London: University of Washington Press.

———. 1995. *World Fire: The Culture of Fire on Earth.* Seattle and London: University of Washington Press.

Shindler, B., and M. Reed. 1996. *Forest Management in the Blue Mountains: Public Perspectives on Prescribed Fire and Mechanical Thinning.* Corvallis, OR: Oregon State University, Department of Forest Resources.

Shindler, B.A., M.W. Brunson, and G.H. Stankey. 2002. *Social Acceptability of Forest Conditions and Management Practices: A Problem Analysis.* General Technical Report PNW-GTR-537. Portland, OR: U.S. Department of Agriculture Forest Service, Pacific Northwest Research Station.

Steelman, T.A., and G. Kunkel. 2004. Effective Community Responses to Wildfire Threats: Lessons from New Mexico. *Society and Natural Resources* 17: 679–699.

———. 2003a. Community Responses to Wildfire Threats in Arizona: Flagstaff. http://www.ncsu.edu/project/wildfire/Arizona/flagstaff/flagstaff.html (accessed August 21, 2005).

———. 2003b. Community Responses to Wildfire Threats in New Mexico: Ruidoso. http://www.ncsu.edu/project/wildfire/ruidoso.html (accessed August 21, 2005).

Steelman, T.A., G. Kunkel, and D. Bell. 2004a. Federal and State Influences on Community Responses to Wildfire: Arizona, Colorado and New Mexico. *Journal of Forestry* 102(6): 21–28.

———. 2004b. Community Responses to Wildland Fire Threats. http://www.ncsu.edu/project/wildfire (accessed August 24, 2005).

Stewart, S., R. Volker, R. Hammer, J. Fried, S. Holcomb, and J. McKeefry. 2005. Mapping the Wildland Urban Interface and Projecting Its Growth to 2030: Summary Statistics. http://silvis.forest.wisc.edu/Library/Stats/uswuistats.pdf (accessed July 13, 2005).

Sturtevant, V., M. Moote, P. Jakes, and A. Cheng. 2005. *Social Science to Improve Fuel Management: A Synthesis of Research on Collaboration.* General Technical Report NC-257. St. Paul, MN: U.S. Department of Agriculture, Forest Service, North Central Research Station.

Tucker, L. 2005. Oregon Society of American Foresters State Chair Elect and District Forester, Oregon Department of Forestry, testimony before the United States House of Representatives Committee on Resources Subcommittee on Forests and Forest Health, USFS and BLM Accomplishment on Healthy Forests Restoration Act. February 17.

U.S. Department of Agriculture (USDA) Forest Service, White House Council on Environmental Quality, and U.S. Department of the Interior (USDI). 2002. Administrative Actions to Implement the President's Healthy Forests Initiative. S-0504.02. December 11. On file with author.

USDA and USDI. 2000. Federal Wildland Fire Management Policy and Program Review. Washington, DC: USDA and USDI.

Vogt, C. 2003. Seasonal and Permanent Homeowner' Past Experiences and Approval of Fuel Reduction. In *Homeowners, Communities, and Wildfire: Science Findings from the National Fire Plan,* P. Jakes compiler, General Technical Report NC-231. St. Paul, MN: U.S. Department of Agriculture Forest Service, North Central Research Station. 63–73.

Vogt, C.A., G. Winter, and J.S. Fried. 2005. Predicting Homeowners' Approval of Fuel Management at the Wildland–Urban Interface Using the Theory of Reasoned Action. *Society and Natural Resources* 18: 337–354.

Waggener, T.R. 1977. Community Stability as a Forest Management Objective. *Journal of Forestry* 75(3): 710–714.

Western Governors' Association (WGA). 2001. A Collaborative Approach for Reducing Wildland Fire Risks to Communities and the Environment: 10-Year Comprehensive Strategy. In *Western Governors' Association, Key Issues in Brief.* http://www.westgov .org/wga/initiatives/fire/final_fire_rpt.pdf (accessed December 21, 2001).

————. 2002. A Collaborative Approach for Reducing Wildland Fire Risks to Communities and the Environment: 10-Year Comprehensive Strategy Implementation Plan. In *Western Governors' Association, Key Issues in Brief.* http://www.westgov.org/wga/ initiatives/fire/implem_plan.pdf (accessed December 21, 2002).

————. 2004. Report to Ann Veneman and Gale Norton from the WGA Forest Health Advisory Committee on the Implementation of the 10-Year Comprehensive Strategy. November. On file with author.

Winter, G., and J.S. Fried. 2000. Homeowner Perspectives on the Fire Hazard, Responsibility, and Management Strategies at the Wildland Urban Interface. *Society and Natural Resources* 13(1): 33–49.

Winter, G.J., C. Vogt, and J.S. Fried. 2002. Fuel Treatments at the Wildland–Urban Interface: Common Concerns in Diverse Regions. *Journal of Forestry* 100(1): 15–21.

Winter, G., C.A. Vogt, and S. McCaffrey. 2004. Examining Social Trust in Fuel Management Strategies. *Journal of Forestry* 102(6): 8–15.

7

Amenity Migration, Rural Communities, and Public Lands

LINDA E. KRUGER, RHONDA MAZZA, AND MARIA STIEFEL

A photo in a magazine advertisement shows friends relaxing around a candlelit dinner table. Through the window, the sun sets behind snow-capped mountain peaks. In the foreground, a kayaker paddles across a lake. The caption below describes a new condominium complex with residences that "showcase dramatic lake and mountain views, complemented by the pleasures of pampered resort services, delightful amenities and a lakeside clubhouse." All of this, the text continues, is just "moments from the urban charms of downtown Sandpoint, the premier resort town offering outdoor fun and family-friendly adventures." On another page, the caption under the picture of a wooded landscape touts the opportunity to buy land with a national forest "at your doorstep." More than a dozen similar eye-catching advertisements are peppered throughout the in-flight magazine, with most highlighting their proximity to public lands (Horizon Air 2004).

These advertisements extol the natural amenities of the locales: the dramatic scenery, recreational opportunities, and an expanse of forest. And indeed these amenities have attracted new residents to rural communities across the country. Often they come first as tourists, attracted to the scenic beauty, adventure, or relaxation. Once there, it may be the local ambience that entices them to stay, retire, and build a second (or third) home. Many of the communities attracting amenity migrants are gateways to public land and previously were economically dependent on timber, mining, and ranching. Examples in the western United States include Bend, Ashland, and Hood River in Oregon; the Lake Tahoe Basin; Missoula, Montana; Boise and Sand Point Idaho; and numerous ski and resort communities in the Rockies. The trend also has been identified across Canada, Mexico, and in some European countries.

As amenity migrants settle in their new communities, the physical changes are readily apparent: new homes, new businesses, new roads, rising real estate values. But the changing relationships and values associated with amenity migration are less evident and also present challenges for community leaders and resource managers. Many of the communities attracting amenity migrants are near public forests. The changing values within the neighboring community may change the issues and concerns residents have about forest management.

This chapter examines who is migrating to amenity-rich areas, why they are coming, and how this change affects communities and forest management. It also discusses gaps in the literature, that when filled, will provide a better understanding of the connections among migrants, their new communities, and forest management. One of these gaps is in understanding the extent of income inequality between immigrants and long-term residents. Although researchers have examined the contribution of tourism and amenity-based development to sustainable rural communities and ecosystems, the effect of this work has been limited by a number of factors, including the dominance of descriptive, case-study research; the lack of funding available for longitudinal studies; the multitude of single-investigator projects with a narrow disciplinary focus; and the lack of careful integration and coordination between research, policy, and community and regional planning processes.

There are few empirical studies that examine nationwide rural effects (Hunter et al. 2005, two exceptions worth reviewing are Deller et al. 2001 and English et al. 2000). It is important to fill these knowledge gaps because policymakers, forest managers, and community leaders lack reliable, science-based information needed to make informed decisions about the future of their communities and forests (communication with Fen Hunt, Cooperative State Research, Education and Extension Service January 23, 2007).

Planned or unplanned, understood or not, development is occurring in communities with natural amenities. For communities wanting to ease the inevitable transition and plan for an envisioned future, understanding how values and socioeconomic factors shape amenity migration and are shaped by it is key.

The Rise of Amenity Migration

Amenity migration is the movement of people to places with attractive environmental and cultural resources (Moss 1994) and recreation opportunities (Garber-Yonts 2004; McCool and Kruger 2003). Amenity migrants may be part-time or full-time residents to their new communities; they may be retirees, professionals able to telecommute, or entrepreneurs seeking to serve the other new residents. They may differ from the resident population in education and income levels and have different perceptions about appropriate resource use and management.

Although amenity migration is occurring across the United States, most areas with this type of growth are found in the mountains of the West and Southwest, coastal areas, and areas near national forests, national parks, or other public land holdings (English et al. 2000). Across the country between 1970 and 2000, population growth was higher in counties with federal land than in counties without federal land (Frentz et al. 2004). Increasing numbers of seniors are settling near amenity-rich national forests (see Figure 7-1). People also are attracted to the lakes and forests of the upper Great Lakes and Northeast that offer summer and winter recreational opportunities (Johnson and Beale 2002). Recreational opportunities, beautiful scenery, lakes, forests, and mountains attract economic development and amenity migrants while retaining existing populations (Johnson and Beale 2002). Rudzitis (1993) found that counties with designated wilderness had population growth through the 1980s that was six times the national average for nonmetro areas and almost twice as much as other rural western counties. Cordell (2006) projects that between now and 2030, counties with national forests (or proximate to national forests) will see significant growth in the number of seniors over 65.

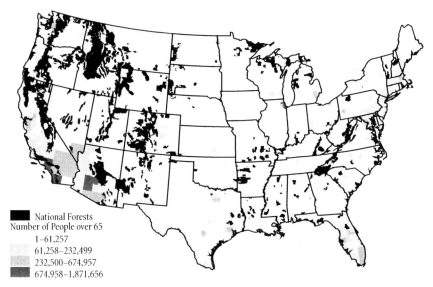

Figure 7-1. Counties with National Forests that Are High in Natural Amenities, Projected Population Age 65 and Over, 2030

Source: Pioneering Research Project, Southern Research Station, USDA Forest Service, Athens, GA, Ken Cordell Project Leader.

In a study of recreation, tourism and rural well-being, Reeder and Brown (2005) used regression analysis to assess and compare socioeconomic conditions in rural recreation and other nonmetro counties. They found that recreation counties grew by 20%—almost three times as fast as other non-metro counties (Table 7-1). During the same period, employment grew 23.7% in recreation counties and only 9.8% in other nonmetro counties. Earnings per job and per capita increased slightly more in recreation counties. The median income was slightly higher in recreation counties but was somewhat offset by higher housing costs. Other studies report similar findings, with long-term residents having higher annual incomes in high-amenity areas offset by higher costs-of-living (Hunter et al. 2005). Reeder and Brown noted that recreation counties are diverse and that the averages they calculated mask considerable variation among counties.

Drivers of Amenity Migration

What is behind the surge in amenity migration? First, rising levels of disposable income among the middle and skilled-working classes and the growth of a "leisure society" with time for recreation and travel have fueled demand for recreation (Whitson 2001, 2005). Increasing demand for recreational oppor-

Table 7-1. Social and Economic Change in Recreation and Other Nonmetro Counties

Indicator	Recreation county	Other nonmetro county
Population growth 1990–2000	20.2 %	6.9 %
Employment growth 1990–2000	23.7 %	9.8 %
Earnings per job in 2000 Change 1990–2000	$22,334 5,340	$22,780 5,140
Income per capita in 2000 Change 1990–2000	$22,810 7,471	$20,727 6,564
Median household income in 1999 Change 1989–1999	$35,001 11,952	$31,812 10,531
Median monthly rent in 2000 Change 1990–2000	$474 134	$384 104

Note: These are county averages (simple means). Data excludes Alaska and Hawaii.

Source: Economic Research Service (ERS) calculations based on data from the U.S. Bureau of the Census, U.S. Department of Commerce, Department of Health and Human Services, and the FBI (adapted from Reeder and Brown 2005).

tunities has provided an opportunity to capitalize on residential and resort development of farm and forestland, particularly near water. Luxury resort communities and second-home developments featuring golf courses and ski areas, often with public land nearby, are booming across the United States.

Second, changes to the federal tax code in 1997 have made second homes a lucrative investment strategy for those looking to diversify their portfolios and invest the equity they have built in their primary residence. Baby boomers began to turn 60 in 2006—retirement age for many and peak years for the purchase of second homes. From 2010 to 2030, the population over age 65 will spike by 75% to more than 69 million people (Hodge 2005). This population spike is coupled with unprecedented growth in home equity and the largest intergenerational transfer of wealth in history that will see more than $10 trillion passed down from elderly parents to boomers (Hodge 2005).

Third, many rural communities have shifted from manufacturing to retail- and service-based economies (English et al. 2000; Shumway and Otterstrom 2001; Whitson 2001). Communities adjacent to public lands are becoming more economically tied to the amenity values of those lands than to resource extraction (Whitson 2005). Montana is a prime example of an economy that now depends on tourism, recreation, retirement living, and health care rather than resource extraction (Diamond 2005). As a region, the Mountain West economy is shifting from dependence on resource-extractive industries to dependence on amenity-based industries, thus making it a retirement and tourist mecca (Shumway and Davis 1996; see also Kraybill 1997; Power 1996; Rasker et al. 2004).

Fourth, outdoor and adventure travel are the fastest growing segments of the travel industry in the United States (Howe et al. 1997). Tourists and retirees are drawn to the natural amenities and opportunities for both tranquility and adventure available in these rural communities (English et al. 2000; Johnson and Beale 2002). Wilderness can be especially attractive (Duffy-Deno 1998) and introduces people to rural and remote locations that many decide to invest in. Resort real estate, full and fractional ownership arrangements (time shares), residence clubs, and a variety of other options provide an array of investment possibilities.

The Lake Tahoe Basin on the California–Nevada border, the Redmond–Bend area in Oregon, and Missoula, Montana, are prime examples of amenity-based migration by retirees and those still working. Historically, migration followed jobs, but with amenity migration, jobs tend to follow people. The working amenity migrants are a diverse group. Some are professionals able to choose where they live and telecommute. Infrastructure such as Internet service and regional airports are built amenities often important to these migrants. Others have more direct employment ties to the community, either as entrepreneurs, often providing services for the other new residents, or as employees of businesses that have moved to the rural area.

Michigan's Grand Traverse County is an example of a rapidly growing, high-amenity, recreation and retirement county (Johnson 2006). Located on the shores of Lake Michigan, the area is known for year-round recreation. It is also a hub of commercial, retail, and health services, with a strong manufacturing and agricultural base. The county's population increased from 39,175 in 1970 to 64,273 in 1990—a 64% increase. By 2000, the population had grown by more than 13,000, adding another 20.8%. Many migrants are retirees who enjoyed the area for vacationing. Additional amenities, including a regional airport with frequent service to Detroit and Chicago; a large, well-equipped medical center; shopping; nightlife; and a variety of recreation opportunities draw retirees and other migrants. Growth has slowed since 2000 to around 6.6%. Growth has brought prosperity and opportunity to many sectors of the community, as well as concern about the effects to the environment and quality-of-life values that have attracted people for more than 50 years (see Johnson 2006 for more details on Grand Traverse County and other examples of amenity-growth communities.)

Amenity Migration Management—Considerations for Community Leaders

Changing demographics have implications for everything from voting to tax receipts. But the social, economic, and cultural changes that accompany amenity migration are not well understood. For example, despite the broad impression that communities adjacent to designated federal lands are economically depressed, counties in western Montana with wilderness, parks, or wildlife refuges had greater employment and personal income growth and lower unemployment between 1969 and 1992 than rural counties without protected lands (Rasker and Hackman 1996). The same pattern holds for counties in other western states (Rasker et al. 2004). This information, often gleaned from census data, is useful to policymakers and community planners, but tells only part of the story. It does not reveal, much less explain, changing relationships among residents, their community, and the land. Understanding these relationships can help community leaders plan for a sustainable future.

Amenity migration stimulates local economies by providing employment and entrepreneurial opportunities (Johnson and Beale 2002). Highly skilled, mobile workers willing to trade higher wages for a higher quality of life are attracted to high-amenity areas (Deller et al. 2001; Rudzitis 1999). Hunter et al. (2005) used longitudinal data from the Panel Study of Income Dynamics to explore rural resident economic well-being. They found that socioeconomically disadvantaged long-term residents may have more economic opportunities in high-growth areas. New development and jobs can slow out-migration of local residents, as long as they can continue to afford to live there. In a 1999 study, Reeder and

Brown (2005) found that poverty was substantially lower in recreation coun-ties than in other nonmetro counties, with 13.2% of residents in poverty in recreation counties and 15.7% in poverty in other nonmetro counties.

Amenity migration also can bring negative consequences, especially when it is characterized by rapid growth. Amenity migration can lead to higher prop-erty taxes resulting from higher assessed values and the need to improve infra-structure, such as sewage-treatment facilities and roads, to accommodate new housing development, resulting in higher infrastructure costs. Rising property costs and rent often result in fewer affordable options for middle- and lower-income residents. Some long-term residents may suffer economic hardship resulting from increased demand for and costs of housing and the inability of some residents to shift from traditional jobs in resource extraction and manu-facturing to available jobs in the service industry (Hunter et al. 2005). While there is little solid evidence, anecdotal reports suggest that this results in some long-term residents leaving, while others stay (Lichtenstein 2004; Sheck 2000).

Long-time residents of gateway communities—communities in close prox-imity to amenity rich national parks, national forests, and other public lands—often have strong relationships with their community and the surrounding landscape. They may support economic development as long as it maintains the local character, natural and historic values, and community identity that they value. Gateway communities thus are faced with the challenge of accom-modating rapid growth and economic development while maintaining the community character and social fabric oriented around a slower pace of life.

Many newcomers become active members of their adopted communities, participating in civic and volunteer groups. Year-round residents often are more engaged than part-time residents. Those who are retired have the time and often the inclination to get involved. Some contribute their time, expertise, and interest to community activities, such as hospital guilds, fundraising, fire pre-paredness planning, Foster Grandparents, or Big Brothers and Big Sisters. Blahna (1990) found newcomers to be more politically active than long-time residents. But community involvement is not a given. Putnam (2000) found newcomers less likely to participate in civic organizations, and those planning to move within five years to be 20–25% less likely to participate than those planning to stay.

The influx of new migrants emphasizes the importance of understanding the underlying social and environmental factors that contribute to the attrac-tiveness of an area. Designing and implementing policies to help maintain those values, and understanding and being prepared to respond to the different atti-tudes, behaviors, expectations, and needs that new residents bring also are important.

When controversy erupts in a community, it is easy to blame the newcom-ers, suggesting that they have brought new values and attitudes that have desta-bilized community solidarity. The literature shows that in some cases differences exist but not always. As Smith and Krannich (2000) point out, though, if the community perceives differences between long-time residents and newcomers, it does not matter if the differences actually exist. Inclusive public involvement in community planning can alleviate such misconceptions. And if differences do exist, acknowledging them can be a first step toward crafting a shared vision.

Infrastructure and Other Challenges for Community Leaders

Migration has led to rapid, unmanaged growth in many communities that simply are not prepared for an influx of new residents (Howe et al. 1997). In some locations, water supplies and sewage-treatment systems are insufficient to accommodate growth. Underground aquifers, mountain streams, and rivers are being tapped at greater rates, while the climate is becoming warmer and drier (Diamond 2005). Water will continue to be a contentious issue across the West and, in some cases, may become the factor that limits growth.

Transportation systems in many growth areas are insufficient to handle the growth, resulting in heavy traffic and congestion. Air quality also is a concern. In Missoula, Montana, and other rapidly developing communities, vehicle emissions, wood-burning stoves, and summer forest fires have resulted in bouts of poor air quality.

Communities that are home to a large percentage of retired and older amenity migrants face a greater need for community hospitals and other health-care facilities. These communities may find themselves choosing between assessing higher taxes to pay for additional services or cutting services that benefit other segments of the population.

The location and pace of amenity-based growth contribute to community vulnerability. Many communities are not equipped to process development permits. Unincorporated areas outside the town's official boundaries often experience some of the heaviest development. These areas have minimal zoning laws, fewer development restrictions than incorporated areas, and lower taxes—factors that attract development (McGranahan 2005). Spatially, the new development may occur far from existing infrastructure, such as water, sewer, and electricity. Per capita, the costs to develop public infrastructure (roads, sewer, electric) at this distance are much higher, and finding the financial capital to make necessary infrastructure improvements can be challenging. New residents outside of town place additional stress on the local community for services they often do not pay for—airports, hospitals, libraries, and other community services.

Amenity migration may populate rural areas and generate property-tax revenues but not necessarily income-tax revenues. Businesses and employment from the mobile workplace may be officially registered elsewhere or individuals may be semi-retired or retired. Municipal planners may anticipate higher tax streams from high-value developments, but costs may exceed expectations, while collection may be less than expected. Policies and incentives that encourage employers to provide jobs with adequate benefits and developers to build affordable housing and pay attention to sustainable practices may help communities proactively anticipate, prepare for, mitigate, and adapt to effects that accompany change.

Community Planning

Natural amenities may be the initial attraction, but certain built amenities help turn the tourist into a new resident. For instance, reliable air transportation and access to an urban center often attract both businesses and retirees. Once resort and recreational development begin, a positive feedback loop is initiated and jobs are generated, fueling the opportunity and need for even more jobs. Likewise, the educated workforce employed by one business may convince outside business owners that relocation is a viable option.

The benefit of these new employment opportunities, however, may be limited for existing residents. Service jobs created through amenity migration and expanded tourism may be seasonal, part-time, and low paying. The local labor pool of traditional resource workers may not have the job skills needed in other types of new businesses. Lower paid service workers and those on fixed incomes can be displaced when the lack of affordable housing and high cost of living drive them out of the community.

In some resort communities, service workers must commute from surrounding areas. For example, in Vail, Colorado, year-round housing is limited, with 75% of residences occupied part-time as second homes. As a result, firefighters and other service workers that the community depends on cannot afford to live in the community (Howe et al. 1997). Lack of affordable local housing often results in lower school enrollment. This, in turn, may harm local schools because revenues are calculated on the number of students. Declining schools can affect the social fabric of a community.

How can community leaders channel the influx of money and energy so that development revitalizes the community rather than alters it in such a way that long-time residents are displaced and newcomers find the charm gone? Community residents—long-term and recent migrant alike—have a stake in deciding what development activities are desirable and appropriate for their community to preserve the quality of life they value. One challenge for community leaders is understanding the values of long-time and new residents regarding natural and built amenities and integrating them into a community vision. (Howe et al. 1997) suggest that successful community development strategies involve inclusive public participation, local initiatives that focus on distinctive features important to the economic future of the community, and innovative approaches to working with developers to create acceptable, livable communities.

Tourism growth and amenity migration are not distributed evenly across the landscape. Communities that want to explore new income and employment opportunities based on their amenity resources may benefit from proactive planning rather than reactive mitigation. For example, assessing the types of businesses and development that might be appropriate and exploring a variety of options is critical. Responding to decisions about what would be most appropriate for the community, economic incentives can be designed to encourage local entrepreneurs and attract outside investors. Attractions such as festivals and special events to extend the tourist season may be an option. Developing facilities that serve both tourist and resident needs maximizes the community's investment and makes the community more attractive for residents and visitors alike. In high-amenity locations, communities may be surprised at the number of amenity migrants already in residence.

Amenity Migration Management: Issues and Challenges for Resource Managers

Amenity migration is blurring the historical differences between urban and rural areas. Rural communities traditionally have been characterized by small the populations sustained by land, whether through timber, mining, ranching, or agriculture. Now the population in many rural, amenity-rich areas is growing rapidly and the livelihoods of the new residents are not tied to these traditional land uses. Nationwide an estimated 22.5 million acres are projected to shift from rural to exurban by 2030, with 21.7 million rural or exurban acres projected to shift to urban (Stein et al. 2005). These changes have implications for natural resource management.

Rising real estate values often mean private forestland is worth more as real estate than as trees. The wildlife habitat, scenic views, open space, and public recreational access often provided by private forestland are lost when this land is developed. Thirty-eight percent of the 311 counties identified by the Economic Research Service as dependent on recreation and tourism have at least 30% of their land in federal ownership (Reeder and Brown 2005). These public lands face increasing pressure to continue to provide and even expand recreation and other services and values.

Fire management is affected as development inches closer to the boundaries of public forestland. Constructing high-priced homes in areas with a high fire risk places an additional burden on agencies responsible for fire protection. When a fire does occur, the presence of homes shifts the focus from protecting forests to protecting homes and lives. The change in land use also limits the ability of forest managers to use fire as a tool to reduce heavy fuel loads. If allowed to accumulate, heavy fuel loads can result in more severe fires than if fuel loads are reduced.

Encroaching development has other management implications. In addition to the ecological footprint left by the new houses, growing subdivisions require additional access roads. Fire roads may be constructed across public land to provide emergency access and escape routes. Invasive species, often introduced as landscaping around new homes or as seeds in horse feed, can be a problem. Sensitive riparian and environmentally sensitive areas are more at risk. Fish habitat may be affected by erosion, flood-control issues may be exacerbated, and the stability of shorelines, dunes, and beaches may be compromised. Concerns extend beyond the United States. Homeowners in the coastal town of Todos Santos on the Pacific shore of the Baja Peninsula in Mexico are concerned that housing construction on sand dunes along their coastline will result in more severe damage to coastal properties when a hurricane strikes (personal conversations with residents in Todos Santos 2007).

Challenges for Forest Planning

Conventional wisdom has been that newcomers bring different values about the environment and natural resource management, but the research in this area is not conclusive. A review of literature by Smith and Krannich (2000) found research from the 1970s and earlier tended to find differences in attitudes, whereas literature from the mid-1980s and 1990s often found similarities. In their own study, Smith and Krannich (2000) found newcomers and long-time residents in three communities in the Rocky Mountain West had similar levels of environmental concern and differed only slightly in attitudes toward development and population growth. Fortmann and Starrs (1990) found that rather than bringing different, pro-environment attitudes to rural areas, migrating urban residents actually shared similar views and brought political savvy and skills for giving voice to preexisting attitudes.

An increasing variety and number of neighbors means additional processes are needed to engage people in decisionmaking that will affect them and the land close by. Issues can be more contentious and difficult to resolve with more people involved and a larger variety of perspectives to accommodate. In the past, a land manager might have had a working relationship with a handful of families who had neighbored public land for generations. Now a continual influx of new residents means relationship building is never done and effective public outreach is a continual process. Discussions about fire management, for instance, need to be held each year because new people unfamiliar with fire activities may have moved to the area.

Attending to forest management under these changing conditions is challenging. Having moved to the area for its amenity values, new residents may vocally oppose timber harvests, fuel reduction, and other commercial harvest activities long practiced on public land. This may pose a challenge for managers with forest plans that call for thinning to reduce fire hazard. It also makes a strong case for extensive, inclusive public participation processes.

Understanding the spectrum of attitudes toward resource management and being aware of the changes in attitudes will help community leaders and natural resource managers do their jobs more effectively. Newcomers without previous experience in forestry may not be aware of the ecological benefits of some common forestry practices, such as thinning or prescribed burns. They may be interested in land stewardship but need direction. Knowing the range of values present will help all sides find common ground and work toward acceptable solutions if conflicts arise. A variety of approaches exist to help managers understand and engage communities (see chapters 2, 3, and 4).

Research Needs

Research on the adaptation of amenity-rich communities can provide a better understanding of ongoing transformation and options of how best to manage the social and economic change that accompany amenity migration. This knowledge could help communities better anticipate, prepare, and adapt to change.

The changing social landscape has a variety of implications for management of both public and private land. In some locations, the value of public lands to nearby communities is changing dramatically. In many cases, public land has become valued more for recreation and amenities than for resource extraction. Little is understood about how resource management affects the values that in turn drive amenity migration. One challenge is that these values are diverse. Social science can help frame and explore research questions to respond to these knowledge gaps.

Increasing demand for amenities provided by public lands, reflected in increased recreation pressure and conversion of private land, is a pressing issue for public land managers (Garber-Yonts 2004). The implications of increasing recreation demand coupled with the conversion of private land largely are unknown. Research in this area could help managers understand this change, its implications and possible responses, and provide tools for engaging communities in land-use planning.

The relationship between management decisions—for both public and private land—and migration is of interest to land managers and community leaders. It is an area largely unexplored by researchers (Garber-Yonts 2004). Additionally, there has been little attention to the more encompassing issue of the effects of resource management decisions on communities and how community change influences resource management.

Urban demand for rural and wildland recreation is increasing. Rapid population growth in the rural–wildland interface increases pressure on recreational resources, natural habitat, wildlife, and water. This demand is fueling many rural economies that have been economically depressed. With the exception of the National Park Service, most public land management agencies are organized around a resource-extraction mission. As resource extraction declines and attracting and retaining businesses and retirees becomes more important for communities in the rural-wildland interface, public land managers must keep pace with the social and environmental aspects of development occurring nearby. Further research can help managers understand the shifting demographics in the local area and implications for management.

Conclusion

Development in amenity-rich areas presents challenges to all involved: long-time residents, new residents, community leaders, and public land managers and decisionmakers. The challenge is to understand the relationships among the groups and their values and to reconcile expectations. A community floundering in the wake of declining timber harvests can be revitalized by a housing boom that brings construction jobs, residents with money to spend, and new businesses to serve the growing population. Some residents may be disheartened if the town they either have long loved or recently moved to fundamentally is changed by growth. Others may be displaced because of rising costs; casualties of a market economy. Change is inevitable and growth, most would argue, is preferable to slow desiccation. The difference between growth that forces some out and creates subdivisions of empty mansions during the off-season versus revitalized communities on a sustainable path toward the future is a vision that integrates the motives and values of residents—the long-time and newly arrived. It is the people who make a subdivision a neighborhood and collective vision that links neighborhoods into communities.

The existing research on differences and similarities among long-time and new residents in rural communities is not complete. As yet, there are not definitive answers to questions such as, "Will newcomers be politically active in their new community?" or "Do they have different environmental values and attitudes toward natural resource management?" What is true in one community may not be true in another. People have different values and, accordingly, will be attracted to different places. The research shows that almost anybody can be an amenity migrant, from the very wealthy to enterprising new business owners hoping to serve the very wealthy. They may be retirees or young people working as guides for recreational outfitters. Many communities offer breathtaking vistas and variations on a host of other natural and built amenities, but an amenity migrant chooses one from the many. Why?

To ask this question in such a way that the answer yields information useful to community leaders crafting a sustainable future requires digging deeper to find answers that go beyond, "I like the scenery," or "I like to fish." A useful question would be framed to understand the deeper values that led the migrant to the community and holds the long-time resident despite the changes. Uncovering base values will facilitate discussions about the future. If successful strategies are documented, this also may facilitate learning among communities that discover they have similar base values, despite differences in location, size, or history. Not all communities will be interested in crafting similar futures. Research that uncovers these similarities and differences among communities will facilitate future discussions; change is constant and amenity migration is simply the next evolution of rural America.

The simple fact that more people are living closer to public land changes natural resource management. Subdivisions bordering public forests change the way fire is managed. More people mean more opinions for resource managers to address. Asphalt roads and concrete foundations alter the landscape more permanently than a clearcut ever would. Irretrievable loss of habitat can necessitate creative public–private partnerships to maintain species that once used the land now under development. For the resource manager, it is a continual process of communication and education because, thus far, the influx of new residents has not abated.

The growing populations and changing relations to the land are blurring the historical differences between urban and rural areas. Yet it is still the land and aspects of rural life that attract new residents. Land managers have the opportunity to nurture the relationships between the new residents and the land, while helping long-time residents maintain those ties. It is a different role than the one they had 50 years ago, when public interaction was working with a few ranchers with generational ties to the land, but it is arguably a more vital role. Facilitating stewardship becomes even more important as the landscape is fragmented.

For many rural communities, amenity migration has meant economic survival. By understanding the values that are driving it, the economic engine can be harnessed so that it also sustains the relationships among residents, the community, and the land. The key consideration for communities is how prepared they are to adapt to change—whatever form it takes—as it comes their way.

References

Blahna, D.J. 1990. Social Bases for Resource Conflicts in Areas of Reverse Migration. In *Community and Forestry: Continuities in the Sociology of Natural Resources*, edited by R.G. Lee, D.R. Field, and W.R. Burch. Boulder, CO: Westview Press, 159–178.

Cordell, H.K. 2006. "Recreation Trends." A talk presented at the Clemson Recreation Management Short Course. September 15. Clemson, SC.

Deller, S.C., T. Tsung-Hsiu, D. Marcouiller, and D.B.K. English. 2001. The Role of Amenities and Quality of Life in Rural Economic Growth. *American Journal of Agricultural Economics* 83: 352–365.

Diamond, J. 2005. *Collapse: How Societies Choose to Fail or Survive.* London: Penguin.

Duffy-Deno, K.T. 1998. The Effect of Federal Wilderness on County Growth in the Intermountain Western United States. *Journal of Regional Science* 38(1): 109–136.

English, D.B.K., D.W. Marcouiller, and H.K. Cordell. 2000. Tourism Dependence in Rural America: Estimates and Effects. *Society and Natural Resources* 13: 185–202.

Fortmann, L., and P. Starrs. 1990. Power Plants and Resource Rights. In *Community and Forestry: Continuities in the Sociology of Natural Resources,* edited by R.G. Lee, D.R. Field, and W.R. Burch. Boulder, CO: Westview Press, 179–194.

Frentz, I.C., F.L. Farmer, J.M. Guldin, and K.G. Smith. 2004. Public Lands and Population Growth. *Society and Natural Resources* 17: 57–68.

Garber-Yonts, B.E. 2004. *The Economics of Amenities and Migration in the Pacific Northwest: Review of Selected Literature with Implications for National Forest Management.* General Technical Report PNW-GTR-617. Portland, OR: U.S. Department of Agriculture, Forest Service, Pacific Northwest Research Station.

Hodge, P. 2005. Living Younger Longer: Baby Boomer Challenges. Statement of Paul Hodge to the 2005 White House Conference on Aging Policy Hearing Committee. www.genpolicy.com/articles/2005 (accessed July 19, 2005).

Horizon Air. 2004. Selected advertisements. *Horizon Air Magazine* 15(12): no page numbers.

Howe, J., E. McMahon, and L. Propst. 1997. *Balancing Nature and Commerce in Gateway Communities.* Covelo, CA: Island Press.

Hunter, L.M., J.D. Boardman, and J.M. Saint Onge. 2005. The Association Between Natural Amenities, Rural Population Growth, and Long-Term Residents' Economic Well-being. *Rural Sociology* 70(4): 452–469.

Johnson. K. 2006. *Demographic Trends in Rural and Small Town America: A Casey Institute Report on Rural America.* Durham, NH: Casey Institute, University of New Hampshire.

Johnson, K.M., and C.L. Beale. 2002. Nonmetro Recreation Counties: Their Identification and Rapid Growth. *Rural America* 17(4): 12–19.

Johnson, K.M., and S.I. Stewart. 2006. Amenity Migration to Urban Proximate Counties. In *Amenities and Rural Development: Theory, Methods, and Public Policy,* edited by G.P. Green, D. Marcouiller, and S. Deller. Northhampton, MA: Edward Elgar Publishing, 177–196.

Johnson, K.M., P.R. Voss, R.B. Hammer, G.V. Fuguitt, and S. McNiven. 2005. Temporal and Spatial Variation in Age-Specific Net Migration in the United States. *Demography* 42(4): 751–812.

Krannich, R.S., P. Petrzelka, and J.M. Brehm. 2006. Social Change and Well-being in Western Amenity-growth Communities. In *Population Change and Rural Society,* edited by W.A. Kandel and D.L. Brown. Dordrecht, The Netherlands: Springer, 311–332.

Kraybill, D.S. 1997. Natural Amenities and Rural Economies. In *Post-Industrial Rural Development: The Role of Natural Resources and the Environment,* workshop proceedings, edited by W.H. Gardiner. Iowa City, IA: Iowa State University Printing Service, 87–92.

Lichtenstein, G. 2004. Part-time Paradise. *High Country News.* October 25: 7–12.

McCool, S.F., and L.E. Kruger. 2003. *Human Migration and Natural Resources: Implications for Land Managers and Challenges for Researchers.* General Technical Report PNW-GTR-580. Portland, OR: U.S. Department of Agriculture, Forest Service, Pacific Northwest Research Station.

McGranahan, D.A. 2005. Returning to Our Roots? County Net Migration in the Non-metropolitan U.S., 1990–2000. Paper presented at the 11th International Sympo-sium on Society and Resource Management, June 16-19, Ostersund, Sweden.

Moss, L.A.G. 1994. Beyond Tourism: The Amenity Migrants. In *Chaos in Our Uncommon Futures*, edited by M. Mannermaa, S. Inayatulla, and R. Slaughter. Turku, Finland: University of Economics, 121–128.

Power, T.M. 1996. *Lost Landscapes and Failed Economies: The Search for a Value of Place*. Washington, DC: Island Press.

Putnam, R.D. 2000. *Bowling Alone: The Collapse and Revival of American Community*. New York: Simon & Schuster.

Rasker, R., and A. Hackman. 1996. Economic Development and the Conservation of Large Carnivores. *Conservation Biology* 10(4): 991–1002.

Rasker, R., B. Alexander, J. van den Noort, and R. Carter. 2004. *Public Lands Conservation and Economic Well-being*. Tucson, AZ: Sonoran Institute.

Reeder, R. and D. Brown. 2005. Recreation, Tourism, and Rural Well-Being. ERR-7, US Department of Agriculture, Economic Research Service.

Rudzitis, G. 1993. Nonmetropolitan Geography: Migration, Sense of Place, and the American West. *Urban Geography* 14(6): 574–585.

Sheck, J. 2000. High Rents, Cost of Living Change Local Congregations. *Mountain View Voice*. December 8, p. 4.

Shumway, J.M., and J.A. Davis. 1996. Nonmetropolitan Population Change in the Mountain West: 1970–1995. *Rural Sociology* 61: 513–529.

Shumway, J.M., and S.M. Otterstrom. 2001. Spatial Patterns of Migration and Income Change in the Mountain West: The Dominance of Service-based, Amenity Rich Counties. *Professional Geographer* 53(4): 492–502.

Smith, M.D., and R.S. Krannich. 2000. "Culture Clash" Revisited: Newcomer and Longer-term Resident's Attitudes Toward Land Use, Development, and Environmental Issues in Rural Communities in the Rocky Mountain West. *Rural Sociology* 65(3): 396–421.

Stein, S.M., R.E. McRoberts, R.J. Alig, M.D. Nelson, D.M. Theobald, M. Eley, M. Dechter, and M. Carr. 2005. *Forests on the Edge: Housing Development on America's Private Forests*. General Technical Report PNW-GTR-636. Portland, OR: U.S. Department of Agriculture, Forest Service, Pacific Northwest Research Station.

Whitson, D. 2001. Nature as Playground: Recreation and Gentrification in the Mountain West. In *Writing Off the Rural West: Globalization, Governments and the Transformation of Rural Communities*, edited by R. Epp, and D. Whitson. Edmonton, Alberta, Canada: The University of Alberta Press, 145–164.

————. 2005. Recreation and Gentrification in Rural Alberta and British Columbia. Paper presented at the Small Cities Forum, May 6, Kamloops, British Columbia.

8

Integrating Commercial Nontimber Forest Product Harvesters into Forest Management

ERIC T. JONES AND KATHRYN A. LYNCH

Forests always have been places for humans to harvest foods, medicines, and materials for clothing, shelter, spiritual practices, and decoration. From prehistoric to contemporary times, forests have provided important resources to human communities (Etkin 1994; Minnis 2003; Moerman 1998). These harvested species, collectively known as nontimber forest products (NTFPs), include wild foods, such as mushrooms, fruits, nuts and honey; medicinal plants; floral greenery and horticultural stock; native seeds; fiber and dye plants; and oils, resins, and saps, such as maple syrup. In the United States, small-diameter poles, posts, and firewood also are considered NTFPs.

People who harvest NTFPs are as diverse as the species they gather. They are known by various names—harvesters, diggers, pickers, tappers, and foragers, to name a few. Today, even in highly industrialized countries such as the United States, people continue to harvest NTFPs for a broad range of reasons. The goal may be to provide food or medicine for their households or community or simply for recreation on the weekend. People may barter, trade, or sell their wild harvests or give them as gifts to build relationships with others in their community. For others, harvesting serves religious or spiritual purposes or is done as part of a scientific study or educational experience. Still others commercially harvest NTFPs for income—either selling it as raw material or processing it into value-added products. These different motivations, although not mutually exclusive, provide a framework for loosely conceptualizing harvesters as communities of interest, linked by their motivation for harvesting of wild species. Of these different communities, this chapter focuses on commercial harvesters and the benefits and challenges to integrating them into forest management.

We focus on commercial harvesters for several reasons. First, there is a distinction between commercial and noncommercial (e.g., personal use, subsistence) harvesting in forest management rules and regulations. Second, commercial harvesters can be found throughout communities in the United States. Third, we are interested in the role of commercial harvesters in the economic diversification of rural economies and their role in the stewardship of forest resources.

Findings from a national project to develop criteria and indicators for NTFPs indicate that despite little tracking of NTFP production, prices, and trade, they clearly contribute billions of dollars annually to the U.S. economy (Alexander 2004). The few economic studies that have been conducted (e.g., Alexander et al. 2002b; Schlosser and Blatner 1995; Weigand 1998) have examined only a few of the hundreds of commercially harvested NTFP species in the United States. The fact that government agencies issue thousands of commercial harvesting permits each year for the collection of a wide variety of NTFPs suggests that they are significant to many people's household economy (Emery 1998; Jones and Lynch 2007; McLain and Jones 2005). In fact, when aggregated over time, NTFPs might produce more economic value than timber production in many regions. Until adequate research is done it will be impossible to discern their true value to forest communities and understand fully what opportunities are being wasted.

Commercial harvesters are not a homogeneous group; there is great diversity of ethnicity, age, gender, education, social class, and income levels within this broad community of interest (Emery et al. 2003; Hansis 1998; Richards and Creasy 1996). Commercial harvesters include morel mushroom pickers in the West; root diggers in Appalachia who tend patches of ginseng, black cohosh, and other medicinal plants; immigrants from southeast Asia and Latin America who pick floral greenery; maple syrup tappers in the Northeast; and Hispanic and Native American Indian pinyon seed gatherers in the Southwest. This community includes African Americans pulling grapevine from the Mississippi Delta for use in making country crafts, those collecting native seeds for ecological restoration efforts or plant nursery stock, and those extracting wild honey from the Tupelo swamp forests of the deep South.

The amount of time commercial harvesters devote to harvesting varies considerably, depending on factors such as seasonal fruiting patterns, the reliability of their transportation, access to harvest areas, and quantities needed. For example, some medicinal plant harvesters may need to gather raw materials only once a year, whereas floral green pickers may spend almost every day out in the woods once the season begins. Harvesters' work locations also vary, as commercial harvesting takes place on a range of land ownerships and jurisdictions, including small, private landholdings; corporate timberlands; and county, state, and national forests. Harvesters can be found living in urban, suburban, and rural settings. Likewise, some people harvest locally, others make daily or overnight commutes to harvest areas, and others, such as mushroom pickers, work often lengthy circuits (Arora 1999; Love et al. 1998).

Dependence on commercial harvesting also differs. For some people, harvesting provides an occasional income supplement, whereas for others it constitutes their primary source of household income (as an example, see Spero and Fleming 2002 for a characterization of commercial users in the Rio Grande National Forest). Commercial NTFP harvesting takes place within both the informal and formal economic sectors and is characterized by its diverse labor structures. Some commercial harvesters are self-employed, functioning as small businesses whether they are registered or incorporated as a business with the state or not. Other harvesters work as contractors and are registered businesses (sole proprietorships or corporations) that enter into legal work contracts with government agencies or other businesses to harvest NTFPs. They either secure contracts through bidding processes or subcontract with another business that has secured a contract. Subcontractors usually work under someone who is licensed and bonded by the state. Still other harvesters work as full-time, part-time, or seasonal employees for hourly wages or a salary.

People are motivated to harvest NTFPs commercially for different reasons. Some are economic, but others are tied to the quality of life this work affords. This can be described as a desire to work in the woods rather than a factory, a desire to work locally rather than commute or move to an urban area, or the desire to carry on cultural or family traditions (Carroll et al. 2005; Hinricks 1998). Many harvesters highly value their independence, privacy, and a lifestyle that gives them the freedom to be out in nature on a regular basis. A strong sense of pride and entrepreneurship exists for many who have started small businesses based on NTFPs. Thus, although some commercial harvesters could earn more income and have more secure livelihoods with other jobs, they prefer harvesting NTFPs. Although we refer to those involved in the commercial harvest of NTFPs as a community of interest, it is important to remember that most harvesters live in or near the forests where they harvest (i.e., are part of a community of place). They may be the least visible, least wealthy, and least knowledgeable about how to influence forest policy, but they have a vested interest and a right to be included in how our public forests are managed.

The culturally rich and diversified world of commercial NTFP harvesting occupies a precarious position in contemporary forest management. In the currently charged and uncertain political terrain, taking advantage of the opportunities offered by NTFPs has been a low priority for forest managers and other stakeholders. Yet, in communities struggling to sustain rural livelihoods, the possibility of developing commercial NTFP operations needs to be reexamined. To help inform future discussions and actions, in the remainder of this chapter we sketch out several of these opportunities, as well as challenges of integrating

NTFPs into sustainable forestry practices. Specifically, we examine opportunities to promote economic diversification and biodiversity conservation through active management of NTFPs. We explore how this integration can enhance public forest management and user stewardship, as well as increase community representation in forest management. We conclude by examining some of the challenges of working with diverse populations of NTFP harvesters and integrating different forms of knowledge about nontimber forest products into forest management.

Opportunities

The following are some of the opportunities to promote economic diversification and biodiversity conservation through active management of NTFPs.

Economic Diversification and Biological Conservation

Mounting scientific evidence shows that biodiversity is a fundamental component of healthy forest ecosystems and that biodiversity conservation is a key principle for ecologically sustainable forest management (Lindenmayer and Franklin 2002; Minnis and Elisens 2000; Pilz and Molina 1996; Shiva and Verma 2002). Managing for NTFPs presents an option to advance rural economic development while maintaining or restoring biological diversity in forests. Although the density and quantity of commercial-grade material varies greatly across locations, active management of NTFPs could increase economic opportunities in many areas of the United States (von Hagen and Fight 1999). As Vance and Thomas note, "Consideration should be given to how this diversity might contribute to stabilizing economies, particularly of communities that have vital relationships with forests. A totally integrated model of ecosystem management or of sustainable forestry would include this kind of interaction" (1997, 4). Linking biodiversity with commodification has its risks, but when done with principles of sustainability in mind, it can be a tool for maintaining biodiversity in the face of competing land uses (Freese 1998).

Linking commodity diversification and biological conservation is compelling because of the negative social, economic, and environmental risks and consequences that often accompany single-commodity extraction on rural, forest-dependent communities (e.g., Power 1996; Robbins 1997; Steen 2004). For example, many towns in the Pacific Northwest experienced unemployment, outmigration, and cultural dislocation, including identity crises, and many other social problems as timber resources were depleted or political conditions disrupted supply (FCR 2002). One response that arose in the 1990s was to resurrect the idea that NTFPs might provide supplemental sources of income to landowners (e.g., Freed 1997; Hammett and Chamberlain 1998; Thomas and Schumann 1993). To this end, several conferences have been held, a few studies have investigated comanagement options with timber (Alexander et al. 2002b; Pilz et al. 1998, 1999; Weigand 1998), and some extension materials, databases, and training programs on procurement and processing have come about. In general, however, NTFP research and management has been minimal compared to other areas of forestry, and the potential contributions of NTFPs to biodiversity conservation and economic diversification remain key questions for future research.

Despite little active management to increase or sustain productivity, NTFPs have played and continue to play important roles in the economies and cultural traditions of communities around the country (Alexander et al. 2002a; Emery 1998; Jones et al. 2004). Matsutake and morel mushrooms, ginseng root, and salal are but a few examples of individual NTFPs that contribute millions of dollars to the economy. Thousands of businesses throughout the country are associated with or dependent on NTFP harvests. More than 1,300 species are or have been commercially harvested in the United States (see www.ifcae.org/ntfp/), and that does not include the hundreds of native species from which seeds are commercially collected. Many of these wild harvested species are processed into a multitude of products. For example, loblolly pine (*Pinus taeda*) cones are processed for their seeds for ecosystem restoration and then sold in arts and crafts stores throughout the country. Western brackenfern (*Pteridium aquilinum*) is used both as a food (boiled spring tips) and floral decoration (fall fronds). Some NTFPs, such as ginseng root (*Panax quinquefolius*), have been commercially traded for hundreds of years and still remain commercially viable (Duke 1989; Hufford 1997). Other NTFPs, such as turpentine (sap from *Pinus sp.*) and cascara bark (*Rhamnus purshiana*), once supplied flourishing commercial industries in the United States but declined due to inventions of alternative products and cheaper sources abroad. However, such products potentially could reemerge as important commodities if market conditions shift to favor domestic production.

A catalyst for looking more seriously at NTFPs in the United States has been growing interest elsewhere around the world in using NTFPs from tropical rainforests as a sustainable economic alternative to logging and other activities threatening biodiversity. Although NTFP market-oriented forest conservation in the tropics has met with mixed success (Crook and Clapp 2002), several factors in temperate forests make conditions more favorable for developing viable businesses. First, tropical forests generally have high plant diversity but individuals from a single species are present at low densities, whereas in temperate forests the reverse often is true (Meffe and Carroll 1994). As a result, in temperate forests it is more feasible to harvest products with lower values by harvesting greater quantities of them in closer proximity, especially for products distributed beyond local markets. Second, access to patches and transport of raw materials often is easier in temperate forests than in tropical forests due to a variety of factors, including higher road densities and better-maintained roads. Roads make it easier to locate climate-sensitive NTFPs like wild mushroom species that are episodic, ephemeral, or may not occur abundantly across the landscape. The ability to access small patches over a larger landscape improves seasonal harvesting averages.

Additional income opportunities for harvesters and forest-dependent communities might emerge by managing forests for NTFPs. For example, it is worth assessing the possibility of linking the widespread popularity of recreational NTFP harvesting with community-organized ecotourism activities, such as guided forays into the forest. Workshops and hikes to teach sustainable harvesting ethics and practices could be included. This could be linked into programs intended to improve urban–rural relationships, dispel cultural misunderstandings, and build respect for rural ways of life. Commercial harvesters could be recruited to play an active role in these types of educational activities by being paid to offer training in harvesting and habitat identification and for leading forays.

Enhancing Forest Management and Stewardship

In addition to promoting economic diversification based on biological diversity, actively integrating NTFPs into forest management also presents an opportunity to enhance forest management and stewardship. Research provides some clues as to how this might happen.

First, NTFP harvesters have useful knowledge about the resources they gather that could enhance forest management (Laird 2002; Turner 1997). As Emery notes, "While formal scientific data on the biological and social ecologies of most NTFPs are limited to nonexistent, long-time gatherers often have extensive experiential knowledge bases. Researchers and managers may overlook this expertise because of assumptions about the nature of knowledge and the identity of individuals who possess valuable information" (2001, *123*). This oversight is a missed opportunity. Commercial NTFP harvesters particularly are likely to develop intimate knowledge of the species they are gathering because they often revisit their harvesting areas during the season and return year after year. Not all of these visits involve harvesting product; some visits are to monitor the plant populations or gauge when an NTFP may be ready to harvest. Additionally, many harvesters often work off-trail, deep in the woods, and potentially could provide valuable insights into cycles and patterns missed by land managers who are unable to spend as much time on the ground as the harvesters (Ballard 2005; Jones 2002). Given their direct experience with the plants they harvest, NTFP harvesters could be valuable allies in the movement to promote sound forest management and stewardship. Conversely, experience has shown that ignoring local knowledge can result in policies and management activities that are not based on local cultural, biological, or ecological realities, which can threaten stewardship and create tension between stakeholders.

Second, ethnographic research has revealed that many commercial harvesters are concerned for the health of the forests where they work and have developed practices to maintain viable plant populations over time (Lynch et al. 2004). Many commercial harvesters (e.g., Buren 2005) also express concern about the potential for overharvesting. This stewardship ethic is evident in the development of ethical harvesting guidelines (e.g., Ambrose and Martinez 1999), web sites advocating wildcrafting ethics (e.g., Newbegin 2005), and multi-party monitoring projects (Bagby 2004). Commercial harvesters may develop informal rules among themselves to discourage overharvesting and some harvesters experiment with harvest techniques and practices aimed at enhancing and sustaining resource productivity (Jones 2002). For many, good harvesting practices include combining trial-and-error techniques with observation of the plants they gather over time and space.

Research studies and demonstration projects show that NTFP harvesters can help managers and scientists learn about NTFPs and help monitor changes in NTFP populations (Ballard 2005; Everett 2001). They also can help assess the effect of management decisions on specific NTFPs and the harvesters who rely upon them, allowing managers to better weigh the ecological, economic, and social tradeoffs of different management actions. For example, a timber sale planned on the Forest Service Crescent Ranger District would have adversely affected mushroom fields, but local harvesters employed there were able to alert managers to the effects (Bagby 2004). This is particularly valuable given that managers are facing declining budgets, decreases in staff, and increasing demands on their time. In a national survey of Forest Service NTFP programs, managers on 58% of 81 responding national forests indicated they supported the idea of harvester involvement in biological inventory and monitoring (McLain and Jones 2005). In recent years, a number of documents have been created to help advance multi-party processes that involve communities in various kinds of social monitoring (e.g., CFRP 2004; Moseley and Wilson 2002). In addition, participatory approaches to biological monitoring are being developed. A handbook by Pilz et al. (2006) provides managers with tools to help create systems so that the biological data gathered through participatory research with harvesters and other stakeholders is reliable and appropriately managed.

Increasing Community Representation in Natural Resource Management

In addition to the economic and ecological opportunities that NTFPs provide, interest is growing in integrating NTFP harvesters into forest management dialogue as a means to promote democratic processes and increase community capacity in natural resource management (Brown and Martín-Hernández 2000; NTFP Working Group 2005). One avenue for improving NTFP harvester representation is through organizations working to advance community-based management approaches. A central pursuit for many community-based forest organizations has been to enhance ecosystem processes, generate investments in communities, and promote civic participation in forest management

(Baker and Kusel 2003). This includes providing community members with training to perform a broad range of forest-related work other than traditional logging and wood processing. Community-based forestry groups could be valuable allies for the dispersed, often invisible, and politically unorganized commercial NTFP harvesters.

Community leaders, forest managers, and anyone else wishing to increase dialogue with harvesters could build relationships with buying and processing companies, which generally are more visible and accessible than harvesters. These firms know who harvests, how much product is being harvested, how often harvesting takes place, whether harvesters reside in the community, and the kinds of problems harvesters are encountering. Buying and processing firms range in size and complexity from small businesses to large, multimillion-dollar processors. These businesses are often a central node of communication in the commercial harvester community, especially in situations where harvesters gather at buying stations at the end of the day to sell their product. Although some buying companies exploit harvesters, many have built reciprocal relationships through activities such as training people how to harvest or loaning them equipment. In turn, harvesters sometimes help out buyers by accepting IOUs when the business is low on operating capital. Some buying companies have expressed interest in partnering with community-based organizations to improve harvester livelihoods, if time and resources permitted.

Researchers also can help to increase the representation and integration of NTFP commercial harvesters into natural resource management. They can help identify and implement methods of participation, document field prices and quantities removed, increase understanding of critical local knowledge, and transfer information from management and science to harvesters and small businesses. Ethnographic research methods have proven appropriate for garnering harvester perspectives and building trusting, long-term relationships with harvesters. Participant observation, in which researchers accompany NTFP harvesters as they work and develop a first-hand understanding of the constraints and opportunities harvesters face, can bring greater depth and understanding to survey or interview data.

Challenges

Although integrating NTFPs into forest management brings many opportunities, significant challenges exist.

Gaining Knowledge and Integration

Despite the increase in public information and scholarly research on NTFPs in the last decade, research is still in its infancy and knowledge gaps are significant. Basic inventories of NTFPs are lacking in many areas. For example, a recent national survey of Forest Service managers found that only 36% of the reporting 84[1] national forests indicated that NTFP inventories on their forests take place (McLain and Jones 2005). As Emery (1998) observes, the lack of knowledge about NTFPs in the Forest Service impedes its ability to sufficiently meet legal mandates to provide for plant and animal community protection on national forests. Information about cultural aspects of NTFPs, such as contemporary subsistence use, also is rare.

Compounding the shortage of basic information is a lack of training for forest managers and policymakers regarding NTFPs. Although a forestry course may mention understory species, such as huckleberry, and an anthropology course may describe Native American subsistence gathering, virtually no academic courses or professional training programs exist specifically to provide land managers or any other decisionmakers with the background and skills needed to manage NTFPs, much less integrate harvesters into forest management.

More researchers are finding that collaborative approaches are needed to integrate scientific and traditional ecological knowledge to strengthen overall understandings of ecosystem functioning (e.g., Davidson-Hunt and Berkes 2001; Michel and Gayton 2002). Resistance exists, however, and many scientists are biased against experientially-based local or indigenous knowledge systems (Chambers 1997). These "expert vs. non-expert" clashes can present a formidable barrier to integrating NTFP issues into forest management. An important justification for including harvesters in forest management is that they often have the most regular contact with specific NTFPs and so are in positions to help monitor the resource. However, ensuring quality control is essential where scientific data is concerned. Thus, involving harvesters in inventory and monitoring requires proper systems of verification that include roles and responsibilities for harvesters, researchers, and managers.

Cultural differences among harvesters, managers, and scientists may hinder communication and understanding. Each group has its own norms, rules, language, and etiquette that, if not understood by the others, could result in miscommunication and conflict. Thus, any effort to integrate commercial harvesters into forest management should seek strategies for improving communication between stakeholder groups. Hiring professional facilitators and translators is one mechanism for overcoming this barrier.

Valuing NTFPs

Although awareness about NTFPs has grown, they generally remain a minor consideration for public and private forest managers (Chamberlain et al. 2002; McLain 2004, Shanley et al. 2002). In part, this reflects the lack of data regarding the current and potential value of NTFPs. It also reflects the tendency to calculate single-species comparisons (e.g., chanterelles vs. timber) at a single moment in time instead of over a period of time (e.g., timber harvest rotation). With this formula, few NTFPs ever will have a value comparable to timber. Most national forests, and state and private forests as well, have the capacity to produce hundreds of NTFP species that could be a part of an annual commercial harvest. By aggregating the potential value of all commercial quality NTFPs in an area over time, more accurate cost comparisons between NTFP production and other land-use options could be derived. In some circumstances, joint production has been found to enhance the commercial value of forests (Pilz et al. 1999). Cost comparisons should include noneconomic factors as well, such as preexisting noncommercial cultural uses and the treaties, laws, and regulations that may require managers and others to understand and possibly protect existing uses.

Management objectives for forests, tree plantations, and agroforestry systems (e.g., alley cropping) play a major role in determining the diversity, quality, density, and accessibility of NTFPs. Management practices designed to simultaneously increase NTFP diversity and availability only recently have begun to emerge in the public forestry sector. Where NTFP management does occur, it is typically only for a few, tree-based NTFPs. Perhaps this is not surprising given the emphasis on trees and timber in the forest-products industry in the last century. When asked about the most significant NTFPs in their forests in a national Forest Service survey, respondents predominantly named tree-based products: firewood, posts and poles, boughs, Christmas trees, and transplants (McLain and Jones 2005). Furthermore, although some Forest Service districts track NTFP sales through their Timber Management Information System database, many users feel this system is inadequate for NTFPs. These facts suggest that of the vast range of extractable products in the National Forest System, tree products are the primary focus of managers.

Increasing the Viability of Commercial Harvesting

Commercial harvesters and NTFP businesses face several challenges to constructing viable livelihoods based wholly or partly on NTFPs. A viable commercial industry requires a reliable supply of raw material. A major problem is the loss of productive NTFP harvesting locations due to logging, cattle grazing, wildlife production, the use of herbicides and fire retardants, and the conversion of forested lands to other uses, such as housing developments and ski resorts (Jones et al. 2004; McGraw and Furedi 2005). As habitat is lost, harvesters may have difficulty obtaining sufficient commercial-quality material and competition at remaining locations may increase.

Although some research has examined the effects of harvesters on NTFPs (e.g., Flaster 2005; Kauffman 2003), we know of few examples where scientists are measuring the effects of other land management practices on NTFP productivity (e.g., Kerns et al. 2004 looked at huckleberry abundance, use, and the role of forest management on its productivity). Nor do we know of research on the effects of management practices such as herbicide application. For example, are wild-harvested products still marketable as "organic"? How much exposure are harvesters and consumers experiencing? A better understanding of the immediate biological and economic effects of land-use management practices could benefit current and future NTFP harvests.

The viability of commercial harvesting also depends on secure access to the raw material. Permitting costs and access restrictions, such as gating, can impede the flow of product needed to develop and maintain markets. Legislation, policies, and regulatory frameworks also can affect harvesters' access to resources. For example, increasing habitat loss can result in an increased concern for the viability of remaining plant populations and thus increased restrictions or prohibitions on harvesting. Mycological clubs in Washington State were instrumental in getting legislation passed that increased the permitting requirements for commercial harvesting in the early 1990s (McLain et al. 1998). In this case, predominantly urban recreational harvesting concerns took precedence over predominantly rural commercial harvesting concerns. Some federal land managers also have restricted access out of concern that commercial harvesting would invoke the National Environmental Policy Act's requirement for an environmental impact statement, a costly and time-consuming process. Such concerns are particularly likely to emerge for NTFP species whose value is not high enough for permit fees to offset their associated management costs. Other Forest Service offices have begun large-scale, competitive-bid, lease systems for floral greens, boughs, and other NTFPs. Evidence from the private sector suggests that such systems are likely to concentrate control over resource access in a few businesses, thus reducing the number of outlets where harvesters can sell raw product and reducing their leverage to demand better working conditions. Furthermore, this lease system may transform labor structures: independent harvesters working alone under individual permits may be replaced by crews working for the company that won the lease or working for an intermediary contractor. The full ecological effect of this transformation is unknown, but preliminary research suggests that this may be changing the relationship of harvesters to the land and undermining stewardship practices (Lynch and McLain 2003).

A challenge facing land managers is developing management strategies informed by an understanding of the informal economic characteristics of NTFPs. Reimer defines the informal economy as those activities involving "the production, distribution, and consumption of goods and services that have economic value, but [that] are neither protected by a formal code of law nor recorded for use by government-backed regulatory agencies" (2000, 2). It encompasses legal economic activities such as barter; volunteer work; unpaid labor, such as child care; and subsistence production; as well as illegal activities (Reimer 2000). Studies examining NTFP social organization show that some harvesters engage in NTFP activities simultaneously for income, subsistence, and to build reciprocity networks (e.g., Hinricks 1998). Promoting commercial NTFP harvesting to strengthen local economies without considering the informal economy would not accurately depict how NTFP economies function or the range of considerations that individuals and firms take into account when making choices about whether and how to participate in NTFP economies (McLain et al. forthcoming). By understanding informal economic behavior at the individual, household, and corporate scale, managers are better equipped to avoid adversely affecting culturally important subsistence and other nonmarket transactions at the household and community levels.

A final point to consider is the effect of globalization on the commercial viability of NTFP economies. Like agricultural workers, commercial NTFP harvesters in the United States are often just one link in a complex global commodity chain in which large brokers and wholesalers rely on multiple sources from around the world to acquire product. Although some native NTFP species are unique to the United States and lack global substitutes, many NTFPs, such as porcini (*Boletus edulis*) mushrooms, are harvested commercially in dozens of countries. Several factors combine to put harvesters in a particularly precarious position. While globalization can create or expand new markets, such as the demand for matsutake mushrooms in Japan, global procurement strategies can result in low prices for raw product or a lack of selling opportunities. At the same time, access fees and permits on federal land, enacted in part to pay for the administration of NTFP programs, are becoming more common and more expensive. Additionally, few associations, unions, or other organizations exist to champion better prices or wages for harvesters (and small businesses). Given that many harvesters are among the most economically marginalized members in rural communities, the combined squeeze of low prices and increased fees (and, often, reduced access) can seriously impede the viability of commercial harvesting. Understanding the global linkages and how these processes affect local harvesters and buyers will help land managers and other decisionmakers to make more informed decisions and mitigate negative consequences (e.g., by adjusting permit prices).

Working with a Diverse Population

As discussed, people engaged in NTFP harvesting come from diverse cultural, ethnic, and class backgrounds. A significant challenge exists in developing processes that are inclusive when working with such diversity. First, commercial harvesters often lack the experience and skills to participate effectively in land management or policy decisionmaking processes. And not all harvesters are interested in getting involved. Even if they have an interest, it often is difficult for harvesters to find time or resources to participate in formal meetings. Second, not all harvesters have the same amount of experience in the woods or knowledge of plants and plant ecology. Some harvesters have gathered for many years, are astute observers, and have knowledge about the plants they gather (e.g., habitat, seasonal variation, growth rates). Others are new to gathering and only beginning to develop experiential knowledge. Thus, land managers seeking to integrate NTFP harvesters face the challenge of developing a process that is inclusive and encourages and enables the participation of the most knowledgeable harvesters.

It is particularly challenging to include migrant or circuit harvesters. As Johnson et al. note, "Migratory peoples such as forest workers in the Pacific Northwest add diversity to communities, but are often left out of communities of place and interest" (2001, 59). In the case of NTFP harvesters, one reason is that many tie harvesting to their seasonal movements as migrant agricultural or forestry workers (e.g., tree planters). For others, especially wild mushroom harvesters, moving seasonally is a strategy adapted to the variable fruiting patterns and quantities of different types of wild, edible mushrooms. Mycorrhizal mushrooms fruit in the same places every year, but quantities differ considerably depending on climatic conditions and forest management practices such as logging or thinning. Morels, for instance, can fruit extensively in conifer forests burned by fire the previous year. Given this variability, harvesters who can travel for different species or different fruiting regions increase their chances for economic success. Although some mobile commercial harvesters develop an affinity for the communities and surrounding forests they regularly visit, call such places home, and are affected by management activities in these areas, they may be excluded from participation in forest decisionmaking processes because they are not permanent residents (Johnson et al. 2001; McLain and Jones 1997).

In addition, in some NTFP sectors, such as floral greens, where the labor force is predominantly Latino, a large percentage of workers may not have citizenship or guest-worker documents (Hansis 2002). Fear of deportation may inhibit the participation of undocumented workers in research or other events designed to help integrate commercial harvesters' knowledge and concerns into forest management. Without their participation, however, these harvesters remain invisible to many forest managers. Lack of English skills among undocumented workers can further complicate the situation. Translation of any outreach or training materials most likely will be needed, as well as the use of translators, as is becoming more common. The example of undocumented workers underscores the fact that commercial harvesters have widely varying degrees of power and political representation.

Conclusion

In recent decades, the shift toward ecosystem management and the growth of community-based and multi-stakeholder approaches to forestry have contributed to the increased visibility of NTFP harvesting. Interest has been growing in how NTFPs might be promoted as a tool to diversify and strengthen rural economies through managing for biological diversity. In this chapter, we focused on commercial NTFP harvesters and explored some of the opportunities and challenges of integrating them into forest management.

One fact is indisputable: despite little active management by foresters, a great diversity of species are harvested commercially. This diversity collectively represents a significant subset of the overall floral diversity found in the temperate, subtropical, and boreal forests of the United States. The potential benefits of active management and further integration of NTFPs into forest management are great and include restoration of unhealthy forests into healthy ecosystems and new economic opportunities. Actively integrating NTFPs into forest management also presents an opportunity to enhance forest management and stewardship. Social scientists have documented that harvesters' on-the-ground knowledge is valuable for enhancing forest management. Likewise, advocates for forest-workers' rights have shown that involving harvesters in the dialogue about forest management fosters better communication across stakeholder groups and promotes democratic participation of a wider group of forest users.

Integrating NTFP issues into forest management faces several challenges, however. Habitat lost to development, logging, mining, grazing, and road building is a significant threat to wild plant populations. This in turn reduces the supply of material available for harvesting. Securing reliable access is another critical factor, and the use of herbicides in the eradication of invasive species and other vegetation control is a potential threat. Policies, regulation, and legislation can reduce access and act as formidable barriers to developing local NTFP businesses. In sum, a variety of factors impede the profitability of harvesting, which weakens the potential of NTFPs to strengthen rural economies.

Integrating NTFPs with traditional forest management requires a shift toward ecosystem management based on holistic and interdisciplinary understandings of the diverse species harvested, as well as the diversity of cultural groups involved in harvesting. Working with diverse populations—all of whom have different "ways of knowing," cultural practices, and widely varying degrees of power and political representation—is another challenge. Effective policies to guide and regulate NTFP industries within a sustainable ecosystem management approach should be careful not to privilege the wealthy but should work instead to advance the knowledge development and stewardship of the resources by harvesters.

Thinking about ways to integrate NTFPs with forest management sparks a whole host of questions for further research. How have the transformation of forests and the loss of biodiversity affected harvesters? Have NTFP harvesters retained or lost access to their traditional gathering areas? What subsistence activities, cottage industries, and small businesses have been overlooked or suppressed in the wake of a forest management paradigm oriented toward "getting the cut out?" We would like to be able to say we are close to answering these and other important questions, but just as harvesters largely have been ignored, so has funding for NTFP research. Although the potential exists for NTFPs and communities of NTFP harvesters to play important roles in the vitality of forest-based communities, much work remains to make it happen.

Note

1. The response number differs from the one reported earlier in the chapter because not all Forest Service national forests responded to each question in the survey.

References

Alexander, S.J. 2004. Criterion 6, Indicator 32 Value of Wood and Non-Wood Products Production as Percentage of GDP. In *Data Report: A Supplement to the National Report on Sustainable Forests—2003*, edited by David Darr. FS-766A. Washington, DC: U.S. Department of Agriculture, Forest Service, 1–16.

Alexander, S.J., J. Weigand, and K.A. Blatner. 2002a. Nontimber Forest Product Commerce. In *Nontimber Forest Products in the United States*, edited by E. Jones, R.J. McLain, and J. Weigand. Lawrence: University Press of Kansas, 115–150.

Alexander, S.J., D. Pilz, N.S. Weber, E. Brown, and V.A. Rockwell. 2002b. Mushrooms, Trees and Money: Value Estimates of Commercial Mushrooms and Timber in the Pacific Northwest. *Environmental Management* 30(1): 129–141.

Ambrose, C., and C. Martinez. 1999. *Standards and Guidelines for the Harvesting of Selected Medicinal Herbs*. Burnt Ranch, CA: Trinity Alps Botanicals.

Arora, D. 1999. The Way of the Wild Mushroom. *California Wild* 52(4): 8–19.

Bagby, K. 2004. Sharing Stewardship of the Harvest: Report on the 2003 Crescent Lake Mushroom Monitoring Project. Taylorsville, CA: Pacific West Community Forestry Center at Forest Community Research.

Baker, M., and J. Kusel. 2003. *Community Forestry in the United States. Learning from the Past, Crafting the Future*. Washington, DC: Island Press.

Ballard, H. 2005. Impacts of Harvesting Salal (*Gaultheria shallon*) on the Olympic Peninsula, Washington: Harvester Knowledge, Science, and Participation. Ph.D. Dissertation. University of California, Berkeley.

Brown, B.A., and A. Martín-Hernández (eds.). 2000. *Voices from the Woods. Lives and Experiences of Nontimber Forest Workers*. Wolf Creek, OR: Jefferson Center for Education and Research.

Buren, B. 2005. Wildcrafting: A "Simple" Life Fraught with a Host of Complex Ethical and Practical Considerations. Rodale Institute. http://www.newfarm.org/features/0304/wilds/wild_ethics.shtml (accessed November 1, 2007).

Carroll, M.S., R.G. Lee, and R.J. McLain. 2005. Occupational Community and Forest Work: Three Cases from the Pacific Northwest. In *Communities and Forests Where People Meet the Land*, edited by R.G. Lee and D.R. Field. Corvallis, OR: Oregon State University Press, 159–175.

Chamberlain, J.L., R.J. Bush, A.L. Hammett, and P.A. Araman. 2002. Eastern National Forests: Managing for Nontimber Products. *Journal of Forestry* 100(1): 8–14.

Chambers, R. 1997. *Whose Reality Counts? Putting the First Last.* London: Intermediate Technology Publications.

Collaborative Forest Restoration Program (CFRP). 2004. The Multiparty Monitoring Handbook Series. Albuquerque, NM: U.S. Department of Agriculture, Forest Service, Southwest Region, State and Private Forestry–Collaborative Forest Restoration Program.

Crook, C., and R.A. Clapp. 2002. The Paradox of Market-oriented Conservation: Lessons from the Tropical Forests. In *Nontimber Forest Products in the United States,* edited by E.T. Jones, R.J. McLain, and J. Weigand. Lawrence: University Press of Kansas, 163–179.

Davidson-Hunt, I.J., and F. Berkes. 2001. Changing Resource Management Paradigms, Traditional Ecological Knowledge, and Non-timber Forest Products. In *Forest Communities in the Third Millennium: Linking Research, Business, and Policy Toward a Sustainable Non-Timber Forest Product Sector,* edited by I. Davidson-Hunt, L.C. Duchesne, and J.C. Zasada. U.S. Department of Agriculture, North Central Research Station: St. Paul, MN. General Technical Report. NC-217.

Duke, J. 1989. *Ginseng: A Concise Handbook.* Algonac, MI: Reference Publications, Inc.

Emery, M. 1998. Invisible Livelihoods: Nontimber Forest Products in Michigan's Upper Peninsula. Ann Arbor, MI: UMI Dissertation Services.

———. 2001. Who Knows? Local Non-timber Forest Product Knowledge and Stewardship Practices in Northern Michigan. *Journal of Sustainable Forestry* 13(3/4): 123–139.

Emery, M.R., C. Ginger, S. Newman, and M.R.B. Giammusso. 2003. *Special Forest Products in Context: Gatherers and Gathering in the Eastern United States.* General Technical Report NE-GTR-306. Burlington, VT: U.S. Department of Agriculture, Forest Service, Northeastern Research Station.

Etkin, N.L. 1994. *Eating on the Wild Side: The Pharmacologic, Ecologic, and Social Implications of Using Noncultigens.* Arizona Studies in Human Ecology. Tucson, AZ: University of Arizona Press.

Everett, Y. 2001. Participatory Research for Adaptive Ecosystem Management: A Case of Nontimber Forest Products. *Journal of Sustainable Forestry* 13(1/2): 335–357.

Flaster, T. 2005. The Medicinal Plant Working Group and Community Conservation: A Work in Progress. *Practicing Anthropology* 27(1): 25–28.

Forest Community Research (FCR). 2002. Assessment of the Northwest Economic Adjustment Initiative. Forest Community Research: Taylorsville. http://sierrainstitute.us/ (accessed November 1, 2007).

Freed, J. 1997. The Future of the Special Forest Products Industry. *Western Forester* 42(6): 6–7.

Freese, C.H. 1998. *Wild Species as Commodities: Managing Markets and Ecosystems for Sustainability.* Washington, DC: Island Press.

Hammett, A.L., and J.L. Chamberlain. 1998. Non-timber Forest Products in Central Appalachia: Development Opportunities in Support of Sustainable Forestry. In *Meeting in the Middle: Proceedings of the 1997 Society of American Foresters National Convention,* Memphis, TN, October 4-8, 1997. Bethesda, MD: Society of American Foresters, 416–418.

Hansis, R. 1998. A Political Ecology of Picking: Non-timber Forest Products in the Pacific Northwest. *Human Ecology* 26(1): 67–85.

———. 2002. Case Study. Workers in the Woods: Confronting Rapid Change. In *Nontimber Forest Products in the United States*, edited by E.T. Jones, R.J. McLain, and J. Weigand. Lawrence: University Press of Kansas, 52–56.

Hinrichs, C. 1998. Sideline and Lifeline: The Cultural Economy of Maple Syrup Production. *Rural Sociology* 63(4): 507–532.

Hufford, M. 1997. American Ginseng and the Culture of the Commons. *Orion* 16(4): 11–14.

Johnson, N., J. Belsky, V. Benavides, M. Goebel, A. Hawkins, and S. Waage. 2001. Global Linkages to Community-based Ecosystem Management in the United States. In *Understanding Community-based Forest Ecosystem Management*, edited by G. J. Gray, M.J. Enzer, and J. Kusel. NY: Food Products Press, 35–63.

Jones, E.T. 2002. The Political Ecology of Wild Mushroom Harvester Stewardship in the Pacific Northwest. Ann Arbor, MI: UMI Dissertation Services.

Jones, E.T., and K. Lynch. 2007. Nontimber Forest Products and Biodiversity Management in the Pacific Northwest. *Forest Ecology and Management.*

Jones, E.T., R.J. McLain, and K.A. Lynch. 2004. *The Relationship Between Nontimber Forest Product Management and Biodiversity in the United States.* Portland, OR: Institute for Culture and Ecology.

Kauffman, G. 2003. Black Cohosh (*Cimicifuga racemosa*) Harvest Monitoring 2002. U.S. Department of Agriculture, Forest Service. http://www.nps.gov/plants/medicinal/pubs/2002bcohosh.htm (accessed November 1, 2007).

Kerns, B.K., S.J. Alexander, and J.D. Bailey. 2004. Huckleberry Abundance, Stand Conditions and Use in Western Oregon: Evaluating the Role of Forest Management. *Economic Botany* 58: 668–678.

Laird, Sarah A. (ed.). 2002. *Biodiversity and Traditional Knowledge. Equitable Partnerships in Practice.* People and Plants Conservation Series. London: Earthscan Publications Ltd.

Lindenmayer, D.B., and J.F. Franklin. 2002. *Conserving Forest Biodiversity. A Comprehensive Multiscaled Approach.* Washington, DC: Island Press.

Love T., E.T. Jones, and L. Liegel. 1998. Valuing the Temperate Rainforests: Wild Mushrooming on the Olympic Peninsula Biosphere Reserve. *Ambio Special Report* 9: 16–25.

Lynch, K.A. 2005. *Nontimber Forest Product Curriculum Workbook.* Portland, OR: Institute for Culture and Ecology.

Lynch, K., and R.J. McLain. 2003. *Access, Labor, and Wild Floral Greens Management in Western Washington's Forests.* General Technical Report PNW-GTR-585. Portland, OR: U.S. Department of Agriculture, Forest Service, Pacific Northwest Research Station.

Lynch, K.A., E.T. Jones, and R.J. McLain. 2004. *Nontimber Forest Product Inventorying and Monitoring in the United States: Rationale and Recommendations for a Participatory Approach.* Portland, OR: Institute for Culture and Ecology.

McGraw, J.B., and M.A. Furedi. 2005. Deer Browsing and Population Viability of a Forest Understory Plant. *Science* 307: 920–922.

McLain, R.J. 2004. Bringing Wildcrafters to the International Policy Table: Reflections on the Nontimber Forest Products Side Event at the 12 World Forestry Congress, Quebec City 2003. Portland, OR: Institute for Culture and Ecology.

McLain, R.J., and E.T. Jones. 1997. Challenging "Community" Definitions in Natural Resource Management: The Case of Wild Mushroom Harvesting in the USA. *Gatekeeper* 68: 1–19.

McLain, R.J., and E.T. Jones. 2005. *Nontimber Forest Products Management on National Forests in the United States.* General Technical Report. PNW-GTR-655. Portland, OR: U.S. Department of Agriculture, Forest Service, Pacific Northwest Research Station.

McLain, R., S. Alexander, and E.T. Jones. Forthcoming. Incorporating Understandings of Informal Economic Activity in Natural Resource and Economic Development Policy. Portland, OR: U.S. Department of Agriculture, Forest Service, Pacific Northwest Research Station.

McLain, R.J., H.H. Christensen, and M.A. Shannon. 1998. When Amateurs Are the Experts: Amateur Mycologists and Wild Mushroom Politics. *Society and Natural Resources* 11: 615–626.

Meffe, G.K., and C.R. Carroll. 1994. *Principles of Conservation Biology.* Sunderland, MA: Sinauer Associates, Inc.

Michel, H., and D. Gayton. 2002. Linking Indigenous Peoples' Knowledge and Western Science in Natural Resource Management: A Dialogue. *B.C. Journal of Ecosystems and Management.* http://www.forrex.org/publications/forrexseries/ss4.pdf (accessed November 1, 2007).

Minnis, P.E. (ed.). 2003. *People and Plants in Ancient Eastern North America.* Washington, DC: Smithsonian Books.

Minnis, P.E., and W.J. Elisens. 2000. *Biodiversity and Native America.* Norman: University of Oklahoma Press, 3–28.

Moerman, D.E. 1998. *Native American Ethnobotany.* Portland, OR: Timber Press.

Moseley, C., and L.J. Wilson. 2002. *Multiparty Monitoring for Sustainable Natural Resource Management.* Hayfork, CA: Watershed Research and Training Center and Eugene, OR: Ecosystem Workforce Program, University of Oregon.

Newbegin, H. 2005. About Us. http://www.juniperridge.com/info_company_about_us.htm (accessed November 1, 2007).

Nontimber Forest Products Working (NTFP) Group. 2005. *Focus: Nontimber Forest Products Practitioner* 23: 30–33.

Pilz, D., and R. Molina (eds.). 1996. *Managing Forest Ecosystems to Conserve Fungus Diversity and Sustain Wild Mushroom Harvests.* General Technical Report PNW-GTR-371. Portland, OR: U.S. Department of Agriculture, Forest Service, Pacific Northwest Research Station.

Pilz, D., E.T. Jones, and H.J. Ballard. 2006. *Broadening Participation in Biological Monitoring: Handbook for Scientists and Managers.* General Technical Report PNW-GTR-680. Portland, OR: U.S. Department of Agriculture, Forest Service, Pacific Northwest Research Station.

Pilz, D., F.D. Brodie, S. Alexander, and R. Molina. 1998. Relative Value of Chanterelles and Timber as Commercial Forest Products. *Ambio: The Journal of the Human Environment* Special Report No. 9: 14–16.

Pilz, D., J. Smith, M.P. Amaranthus, S. Alexander, R. Molina, and D. Luoma. 1999. Mushrooms and Timber: Managing Commercial Harvesting in the Oregon Cascades. *Journal of Forestry* 97(3): 4–11.

Power, T.M. 1996. *Lost Landscapes and Failed Economies: The Search for a Value of Place.* Washington, DC: Island Press.

Reimer, B. 2000. *The Informal Economy in Rural Canada.* Presentation to the Canadian Employment Research Forum, July 30. www.cerf.mcmaster.ca/conferences/rural/papers/reimer.pdf (accessed November 1, 2007).

Richards, R.T., and M. Creasy. 1996. Ethnic Diversity, Resource Values, and Ecosystem Management: Matsutake Mushroom Harvesting in the Klamath Bioregion. *Society and Natural Resources* 9: 359–374.

Robbins, W.G. 1997. The Social Context of Forestry: The Pacific Northwest in the Twentieth Century. In *American Forests: Nature, Culture and Politics*, edited by C. Miller. Lawrence, KS: University Press of Kansas, 195–207.

Ruth, P. 1997. Biodiversity: Why Is It Important? In *Biodiversity II: Understanding and Protecting our Biological Resources*, edited by M.L. Reaka-Kudla, D.E. Wilson, and E.O. Wilson. Washington, DC: Joseph Henry Press, 15–24.

Schlosser, W., and K. Blatner. 1995. The Wild Edible Mushroom Industry of Washington, Oregon and Idaho: A 1992 Survey of Processors. *Journal of Forestry* 93(3): 31–36.

Shanley, P., A.R. Pierce, S.A. Laird, and A. Guillén (eds.). 2002. *Tapping the Green Market: Certification and Management of Non-timber Forest Products*. London: Earthscan Publications Ltd.

Shiva, M.P., and S.K. Verma. 2002. Approaches to Sustainable Forest Management and Biodiversity Conservation: With Pivotal Role of Non-timber Forest Products. Dehradun, India: International.

Spero, V., and C. Fleming. 2002. Case Study: Rio Grande National Forest. In *Nontimber Forest Products in the United States*, edited by E.T. Jones, R.J. McLain, and J. Weigand. Lawrence: University Press of Kansas, 108–112.

Steen, H.K. 2004 (1976). *The U.S. Forest Service: A History*. Durham, NC: Forest History Society in collaboration with the University of Washington Press.

Thomas, M.G., and D.R. Schumann. 1993. Income Opportunities in Special Forest Products. Self-Help Suggestions for Rural Entrepreneurs. *Agriculture Information Bulletin 666*. Washington, DC: U.S. Department of Agriculture, Forest Service.

Turner, N.J. 1997. Traditional Ecological Knowledge. In *The Rainforests of Home: Profile of a North American Bioregion*, edited by P.K. Schoonmaker, B. von Hagen, and E.C. Wolf. Washington, DC: Island Press, 275–298.

Vance, N.C., and J. Thomas (eds.). 1997. *Special Forest Products: Biodiversity Meets the Marketplace*. Sustainable Forestry Seminar Series, Oregon State University, Corvallis, OR, October-November 1995. General Technical Report GTR-WO-63. Washington, DC: U.S. Department of Agriculture, Forest Service.

von Hagen, B., and R. Fight. 1999. *Opportunities for Conservation-based Development of Nontimber Forest Products in the Pacific Northwest*. General Technical Report. PNW-GTR-473. Portland, OR: U.S. Department of Agriculture, Forest Service, Pacific Northwest Research Station.

Weigand, J.F. 1998. *Management Experiments for High-elevation Agroforestry Systems Jointly Producing Matsutake Mushrooms and High-quality Timber in the Cascade Range of Southern Oregon*. General Technical Report PNW-GTR-424. Portland, OR: U.S. Department of Agriculture, Forest Service, Pacific Northwest Research Station.

9

Job Quality for Forest Workers

Cassandra Moseley

Work long has been a fundamental way that people relate to forests. After World War II, communities near national forests developed an intimate economic relationship with these lands by participating in industrial-scale timber harvest. Prior to the 1990s, rural forest community development efforts, especially those of the Forest Service, focused on sending large volumes of timber to mills (Clary 1986; Hirt 1994; Waggener 1977). This was true across the country, whether in the Pacific Northwest, South, or interior West. Although many forest communities suffered from the high poverty rates of rural America, especially after the early 1980s recession, wages in the forest-products sector generally were considered sufficient to support a family (Freudenburg and Gramling 1994). With a focus on fallers, truck drivers, and mill workers, the forest-products industry seemed to create high-quality jobs in forest communities.

Over the past several decades, however, rural America and particularly resource-based communities have undergone significant change. Rural America has come to have higher poverty, unemployment, and underemployment rates than urban and suburban America (Findeis and Jensen 1998). Although some rural areas, especially in the West and South, have seen rapid population growth, it often has been accompanied by increasing economic inequality and limited growth of high-quality jobs for long-time residents. In addition, many rural communities that lack amenities or otherwise have not attracted urban and suburban migrants have seen little or no benefit from these demographic changes. Rather, their economic well-being has declined with the deterioration of the natural resource and farm sectors (Danks and Jungwirth 1999; Wilson 2000). In this context, it particularly is important that rural economic development efforts focus attention on economic development that creates high-quality jobs. High-quality jobs—jobs that are well paying, stable, safe, and close to home—are vital to the well-being of families and communities.

With the reduction in the federal timber-sale program and the shift in focus to ecosystem management in the early and mid-1990s, the Forest Service and rural communities began to turn away from industrial-scale forest management to forest and watershed restoration and ecosystem management as an economic development opportunity (DeForest 1999, *572*; U.S. Fish and Wildlife Service 2003). Rather than relying on timber sales as the only source of economic opportunity, the focus shifted to implementing forest and watershed restoration through service contracting with businesses and grants and cooperative agreements with nongovernmental organizations.

Forest and watershed restoration and maintenance include a variety of work that roughly can be divided into three categories. Labor-intensive activities involve many people doing significant, heavy physical labor, such as tree planting and thinning using chain saws. Other labor-intensive activities include brush piling and the manual components of stream restoration. Equipment-intensive activities use capital-intensive pieces of equipment, such as backhoes or excavators, and typically involve activities such as road building or decommissioning, as well as many stream-restoration activities such as bank stabilization, culvert replacement, removal of fish-passage barriers, and restoring natural meandering patterns. Technical work involves high-skill activities such as surveying for endangered species, plant identification, data collection for monitoring activities, native grass seed collection, road engineering, and project design and engineering. Job quality differs across these types of work: labor-intensive activities typically have lower job quality, whereas equipment and technical jobs have higher job quality (Moseley 2006b). These activities can occur on public or private lands, although much of the political attention has been on public lands in the American West.

Some people have seen forest and watershed restoration as a potential high-quality economic opportunity for rural, public-lands communities. For example, it was hoped that the Jobs-in-the-Woods Program, which began in the mid-1990s in the Pacific Northwest, would generate demand for highly skilled restoration and maintenance jobs that could be compensated with high wages (Hallock 1998; Spencer 1999). More sophisticated management approaches, it was thought, would require workers who could implement complicated thinning prescriptions, undertake complex stream restoration, and survey a diversity of plants and animals.

Over the past several years, however, research about forest work increasingly has made it clear that contract forest management services have not provided consistently high-quality jobs, as was hoped. With the exception of some niche markets, forest work typically provides fairly low job quality, with worse conditions for labor-intensive workers, people working on private lands, and

Hispanics (Brown 2001; Casanova and McDaniel 2005; McDaniel and Casanova 2003; Moseley 2006a, in prep; Moseley et al. 2006).

Using forest and watershed restoration as an economic development strategy to transform loggers, truck drivers, and mill workers into restoration workers ignored the fact that a well-developed restoration-contracting market already existed, largely focused around reforestation (Brown 2000). This reforestation market long has been a labor market with poor working conditions for many workers.

Why has job quality been poor in much of the federal, contract forest management sector? This question particularly is puzzling because of the abundance of labor and immigration laws in place that are designed to ensure high wages and good working conditions for contract forest workers.

As with almost all workers, forest and watershed-restoration workers working on both public and private lands have full protections under the Fair Labor Standards Act, which sets the federal minimum wage, and the Occupational Safety and Health Act. Federal contract workers also are protected under the Service Contract Act (SCA) or the Davis-Bacon Act and the Contract Work Hours and Safety Standards Act (CWHSA). The SCA and Davis-Bacon Act require that contractors pay prevailing wages, payments in lieu of benefits, and overtime or paid vacation on certain federal holidays when working on federal service and construction contracts. The CWHSA requires that federal contract workers be paid time-and-a-half whenever they work more than 40 hours per week. In addition, labor-intensive forest workers are protected by the Migrant and Seasonal Agricultural Worker Protection Act (MSPA), and, in Oregon, the Farm Labor Law (Bureau of Labor and Industries 2005). The MSPA and the Farm Labor Law require that employers provide workers with information about legal entitlements, detailed accounting of their pay, transportation in safe, insured vehicles, and other items. These requirements are stated explicitly in federal contracts, and failure to follow these laws when working under federal contract puts contractors in violation of the contract, thereby risking disbarment from federal contracting.

Given the abundance of labor and contract law, one might expect forest workers to have fairly high job quality, even for activities involving considerable physical labor. Despite considerable labor laws designed to create high-quality jobs for federal contract workers and recent policy efforts to create high-skill, high-wage employment opportunities restoring national forests, there are several other political institutions in place that serve to limit job quality for forest workers and economic opportunity for public-lands communities.

This chapter argues that the forest- and watershed-restoration industry has not become a new industry, as many had hoped, but rather is a continuation of a long-standing industry that has evolved to have varying job quality, including poor job quality and chronic problems with immigration, labor, and workers-compensation violations for labor-intensive activities. The labor-intensive forest- and watershed-restoration industry has inherited these problems. Immigration policy has had the opposite effect than intended—by creating a discriminatory labor market, it has lowered wages and job quality for both documented and undocumented workers. In addition, the federal land management agencies have a culture and institutional incentives that place land management accomplishments and efficiencies above economic development and the working conditions of its external workforce. To make this argument, this chapter reviews the literature about job quality in the woods, discusses the development of the contracting and labor market, and considers the institutional structures that inhibit the creation of high-quality jobs in the woods.

Job Quality

Job quality can be measured several ways. In forest management, the focus primarily has been on: 1) wages and benefits; 2) workplace safety and health; 3) job durability across seasons and across years; 4) opportunity for advancement; and 5) the ability to work near where one lives (Ecosystem Workforce Program 2003; see also, Doeringer and Piore 1970; Kalleberg et al. 2000). This section reviews what is known about each of these components of job quality.

Although the stereotypical person who works in the woods is a white, rural-dwelling male, in fact the forest- and watershed-restoration workforce is ethnically diverse. In the Pacific Northwest at least, the forest and watershed workforce primarily is made up of whites and Hispanics (largely from Mexico). Hispanics predominate in labor-intensive activities, such as tree planting, thinning, piling brush, and, increasingly, fire suppression and mop-up. In the Southeast, where Hispanics dominate the labor-intensive labor market, immigrants also come from Central America and Brazil (Casanova and McDaniel 2005). A survey of contractors from six national forests across the country found that Hispanics made up 43% of all workers and 66% of labor-intensive workers. Hispanic workers are more likely than white workers to hold labor-intensive jobs, and they appear to have lower quality jobs than white workers (Brown 2000, 2001; Brown and Martín-Hernández 2000; Mann 2001; Moseley 2006a, in prep).

Workers may be citizens of the United States, legal permanent residents, guest workers, or undocumented workers (Bowman and Campopesco 1993; Knudson 2005). In the Southwest, it appears that guest workers are fairly common (McDaniel and Casanova 2005). By contrast, in the Pacific Northwest, contractors rarely use guest workers, and undocumented workers and legal permanent-residents workers appear to be more common (McDaniel 2006).

Because of several recent studies about labor-intensive forest workers, as well as repeated political controversy over their working conditions and immigration status, much more is known about the job quality of labor-intensive forest workers than equipment-intensive and technical workers. In addition, labor-intensive forest workers are concentrated under a single industrial code, called "forestry services" (SIC 0851) in the Standard Industrial Code system or "support activities for forestry" in the North American Industrial Code System (NAICS 11531), which allows for some quantitative analysis that is not possible for equipment and technical workers, whose companies are not concentrated under unique industry codes.

Given that different labor laws, particularly prevailing wage laws, apply when an employee is working on public lands, job quality is likely to be poorer for private-land workers than for federal-land workers. However, studies either include all workers or focus only on federal-land workers, making comparison across land ownerships difficult.

Wages and Benefits

When working under contract with the federal government, contractors must pay at least the prevailing wages set under the SCA for labor-intensive activities, such as tree planting, brush piling, and thinning, and Davis-Bacon prevailing wages for construction activities, including equipment-intensive work such as road construction. Davis-Bacon wages typically are higher than SCA. For example, in Oregon (and in other western states) in 2004, the SCA minimum wage was $12.90 per hour for pre-commercial thinning, $11.69 per hour for tree planting, and $8.30 for slash piling, plus $2.59 per hour in lieu of benefits (U.S. Department of Labor 2004). The median hourly wage in Oregon in forestry services (NAICS 11531/SIC 0851) was $11.57 an hour (compared to $16.15 per hour for logging) (Moseley et al. 2006). Determining heavy-equipment wages for forest-restoration work is more complicated, but heavy-equipment operators in Oregon constructing roads were to be paid $27.47 per hour plus $9.70 in lieu of benefits and up to $3.00 per hour for working far from town (Office of Management and Budget et al. 2004). Not all forest restoration activities involving heavy equipment are classified as road construction, and wages may be less.

Although the hourly wages appear substantial for equipment-intensive workers and reasonable for forestry-services workers, these hourly wages do not necessarily translate to family-supporting wages on an annual basis. An analysis of unemployment insurance data in Oregon reveals that the annual median wage for forestry-services workers was $4,355 in 2003, whereas the annual median wage for loggers was $17,810 (Moseley et al. 2006).

For undocumented workers, wages may be less than reported because some undocumented workers are hired through "subcontractors" who take part of their hourly wage ($1.00–$4.00 per hour) in exchange for continued employment. In addition, many workers typically are paid for eight hours of work per day even if they work more; overtime and travel time rarely are paid except when firefighting (Moseley in prep).

A survey of forest contractors from six national forests found that 39% of all workers and 64% Hispanics worked for companies that did not offer health insurance (Moseley 2006a).

Workplace Safety and Health

The Bureau of Labor Statistics collects workplace illness, injury, and fatality data by industry. As with wage data, these data allow a comparison to injury and accident rates in logging (NAICS 11310/SIC 2411) and support activities for forestry (NAICS 11531/SIC 0851). In 2003, logging had an injury/illness rate of 6.4 incidents per 100 workers nationwide, whereas support activities for forestry had a rate of 2.7 incidents per 100 nationwide, making logging a far more dangerous activity than forestry services. Of these incidents, 69% of logging and 48% of forestry-services accidents resulted in time away from work, suggesting that logging injuries and illnesses frequently are more serious than forestry-services injuries and illnesses. In addition, the fatality rate in logging was .177 per 100 workers, whereas it was .067 in forestry services, making the fatality rate in logging more than twice as great than in forestry services (Bureau of Labor Statistics 2005a, 2005b).

Interviews with Hispanic labor-intensive forest workers suggest that many injuries may go unreported, particularly among vulnerable workers, such as undocumented workers (Knudson 2005; Moseley in prep). In some instances, it also appears that companies pay for injuries out of their own pockets rather than having their workers file a claim in order to keep their insurance rates down. Thus, the reported accident rates for forestry-services workers may be somewhat low, although it is impossible to say how significant this underreporting is to the overall incident rate. Another way in which injuries and illnesses are likely underreported in forestry services is cumulative or repetitive injury that occurs as a result of the considerable physical activities involved in some forestry-support activities, such as tree planting, thinning, and manual activities associated with wildland fire suppression. Assuming that these rates are approximately accurate, however, these data suggest that forestry services work is considerably safer than logging and safer even than the overall private industry rate of 5.0 incidents per 100 workers (Bureau of Labor Statistics 2005). This is the only area in which logging may have poorer job quality than forestry services.

Job Duration

Forest work of all types is a seasonal activity that varies with the weather and the biological windows for achieving particular tasks. Depending on their employer, workers may have frequent gaps in their employment over the course of a year, or their employment may be somewhat steady. In forestry services in

2003, for example, 44% of workers in Oregon worked in only one quarter and less than 17% worked all four quarters of the year. By contrast, 21% of loggers worked only one quarter and 51% worked four quarters. Also in 2003, almost 50% of forestry-services workers (but only 28% of loggers) worked outside of their industry over the course of the year. In addition to offering more seasonal employment, forestry services appear to offer less durable jobs across years than logging. For example, 46% of forestry-service employees working in 1997 were still working in the industry two years later and only 28% were still working in the industry in 2003. By contrast, 64% of loggers working in 1997 were working two years later and 44% were still working in 2003. These differences exist despite the fact that overall employment in forestry services has been increasing while overall employment has been decreasing in logging (Moseley et al. 2006).

Ability to Work Near Where One Lives

Studies of the labor-intensive forestry-services contracting market suggest that this market has regional and national linkages (Casanova and McDaniel 2005; Moseley and Shankle 2001). Workers may travel long distances over the course of their work year because contractors typically bring their workers with them when working far from home (Moffett et al. 2005). In Oregon, Washington, and Northern California, the service-contracting market for federal forestry management services contains small firms that work close to home. These contractors typically perform equipment-intensive activities such as road and stream-restoration work. The Pacific Northwest contracting marketplace also includes larger firms located along the Interstate 5 corridor in western Oregon and Northern California that work across Oregon, Washington, and Northern California. These mobile contractors typically perform labor-intensive activities such as pre-commercial hand thinning (with a chainsaw) and brush piling throughout the Northwest (Moseley et al. 2003; Moseley and Shankle 2001). A similar pattern occurs in the Southeast. Hispanic tree planters from Central America and Mexico may work part of the year in Alabama, for example, and then travel to Idaho or elsewhere in the West as the work season progresses (Casanova and McDaniel 2005).

Summary—Job Quality

The job quality of forest-restoration work varies considerably. Labor-intensive forest workers may have high hourly wages when working on federal lands, but this does not amount to much in the way of an annual wage because jobs often are seasonal and employment erratic. The limited information that has been gathered about equipment-intensive and technical workers suggests that their job quality is higher than labor-intensive forest workers. All kinds of forest workers work away from home, although labor-intensive workers are more likely to do so. Similarly, few forest workers are offered health insurance, although technical and equipment-intensive workers are somewhat more likely to be offered such benefits. In all of these categories, Hispanic workers are more likely than non-Hispanics to have poorer job quality.

Contracting and Labor Market Development

Today's labor and contracting markets are not simply the result of current conditions. They did not arise with the notion of ecosystem management in the 1990s but are the by-products of economic and political developments that occurred during the 1960s, 1970s, and 1980s. They emerged during the period of industrial-scale forestry on public lands, particularly in the 1970s, when clearcutting became ubiquitous on public lands and reforestation emerged as a requirement for both public and private lands. The Oregon Forest Practices Act, passed in 1971, and the Washington Forest Practices Act, passed in 1974, require the reforestation of harvested land. Several other forested states followed with forest-practices laws that required reforestation. The National Forest Management Act of 1976 further strengthened Forest Service reforestation requirements. These new laws created new markets for reforestation activities.

Similarly, equipment-intensive markets developed as the Forest Service and private industrial landowners undertook massive road-building projects during this same period to make timber removal possible. Finally, there were also technical activities such as timber cruising and stand exams, which helped land managers determine how much standing timber was available for harvest. Road-building activities often were included in timber-sale contracts and the purchasers subcontracted these activities or used in-house crews. By contrast, government employees did much of the technical work on federal land. Relatively little is known about the details of the political–economic development of the equipment and technical markets. Consequently, the remainder of this chapter focuses on the development of the labor-intensive contracting and labor markets.

During the period of industrial-scale forest management on public lands, tree planting was one of the major labor-intensive activities that the Forest Service and Bureau of Land Management contracted out. Pre-commercial thinning, plantation thinning, and timber-stand improvement—all thinning of small trees—also were important, as was site preparation, brushing, gopher baiting, and application of big-game repellent. Tree planting is a seasonal activity that only can be undertaken at a particular elevation, latitude, and aspect a few weeks a year. To assemble steady work from tree planting, individuals and companies must move across the landscape over the course of a year and supplement tree planting with other reforestation activities (Mackie 1990).

Early reforestation crews were made up of college-age youth, skid-row transients, and others from the agricultural labor pool. Reforestation work was considerably higher paying than agricultural work, although physically more demanding. Barriers to entry were low, personnel turnover large, working conditions poor, and failure to pay promised wages common (Mackie 1990).

In the 1960s, Mexican immigrants were relatively rare outside of California and Texas. Hispanics were not tracked in the 1960 census, but in 1970, Hispanics made up 1.7% of the population in Oregon and 2.9% in Washington (compared to 13.7% in California) (U.S. Census Bureau 2005). Oregon farmers made some use of the Bracero guest-worker immigration program to import Mexicans to work in the pear orchards of southern Oregon and in other types of agriculture in the northern Willamette Valley during the 1960s and 1970s. The Washington State fruit industry made larger use of the program. Even after the Bracero program ended in 1965 and into the mid-1980s, Mexican immigrants were concentrated in a few states, primarily California and Texas. Oregon and Washington each absorbed considerably less than 1% of new Mexican immigrants each year (Durand et al. 2000). Until 1986, it was not illegal to employ undocumented workers and some reforestation contractors in the Northwest hired them (Hartzell 1987).

In the late 1960s and early 1970s, counter-cultural youth began to work as tree planters because the work was outside, casual, and relatively high-paying. Experiencing poor working conditions, failure to receive promised wages, and extensive tree stashing—burying large groups of tree seedlings rather than planting them—counter culturalists began to form worker cooperatives across the Pacific Northwest. Hippie planting crews realized they could work without the supervision of a contractor's foreman and that all they needed to start their own business were hoedads—tree planting tools—tree bags, and a crummy—a crew van (Hartzell 1987). Hoedads, perhaps the largest and most well-known of the reforestation cooperatives, incorporated in 1974 after forming as a partnership in 1970. By the late 1970s, there were no fewer than 23 cooperatives and 1,000 cooperative workers in Oregon, Washington, California, Idaho, and Montana (Gunn 1984).

As the cooperatives grew, the wages of reforestation workers increased as well, not only for the cooperative workers but also for workers employed by traditionally organized contractors. This was in part because of the expanding tree-planting market caused by increased Forest Service and Bureau of Land Management clearcut timber harvesting and a strong economy. The cooperatives also put pressure on the other reforestation contractors to raise wages and improve working conditions by hiring away their better workers with promises of higher wages, self-management, and better working conditions. But "because of entry ease, a plethora of shifty small outfits remained, here today, gone tomorrow" (Mackie 1990, *119*).

In 1976, both the cooperatives and traditionally organized contractors formed associations to act politically on their own behalf (Mackie 1990). The

Association of Reforestation Contractors began to lodge complaints and encourage legal investigations of Hoedads, accusing them of various violations. For example, the association argued that the policy of paying tree planters piece-rate without guaranteeing minimum hourly wages violated the SCA. Hoedads management became increasingly absorbed with responding to legal challenges. On the cooperative side, the Northwest Forest Workers Association and Hoedads began to lodge complaints and file lawsuits to protect workers rights.

In the early and mid-1970s, the use of undocumented workers was fairly rare both in reforestation and in agriculture in Oregon. However, it began to increase in the latter 1970s, particularly in Medford and in Woodburn and other northern Willamette Valley agricultural areas. Contractors began to smuggle Mexicans into Oregon to perform reforestation work as well. By 1978, it had become obvious that contractors were importing and employing undocumented workers (Mackie 1990). Still, wages were high in 1979. However, when a severe recession hit Oregon in 1980, wages began to fall. In 1980, the Salem *Statesman Journal* ran the first series of articles about exploitation of undocumented Mexican reforestation workers. In the early 1980s, reforestation contractors who used undocumented workers rapidly became dominant because they paid workers considerably less, thereby out-competing contractors and cooperatives that were not using undocumented workers. The vulnerability of undocumented workers meant that few if any labor complaints were filed against these contractors. Because wages were so much lower, they eliminated the comparative advantages of experienced, organized cooperatives. As the reforestation market worsened in the early 1980s, wages and bid prices fell. Contractors and cooperatives began to decline or go out of business entirely. By 1986, there were probably fewer than 100 cooperative workers left in the Pacific Northwest (Mackie 1990).

In the late 1980s, the contracting market improved somewhat with renewed federal and private timber harvests, which lasted into the early 1990s. By 1993, however, timber-sale injunctions, followed by budget cuts, dramatically reduced the amount of contracting that the Forest Service was doing in the Pacific Northwest, particularly for tree planting and other activities associated with intensive forest management (Moseley 2005). This dramatic decline finished off nearly all of the remaining cooperatives.

It is not clear how many contracting companies went out of business entirely and how many simply stopped contracting with the Forest Service in the 1990s. However, in western Oregon, Washington, and Northern California, 78% of the forest management contractors that had worked for the Forest Service between 1990 and 1992 were no longer working for the agency a decade later (Moseley 2005). Some of these departures would have happened anyway, a by-product of long-term instability in the contracting market caused by low barriers to entry in the labor-intensive portion of the market. Still, the number of contractors working for the Forest Service declined considerably as a result of fewer contracting opportunities, not simply natural turnover.

Changes in federal land management in the 1990s and early 2000s led to further shifts in the industry. When the Forest Service employed a large workforce to perform timber stand examinations, timber cruising, and other activities, these workers were available to fight fires when demand outstripped regular fire personnel. The Pacific Northwest, where employment was the greatest, provided many of these fire suppression staff nationwide. When Forest Service employment declined in the 1990s, the greatest declines were in the Pacific Northwest and in low service grade staff (National Federation of Federal Employees 2000). This decline of low service grade staff in the Pacific Northwest left the Forest Service nationwide short of staff for fire suppression, which resulted in a rapid increase in the need for contract fire suppression crews (U.S. Government Accounting Office 2004; Pulaski 2002, 2003). With a shift to contract fire suppression, wildfire work has become predominately Hispanic (Johnson 2006; Knudson 2006; USDA Office of the Inspector General 2006). The forestry services contracting market now is dominated by two kinds of contractors: those who take advantage of vulnerable workers by paying below SCA minimum wage and failing to pay overtime and those who can bid low and pay SCA wages on less lucrative projects such as thinning because their income primarily is from lucrative fire suppression work (Desmond 2004).

Institutional Reinforcements

With the Latinization of the labor-intensive contracting labor market, it would be tempting to argue that low job quality simply is a result of the immigration of Mexican workers who are willing to work for low wages. This common argument, which in fact underlies much of U.S. immigration policy, is that living standards and economic opportunity are so much lower in Mexico than they are in the United States that it creates a large pool of labor that is willing to come to the United States and work for low wages (Mann 2001; Massey et al. 2002). This explanation misses the major role that immigration and labor policy and forest management institutions play in creating and maintaining a system of low-quality jobs in labor-intensive forest work. Rather than being a by-product of "natural" market forces, this marketplace has been structured by government institutions.

Immigration Policy

From 1965 to 1986, most Mexicans went to Texas and California to work (Durand et al. 2000; Wells 1996). During this period, documented and undocumented workers were paid approximately the same wages, after controlling for factors such as educational attainment, facility with English, and social capital (Donato et al. 1992).

Although the number of Mexicans coming into the United States had not increased dramatically, Congress passed the Immigration Reform and Control Act (IRCA) in 1986 to reduce the number of undocumented workers entering the country (Massey et al. 2002). The law used four central strategies: amnesty for long-time residents and agricultural workers; a guest-worker program to allow people to work seasonally in the United States; increased resources for the Border Patrol; and requirements that employers check the work documents of their employees, with civil and criminal penalties for employees who failed to do so. This law might have reduced the number of undocumented workers working in forestry services either by increasing the number of documented Hispanic workers in the United States or by deterring Mexicans and others from immigrating to the United States for work (Wyant 1988). But by the 1990s, Mexican immigration rates had returned to pre-IRCA levels (Massey et al. 2002). If forestry services reacted similarly to other sectors of the economy, it is likely that over time the IRCA lowered wages and worsened working conditions.

It is difficult to tell exactly what happened in the forestry-services labor market as a result of the IRCA because historical quantitative data are slim. But despite early hopes that IRCA would improve conditions by eliminating undocumented workers from the labor pool, by the early 1990s it was apparent that some contractors were continuing to use undocumented workers and that in some instances these workers were subject to considerable abuse. In 1993, a CNN special report and an investigative report published in the *Sacramento Bee* chronicled undocumented forest workers working in deplorable conditions in California (Bowman and Campopesco 1993). These reports led to a congressional investigation in which several people testified, including some public employees, that labor law and immigration violations were common (U.S. Congress House 1993). One person estimated that approximately 50% of workers in reforestation were undocumented, with a higher percentage in California (Desmond 1993). In 2005, there was another series of articles in the *Sacramento Bee* and a subsequent congressional hearing, this time focused on guest workers who also faced poor working conditions and, significant exploitation, including illegally pay docking and unsafe vehicles (Knudson 2005; U.S. Congress Senate 2006).

Although there is limited information about the effect of the IRCA in forestry services, the effect on the broader economy has been well researched. Undocumented workers came to the United States in similar numbers after the law as before but saw their wages drop relative to documented immigrants. After the IRCA, undocumented workers with the same background as documented immigrants were paid approximately 22% less than documented immigrants and undocumented agricultural workers were paid another 33% less

(Phillips and Massey 1999). These wage differences appear to have come about because of the increased risk the employers faced when hiring undocumented workers after the IRCA. The new law also gave rise to labor subcontractors, who acted as employers of undocumented workers in exchange for part of the employees' wages, thereby assuming the risk that business owners faced, further reducing wages (Phillips and Massey 1999).

Other immigration laws and the militarization of the Border Patrol followed the IRCA. The 1990 Immigration Act focused further on border control. The Border Patrol's budget skyrocketed in the early 1990s, with particular efforts on slowing undocumented crossings at San Diego and El Paso (Durand and Massey 2003). California's Proposition 187, which passed in 1994, sought to prevent undocumented immigrants from accessing public health, education, and welfare services. Increased patrols of the California–Mexico border and the hostile environment in California served to disperse Mexican immigrants to other states. In addition, the increased risk of crossing the border did not so much deter people from crossing in the first place but encouraged people to settle in the United States once they arrived. By the mid-1990s, the Pacific Northwest had become an increasingly important settlement location (Durand et al. 2000). In the 1990 Census, Hispanics made up 4% of Oregon's population and 4.4% of Washington's. In the 2000 census, Hispanics had reached 8% of the population in Oregon and 7.5% in Washington (U.S. Census Bureau 2005).

Immigration policy, which was designed to reduce the flow of documented and undocumented migrants and presumably lead to increased wages and improved working conditions as labor markets tightened, in fact had the opposite effect. The IRCA increased discrimination against undocumented workers, and even against documented immigrants, and led to a decay of wages in sectors dominated by Hispanic workers. And, along with other immigration policies, the IRCA increased the settlement of Hispanics outside of California and Texas, in places such as the Pacific Northwest and the Southeast, creating an increasingly permanent pool of workers who are more readily discriminated against in the workplace.

In addition, the IRCA also created a guest-worker program for seasonal laborers. The so-called H2A program is for agricultural workers and the H2B program is for other types of work, including forestry, service sector jobs, and landscaping. The H2B program allows companies to apply for visas after advertising job openings at the prevailing wage and failing to get enough qualified applicants. Labor-intensive contractors in the Pacific Northwest rarely have used the guest worker program, but forestry is one of the largest segments of the guest-worker program and its use in the South is pervasive. Although the H2B program provides legal status to workers, these workers are beholden to a single employer, which makes them vulnerable to exploitation. Quitting an abusive job voids a worker's visa, requiring him to return home or become undocumented. Unlike the H2A program, there are relatively few protections put in place to prevent such abuses, and H2B workers are prohibited from accessing legal-aid programs provided to H2A workers.

Federal Land Management Institutions

The U.S. immigration system—particularly the militarized border and components that effectively deny immigrant workers equal protection as other workers—has created a low-cost, poor-job-quality labor market for labor-intensive forest work. This labor market, combined with institutional incentives in the federal land management agencies and limited labor-law enforcement, serves to keep job quality poor despite significant labor law designed to protect the job quality of federal contract workers.

Because the Forest Service is part of the federal government, it is tempting to expect it to be responsible for ensuring that its contracts are awarded only to businesses that are in strict compliance with all federal laws. There are, however, other institutional processes at work that affect Forest Service behavior. The three most important of these are weak law-enforcement mechanisms, the importance of meeting natural resource accomplishment targets, and the historical use of sealed, low-bid contracting mechanisms.

The Forest Service does not have primary enforcement responsibility for enforcing the SCA, Davis-Bacon Act, or MSPA. Investigation and enforcement of these laws are the purview of the Department of Labor's Wage and Hour Division (WHD). But forestry work occurs in isolated locations far from WHD offices, and on-site inspections appear to be rare (Moseley in prep.). The Forest Service, however, is not supposed to award contracts to businesses in violation of these laws and should report suspected violations to the WHD. Historically, however, coordination between the WHD and the Forest Service has been poor (U.S. Congress House 1993). Given that enforcement authority rests elsewhere, other institutional pressures can lead staff to ignore job quality.

The Forest Service's budget and staff performance evaluations and advancement long have been tied to targets. During the period of industrial-scale forestry, the most obvious target was the volume of timber harvested. Each year, the president's budget for the Department of Agriculture included a proposed timber volume target and total budget. The volume was apportioned to each national forest. Meeting the cut target in one's area of control was related to increasing budget and staffing for one's area, as well as promotion. Although timber volume was the most well-known target, reforestation and timber stand improvements and other thinning activities also were important because the assumption that the Forest Service could sustain and increase timber harvest levels rested on successful reforestation and timber stand improvements.

Accomplishments in these areas were reported annually to Congress and subject to review at budget hearings (e.g. U.S. Congress House 1982, 1983). The targets are quantifiable—volume harvested, acres treated, miles of stream or road restored—and focused on natural resources, rarely, if ever, related to achieving social or economic goals. Although the Forest Service has policies designed to create economic opportunity, it always has been a natural resource agency, with its primary focus on the management of resources.

The focus on timber targets lessened during the 1990s, but accomplishment targets remained in place. The Government Performance Results Act of 1993 was designed to shift government evaluation from outputs to outcomes. But the performance measures, as targets are now called, continue largely to be output oriented and under the George W. Bush administration have increased in importance again. Programs failing to meet their targets are subject to budget cuts or outright elimination in the president's proposed budgets (Sarasohn 2005). With declining forest-level budgets and direction to do more with less, the need for low-cost contractors has become even stronger.

The focus on maximizing natural resource accomplishments in terms of volume, acres, and miles creates little institutional mandate for attending to the job quality of the contract workforce or ensuring that contractors strictly follow labor and immigration laws. Because Forest Service staff are rewarded for natural resource accomplishments, program staff and managers have strong incentives to complete as much work as possible for the lowest possible cost.

Another institution that has created incentives to limit attention to working conditions is the low-bid contracting system. Prior to the mid-1990s, the Forest Service had little choice but to award contracts to the lowest qualified bidder, almost regardless of the quality of the work they performed. Companies could be barred from bidding by not completing previous contracts or if found in violation of labor laws, such as SCA, the Davis-Bacon Act, MSPA, or by operating without workers-compensation insurance. In the mid-1990s, federal procurement contracting laws changed, and the Forest Service and Bureau of Land Management were able to use a negotiated contract, which no longer required the agencies to consider only price when awarding contracts. Other factors could be considered, such as past performance and technical capability. This created a mechanism to refuse offers from contractors with reputations for poor quality work. The emphasis was on creating the best value to the government, primarily understood as the best-quality services for the lowest price. This system can reward contractors who perform high-quality work with increased awards, which in turn can be passed onto workers as higher wages. But, until 2006, the Forest Service did not have a system in place for contracting offices to learn from each other about contractors that had problems with labor law, safety compliance, or job performance. After the political controversies over working conditions of labor-intensive forest workers that began in the fall of 2005, the Forest Service created an agency-wide reporting system to share information among its contracting officers about contractors who appear to be not complying with labor or safety laws.

It is challenging to use solicitation and award practices to create high-wage work because there are other institutional structures that create incentives for both contracting officers and program staff to prioritize low-cost treatments. Agency managers and their staff are rewarded for the number of acres of land treated. They are not rewarded for promoting high-quality jobs or ensuring that the contractors pay their workers well. In tight budgets, these employees have strong incentives to find the least expensive contractor so that they can accomplish the most work. Contracting officers consider it their role to protect the interests of the government (and taxpayers). Their task is to get the best value for the government. Contractors that perform adequately for a low cost will be chosen over contractors who are more expensive.

Conclusion

Forest- and watershed-restoration workers face a variety of working conditions. Some workers earn family wages and work almost year round. Many more, however, have highly seasonal opportunities, low annual wages, and are not offered benefits such as health insurance. Workers of all sorts regularly travel away from home overnight to work. Hourly wages likely are better for forestry-services workers than agriculture laborers and those who work in retail sales, which may be a by-product of the considerable labor protection that federal contract-forest workers have. But, forestry services wages are considerably lower than logging.

Although federal land management policy shifted in the early 1990s toward ecosystem management, the contract and labor markets of forest management are connected strongly to the earlier period. The forest- and watershed-restoration labor and contracting markets did not emerge in the 1990s with the rise of ecosystem management but in the 1970s with the intensification of industrial-scale forest management on national forests. Job quality increased in the 1970s with the rise of reforestation cooperatives but declined again with the Latinization of reforestation work in the 1980s.

Ecosystem management came with goals of creating quality jobs for public-lands communities. Subsequent laws gave the Forest Service authority to direct work to local communities, but strong historical institutional pressures that structure the labor and contracting markets and limit job quality have continued from the earlier period. For the Forest Service, the use of natural resource targets, which are central to budget growth, staffing, and promotion, keep the agency focused on natural resource objectives rather than the job quality of its contracted workforce. This is reinforced by the agency's ambiguous role in labor-law enforcement. In addition, and much larger than the Forest Service, federal immigration policy has served to worsen job quality where there are considerable numbers of undocumented workers, particularly after 1986.

References

Baker, M. 2004. *The Organization of Natural Resources Restoration Work. Trinity County: An Overview.* Greenville, CA: Forest Community Research.

Baker, M.J. 2005. Socio-economic Characteristics and Contributions of the Natural Resource Restoration System in Humboldt County, California. *Ecological Restoration* 23(1): 5–14.

Bowman, C., and M. Campopesco. 1993. Shame in the Forest: U.S. Hires Undocumented Workers. *Sacramento Bee,* June 8, p. A1.

Brown, B. 2000. The Multi-ethnic, Nontimber Forest Workforce in the Pacific Northwest: Reconceiving the Players in Forest Management. In *Sustaining the Forests of the Pacific Coast,* edited by D.J. Salazar and D.K. Alper. Vancouver, Canada: UBC Press, 148–169.

———. 2001. *Analysis of Challenges Facing Community Forestry: The Role of Low Income Forest Workers.* Wolf Creek, OR: Jefferson Center for Education and Research.

Brown, B., and A. Martín-Hernández. 2000. *Voices from the Woods: Lives and Experiences of Non-timber Forest Workers.* Wolf Creek, OR: Jefferson Center for Education and Research.

Bureau of Labor and Industries. 2005a. Oregon Farm/Forest Labor Contractor Handbook, 2005 Edition. Salem, OR: Bureau of Labor and Industries.

Bureau of Labor Statistics. 2005a. Census of Fatal Occupational Injuries, Table A-1. Fatal Occupational Injuries by Industry and Event or Exposure, All United States, 2003 http://stats.bls.gov/iif/oshwc/cfoi/cftb0177.pdf. (accessed January 21, 2005).

———b. Industry Injury and Illness Data, Table 1: Incidence Rates of Nonfatal Occupational Injuries and Illnesses by Industry and Case Types, 2003. http://www.bls.gov/iif/oshwc/osh/os/ostb1356.pdf (accessed January 21, 2005).

Casanova, V., and J. McDaniel. 2005. "No Sobra y No Falta": Recruitment Networks and Guest Workers in Southeastern U.S. Forest Industries. *Urban Forestry* 34(1): 45–84.

Clary, D.A. 1986. *Timber and the Forest Service.* Lawrence, KS: University of Kansas Press.

Danks, C., and L. Jungwirth. 1999. *Community-based Socioeconomic Assessment and Monitoring of Activities Related to National Forest Management.* Hayfork, CA: Watershed Research and Training Center.

DeForest, C.E. 1999. Watershed Restoration, Jobs-in-the-Woods and Community Assistance: Redwood National Park and the Northwest Forest Plan. General Technical Report PNW-GT2-449. Portland, OR: U.S. Department of Agriculture, Forest Service, Pacific Northwest Research Station.

Desmond, M.J. 1993. Testimony Before the Subcommittee on Information, Justice, Transportation, and Agriculture of the House Committee on Government Operations. Washington, DC: U.S. Government Printing Office.

———. 2004. Personal Communication, n.d. Eugene, Oregon.

Doeringer, P.B., and M.J. Piore. 1970. Equal Employment Opportunity in Boston. *Industrial Relations* 9(3): 324–339.

Donato, K.M., J. Durand, and D.S. Massey. 1992. Changing Conditions in the US Labor Market: Effects of the Immigration Reform and Control Act of 1986. *Population Research and Policy Review* 11(2): 93–115.

Durand, J., and D.S. Massey. 2003. The Costs of Contradiction: US Border Policy, 1986–2000. *Latino Studies* 1(2): 233–252.

Durand, J., D.S. Massey, and F. Charvet. 2000. The Changing Geography of Mexican Immigration to the US: 1910–1996. *Social Science Quarterly* 81(1): 1–15.

Ecosystem Workforce Program. 2003. Definition of a Quality Job. Ecosystem Workforce Program. http://www.uoregon.edu/%7Eewp/index.html (accessed July 1, 2003).

Findeis, J.L., and L. Jensen. 1998. Employment Opportunities in Rural America: Implications for Poverty in a Changing Policy Environment. *American Journal of Agricultural Economics* 80(5): 1000–1007.

Freudenburg, W.R., and R. Gramling. 1994. Natural Resources and Rural Poverty: A Closer Look. *Society and Natural Resources* 7: 5–22.

Gunn, C. 1984. *Workers' Self-Management in the United States.* Ithaca, NY: Cornell University Press.

Hallock, M. 1998. *Improving Jobs, Community, and the Environment: Lessons from the Ecosystem Workforce Project.* Eugene, OR: Labor Education Research Center, University of Oregon.

Hartzell, H.J. 1987. *Birth of a Cooperative: Hoedads, Inc., a Worker Owned Forest Labor Co-op.* Eugene, OR: Hulogos'i.

Hirt, P.W. 1994. *A Conspiracy of Optimism: Management of the National Forests Since World War Two.* Lincoln, NE: University of Nebraska Press.

Johnson, K. 2006. With Illegal Immigrants Fighting Wildfires, West Faces a Dilemma. *New York Times,* May 28, p. 1.

Kalleberg, A.L., B.F. Reskin, and K. Hudson. 2000. Bad Jobs in America: Standard and Nonstandard Employment Relationships and Job Quality in the United States. *American Sociological Review* 65(April): 256–278.

Korten, D.C. 1987. Third Generation NGO Strategies: A Key to People-centered Development. Word Development 15 (Supplement): 145-159.

Korten, D.C. 1990. Getting to the 21st Century: Voluntary Action and the Global Agenda. West Hartford, CT: Kumarian Press.

Knudson, T. 2005. The Pineros: Men of the Pines. *Sacramento Bee,* November 13–August 6, series. http://www.sacbee.com/content/news/projects/pineros/ (accessed October 30, 2007).

———. 2006. Untrained Migrants Fight Fires: Inexperienced, Undocumented Hired by Private Contractors. *Sacramento Bee,* May 7, http://www.sacbee.com/content/news/projects/pineros/ (accessed October 30, 2007).

Mackie, G. 1990. Rise and Fall of the Forest Workers' Cooperatives of the Pacific Northwest. M.S., Political Science, University of Oregon, Eugene, OR.

Mann, G. 2001. The State, Race, and 'Wage Slavery' in the Forest Sector of the Pacific Northwest United States. *Journal of Peasant Studies* 29(1): 61–88.

Massey, D.S., J. Durand, and N.J. Malone. 2002. *Beyond Smoke and Mirrors: Mexican Immigration in an Era of Economic Integration.* New York: Russell Sage Foundation.

McDaniel, J. 2006. Personal communication via email, February 10.

McDaniel, J., and V. Casanova. 2003. Pines in Lines: Tree Planting, H2B Guest Workers, and Rural Poverty in Alabama. *Southern Rural Sociology* 19(1): 73–96.

———. 2005. Forest Management and the H2B Guest Worker Program in the Southeastern United States: An Assessment of Contractors and Their Crews. *Journal of Forestry* 103(3): 114–119.

Moffett, S., C. Mater, C. Moseley, V.A. Sample, and S. Kavanaugh. 2005. *Assessing Community Benefits from Land Management Activities on National Forests.* Washington, DC: Pinchot Institute for Conservation.

Moseley, C. 2002. *A Survey of Innovative Contracting for Quality Jobs and Ecosystem Management.* General Technical Report PNW-GTR-552. Portland, OR: U.S. Department of Agriculture, Forest Services, Pacific Northwest Research Station.

———. 2006a. Ethnic Differences in Job Quality Among Contract Forest Workers on Six National Forests. *Policy Sciences* 39(2): 113–133.

———. 2006b. Procurement Contracting in the Affected Counties of the Northwest Forest Plan: Twelve Years of Change. General Technical Report PNW-GTR-661. Portland, OR: U.S. Department of Agriculture, Forest Services, Pacific Northwest Research Station.

———. in prep. Working Conditions of Latino Labor Intensive Forest Workers. Manuscript in development.

Moseley, C., and S. Shankle. 2001. Who Gets the Work? National Forest Contracting in the Pacific Northwest. *Journal of Forestry* 99(9): 32–37.

Moseley, C., and N. Toth. 2004. Fire Hazard Reduction and Economic Opportunity: How Are the Benefits of the National Fire Plan Distributed? *Society and Natural Resources* 17(8): 701–716.

Moseley, C., Y. Reyes, and B. Melton. 2006. *Job Quality among Forestry Services Workers and Loggers in Oregon.* Ecosystem Workforce Program Working Papers. Eugene, OR: Ecosystem Workforce Program, University of Oregon.

Moseley, C., M. Balaev, and A. Lake. 2003. Long Term Trends in Contracting and the Impact of the National Fire Plan in Northern California. Eugene, OR: Ecosystem Workforce Program, University of Oregon.

National Federation of Federal Employees. 2000. Open Letter to the Chief of the Forest Service: Local 457.

Office of Management and Budget, Department of Labor, Department of Defense, General Services Administration, Department of Energy, and Department of Commerce. 2004. Wage Determinations Online. http://www.wdol.gov/(accessed September 14, 2004).

Phillips, J. A., and D.S. Massey. 1999. The New Labor Market: Immigrants and Wages after IRCA. *Demography* 36(2): 233–246.

Pulaski, A. 2002. State Tightens Fire Crew Enforcement. *Oregonian*, September 22, p. A01.

———. 2003. Fire Crew Crackdown Proposed. *Oregonian*, January 29, p. B01.

Sarasohn, J. 2005. Bush '06 Budget Would Scrap or Reduce 154 Programs. *Washington Post*, February 22, p. A13.

Spencer, C. 1999. Linking Forest Employment and Forest Ecosystem Objectives in the Pacific Northwest. *Community Development Journal* 34(1): 47–57.

U.S. Census Bureau. 2005. Census 2000 Summary File 1 (SF 1) 100-Percent Data and1990 Summary Tape File 1 (STF 1) 100-Percent Data. http://factfinder.census.gov/servlet/DatasetMainPageServlet?_lang=en&_ts=126550852362&_ds_name=DEC_1990_STF1_&_program= (accessed February 15, 2005).

U.S. Congress. 1982. Department of the Interior and Related Agencies Appropriations for 1983—Part 10: Hearings Before a Subcommittee of the House Committee on Appropriations, 97th Congress, Second Session.

———. 1983. Department of the Interior and Related Agencies Appropriations for 1984—Part 11. Hearings Before a Subcommittee of the House Committee on Appropriations, House of Representatives, 98th Congress, First Session.

———. 1993. Allegations of Contract Abuse in the U.S. Forest Service Reforestation Program. Information, Justice, Transportation, and Agriculture Subcommittee of the House Committee on Government Operations, 103rd Congress. Washington, DC: U.S. Government Printing Office.

———. 2005. Race and Hispanic Origin: 1850 to 1990 Tables, for California (Table 19), Oregon (Table 52) and Washington (Table 62). U.S. Census Bureau. http://www .census.gov/population/www/documentation/twps0056.html (accessed February 16, 2005.

U.S. Department of Agriculture (USDA) Office of the Inspector General. 2006. Audit Report: Forest Service Firefighting Contract Crews. Washington, DC: U.S. Department of Agriculture, Office of Inspector General, Western Region.

U.S. Department of Labor. 2004. Register of the Wage Determinations Under the Service Contract Act, SCA No: 77-0079 Rev 30 Forestry and Land Management Services. Washington, DC: U.S. Department of Labor, Employment Standards Administration, Wage and Hour Division.

U.S. Fish and Wildlife Service. 2003. Jobs-in-the-Woods Program. http://pacific.fws.gov/ jobs/orojitw.overview.htm (accessed June 20, 2003).

U.S. Government Accounting Office. 2004. Biscuit Fire: Analysis of Fire Response, Resource Availability, and Personnel Certification Standards. Washington, DC: Government Accounting Office.

U.S. Senate. 2006. Energy and Natural Resources Subcommittee on Public Lands and Forests. No title. 109th Congress, Second Session. March 1.

Waggener, T.R. 1977. Community Stability As a Forest Management Objective. *Journal of Forestry* 75(3): 710–714.

Wells, M.J. 1996. *Strawberry Fields: Politics, Class, and Work in California Agriculture.* Ithaca, NY: Cornell University Press.

Wilson, L. 2000. Census 2000: A Summary of the Key Findings, Data, and Graphs. Hayfork, CA: Watershed Research and Training Center.

Wyant, D. 1988. Law Aids Forestry Workers. *Register Guard,* February 23, pp. 1C, 2C.

Part III
Communities and Forest Governance

10

Institutional Arrangements in Community-based Forestry

CECILIA DANKS

Part I of this book focused on social science considerations for understanding community and forest connections. Part II explored how forest management issues shape communities and communities in turn affect forest management. In Part III, this chapter and the three chapters that follow examine the ways that forest and community connections develop into unique forms of forest governance, each emphasizing the integration of community health with forest health.

Over the past decade, a number of action-oriented groups have sprung up in forest communities that are struggling with the decline of the traditional timber industry and the shifts in how forests are managed. These nonprofit groups, which are fairly new players in U.S. forestry, have played innovative roles in redefining the relationship between communities and forests. Dubbing their work "community-based forestry," they have sought both to build local capacity and to reorient the practice of forestry on public and private land to better meet the needs of human communities while promoting long-term ecosystem health. These grassroots efforts have made progress by working in partnership with government agencies, businesses, universities, private landowners, and other nonprofit organizations on local, regional, national, and even international scales. In doing so, they are creating a new, alternative set of institutional arrangements through which forest resources are managed and forest products are produced, processed, and marketed. The ability of community-based forestry to achieve its goals of healthy forests and healthy communities depends, in part, on the viability of these new institutions.

This chapter describes the organizations, relationships, and activities that make up the emerging institutional arrangements of community-based forestry. I discuss how they have evolved and the challenges they face. In doing so, I look to the literature on international community development for insights regarding

similar organizational issues. In conclusion, I discuss some challenges to growing and sustaining community-based forestry approaches, drawing on both the
literature and the observations of community-based forestry practitioners.

Defining Terms

Community-based forestry is an approach to achieving the dual goals of ecological health and socioeconomic well-being by incorporating local communities into sustainable forest management. Supporters of community-based
forestry have sought institutional arrangements that allow communities to
share in the decisionmaking and benefits associated with forest management,
while contributing expertise and labor (Danks and Fortmann 2004). There is
a great diversity of tenurial arrangements in the United States and around the
globe that can be considered community-based forestry, including small private ownerships (e.g., Bliss, Chapter 11 in this volume), communities that own
and manage their own forestland (e.g., Belsky, Chapter 12 in this volume), and
communities that collaborate in management of forestland owned by national
governments (e.g., Moote, Chapter 13 in this volume). What brings these efforts
under the umbrella of community-based forestry as described in this chapter
is the common desire to reorient forestry so as to achieve community development goals such as sustainable livelihoods, effective participatory institutions,
and a healthy environment.

   The term community-based forestry is used here to distinguish it from
urban tree planting and care programs that are commonly referred to throughout the United States as "urban forestry" but also sometimes as community
forestry. In many developing countries, however, for the past three decades
"community forestry" has referred to forest-based community development
that seeks to secure tenurial rights as well as livelihoods (c.f. Menzies 2007).
The breadth of the term is captured in the work of Dr. Wangari Maathai, winner of the 2004 Nobel Peace Prize for "her contribution to sustainable development, democracy and peace" by combining human rights and reforestation
in a single movement that would "secure and strengthen the very basis for ecologically sustainable development" (Nobel Prize 2004).

   Community forestry includes a broad range of initiatives, such as Nepali
Forest User groups (Acharya 2002) and the legalization of indigenous forest
rights in the Philippines (Contreras 2004). Since the mid-1990s in some former timber towns of the western United States, local groups of diverse stakeholders collaborating with agencies to sustain local livelihoods based on
public forest resources have called their work "community forestry" partly in
reference to developing-country models (Danks 1997). Increasingly, rural
community-based forestry practitioners in the United States use the term
community-based forestry to distinguish it from urban initiatives, although

they acknowledge the interconnected social and ecological goals that drive both urban and rural efforts.

The term community-based forestry is also a useful distinction from "community forestry," given that community forestry often implies ownership or some type of tenurial arrangement related to the forestland, and these types of arrangements are rare in the United States. In New England, town forests and landowner cooperatives might be considered types of community forestry, although they long precede the recent use of the term. Ownership is one characteristic that aligns this type of community-based forestry with the community forestry efforts occurring in some developing countries. As diverse as these contexts are, community-based forestry practitioners in many of these places share common goals and challenges (Danks 2002).

Forest communities, as discussed in this chapter, refer to small, rural, human communities that are linked culturally and economically to nearby forestlands. In the United States, forest communities differ tremendously in many respects. They range from commuter suburbs of urban areas to remote towns surrounded by national and industrial forests. They also include communities of forest workers who are economically and culturally tied to forests through seasonal work but may not reside immediately adjacent to them. Communities that are more isolated and more economically tied to forests are more likely to seek community-based forestry approaches. Much of the discussion here is influenced by the types of communities and community-based forestry efforts found amid the western public lands; however, some cases and insights are drawn from the eastern United States, where forests largely are privately owned.

The main activities and challenges in community-based forestry have not been silvicultural or even political (in the sense that often there is broad political support for such initiatives) but rather institutional. The term institution, as discussed here, includes groups, organizations, agencies, and partnerships, as well as laws, regulations, and established, rule-bound behavior such as economic markets and certain cultural or professional norms. Institutional arrangements refer not only to the array of institutions involved but also to the relationships among them through which community-based forestry is put into practice.

The term "sustainable forest management" can mean different things to different people. In this chapter, the term is used as shorthand to indicate a broad set of forestry activities—encompassing forest ecosystem management as well as the production, processing, and marketing of forest products—that seeks to sustain a diverse combination of ecological and social values. Such broad-ranging goals perhaps are best expressed in the Montreal Process criteria and indicators for sustainable forest management (Montreal Process Working Group 1995) and stand in contrast to commodity-based, timber-oriented forest management and industries.

The Emergence of Community-based Forestry

Until about 1990, forestry in the United States primarily was the domain of private industry and government, with limited involvement of the nonprofit sector. The timber industry was, and still is, the primary harvester, processor, and marketer for timber from all ownerships, as well as a principal landowner and manager. The federal government is a major landowner and manager and has played significant roles in research, regulation, and outreach. Small, private landowners have held the most forested acres in many regions of the United States, but their management has been influenced by the timber market and industry practices and by governmental regulations and technical assistance. Most states offer forestry extension services, many regulate timber harvests and offer tax incentives for private forestland, and some manage their own forests. A number of municipalities manage forestland, mostly in the Northeast. Fire-suppression capacity resides in a mix of government agencies and private contractors. Thus, forest management has truly been a joint public–private endeavor in the United States since the late 1800s. Although nonprofits have been present in past decades, they have had relatively small roles that focused largely on planting trees and promoting good forest management through groups such as American Forests, woodlot associations, and the American Tree Farm System.

Since the late 1980s, due to the reduced number of mature trees, increasing environmental regulations, and more lucrative options elsewhere, the timber industry has declined in some traditional strongholds in the West and the Northeast (while expanding production in the South). Timber companies have closed mills and put large tracts of land up for sale. Loggers moved or sold equipment. At the same time, timber harvests on federal lands dropped dramatically, especially in the Northwest, due to court injunctions in the early 1990s related to the spotted owl and other endangered species affected by timber harvests. The 1994 Northwest Forest Plan, which was developed in response to the injunctions, reduced timber harvests by more than 90% from the historic highs of the 1980s. In many places, the Forest Service downsized and consolidated administrative units, resulting in further loss of local jobs and the skilled personnel who worked at district offices. For towns that had unusual beauty or proximity to urban areas, economic alternatives to timber, including tourism, commuting, and second-home development, existed. However, for the more isolated forest communities that had depended heavily on timber extraction, these rapid changes left a gaping hole in their local economies and social fabrics. It contributed to finger-pointing and conflict among distressed community members who did not see a clear future. The self-help activities that community members excelled in—the spaghetti dinners, raffles, and work parties to help support kids' programs or families in crisis—could not lift their communities out of this socioeconomic crisis.

Community-based forestry arose in the early 1990s in several western forest communities as an effort to find a positive way forward that reduced conflict, promoted economic alternatives, and helped community members envision a future with positive options. The first steps often were led by local leaders, who convened key local players, including influential stakeholders representing timber, ranching, environmental, and local business interests, as well as agency personnel and Native American tribes. The participants in these new collaborative groups put their heads and resources together to identify and tackle problems related to resource management that were affecting communities. Participants hoped that such collaboration would yield widely agreed upon, win–win solutions that would break the gridlock in public forest management. Initially, these groups were fairly informal, and government resources often helped to support their limited infrastructure. Broad participation in deliberative forums like the Wallowa County/Nez Perce Tribe Salmon Recovery Plan in Oregon, the Flathead Forestry Project in Montana, and the Trinity Bioregion Group in California showed that diverse community members could agree on forest-management issues. Through these efforts, they developed a vision for sustaining their communities by working to steward forest ecosystems. However, implementation of agreed-upon projects was frustratingly slow. In order to promote implementation, some local civic leaders started nonprofit organizations that could handle the finances and had the paid staff needed to conduct training, secure funds, and carry out projects. Although these grassroots nonprofit organizations are significant innovators and catalysts in the forestry sector, they rarely work alone. Rather, just as forestry and community development has always involved a mix of actors from different sectors working at different scales, community-based forestry has been carried out by a diversity of organizations, usually acting in partnerships, as described below.

Typology of Institutions for Community-based Forestry

There are several different types of organizations working together to promote ecosystem health and community well-being through community-based forestry. Throughout this chapter, the first three categories of actors below are called "community-based forestry groups" and the other actors described below collectively are called "partners" or "participants." The institutional arrangements of community-based forestry involve all of these actors.

Community-based Forestry Groups

Among the newest players in U.S. forestry are the grassroots groups that sprang up in local communities that were experiencing some crisis related to forest management. These groups often sought to ease the economic and social transition from a timber-dependent economy to an uncertain future. Examples of these groups include the Flathead Forestry Project in Montana, the Watershed Research and Training Center in California, Wallowa Resources in Oregon, the Partnership for Public Lands in Colorado, and Framing Our Community in Idaho. Each started informally with local leaders who realized that the problems confronting their communities and forests required a collaborative approach. These groups became more formalized over time and several, but not all, have incorporated as nonprofit 501c(3) organizations with local boards and paid staff. Although these groups may not represent their communities in the sense that elected officials do, they generally seek to include diverse interests in their communities. Grassroots groups, with the help and participation of the other groups listed below, have pioneered community-based forestry in the United States. While rooted in their communities, these groups have taken on an impressive range of activities locally, regionally, and nationally in service of their missions to promote community well-being and environmental sustainability. They have sought to build a new local consensus around sustainable forest management while promoting local, forest-based businesses and pushing government agencies to adjust policies and practices to address local needs.

A number of regional organizations also have developed programs specifically to address community-based forestry concerns, especially regarding poverty, social well-being, economic opportunity, resource sustainability, and social justice. These include diverse groups like the Alliance of Forest Workers and Harvesters, based in California; Sustainable Northwest in Oregon; the Federation of Southern Cooperatives, based in Alabama; the New England Forestry Foundation, based in Massachusetts; Rural Action, based in Ohio; and the Forest Guild, based in New Mexico. Although these groups may have a number of local initiatives, their work often spans several states. A number of these regional groups have a long history of supporting community development or forestry in their regions; however, community-based forestry may be just one program area among several. Although these groups differ significantly from each other, they generally build local capacity for community-based forestry approaches by providing technical support and training for place-based projects, assisting in market development, conducting policy dialogues, and promoting formal and informal networking at the regional and national levels. They work with grassroots groups, as well as directly with local landowners, nontimber forest product harvesters, and wood product manufacturers on some initiatives. Some of these groups help bridge the urban–rural divide by connecting forest communities with urban-based markets, funding sources, policymakers, and technologies. Similarly, some groups focus on linking underserved populations to government programs, advocacy networks, and entrepreneurial opportunities.

There are several national organizations that work on community-based forestry issues. These include longstanding nonprofit organizations such as

American Forests, the National Forest Foundation, and the Pinchot Institute, as well as more recently established groups such as the Communities Committee of the Seventh American Forest Congress. The National Network of Forest Practitioners, one of the few national-level membership organizations in U.S. community-based forestry, promotes networking among its members, facilitates research and policy activities, and partners with other support organizations on capacity-building activities. These groups collaborate with each other and with grassroots and regional groups in efforts to bring the community voice to national-level dialogues and policy initiatives.

Partners, Participants, and Promoters

In addition to these three levels of nonprofit organizations that have taken the lead in envisioning and enacting community-based forestry, there are several other sets of actors that are major forces in supporting and participating in community-based forestry activities. These may be considered partner or participating organizations and individuals. The institutional arrangements of community-based forestry are comprised of the relationships between and among all of these groups—the community-based forestry organizations above and their partners below.

Private for-profit businesses and private landowners are active and essential participants in most community-based forestry efforts. The expressed goal of many community-based forestry activities—such as job training programs, technical assistance, product research and development, marketing initiatives, business incubators, and cost-sharing programs—is to promote the viability of these private-sector actors, who in turn contribute to community well-being.

Government agencies, especially the Forest Service and the Bureau of Land Management, have served multiple roles at multiple levels in community-based forestry activities in the United States. As major players in land management and local economic well-being, these agencies have served critical roles as collaborators, project partners, funders, and implementers. They have both contributed to and benefited from capacity-building efforts. Individual innovators and risk-takers within the agencies have been instrumental in helping community-based forestry activities to grow. Likewise, the nongovernmental funders of community-based forestry at all levels have not only supported the vision of community-based forestry groups but helped them to develop it. Through both personal contacts and strategic investments in networking, exchange visits, demonstration projects, and research, several funders, most notably the Ford Foundation, have proven to be partners in capacity building for community-based forestry in ways that go beyond the sums granted.

In the United States, the field of natural resource management has a number of types of quasi-governmental collaborative groups that work at the multi-community or county level. These include Resource Conservation Districts,

Resource Conservation and Development councils, Coordinated Resource Management Program groups, and most recently Regional Advisory Committees (created in 2000 by P.L. 106–393). These groups tend to be made up of local representatives of diverse interests. Some take on the governance task of reaching agreement about how to allocate resources, while others focus on implementing projects that help forests and forest communities. Although they may not identify themselves as doing community-based forestry, they may be contributors or key partners when their resource management work is infused with community development goals. In the field of community development, regional economic development corporations and councils and job training groups also frequently become partners in community-based forestry efforts.

Universities and other nonprofit and government research organizations have conducted, promoted, or funded action-oriented research that has built capacity for community-based forestry by providing valuable information for community-based forestry efforts. University-based efforts include the Community Forestry Research Fellowship Program, which funds graduate students to do participatory research with community partners; individual researchers who have provided expertise in fields such as GIS and monitoring; and organized visits of scholars and practitioners from other countries. There also are nonprofit research organizations active in community-based forestry, including the Sierra Institute for Community and Environment in California, the Institute for Cultural Ecology in Oregon, and the former USDA-funded National Community Forestry Center, which had four research centers across the United States. The research branch of the Forest Service, including the Pacific Southwest and Pacific Northwest Research Stations and the Forest Products Laboratory, also has conducted and funded projects on topics central to community-based forestry efforts. In many cases, the research efforts of these organizations were done in collaboration with grassroots, regional, and national community-based forestry groups. In addition, traditional educational institutions, such as local schools, community colleges, and universities, have been active partners in developing and delivering youth activities, college courses, job retraining, and internship opportunities.

What Community-based Forestry Groups Address: Governance, Implementation, and Capacity Building

Community-based forestry groups have sought to provide a greater community role in two areas of resource management—governance and implementation—to promote forestry activities that are both ecologically sustainable and beneficial to local communities. Aspects of governance addressed in community-based forestry include participatory decisionmaking, ensuring equity, gaining consensus on objectives, incorporating local and indigenous knowledge, resolving conflict, influencing policy and practice, and managing interorganizational relationships. Involvement in "governance" does not imply taking on the role of "government." Nor does improved governance imply "local control," as advocates of U.S. community-based forestry point out (Jungwirth 1997). It does, however, mean ensuring that diverse community voices are heard in fair and transparent processes. Some governance activities overlap with implementation. For example, groups may implement a monitoring program examining the ecological or social effects of a fuels-reduction project to contribute to transparency and to provide information for better decisionmaking.

Implementation includes facilitating or carrying out activities that often are chosen through participatory decisionmaking. Implementation activities in community-based forestry can include project planning, data collection and analysis, research, training, mapping, gathering, contracting, treating vegetation, processing raw materials, marketing, monitoring, and securing the resources to make these things happen. Grassroots and regional nonprofit groups typically have become involved in implementation when the traditional practitioners of forest management—public agencies and private businesses—were unable to carry out activities due to lack of funding, perceived risks of innovation, lack of expertise, or differing priorities.

Community-based forestry groups also have sought to experiment with and model how implementation can be done in ways that better involve and benefit forest communities. Their adaptations to implementation include utilizing local expertise, providing on-the-job training, developing new markets for forest products, and introducing low-cost, eco-friendly technologies. The emphasis on facilitating implementation in ways that benefit communities distinguishes community-based forestry from other efforts at collaborative governance of natural resources.

To enhance the success of governance initiatives and program implementation, community-based forestry groups have engaged extensively in capacity building, the development of skills, knowledge, attitudes, institutional infrastructure, and resources to get things done. Groups in each type of community-based forestry organization and participating entity listed above have been both the beneficiaries and providers of capacity-building activities. Such activities typically include workshops and training programs. However, community-based forestry actors also generally infuse all activities, be it research, monitoring, policy education, tree planting, or brush control, with elements of capacity building. They do so in the context of project implementation by providing on-the-job-training, by incubating new businesses, by experimenting with new approaches to implementation, by giving field tours, and by recording, reflecting on, and sharing the innovative aspects of their work. Capacity building is viewed as essential to helping all actors, from community members to businesses to government officials, participate in a new set of institutional arrangements that enhance community well-being and ecosystem health.

Community-based Forestry Groups Working as Bridges, Catalysts, and Service Providers

As noted above, community-based forestry groups almost always work in partnership with other players to achieve their goals. The emphasis on partnerships is a reflection both of a commitment to inclusive collaboration that these groups share and a recognition that community-based forestry groups rarely control the forests, policies, and markets they seek to influence. Within these partnerships, they serve the often overlapping roles of bridges, catalysts, and service providers, as described below.

Bridging Sectors, Scales, and Interests

A distinctive role of community-based forestry groups has been to serve as bridges that connect potential partners in sets of institutional relationships that better address community concerns. In carrying out both governance and implementation activities, community-based forestry groups often function at the boundaries of or overlap between the public and private sectors. For example, in governance, community-based forestry groups often have been the conveners of collaborative groups that combine several different federal and state agencies, industry representatives, local businesses, and other community members of diverse perspectives. Regarding implementation, nonprofit community-based forestry groups have secured government funding to retrain private-sector workers to eventually bid on government forestry projects. They also have sought private foundation funding to carry out research related to government agency projects that would benefit private-sector businesses. Community-based forestry groups thus act as bridges that connect people and resources that are otherwise separated by institutional, ideological, jurisdictional, or sectoral boundaries or that fall in the gaps between them.

The importance of "bridging organizations" is noted in the sustainable development literature. For example, Brown (1991) argued that nongovernmental bridging groups were central to a multi-sectoral development approach that was likely to be more successful than strictly market-driven or government-led development activities. Bridging private and public sectors is important not only to reach community development goals but also resource management goals. U.S. forestland is owned and managed by a diverse mix of public and private entities. Sustainably managing forest ecosystems often involves working with multiple ownerships and regulations that include local, state, or federal governments, as well as industrial and nonindustrial private owners. Wallowa Resources's weed control program and the Watershed Research and Training Center's Post Mountain wildfire risk reduction project, both of which helped promote, coordinate, and implement vegetation treatment on adjacent public and private property, are examples of how community-based forestry groups have bridged ownership boundaries for community and environmental benefit.

Community-based forestry groups not only connect the public and private sectors but also function as bridges between different levels or scales within a sector. For example, there are several cases in which a grassroots community-based forestry group worked extensively with a local district ranger on a specific project and also sought resources and support from the forest supervisor or regional forester and even the Forest Service's Washington office and members of Congress. They have come to understand the different priorities and decisionmaking capacities of different levels of government. Much of their policy work seeks to align these levels so that government agencies can best serve forest communities. A good example of community-based forestry groups bridging scales within the public sector is the work to promote, pilot, and monitor stewardship contracts—a form of federal contracting for forest management services that seeks to achieve ecological objectives and community benefits (USDA Forest Service n.d.).

In the private sector, a community-based forestry group promoting marketing of forest products is likely to be the one connecting local producers and processors to each other and to regional buyers. An example of that kind of bridging activity is the Healthy Forest, Healthy Communities (HFHC) Partnership, a membership-based initiative of Sustainable Northwest established to help small wood-products companies market their sustainably produced goods. The HFHC Partnership has brought together nonprofit organizations, small manufacturers, and high-end urban markets through capacity-building workshops, brand development, product shows, and other activities. In Ohio, Rural Action established the Roots of Appalachia Growers Association, a nonprofit organization of medicinal herb growers that serves as a support network for growers, providing information about how to grow and market woodland medicinals and how to develop their operations into businesses. These cross-scale linkages are critical for the success of business ventures based in isolated, forest communities where access to capital, specialized expertise, and markets often is limited. Moreover, the relationships formed among peers involved in these programs have yielded information and collaborations that have enhanced the success of participants.

On private lands, market-based approaches such as Forest Stewardship Council certification have been an important element of several community-based forestry efforts. The development and promotion of forest certification is itself a case of cross-sector cooperation in which business and nonprofit organizations join under a nonprofit umbrella to promote sustainable forestry through the market rather than by government regulation. In theory, it can connect a single landowner with a global market in which consumers will pay extra—a green premium—to cover the costs of good forest management when they buy lumber, furniture, flooring, or paper. In practice, the costs of certification and difficulties in developing and accessing the certified market are barriers for some potential participants, especially small operations in relatively isolated areas. Some community-based forestry groups, such as the Vermont Family Forest Partnership, have served as a bridges by providing small landowners and community-based businesses with the resources or information they need to become certified and then by connecting producers with local institutional buyers, such as universities and museums.

The ability to bridge scales in the public and private sectors has relied in large part on the cross-scale connections and working relationships among community-based forestry groups at the local, regional and national levels. A good example of a program the crossed both sectors and geographic scales is the multi-party monitoring of congressionally authorized forest stewardship projects mentioned above (Pinchot Institute n.d.). In this program, the Washington Office of the Forest Service funded the Pinchot Institute, a national nonprofit organization, to work with local and regional multi-party teams to monitor local Forest Service projects involving for-profit contractors. It made good use of the knowledge and organizational skills at each level and was conducted in a way that shared learning and built capacity among all involved. Moreover, it was a multi-party effort, which means that representatives of different interests were all part of the monitoring effort at each level. Other good examples of bridging scales and interests are found in policy work. Efforts to educate policymakers about community-based forestry issues make good use of the relative strengths of local, regional, and national groups in bringing community issues into national policy debates. National groups that support community-based forestry like American Forests, the Pinchot Institute, and the National Network of Forest Practitioners have collaborated on "Week in Washington," an annual event that brings members of forest communities to Washington, DC to learn how to access their federal representatives and agency leaders. The regional group Sustainable Northwest also helped to organize Rural Voices for Conservation Coalition, which fostered collaboration among local, community-based groups to identify and communicate key policy issues affecting forest communities. Through efforts such as these, local forest workers have been able to testify to Senate and House committee hearings about concerns and stories that appeal to both Democrats and Republicans.

Catalyzing Change While Providing Services

In the international development literature, some authors distinguish between the roles of service provider and catalyst played by nongovernmental organizations in promoting community development (e.g., Carroll 1992; Korten 1987; Lewis 2001). They note that these roles can be played by the same organization but require somewhat different organizational orientation, abilities, and management. Service and social change roles can be reinforcing when both are conducted in ways that build capacity among participants (Carroll 1992). To reorient forestry to better address community needs and forest health, community-based forestry groups seek above all to change the existing system of forest management and utilization, which is no longer working, and perhaps never worked well, to serve community needs. As typically practiced in community-based forestry, services usually are provided as a way to catalyze change, and almost all efforts are infused with capacity building.

These groups act as catalysts by building capacity, advocating for policy change, leading demonstration projects, providing seed money and matching funds, conducting innovative research, and introducing new ideas and information. Their efforts to bridge diverse interests, geographic scales, and the public and private sectors also are catalytic in that they are intended to create new relationships that result in new ways of doing business for both the public and private sectors.

One major area in which grassroots community-based forestry groups play a catalytic role is in fostering for-profit activities for community benefit. The livelihoods and civic engagement associated with appropriately scaled, ecologically sustainable, community-oriented business contribute to their mission of promoting family and community well-being. Many groups, such as the Watershed Research and Training Center, Framing Our Community, Rural Action, and the Vermont Family Forest Partnership have promoted commercial opportunities involving underutilized timber sizes, grades, and species or nontimber forest products. Wallowa Resources even bought part ownership of a local sawmill in an attempt to keep it open and later started a new for-profit enterprise, Community Smallwood Solutions. These grassroots organizations have stepped in to raise capital, develop products, experiment with processing, and research markets where entrepreneurs and economic development specialists perceive too much risk. These groups do so because they care deeply about their local communities, not as a way to generate revenue. They are eager for these businesses to operate independent of the nonprofit group as soon as possible.

Community-based forestry groups also offer services that typically are provided by the government or the private sector. For example, several community-based groups, such as Wallowa Resources, the Watershed Research and Training Center, and Rural Action, have started their own natural resources-oriented summer camps and youth programs. Although a camp may seem like a routine activity rather than a catalyst for changing the local economy and forest management practices, it serves both functions. Youth programs and camps are central to the concerns that prompted the formation of these groups—the need to provide options for local families and to help them see a future at home. Youth programs are visible, positive forces in the community that help local people understand and support the work of community-based forestry organizations. Moreover, to help develop and deliver camp activities these organizations draw on local natural resource managers from a diversity of government agencies and the private sector with whom they work on other projects. In doing so, they build connections and understanding among agency personnel, local businesses, and community members. Thus the youth programs not only help kids see a positive future but also build social capital that spills over into other collaborations.

Even for fairly routine goods and services typically provided by government or for-profit entities (such as extension, business incubation, job training, project planning, data collection, information dissemination, and college courses) nongovernmental organizations, especially community-based ones, often are better able to deliver services in ways that help communities address community and forest goals. The literature suggests that this ability is due, in part, to the better "reach" that nongovernmental organizations may have compared to government agencies in addressing the needs of underserved populations, such as poor families, indigenous peoples, and ethnic minorities (Carroll 1992; Chambers 1987; Lewis 2001). Reach is the ability to connect with and deliver services to marginalized sectors of the population that may require extra effort to engage due to issues including trust, legal status, culture, language, and physical remoteness. Nongovernmental groups also offer innovation, both in service delivery mechanisms and in research into unmet needs, and they take risks that may exceed the comfort zones of bureaucracies or businesses. For example, in the Philippines a nongovernmental organization helped define and address the soil fertility issues of poor, upland farmers who were overlooked by government extension programs that provided more traditional assistance to wealthier farmers (Lewis 2001). In cross-sector partnerships, the strengths of nongovernmental groups can complement the strengths of governmental and business partners, which often include resources, authority, and technical expertise, resulting in synergies that can better provide community-level benefits than single-sector approaches (Evans 1996a, 1996b; Ostrom 1996).

Worker retraining programs and business incubators, started by groups like the Watershed Research and Training Center, the Rogue Institute of Ecology and Economy, and Framing Our Community, are good examples of community-based forestry groups functioning as service providers in order to extend the reach of government-sponsored development activities into forest communities. These groups sought out partners, raised matching funds, and developed their own capacity to conduct these activities from scratch to ensure that their communities were served. Without a local job training venue, local human capital actually could be depleted by government-sponsored retraining programs that require participants to travel to classes in a neighboring urban center to be trained for urban-based jobs. These local training programs are valuable as catalysts for change because they do not just turn out graduates but serve as opportunities for innovation. Retraining crews have tested new resource management approaches and technologies and contributed to government-sponsored research projects. And like the local camps, because they were place-based, conducted in partnership with local agencies, and had positive community effects, these training programs have built local capacity while strengthening nongovernmental organizations' relationships with the business community, economic development organizations, and land management agencies, which formed the foundation for potential future collaboration (Danks and Aldinger 1998).

Change and Challenges for Community-based Forestry

The work of community-based forestry organizations and their relationships with their partners have evolved over time in response to perceived needs. Some practitioners have likened their problem-solving work to peeling an onion: once one barrier is removed, they find yet another that constrains the ability of their communities to thrive through forest stewardship. As a result, the initial emphasis on the local governance work of developing collaborative consensus has shifted in two directions: toward regional and national governance issues and toward implementation of agreed upon projects in ways that help forest communities. Such shifts present institutional challenges as groups and their relationships change to address these needs.

Evolving Governance and Implementation Activities

In some places, new forms of local governance have become institutionalized in the form of multi-party decisionmaking councils, such as the Resource Advisory Committees established by the Secure Rural Schools and Community Self-Determination Act. As trust has grown, agreements have been reached, and local collaboration has become the norm, many community-based groups have turned their attention to policy issues that had once seemed beyond local reach, such as federal contracting practices and influencing the appropriations process. These efforts have stretched the volunteers and staff of grassroots groups and have been harder to fund than project implementation. Partnerships with regional- and national-level community-based forestry organizations have been critical for providing training opportunities, access to staff on key legislative committees, invitations to hearings, participatory forums for discussing policy needs, and field trips for congressional staff to visit the grassroots groups on site.

As grassroots groups moved from dialogue to implementation, many found that they needed to formalize their structure and membership. Local groups such as the Public Lands Partnership in Colorado, which began as an informal, common-ground-seeking grassroots forum, have moved from talking to implementing projects in order to realize the fruits of their discussions. In doing so, they have had to consider whether to formalize their nonprofit status in order to manage grants and contracts with government agencies and funders. Concerns about the potential trade-offs regarding inclusiveness, flexibility, funding, and accountability accompany the formalization of groups. Moreover, they must confront the issue of whether they primarily are a catalyst versus a service provider. They must answer the question of whether they are trying to promote change in the public sector that will help community-oriented businesses flourish or they are trying to fill a gap that neither government nor business is expected to fill?

Evolving Roles as Catalysts and Service Providers

Within the realm of implementation, the more catalytic activities offering training programs and demonstration projects have evolved into the more regular implementation of field projects via federal contracts. Examples of these contract services include community wildfire planning, ecological monitoring, and implementation of fuel-reduction projects. This expansion of government contracting with community-based, nonprofit organizations, which did not exist five or 10 years ago, reflects several changes, including the downsizing of federal capacity and recognition of the expertise and capacity now residing in the nonprofit sector. Some of that nonprofit expertise is due to the presence of individuals who formerly worked for business or government and chose to stay and work in their communities when sawmills closed or agencies offered them early retirement. Other factors include the new capacities needed in collaborative processes, community participation, and multi-party monitoring that agencies and the private sector did not offer. It also reflects the success of community-based forestry efforts: the voices of communities have been heard and land management agencies have made an effort to work with community-based groups as a way to support local communities.

Despite these potential advantages to the involvement of community-based forestry organizations in implementing projects and delivering services, there may be some trade-offs involved. For instance, if a need is met by a nonprofit organization, will government ever step up to the plate or will businesses be able to step in? Lewis states that "while there may be good short-term reasons for 'gap filling' in public provision, NGO service delivery should ultimately be judged on its developmental impact" (2001, 70). He and others (e.g., Poole 1994) suggest a "pragmatic approach" that "stresses a limited time frame scale and the ultimate goal of having the state (or the private sector) take over provision [of services] once new skills and approaches are acquired and resources mobilized" (Lewis 2001, 70). Korten (1990) also warns of the dangers to the nonprofit itself. He argues that the "public service contractor" role may deflect a nongovernmental organization from its mission, detracting from its creative and value-driven qualities and leading it to act more like a business that focuses first on organizational needs. On the other hand, Carroll (1992) found that service and social change roles can be complementary, rather than conflicting, when both seek to develop the abilities of and connections among participants that enable them to meet community needs over time.

Future Roles of Community-based Forestry Organizations

Although the roles of service provider and catalyst can be compatible, the differences between these strategies become important when considering the future of institutional arrangements through which community-based forestry goals are achieved. Will community-based forestry organizations catalyze the changes needed to create a new set of institutional arrangements among the public and for-profit sectors to benefit forest communities and sustain forests and then close their doors because they have accomplished their goals? Or will they become players in these new institutional relationships with lasting roles? Put another way, if community-based forestry groups are helping with the transition to a new kind of forestry and forest-based economy that addresses community needs, does their work end when the transition is complete or do they have an ongoing role in that new economy? This question has implications for "scaling up" community-based forestry to reach more communities on a more regular basis. If a few highly effective community-based forestry groups can catalyze systemic change, this could benefit all forest communities. If an effective, grassroots community-based forestry organization is needed in every community to help achieve community well-being and forest health, then considerable investment in capacity building is required across the board and some communities likely will be left out.

To date, field work suggests that grassroots community-based forestry organizations have remained agile, problem-solving organizations, even as they have taken on more routine services (Danks et al., forth coming). They have sought to provide innovative, yet grounded, approaches for addressing management practices as well as accessing markets. They are willing to spinoff stand-alone activities, such as camps, cooperatives, contractors, and sawmills, but have met with limited success in such efforts. Given the small size and remoteness of forest communities, which affect both market and political success, and given the mixture of public and private goods expected from sustainable forest management, a public–private partnership likely will be needed to achieve the diverse goals of community-based forestry. As noted in the beginning of this chapter, there has been a private–public partnership in U.S. forestry in the past, but it has not always benefited forest communities. Community-based forestry practitioners have expressed an ongoing need for the community perspective to be present and active in order to sustain both the ecological and human communities (Danks 2007; Rural Voices for Conservation Coalition 2005).

There are a number of challenges to a sustained role for community-based forestry organizations at all scales. Both funding and energy can decline after the initial onset of the crisis that typically precipitate community-based forestry in the United States. Groups have been adept at keeping current with evolving forest management priorities, such as a shift in emphasis from the Northwest Forest Plan to community wildfire planning. However, some of the noteworthy achievements of community-based forestry have been due to the extraordinary efforts of extraordinary individuals. Sustaining and routinizing that level of engagement in a small forest community—much less replicating it elsewhere—can be difficult. Working with and through networks and partnerships that allow groups to share the heavy lifting will remain critical to their work.

Growing partnerships among groups across scales and sectors also can be challenging. Diverse capacities are needed to engage the complex set of institutions involved in forest management and the forest-based industries on private and public lands. If community-based forestry groups have an ongoing role, current practitioners suggest that it will be one in which they serve as bridges for ideas, actions, policies, and relationships that can catalyze new approaches. They feel that there still is much to learn about the sustainable management of forest resources and that communities can play a vital role. It is their hope that the ongoing provision of routine goods and services will be conducted by businesses and government agencies (Danks 2007; Danks et al. forthcoming).

Current political discourse in the United States suggests that community groups and the private sector should take on much of the resource management and conservation activities historically undertaken by government on public lands (e.g., the Cooperative Conservation initiative of the Bush administration at http://cooperativeconservation.gov/). However, it would be unrealistic to assume that community-based forestry organizations could take over the roles of either for-profit businesses or government and that is expressly not their intent. International development literature stresses the need for nonprofit groups to reorient government rather than replace it. For community-based forestry groups to be effective, they need to engage in "active partnerships" (Lewis 2001) in which ongoing negotiation, debate, and adaptation characterize the relationship among partners, rather than rigid roles and prescribed actions. Such a partnership requires a healthy public sector in which time is allocated to partnerships and incentives reward agency personnel for innovation and collaborative work.

Interviews and situation-mapping exercises with the staff, boards, and partners of several grassroots and regional community-based forestry groups in 2005 suggest that these groups are aware of these challenges and yet remain optimistic (Danks 2007). They cite the regional and national networks that are linking community-based forestry efforts across scales. They have noticed a small but vibrant number of young workers and professionals who can see their future in community-based stewardship of forest lands. They can claim a number of legislative successes in Congress and more community-oriented practices and programs within the land management agencies. Their agency partners express a growing interest in collaboration and many are grateful for the role that these groups have played in helping agencies meet their management goals. Business incubation efforts can claim real, though modest, successes in fledging new, forest-based businesses. And the forest products of these communities are making it into local, regional, and national markets. Although many forest communities still are struggling economically and socially, community-based forestry is creating new models, and with them, new hope for the future.

Although community-based groups have proven to be able catalysts, it must be recognized that successes to date have not been achieved by local groups working alone but through active partnerships that bridge scales and sectors. The ability of community-based forestry to foster strong, resilient forests and communities depends on the health and commitment of all partners—be they local or national, public or private, for-profit or nonprofit.

References

Acharya, K.P. 2002. Twenty-four Years of Community Forestry in Nepal. *International Forestry Review* 4(2): 149–156.

Brown, D.L. 1991. Bridging Organizations in Sustainable Development. *Human Relations* 44(8): 807–831.

Carroll, T. 1992. *Intermediary NGOs: The Supporting Link in Grassroots Development.* West Hartford, CT: Kumarian Press.

Chambers, Robert. 1987. *Sustainable Rural Livelihoods: A Strategy for People, Environment and Development.* Commissioned study; no. 7, Institute of Development Studies. Brighton, England.

Contreras, A. 2004. Creating Space for Local Forest Management: The Case of the Philippines. In *Local Forest Management: The Impacts of Devolution Policies,* edited by D. Edmunds and E. Wollenberg. London: Earthscan, 127–149.

Danks, C. 1997. Developing Institutions for Community Forestry in Northern California. *Rural Development Forestry Network* 20a (Winter): 4–23.

———. 2002. International Experiences: Learning from Innovations in Community Forestry. Planting Seeds. Washington, DC: Aspen Institute.

———. 2007. Picturing the Future: Situation-Mapping as a Participatory Research Tool. A paper presented at the 13th International Symposium on Society and Resource Management, June 17–21, Park City, UT.

Danks, C., and S. Aldinger. 1998. *Review of the Ecosystem Management Technician Training Program, 1994–1997.* An unpublished report to the Trinity County Office of Occupational Training.

Danks, C., and L. Fortmann. 2004. Social Forestry: Forest and Tree Tenure and Ownership. In *Encyclopedia of Forest Sciences,* edited by J. Burley, J. Evans, and J. A. Youngquist. Oxford: Elsevier Ltd., 1157–1162.

Danks, C., S. Broussard, and A. Cheng. Forthcoming. Community-based Forestry Organizations as social entrepreneurs. A manuscript prepared for the Ford Foundation.

Evans, P. 1996a. Introduction: Development Strategies Across the Public-private Divide. *World Development* 24(6): 1033–1037.

———. 1996b. Government Action, Social Capital and Development: Reviewing the Evidence on Synergy. *World Development* 24(6): 1119–1132.

Jungwirth, E. L. 1997. Testimony as Chair of the Communities Committee at the Senate Learning Session on Community Based Forestry, May 22, convened by the Senate Committee on Energy and Natural Resources Subcommittee on Forests and Public Land Management.

———. 2000. Who Will be the Gardeners of Eden? Some Questions about the Fabulous New West. In *Across the Great Divide: Explorations in Collaborative Conservation and the American West*, edited by P. Brick, D. Snow, and S. Van de Wetering. Washington, DC: Island Press, 58–63.

Lewis, David. 2001. The Management of Non-governmental Development Organization: An Introduction. London and New York: Routledge.

Menzies, N. 2007. *Our Forest, Your Ecosystem, Their Timber: Communities, Conservation, and the State in Community-based Forest Management.* New York: Columbia University Press.

Montreal Process Working Group. 1995. Criteria and Indicators for the Conservation and Sustainable Management of Temperate and Boreal Forests. http://www.mpci .org/rep-pub/1995/santiago_e.html (accessed June 27, 2006).

Nobel Prize. 2004. Press Release: Winner of the 2004 Nobel Peace Prize. www.nobel-prize.org (accessed December 28, 2004).

Ostrom, E. 1996. Crossing the Great Divide: Coproduction, Synergy, and Development. *World Development* 24(6): 1073–1087.

Pinchot Institute for Conservation. n.d. Stewardship Contracting on Federal Forest Lands. http://www.pinchot.org/what_we_do/sustainable/contracting (accessed August 28, 2006).

Poole, Nigel. 1994. "The NGO Sector as an Alternative Delivery System Agricultural Public Services". Development in Practice 4(2): 100-111

Rural Voices for Conservation Coalition. 2005. RVCC Mission. http://www.sustain-ablenorthwest.org/programs/rvcc.php (accessed November 16, 2007).

U.S. Department of Agriculture (USDA)Forest Service. n.d. Stewardship Contracting: Collaboration. http://www.fs.fed.us/forestmanagement/projects/stewardship/collaboration/index.shtml (accessed September 8, 2006).

11

Family Forest Owners

JOHN C. BLISS

Families own more than four in 10 forested acres in the United States and dominate the rural landscape east of the Mississippi River. Comprising the largest forest ownership category in the country, family forest owners grow the wood that feeds most local mills and employs most forest workers; they are the social and economic backbones of many rural communities. Family forests bring diversity to rural and urban fringe landscapes, supplying environmental values and services. Family forest owners provide many of the benefits desired of community-based forestry, including local knowledge, values, and decision-making; human-scale management applications; and multiple, creative alternatives to modern industrial forestry practices. For all these reasons, family forest owners are central players in community-based forestry in the United States.

This chapter presents a brief primer on family forest owners and explores their current and prospective roles in enhancing the communities they surround. First, I make the case that family forestlands and their owners are indispensable contributors to the ecological, economic, and social well-being of the landscapes in which they occur. Second, I outline a variety of challenges, from local to global, that put these ownerships, and the contributions they make, at risk. I conclude with observations on the similarities and differences between community-based forestry and family forestry and suggest ways for developing greater synergy between family forest owners, their neighbors, and the communities in their neighborhoods.

Definition and Extent of Family Forests

For the first time in its history, the 2004 Forest Service National Woodland Owner Survey classified family forests as a separate ownership category (Butler and Leatherberry 2004). It defines family forests as lands that are at least one acre in size, 10% stocked, and owned by individuals, married couples, family estates and trusts, or other groups of individuals who are not incorporated or otherwise associated as a legal entity. The survey determined that family forest owners comprise the dominant forest ownership group in the country, holding four of every 10 forested acres (Butler and Leatherberry 2004). An estimated 10.3 million family forest owners control 262 million acres, or 42%, of the nation's forestland. Nearly nine out of 10 family forest ownerships (88%) are in the East, where they dominate most forested landscapes. The remaining 12% are in the West, where they frequently occupy ecologically and culturally significant lower elevation sites and riparian corridors (Mac-Cleery 1993).

Until the mid-1990s, forests owned by private individuals and families who do not own or operate wood-processing facilities were categorized as "nonindustrial private" forests. The negative nomenclature was intentional: from the forestry profession's perspective, these forests were viewed as neglected, mismanaged, or, at best, managed by millions of untrained, irrational owners following wildly diverse objectives. They decidedly were not industrial forests. Generations of foresters (the author of this chapter included) accordingly were trained to chip away at "the small woodland problem," as this failure to emulate industrial forestry on family forests came to be known. With the industrial model of efficiency and orderly plantation management as the standard against which family forests were compared, the diversity of conditions found on family forests were viewed as a problem rather than a source of ecological value or economic resilience.

More recently, the term "family forest" increasingly is being used to highlight the distinctive characteristics of ownerships for which personal and family values are strong management motivators and to increase awareness of the unique contributions these lands make to society. In the political arena, where monikers matter, family forests, and the objectives, values, and challenges of their owners, often are sharply contrasted with those of public and industrial forests.

Forestry and Identity

For many family forest owners, the family forestland is a visceral component of individual and family identity. When asked, "Who are you?" many respond, "I am a forest owner." Forest ownership, in this context, is more akin to religious or ethnic identification than to ownership of automobiles, homes, or other consumer goods. The archetypical family forest owner embodies strong ties to the land, familiarity with the seasons, a long-time perspective, a strong work ethic, and a commitment to stewarding the resources in one's care for future generations. She also has a strong tendency toward independent thinking, an equally strong distrust of government, and a disinclination to get involved in the affairs of her neighbors. Although such an archetype is, of course, a gross generalization, and although few individuals actually might be accurately described by it, it does suggest themes that resonate with many owners.

Most importantly, family forest owners commonly profess to have a strong, personal relationship with a particular "piece of ground." In some cases, this relationship has been forged over several generations. Many family forests contain the graves or memorials of deceased family members. More often, family forest owners aspire unsuccessfully to develop multi-generational ties to a forest property. Nonetheless, they often cultivate within themselves a strong sense of "rootedness" to forestland they might have owned only a few years.

Owners who reside on their forestland or rely significantly upon it for their livelihoods develop especially strong relationships to their forests. These owners' material well-being is affected directly by changing forest conditions, timber markets, regulatory requirements, and other external factors affecting production of income from the forest. An ice storm might destroy one's investment in reforestation or necessitate harvest of trees intended to stand another decade, perhaps to be turned to cash when a child reaches college age. And trees held as a retirement account might not bring the anticipated return if markets turn soft. Such shared experiences, risks, and values create among family forest owners an occupational community of sorts.

These direct, material links between family forest owners and their forestlands distinguish family forest owners from stakeholders in other forest tenures. They tend to make family forest owners cautious and conservative. They make many suspicious of any program, regulation, or scheme that might add more uncertainty to an already uncertain future. And they lead family forest owners to direct their attention, time, and energy to their own properties and expect others to do the same. A small proportion of the nation's family forest owners belong to forest owner associations, such as the National Woodland Owners Association or its state affiliates. Forest owner cooperatives have sprung up from time to time across the country, but very few, if any, have had much lasting success. Although landscape-scale, cross-boundary cooperation, and landowner cooperatives currently are receiving much attention from academics, conservationists, and environmental activists, actual examples of long-term collaboration involving family forest owners in mixed-ownership landscapes are relatively few and far between (Knight and Landres 1998; Rickenbach et al. 2004; Wondolleck and Yaffee 2000).

Significance of Family Forests

The significance of family forests includes their economic contribution, ecological diversity, and social vitality.

Economic Contribution

Historically, family forests have been valued principally for their contribution to the nation's wood supply. Historically, nonindustrial, private forestlands (of which family forestlands are the largest part) have produced well over half of the nation's annual timber harvest (Powell et al. 1993); in 2001, they accounted for 63% of the nation's timber harvest (Smith et al. 2004). As timber harvesting has been curtailed on federal lands, forest-products companies have had to look to their own lands and the lands of other private owners to find wood for their mills. Between 1986 and 2001, timber harvest on nonindustrial, private forestlands increased by some 46%, in part in response to the shift in harvesting from the Pacific Northwest, where public forests dominate, to the South, where private forests are concentrated (Smith et al. 2004).

Family forestlands may provide some balance to the unpredictable, sudden swings currently being experienced by large corporate forestry players. The forest industry once was seen as a steady and dependable owner of forestland. Family forest owners, by contrast, were viewed by many in the forestry profession as fickle, subject to the vagaries of the marketplace, and unreliable as long-term stewards. Today, however, mounting global competitive pressures are forcing large forest-products companies to merge and take over other companies or be taken over. This is fueling unprecedented debt loads, with predictable consequences, including ever-shorter rotations, liquidation of standing timber assets, and conversion of timberland to real estate development, where such markets exist. In 2002, Plum Creek, which is among the nation's largest holders of private timberland, announced plans to "develop" 3.2 million ha of its land throughout the United States, including 162,000 ha for urban-fringe development (Forestry Source 2002b). Clearly, industrial timberland no longer can be considered forest in perpetuity, which makes family forests even more important.

Ecological Diversity

The ecological importance of family forests is profound. The forests of the East coast, Midwest, and South all are dominated by private ownership, and especially family forests (Table 11-1). Although public ownership is the dominant forest tenure in the West, the location of family forests in this region gives them an importance beyond the proportion of land area they occupy. As a result of early settlement patterns, family forests in the West are prevalent at lower elevations and dominate riparian corridors. These ecologically significant lands host important habitat for northern spotted owls, marbled murrelets, and the salmon for which the Pacific Northwest is famous.

An examination of the relationship between forest ownership patterns and patterns of forest habitat diversity in the Coast Range (Stanfield et al. 2002) confirmed that the spatial arrangement of public, industrial, and family forestlands has a large effect on the forest diversity present in any given watershed. Moreover, each ownership type contributes a different mix of forest conditions to the landscape. Family ownerships, for example, provide a mixture of young-to-medium age conifer stands, extensive hardwood stands, and a high proportion of nonforest land (often abandoned farmland). Notably missing

Table 11-1. Forestland Ownership in the United States, 2002

| Region | *Thousand acres (%)* | | | | |
	All ownerships	*Total public*	*Total private*	*Forest industry*	*Nonindustrial private*[1]
North	169,685	41,368 (24)	128,317 (76)	14,827 (9)	113,489 (69)
South	214,603	25,758 (12)	188,845 (88)	35,916 (17)	152,929 (71)
Rocky Mountain	144,344	106,134 (74)	38,209 (26)	2,926 (2)	35,283 (24)
Pacific Coast	220,291	145,901 (66)	74,390 (34)	12,711 (6)	61,679 (28)
United States	**748,922 (100)**	**319,161 (43)**	**429,761 (57)**	**66,380 (9)**	**363,381 (49)**

[1] Includes family forestlands and other private ownerships whose owners do not operate wood processing facilities.

Note: Data may not add to totals because of rounding.

Source: Smith et al. 2004.

from these ownerships are stands of large, old trees, which generally are harvested and marketed before reaching biological maturity. For old growth, one must look to the public forests in the region.

Throughout the nation, family ownerships dominate forestland at the fringes of many metropolitan areas, where the ecological services, open space, and aesthetic beauty they provide add immeasurably to urban dwellers' quality of life.

A history of human habitation and use, combined with the wide range of ownership objectives, capabilities, and constraints of family forest owners, is responsible for the diverse ecological outcomes observed on family ownerships. To be sure, not all such outcomes are equally desirable from an ecological point of view; suboptimal species composition, invasive species, and poor management practices characterize some family forest ownerships. Yet the small scale of most family ownerships may have a limiting effect on the extent of abusive mismanagement, especially in states where forest practices acts are in place and enforced. Relatively few family forest owners report following a written management plan (an estimated 3% of the owners) or seeking professional management advice (16%); however, those who do tend to own relatively large acreages (Butler and Leatherberry 2004).

Social Vitality

The unique economic and ecological values that family forests bring to the landscape derive from the human characteristics of family forest owners. The diversity of human aspirations, capabilities, values, and knowledge drives the diversity in forest conditions observed among family forestlands. Family forest owners bring a human scale to the landscape, integrating elements of wildness and cultivation, protection and production into management of their properties. They provide a link to the past by preserving special places, buildings, and even individual trees that have some special historical or family significance (Bliss 1992; Bliss and Martin 1989).

Family forest owners also are members of rural communities, contributing to rural vitality at a time when many rural areas are undergoing out-migration and decline. About 40% of all private forest owners reside on their forestland (Birch 1996). Many are active members of rural communities; they have children in public schools, serve on school boards, participate in local churches, run local businesses, and serve on chambers of commerce.

Family forest owners help maintain a connection between society and the resources on which it depends—a connection most in society have lost sight of. A large and growing percentage of family forest owners are suburbanites themselves. Many have one foot firmly planted in the culture of forest management and the other in the mainstream suburban culture. Survey research indicates that they share the same core environmental values as the general American public (Bliss et al. 1997). These family forest owners could play a major role in raising public consciousness regarding forestry.

Challenges to Sustaining Family Forests

There are several challenges facing family forests in terms of sustainability, including changing forestland tenure patterns, changing markets, and changing social values.

Changing Forestland Tenure Patterns

At the fringes of urban centers across America, family forests are being subdivided to serve their "highest and best use" as residential mini-nature preserves for the wealthy, subdivisions for the middle class, retirement destinations for the aging, and shopping malls for everyone. In the Southeast, uncontrolled suburban sprawl is converting thousands of hectares of productive forestland into concentric circles of shopping malls, townhouses, faux antebellum mansions, and congested commuter beltways surrounding every metropolitan area. The Forest Service estimated that almost 4.9 million ha of forestland in the southeastern United States were lost to urban development between 1982 and 1997 (Forestry Source 2002a). Forest Service researchers anticipate the region could lose an additional 7.7 million ha by 2040, most of it nonindustrial, private, particularly family, forestland.

In the Pacific Northwest, the temperate rainforests that drew so many to Seattle now are being felled to accommodate the burgeoning population. Even in Oregon, the state that leads the nation in land use planning and zoning, as much as one-third of the family forestland in the Coast Range could surrender to urban growth over the next 50 years, despite laws enacted to prevent such a loss (Johnson 2002). The consequences of this parcelization are many and familiar: forest fragmentation and the resultant habitat destruction; loss in management options and the concomitant decline in timber productivity; conversion of forest to non-forest land uses, and increased social conflict as rural and urban lifestyles collide (Egan and Luloff 2000; Sampson and DeCoster 2000).

In the major timber-growing regions of the country, family forests are being gobbled up by multinational mega-corporations to serve more efficiently the insatiable appetites of consumers and investors around the globe. Family forests make attractive additions to adjacent corporate timberlands, especially where they can be converted profitably to intensively managed tree farms. Over the past decade in western Oregon alone, about 8,000 ha have moved out of non-industrial, private (mostly family) forestland ownership every year, and most have moved into corporate ownership (Zheng and Alig 1999).

But the largest industrial forestry players also are undergoing significant change in forestland ownership. In pursuit of ever-higher returns to shareholders, many companies have spun off their timberland holdings in order to concentrate on their core wood-processing businesses. Timber Investment Management Organizations (TIMOs) and Real Estate Investment Trusts (REITs), which acquire and manage timberlands for investors, now constitute the fastest-growing forestland tenures in America. The Pinchot Institute predicts that 5–6 million ha of timberland will move out of industrial ownership by 2010, with much of it moving into TIMO ownership (Block and Sample 2001). As TIMOs consolidate their land-base, they too seek to acquire adjacent family forestlands. There may be some counter-balance to this trend, as TIMOs and REITs sell-off marginal or isolated properties to families, individuals, and other nonindustrial owners.

Changing Markets

These developments not only result in a direct loss of family forestland but also make it increasingly difficult for the remaining family forests to compete and survive. Gone are the days when farmers sold timber to the neighborhood sawmill to be processed into lumber for local consumption. The local mill, if it still exists, is a small part of a conglomerate that has owners in far-off places who answer to distant shareholders. The family forest owner is in direct competition with corporate owners that dominate the marketplace, determining which products are in demand and at what price. In the Pacific Northwest, the forest industry's shift to growing shorter rotation, smaller diameter Douglas-fir

(*Pseudotsuga menziesii*) significantly has reduced the market for large, high-quality logs. Mills capable of processing large logs now are scarce. Family forest owners who have for decades nurtured stands of older, large Douglas-fir now find themselves searching for markets in which to sell. These market realities likely will force many owners to abandon their current management strategies and adopt the industry's short-rotation plantation model.

Changing Social Values

When the United States was in its infancy, most citizens lived on farms, grew much of their own food, and burned firewood from their own woodlots to heat their homes. Society looked to rural America primarily as a source of food and fiber to feed, clothe, and house the nation. Today, some citizens still can recall visiting the farm of a grandparent or cutting firewood in the old family forest, but the number of Americans with such memories is dwindling. As the 2000 U.S. Census (U.S. Census Bureau 2000) indicates, America is now a suburban nation, with a majority of its population, and most of its political power, in the suburbs. Most Americans are not even rural–urban migrants—they have no personal memory of America's rural past and little personal relationship with land resources. One result is that few citizens make the conceptual connection between the wood houses they live in, the paper that fills their mailbox, and the forests from which those products come. Many, and perhaps most, Americans are unaware that family forests even exist. If they ever think of forests, they likely picture the "untouched" wilderness of national parks or the clearcut plantations of industrial forests. Being unaware of family forests, they cannot be expected to understand the valuable contributions that these lands make to society, let alone the challenges involved in sustaining them. This lack of awareness is symptomatic of the weak social contract between society and forest owners, or, to put it another way, between those who consume and those who produce the nation's forest products, amenities, and values. This weak social contract presents a challenge as daunting to the sustainability of family forestlands as the formidable challenges of competing in the global economy.

Family Forests and Community-based Forestry

Arguably, family forests provide many, if not all, of the social benefits aspired to through community-based forestry (Danks, Chapter 10 in this volume) and face many of the same challenges. If the essence of community-based forestry consists of: a) local involvement; b) local benefits; c) management reflecting the values and objectives of local people; and d) a broader range of values in the management mix than is found in industrial or government ownership, then one might conclude that family forestry provides much of the essence of community-based forestry. Ownership of forests is the obvious similarity between family forest owners and community groups involved in community forestry projects (Belsky, Chapter 12 in this volume). To the extent that family forest owners can be considered a "community" of forest users, they share many of the goals and values exhibited in community forestry and community-based forestry efforts.

Most family forest owners are local, living on or near their forestland. They have kids in the local school and parents in the local retirement facility. They buy their groceries, work boots, and fence posts from local stores. Local foresters, surveyors, and environmental consultants assist in managing their properties. Local loggers harvest their timber for local mills to process. In general, family forest owners do not outsource their management planning either. Very few manage according to a written plan—a source of great frustration and concern for generations of college-trained foresters. The lack of a written management plan, however, is not necessarily evidence of a lack of owner intention. Their forest management—for good or bad—reflects personal knowledge and values as much as it reflects financial need or greed. Application of this knowledge and these values through management may be inconsistent across the landscape, but the intention to be good stewards is ubiquitous among family forest owners and is a primary driver of such management.

The diversity of family forest owner objectives, values, and capabilities implies a similarly diverse set of outcomes on the land. Indeed, despite the best efforts of generations of professional foresters to convince family owners to mimic industrial forestry practices, the multi-species, multi-age, small-scale conditions that typify family forestlands contrast starkly with the intensively managed, even-aged, single-species plantations of neighboring industrial and corporate lands.

Although family forests dominate the landscape surrounding many communities, their current and potential contributions to community well-being have received relatively little attention. Yet, as community residents, watershed landowners, stakeholders in public forests, shareholders in corporate forests, voters, and consumers, family forest owners would seem to hold potential as key players in community-based forestry. They potentially bring not only their land-base and all the functions and values associated with it, but also a tremendous store of human capital, passion, experience, and knowledge. As a demographic group, they tend to have more formal education and be older than the general population, suggesting that their stores of human capital are indeed high (U.S. Census Bureau 2000).

However, available evidence suggests that family forest owners are less involved in cross-boundary, collaborative forestry activities than would be predicted based upon land ownership patterns (Rickenbach et al. 2004). Regional and national surveys of private forest owners generally have found that although these owners share many values regarding forest health, ecosystem processes, and conservation of special habitats, they are wary of participating in large-scale, collaborative processes (Brunson et al. 1996). Many family forest owners are cautious about becoming involved in managing resources beyond their ownership boundaries, and some are downright resistant to the idea (Bergmann and Bliss 2004; Fischer and Bliss 2006). Many own forestland, in part, because of the sense of autonomy and independence they derive from making and implementing their own management decisions (Bliss and Martin 1989). Fear of losing autonomy, distrust of government, weak rural social networks, and a lack of perceived incentives to cooperate with others may explain the relatively low levels of cross-boundary cooperation observed among family forest owners around the country (Bergmann and Bliss 2004; Edwards and Bliss 2003; Fischer and Bliss 2006).

In recent research on family forest owners in western Oregon, owners were found to value and be generally knowledgeable of the biodiversity present on their properties; they were less familiar with the landscape context within which their properties occur and not inclined to discuss it (Fischer 2004). Although most sought advice and assistance on managing their own forest resources, few took advantage of opportunities to collaborate with neighboring landowners in watershed councils or forest owner organizations. Bergmann and Bliss (2004) found ranchers in eastern Oregon as reticent to cooperate on fire and fuel management with neighboring ranchers as they were with the Forest Service. Lack of trust, risk aversion, regulatory insecurity, and the short tenure of Forest Service personnel were among the explanatory factors.

Their reluctance to engage in cross-boundary collaboration not withstanding, family forest owners would seem to have much to gain from increased communication and interaction with neighboring landowners and communities. Some owners would welcome a clearer understanding of how their individual ownership fits into the landscape. Those landowners with a concern for practicing good stewardship are being drawn with increasing frequency into conversations with their neighbors regarding species habitat, fire protection, water management, and other landscape-level issues. Enlightened self-interest also would seem to encourage cross-boundary communication, particularly where legal requirements such as protection of threatened or endangered species habitat compel adjacent owners to coordinate management activities.

Similarly, some family forest owners might find cooperation with neighbors to be of benefit in the marketplace. Despite their mixed record of success, forestry cooperatives currently are gaining momentum as owners seek ways to reduce management costs and improve market competitiveness through achieving efficiencies of scale.

Perhaps the most compelling reason for increased communication, interaction, and cooperation between family forest owners and their neighbors is political. By in large, family forest owners have not spoken effectively with a unified voice on issues that affect their well-being. Nor have they sought political alliances with others who share similar core values. Yet, many of the values that drive the management of many family forests also are held by community-based forestry activists, including a strong stewardship ethic and identification with the land, a long-term perspective, and an emphasis on human–forest relations. Increased involvement with an expanded community of interest would serve to raise the profile of family forest owners and their issues.

Community-based forestry is about strengthening the relationships between communities and the forests which surround and sustain them. If community-based forestry is to thrive in the United States, it must be responsive to the dominant forest tenure in the country—family forestland. The potential for strengthening and enhancing the flow of benefits and services from family forestlands to local communities, while supporting and nurturing productive stewardship of those lands, is tremendous.

Realizing this potential requires a greater awareness of the extent and significance of family forests. Understanding family forests and their owners as resources to be valued and nurtured is prerequisite to fostering constructive, long-term working relationships. Yet, the forestry profession historically has viewed family forestlands less as a resource to be cultivated and more as a problem to be solved (e.g. Fedkiw 1983; McMahon 1964; Sedjo and Ostermeier 1978). For decades, "the small woodland problem" as it came to be known, has referred to the difficulty of coercing millions of individual, independent-minded private forest owners to behave more like industrial owners. The great diversity of owner objectives, the small scale of their ownerships, and the general lack of formal, written management plans among family forest owners have been viewed as hindrances to achieving optimal timber production from these lands. Today, although the profession's objectives have broadened beyond timber production, "the small woodland problem" perspective still is evident in claims that only through regulation, certification, or easements can family forests be conserved (e.g. Best 2004; Best and Wayburn 2001; Yale School of Forestry and Environmental Studies 2005).

Identifying shared values and aspirations would do much to build more collaborative relationships with and among family forest owners. Two decades of research suggest that family forest owners throughout the United States share the bedrock environmental values of the American citizenry (Bliss 1993; 2000; Bliss et al. 1994, 1997; Dunlap 1992; Luloff et al. 1993). Like the majority of Americans, family forest owners cherish and desire to conserve the ecological values of the forest. Indeed, in the most recent national survey of family forest owners, the most common reasons cited for owning forestland were: 1) to enjoy beauty; 2) to protect nature and biological diversity; 3) because the forest is part of a farm or residence; and 4) to pass the land on to heirs (Butler and Leatherberry 2004). Owners take pride in their efforts to leave their forestland better than they found it and invest heavily in restoring and stewarding their land. Many, perhaps most, take seriously their obligation to be accommodating hosts to threatened and endangered species, despite the managerial and financial burdens that accompany that role (Fischer and Bliss 2006; Giampaoli 2004).

Developing empathy with family forest owners for the legitimate constraints and challenges they face in practicing good stewardship is essential to achieving their trust and collaboration. Family forest owners manage their forests in a world of unpredictable markets; constantly evolving regulatory requirements; family contingencies such as illness, college, and retirement expenses; and concern over intergenerational land transfer. These constraints and challenges mold what is possible on family forestland and shape family forest owners' capacity for cooperating beyond the limits of their own property.

Cooperating with one's neighbors in landscape-scale initiatives adds additional layers of social, financial, political, and managerial complexity to an already complex enterprise. With additional complexity comes additional risk. For family forest owners to engage in cross-boundary cooperation, they must make the calculation that with the additional risk comes commensurate rewards. For many owners, knowing that they are contributing to the restoration of degraded habitat, or improving the survival of threatened populations, or enhancing forest health is reward enough. For others, cooperation with neighboring landowners becomes a rewarding social interaction. Many are reluctant to engage in any activity that threatens their sense of autonomy and only may participate in programs for which the financial rewards outweigh the perceived risks.

Acknowledgments

The research from which much of this chapter is drawn is supported by the Starker Program in Private and Family Forestry at Oregon State University. The text on the roles and challenges of family forestlands was adapted from Bliss (2003). Thanks to Mark Rickenbach, Tom Beckley, Ellen Donoghue, and Victoria Sturtevant for their ruthlessly honest reviews of early drafts of this chapter.

References

Bergmann, S., and J.C. Bliss. 2004. Foundations of Cross-boundary Cooperation: Fire Management at the Public-private Interface. *Society and Natural Resources* 17(5): 377–393.

Best, C. 2004. Non-governmental Organizations: More Owners and Smaller Parcels Pose Major Stewardship Challenges. America's Family Forest Owners. *Journal of Forestry* 102(7): 10–11.

Best, C., and L. Wayburn. 2001. *America's Private Forests: Status and Stewardship.* Washington, DC: Island Press.

Birch, T. 1996. *Private Forest-land Owners of the Western United States, 1994.* Resource Bulletin NE-137. Radnor, PA: U.S. Department of Agriculture, Forest Service, Northeast Forest Experiment Station.

Bliss, J.C. 1992. Evidence of Ethnicity: Management Styles of Forest Owners in Wisconsin. *Journal of Forest and Conservation History* 36(2): 63–72.

———. 1993. Alabama's NIPF Owners: Snapshots from a Family Album. Agriculture and Natural Resource Circular ANR-788. Auburn, AL: Alabama Cooperative Extension Service.

———. 2000. Public Perceptions of Clearcutting. *Journal of Forestry* 98(12): 4–9.

———. 2003. Sustaining Family Forests in Rural Landscapes: Rationale, Challenges, and an Illustration from Oregon, U.S.A. *Small-scale Forest Economics, Management, and Policy* 1(2): 1–8.

Bliss, J.C., and A.J. Martin, 1989. Identifying NIPF Management Motivations with Qualitative Methods. *Forest Science* 35(2): 601–622.

Bliss, J.C., S.K. Nepal, R.T. Brooks, Jr., and M.D. Larsen. 1994. Forestry Community or Granfalloon? *Journal of Forestry* 92(9): 6–10.

———. 1997. In the Mainstream: Environmental Attitudes of Mid-South NIPF Owners. *Southern Journal of Applied Forestry* 21(1): 37–42.

Block, N.E., and V.A. Sample, 2001. *Industrial Timberland Divestitures and Investments: Opportunities and Challenges in Forestland Conservation.* Washington, DC: Pinchot Institute for Conservation.

Brunson, M.W., D.T. Yarrow, S.D., Roberts, D.C. Guynn, Jr., and M.R. Kuhns. 1996. Nonindustrial Private Forest Owners and Ecosystem Management: Can They Work Together? *Journal of Forestry* 94: 14–21.

Butler, B.J., and E.C. Leatherberry. 2004. America's Family Forest Owners. *Journal of Forestry* 102(7): 4–9.

Dunlap, R.E. 1992. Trends in Public Opinion toward Environmental Issues, 1965– 90. In *American Environmentalism: The U.S. Environmental Movement, 1970-90,* edited by R.E. Dunlap and A.G. Mertig. New York: Taylor and Francis, 89–117.

Edwards, K.K., and J.C. Bliss. 2003. It's a Neighborhood Now: Practicing Forestry at the Urban Fringe. *Journal of Forestry* 101(3): 6–11.

Egan, A.F., and A.E. Luloff, 2000. The Exurbanization of America's Forests: Research in Rural Social Science. *Journal of Forestry* 98(3): 26–30.

Fedkiw, J. 1983. Background Paper on Non-industrial Private Forest Lands, Their Management, and Related Public and Private Assistance. Washington, DC: U.S. Department of Agriculture, Forest Service, Office of Budget Program Analysis.

Fischer, A.P., and J.C. Bliss. 2006. Mental and Biophysical Terrains of Biodiversity: Conservation of Oak Woodland on Family Forests. *Society and Natural Resources* 19(7): 625–645.

Forestry Source. 2002a. Urban Sprawl Threatens Southern Forests. *The Forestry Source* 7(1): 1– 5.

———. 2002b. Plum Creek to Develop Timberlands. *The Forestry Source* 7(1): 7.

Giampaoli, P. 2004. Extent and Implications of Specified Resource Site Protection in Oregon. Unpublished Master of Science thesis, Oregon State University, Corvallis, OR.

Johnson, K.N. 2002. Personal communication with author, Oregon State University, Corvallis.

Knight, R.L., and P.B. Landres. 1998. *Stewardship Across Boundaries.* Washington, DC: Island Press.

Luloff, A.E., K.P. Wilkinson, M.R. Schwartz, J.C. Finley, S.B. Jones, and C.R. Humphrey. 1993. Pennsylvania's Forest Stewardship Program's Media Campaign: Forest Landowners and the General Public's Opinions and Attitudes. Unpublished report submitted to the State Forester, Commonwealth of Pennsylvania and the U.S. Department of Agriculture, Forest Service, Pennsylvania State University.

MacCleery, D.W. 1993. *American Forests: A History of Resiliency and Recovery.* Durham, NC: Forest History Society.

McMahon, R. 1964. Private Nonindustrial Ownership of Forest Land. Yale University School of Forestry Bulletin No. 68. New Haven, CT: Yale University.

Powell, D., J. Faulkner, D. Darr, Z. Zhu, and D.W. MacCleery. *1993. Forest Resources of the United States, 1992.* General Technical Report RM-234. Fort Collins, CO: U.S. Department of Agriculture, Rocky Mountain Forest Service and Range Experiment Station.

Rickenbach, M.G., J.C. Bliss, and A.S. Reed. 2004. Collaboratives, Cooperation, and Private Forest Ownership: Implications for Voluntary Protection of Biological Diversity. *Small-scale Forest Economics, Management, and Policy* 3(1): 69–83.

Sampson, N., and L. DeCoster. 2000. Forest Fragmentation: Implications for Sustainable Private Forests. *Journal of Forestry* 98(3): 4–8.

Sedjo, R., and D. Ostermeier. 1978. *Policy Alternatives for Nonindustrial Private Forests.* Washington, DC: Resources for the Future.

Smith, W.B., P.D. Miles, J.S. Vissage, and S.A. Pugh. 2004. *Forest Resources of the United States, 2002.* General Technical Report NC-241. St. Paul, MN: U.S. Department of Agriculture, Forest Service, North Central Research Station.

Stanfield, B.J., J.C. Bliss, and T.A. Spies. 2002. Land Ownership and Landscape Structure: A Spatial Analysis of Sixty-Six Oregon Coast Range Watersheds. *Landscape Ecology* 17(8): 685–697.

U.S. Census Bureau. 2000. United States Census 2000. http://www.census.gov (accessed November 16, 2006).

Wondolleck, J.M., and S.L. Yaffee. 2000. *Making Collaboration Work: Lessons from Innovation in Natural Resource Management.* Washington, DC: Island Press.

Yale School of Forestry and Environmental Studies. 2005. *Family Forest Owners: An In-depth Profile.* Unpublished manuscript prepared for the Sustaining Family Forests Initiative.

Zheng, D., and R.J. Alig. 1999. *Changes in the Non-Federal Land Base Involving Forestry in Western Oregon, 1961–94.* Research Paper PNW-RP-518. Portland, OR: U.S. Department of Agriculture, Forest Service, Pacific Northwest Research Station.

12

Creating Community Forests

Jill M. Belsky

Community forests have existed around the world for centuries. Community forests are properties historically owned and managed for a variety of forestry values by a village, city, town, school district, township, county, or other political subdivision of the state. In the United States, community forests have been owned and operated for more than a century by Native Americans, Spanish land-grant (Hispano) settlers in the Southwest, and by early colonists in New England (Baker and Kusel 2003; McCullough 1995). In the early twentieth century, the establishment of community forests was advocated by a small group of professional U.S. foresters, but their advice went largely unheeded (Brown 1941; Reynolds 1939). Today, efforts to establish community forests are coming from a new source—community-based conservation organizations seeking to avoid landscape parcelization and to maintain local access to and control of nearby working forests for the conservation of wildlife, rural lifestyles, jobs, recreation, and ecosystem services (Belsky 2004; Braxton-Little 2006; Duvall and Belsky 2005).

Creating community forests represents a new strategy in the U.S. community-based forestry toolbox. Whereas community-based forestry usually involves local communities and their allies collaboratively interacting to increase their involvement in sustainable public forestland management, community forests refer to forests that collectively are owned and managed by communities, towns, municipalities and, in the case discussed below, by community-based conservation organizations.

This chapter provides a history and analysis of a community forest being created in the U.S. Intermountain West in the twenty-first century. The chapter begins with an overview of community forests, including a typology of their major forms. Insights from the literature on common property and community-based conservation follow to highlight challenges regarding the definition and nature of "community" in conservation and the complexities involved in coordinating conservation across mixed-ownership landscapes. The following section discusses corporate timber divestiture, a driving force behind current efforts to purchase and create community forests in the United States. The chapter then turns to the experience of the Blackfoot Challenge, a community-based conservation organization in western Montana that has been successful in acquiring former corporate timberlands and is in the process of establishing a community forest on a portion of them. The chapter highlights key lessons, caveats, and possibilities for community forests pursued by community-based conservation organizations in the United States today.

Understanding Community Forests

Community forests involve the ownership and management of forest resources by groups of people who establish rules for whom and how these forest resources can be used and may be viewed as a kind of common-property regime. A common-property regime involves resources that jointly are owned and managed by groups of people who use them and who have a set of rules (formal or informal) defining rights and duties to access, withdrawal, management, exclusion, and alienation (Schlager and Ostrom 1992). Common property (be it forests, fisheries, waterways, or otherwise) often has been misunderstood and confused with "open access" properties, which are defined by a lack of clear ownership and exclusion-of-use rights. Common property has clear ownership and exclusion-of-use rights (at least it strives to have them). As such, it is useful to think of community forests as common property involving collective ownership and management of a forest parcel.

Definitions and Types

Community forests are owned, managed, and used by different types of communities, with different authority and ownership arrangements. The main types of communities who own and manage forests include two historical or archetypical examples and a third, emergent type. The three types are:

Indigenous Community Forests: The community is defined by shared residence, culture, and (mostly) customary forest access and resource use.

Town or Municipal Community Forests: The community is defined by shared residence and forest use administrated through a town or municipal (local) government.

Community-based Conservation Organizations Community Forests: The community is defined by community-affiliated landowners, partner organizations, and legal arrangements (see Table 12-1).

Table 12-1. Types of Community Forests

	Indigenous community forests	*Town or Municipal community forests*	*Community-based conservation organization(s)*
Ownership	Community, tribe, or village	Town, municipality	Nongovernmental organizations including foundations, land trusts, and limited liability companies
Community	Community defined by shared residence, culture	Community defined by shared residence, political jurisdiction	Community defined through affiliation with place and/or interest
Access and control	Customary and legal	Legal	Legal
	Clear delineation of who constitutes forest users and managers	Clear delineation of who constitutes forest users and managers	Evolving delineation of who constitutes forest users and managers
	Forest land and use rights held in common for all community members	Forest land and use rights not held in common for all community members	Forest land held on behalf of community members or as a share
Governance	Tribal council or council of elders	Elected or appointed town or municipal officials, advisory council	Elected or appointed subcommittees, advisory councils
Examples	Dayak, Borneo	North Cowichan (British Columbia)	Blackfoot Community Conservation Area (Montana)
	Ejidos, Mexico	Mission Municipal (British Columbia)	
		Hampshire Town Forest Forest (Massachusetts) Forestry Partnership (Maine)	Vermont Family Foresters (Vermont)

Each of these three types of community forests is examined below, highlighting the definition of community, ownership, and collective-management institutions. The third type of community forest particularly is relevant to this chapter because it includes new community forests being established in the United States. After introducing these three types of community forests, the chapter returns to issues regarding common property ownership, governance, and community in conservation.

Indigenous Community Forests

Perhaps the most widely held notion of community forests are those associated with indigenous or native peoples in remote locations. These include ancient community forests, such as those found in upland Asia (Conklin 1957; Kunstadter 1978; Lynch and Talbott 1995; Poffenberger 1990; Peluso et al. 1995), or more recent ones established as a result of peasant struggles such as the *ejidos* of Mexico (Bray et al. 2003). These community forests typically are connected to discrete villages with well defined physical and social boundaries and cultures. They are self-governed by long-established traditions and rules, often involving leadership by community elders. The function of traditional community forest authorities and governance institutions in this type of community forest includes setting rules on community membership and allocating forestland for various uses, including cultivating rotational agricultural plots (or "swiddens"); gathering wild foods, herbs, medicinal and other useful plants; hunting or fishing; and cutting timber to build homes and other structures. In addition to allocating forest and appropriate forest uses, local community-forest authorities also are responsible for meting out penalties and fines to those who disobey local forest management rules and for negotiating conflict and disputes.

Much has been written about the co-evolution, adaptability, and resiliency of traditional community forest knowledge and governance institutions, including the challenges they face in the modern era (Berkes 1989; Poffenberger 1990). Many indigenous community forests only are locally recognized based on customary use and local governance institutions. The territorializing and modernization interests of nation–states, as well as their interest in rapid resource exploitation for export production, has led most colonial and modern states to disregard customary community forests and to not protect them from competing interests. For example, earlier legal protections afforded to lands communally owned and managed in Mexico, known as *ejidos*, have been eroded with the passage of the North American Free Trade Agreement and state authorization of logging concessions (Bray et al. 2003). Today numerous transnational efforts are underway to gain legal protection of native land claims, culture and community-based forestry, and natural-resource management regimes (Brosius et al. 1998; Global Caucus on Community-based Forest Management 2005; Li 1996).

Town or Municipal Forests

Community forests based on geographically defined communities with town or municipal government jurisdiction represent the second type of community forests. Most common examples of these include town and municipally owned and managed forests in New England (McCullough 1995), Western Europe (Jeanrenaud n.d.), Latin America (Ferroukhi 2003), and British Columbia (Canada) (Brown et al. 2004; McCarthy 2006).

Town forests are a tradition in New England. Some have been around for centuries, established by English immigrants to America in the mid-1600s. Colonial authorities granted land to groups of individuals who established communities and were known as "town proprietors." Proprietors determined the form of their village boundaries, assigned land for individual and community purposes, and kept remaining lands in common or what McCullough describes as "technically a form of undivided ownership, with each owner sharing a proportional right to use the whole subject to limitations against abuse or waste" (1995, *15*). Initially, councils of town proprietors collectively decided and enforced rules for different communal lands use. Later, some communal lands were transferred to public lands to benefit a broader, nonresidentially defined community or shifted into private ownership.

In the early twentieth century, all six states comprising New England passed laws allowing the establishment of town forests. Forests were acquired through donation, purchase, or seizure when tax bills went unpaid. Today, most are managed by local town councils for a combination of forest-commodity production, watershed protection, and recreation (McCullough 1995). In Vermont alone, it is estimated that about 120 of the state's 251 municipalities already own a total of 140 forests and new ones are being established (Curtis 2006). Acquisitions include the purchase by Randolph, NH, of a 10,000-acre forest slated for development and a 5,300-acre community forest known as the 13 Mile Woods purchased by the town of Errol, NH, with the assistance of the Trust for Public Land. New England has been a leader in both historic maintenance as well as recent establishment of town or municipal community forests. The region also has been successful in hosting the third type of community forests, where ownership and management moves into the hands of community-based conservation organizations.

Community Forests of Community-based Conservation Organizations

The third type of community forest is the newest form and represents a growing area of interest, not only in New England but elsewhere in the United States. It involves forests owned and managed by community-based or affiliated nonprofit conservation organizations, frequently collaborating or partnering with

other nonprofit groups, landowners, local or regional land trusts, and state or
federal resource-management agencies. These organizations go by a number
of different names (e.g., partnerships, consensus groups, community-based
forestry, community-based conservation, collaborative conservation, community-based ecosystem management, and grassroots ecosystem management),
and literally have exploded in numbers since the 1990s (Conley and Moote
2003). A focus on local community and place differentiates these organizations
from national-level, nongovernmental organizations working largely on policy or issues of a broader scale, such as the Sierra Club, Wilderness Society, or
National Wildlife Federation (Cestero 1999). Many have evolved from informally organized associations meeting periodically to becoming more formally
organized 501(c)(3) nonprofit organizations, legally able to negotiate government and other financial contracts. The long-term goals of many community-
or placed-based organizations are to resolve local resource management conflicts through alternatives to litigation, to get forest management activities moving, and to raise the capacity of their organizations to influence decisions
affecting both the social well-being of their communities and the ecological
quality of their lands. Indeed, the mission statements of many community-
based conservation organizations explicitly seek to maintain and nurture connections between people and forests (Baker and Kusel 2003; Cestero and
Belsky 2003; Gray et al. 2001; Moote and Bedel Loucks 2003).

As noted above, community-based conservation organizations often work
collaboratively with land trusts, foundations, state and federal resource agencies, and limited liability corporations to acquire land and establish community forests. Land trusts have played a particularly important role in such
efforts. Land trusts are local, regional, or statewide nonprofit conservation
organizations that help protect natural, scenic, recreational, agricultural, historic, or cultural property through assisting direct land transactions, primarily
the purchase or acceptance of donations of land or conservation easements.[1]
Land trusts often work to preserve open land that is important to particular
communities and regions where they operate. There are nearly 900 independent land trusts in the United States. Foundations also can be affiliated with particular people and places and vary in size and scope but largely are defined by
their nonprofit status. Limited-liability companies are organizations created
under state law that are recognized as legal entities separate from their owners
and offer their members' protection from personal liability for the debts of the
company's business, similar to the liability protection that a corporation offers
to its shareholders.

A recent legal change in the United States signals growing recognition of this
third form of community forests. It is House Bill 2729, passed in Oregon in
May 2005. The bill authorizes a city or county to create a special community
forest authority that is able to issue revenue bonds or other revenue obligations

for towns, municipalities, or possibly local community organizations to acquire and maintain community forests on collectively owned, private forestlands. The bill defines "community forestlands" as "private lands that are zoned and permanently managed for commercial forestland use and any interests in those private lands, including related roads or other improvements financed by a community forest authority." This legislation was sought to ensure the legal ability of towns, municipalities, and community-based conservation organizations to acquire and own community forests for both commercial and conservation means.

Insights from Common Property and Community-based Conservation Research

Community-based conservation organizations face considerable challenges as they become involved in the community forest movement in the United States. A first set of issues involves ideas about property. Although numerous ideas of property exist in the United States, two narratives are particularly salient: the first emphasizes inherent rights and characteristics associated with property as a material entity, whereas the second approaches property as a more socially oriented process and set of relationships (Freyfogle 1998). In the first narrative, the sanctity of individual, private-property rights is a central tenet, as is a belief in the essential right of individuals to participate in a vigorous, self-regulating market without interference by government. This approach builds on the seventeenth-century work of John Locke and emphasizes a laissez faire approach to regulation, positing that the greatest efficiency in resource use and long-term protection of the resource stems from the voluntary efforts of private owners. Accordingly, in this view, the most effective land-use decisions are those made by individual landowners due to their confidence in their ability to control future products of their efforts. This tradition has bolstered the growth of a private-property rights movement in the United States that has great support in the Intermountain West (Brick and Cawley 1996).

The second narrative does not view property arrangements as inherent (or natural) but as evolving cultural creations influenced by particular historical contexts. The rise of modern business enterprises and corporate charters in the late nineteenth century challenged the above ideas about property and put pressure on them to change. Property rights evolved from a focus on the physical thing, such as land, to its market value. This shift enabled the development of the now familiar view of property as a bundle of sticks. In this metaphor, property is treated not as a single right, but rather as a collection of specific powers (or "sticks") where property rights more easily could be divided, with different individuals holding different sticks in the bundle (Bromley 1991).

This second property narrative has paved the way for a growing complexity of property arrangements. The increasing popularity of purchasing development rights (or conservation easements) illustrates that Americans are able to separate the different rights bundled together in private ownership and make arrangements for protecting those rights that markets alone fail to protect (Geisler and Danker 2000). Easements also suggest an evolving ecological approach to property that has generated momentum to update U.S. common law and evolving meanings of ownership, including what it would take in property law to enable greater coordination among levels of government, meaningful citizen involvement, and understanding of the weaknesses as well of the strengths of markets in providing public goods (Freyfogle 2003). Fairfax et al. (2005) use the term "mosaics" to draw attention to the diversity of ownership arrangements under which land is purchased by different acquirers under varying terms and conditions and is managed to meet very different goals.

Common-property regimes, widely misunderstood in the past, have received considerable attention over the last few decades, in part because of increasing recognition of the benefits of community-level ownership and management. An important benefit of group ownership is that it can avoid the parcelization associated with individual ownership and land markets, such as with forest landscapes, which are more likely to sustain multiple ecological functions if they remain intact and connected rather than sliced into uncoordinated parcels. A second advantage is that because of long-standing rules, customs, and local knowledge, rural communities often are capable of self-regulating resource management (Lynch and Talbott 1995; Western and Wright 1994). Third, group ownership can promote social justice because it nurtures community participation and inclusive decisionmaking procedures and restores customary resource access and control where these have been ignored, overwritten, or forcibly appropriated (Brechin et al. 2002).

Advocates of common property regimes recognize the practical difficulties of implementing them on the ground and suggest a high priority should be identifying conditions under which such regimes actually work (McKean 2000; Ostrom 1999). These terms and conditions have clear implications for community forests in the United States and include: 1) clearly specified property rights among potential users; 2) appropriate legal support from governments; 3) clear boundaries of the common resource; 4) clear criteria for membership in the group of eligible users of the resource; 5) rules that are clear and enforceable; 6) the right of users to modify their use rules over time; 7) rules that correspond to what the system can tolerate and be environmentally conservative; 8) infractions of use rules must be monitored and punished appropriately; and 9) distribution of decisionmaking and use rights to co-owners of the common need not be equal but "fair" (i.e., acceptable to members).

Community-based Conservation

Creating the conditions under which common-property regimes work is extremely difficult. Whereas communities among indigenous groups and municipal or town forests are defined by fixed residence, shared culture and local government, this definition of community is neither stable nor universal (Agrawal and Gibson 1999). Community-based conservation organizations in the United States face vastly different social and political conditions than found in these archetypal types. As such, they need to be wary of uncritically transferring community management and property models. Critics of community-based conservation and collaborative conservation have been quick to point out the limitations of these approaches for the United States. Two key criticisms are first, that they redirect attention away from gains achieved in the United States through passage of environmental rulings, regulations, litigation, and land purchases or exchanges (Coggins 1996), and, second, while community-forestry advocates lament interest-group politics for disadvantaging marginal groups and the considerable time embroiled in conflict and litigation, community- or place-based collaborative planning privileges local residents and communities who also are more vulnerable to elite, and especially corporate, capture (McCloskey 1999).

Questions regarding the ability of community-based conservation efforts to effectively engage and represent broad interests across their communities have been raised by those who otherwise are sympathetic to community-based resource management. Common property scholar McCay (2001) is concerned that those living in highly capitalistic, industrialized worlds may be prone to mythologize an earlier, pre-capitalistic time and romanticize "the commons" as part of a Western suspicion regarding unrestrained individualism, as well as romanticize small, rural communities as democratically sharing and sustainably using forests. Empirical studies document that small, rural communities are not always homogenous, harmonious, and built around shared values and governance capability (Agrawal and Gibson 1999; Brosius et al. 1998). On the contrary, the costs and benefits of participating in community-based, natural resource programs are not always borne equally or fairly across members within small, rural communities. Differences based on class, race, gender, or age can influence how community members are involved in resource management and the particular knowledge they potentially bring to bear on it. Even in well-intentioned, community-level focused efforts, unintended consequences occur that intensify state control over local resources, lives, and livelihoods (Li 2002) and even involve sabotage by factions within communities who think they are excluded from the benefits of community conservation efforts (Belsky 1999). Community-based conservation organizations must grapple with the complexities involved in justifying who they define as "the community" in conservation, who decides this based on what criteria, and how they go about being inclusive. These issues are most contentious where demographic change and resource conflicts are highly dynamic, such as in the U.S. Intermountain West.

Lastly, there is a question of the stability and endurance of community-based conservation organizations. Many community-based conservation organizations have not been around for more than a decade or two. It is not clear if they will be able to maintain the necessary, long-term commitments involved in forest ownership, planning, monitoring, and reinvesting. It also is unknown if they can be sophisticated and resilient enough to deal with the tensions and challenges they face in defining community, property, and governance regimes, let alone how to resolve conflicts among competing forest users. I turn now to a discussion of the restructuring of the timber industry, as it sets the current context for community-based conservation organizations' involvement in land acquisition and establishment of community forests.

Converting Working Forests to Real Estate with Corporate Timberland Divestment

Restructuring within the corporate timber industry provides a context for recent interest of community-based conservation organizations in creating community forests. In the 1990s, private industrial forestlands produced one-third of the total timber in the country (Best and Wayburn 2001). Over the last decade, however, this percentage declined as the forest-products industry substantially changed. Some estimates suggest that about 25 million acres have been sold by the forest industry and acquired by investment-oriented landowners since 1985 (Stein 2005), with 15 million acres nationwide changing ownership between 1998 and 2002 alone (Ingerson 2003). Timber companies have sold timberlands to alleviate debt and to shift capital toward more economically productive activities. Some strategies include moving capital away from less productive timberlands into lower cost, higher productivity timberlands or moving out of timber completely; some companies also are refocusing on production manufacturing and biotechnology research (Block and Sample 2001). Some divested timberlands are being purchased by institutional timberland investors outside the forest-products industry known as Timber Investment Management Organizations, while some are sold to support environmental conservation (Block and Sample 2001).

Of most concern to many local communities and community-based conservation organizations is the recent trend for corporate timber companies to value some of their lands as having a "higher and better use" as real estate than for timber or providing ecological services (Stein 2005). Many soon-to-be-sold "higher and better use" parcels are heavily cut before they are subdivided and placed on the market (known as "liquidation harvesting"). Even as clear-cut parcels, they are desirable to those seeking to live in less crowded, less polluted, and less crime-filled areas near scenic public lands with public services such as airports, found in the Intermountain West states of Montana, Colorado, and Idaho (Rasker et al. 2004). Strong pressure from the environmental and preservationist sectors to maintain lands for biodiversity value, paradoxically, also have contributed to the rising value of western lands for real estate. The idea that nature can be restored to a "pristine" condition has motivated campaigns to remove cattle from public rangelands and to reduce timber harvesting, presuming that the shift away from a landscape based on resource production would necessarily benefit wildlife and biodiversity. But as Sayre (2002) writes, opposition to natural resource-based livelihoods actually aided and abetted the subdivision and suburbanization of the West by appearing environmentally benign if accompanied by the elimination of timber cutting and cattle grazing on public lands. The restoration of these lands, in a perverse way, has encouraged other rural lands to be developed.

Plum Creek Timber Company is a major player in the divestiture trend. The Plum Creek CEO actively promotes Plum Creek as a land company and is often quoted as saying "It's not just trees; it's the underlying value of the land." Plum Creek estimates the value of its targeted 1.3 million acres of "higher and better use" lands at nearly $2 billion, most of it in Montana, Wisconsin, Georgia, Florida, and Maine (Ward 2006). Conservation organizations, government agencies, and local communities in western Montana are extremely concerned about Plum Creek timberland divestiture and future land sales. Alan Wood, Wildlife Mitigation Coordinator for Montana Fish and Wildlife and Parks, sums up his concerns:

> These lands are valuable and are at risk of being lost. Who will own these lands? What will be the forest management? How will they contribute to the local economy, community and jobs? All these questions are important, but once the lands are sold and subdivided those options are gone...forever. (Wood in Hartmann 2004, *40*)

To date, 7,000 acres of Plum Creek "higher and better use" lands have been sold to the Forest Service, 1,400 acres have been sold as real estate, and 1,500 acres remain on the market (Parker 2005). Rural communities and affiliated community-based conservation organizations, not willing to let the market determine that the highest value of these lands is for residential development, are raising funds to purchase former timberlands and manage them for an array of social and ecological concerns, including broad, landscape-level forest conservation. Although this trend is occurring across the country, below we take a brief look at the experience of the Blackfoot Challenge in Western Montana.

Creating Community Forests: The Experience of the Blackfoot Challenge in Western Montana

While several community-based conservation organizations in western Montana in the Yaak, Flathead, and Upper Swan Valleys are seeking to acquire Plum Creek timberlands that are for sale, the Blackfoot Challenge has had the most success. A brief examination of the Blackfoot Community Project suggests factors that account for this organization's successes, as well as future challenges it faces to develop and operate a community forest.

The Blackfoot Challenge is a community-based conservation organization that began with the efforts of local landowners and ranchers to conserve the famous Blackfoot River and its spectacular watershed. In 1993, it incorporated as a 501(c)(3) nonprofit organization with the mission to protect native streams, habitat, open lands, ranching, and a rural way of life across the 1.5 million-acre watershed from "ridge to ridge." The organization consists of an executive director, a board representing diverse interests of residents, and employees from local government resource agencies and nongovernmental organizations; subcommittees are tasked to do the actual work. The Blackfoot Challenge and its many partners have, over the years, accomplished an impressive array of conservation projects that have gained them national prominence. These include extensive stream and grassland restoration, weed control, and brakes on development involving conservation easements on some 90,000 of the 300,000 acres of private land in the Blackfoot Valley (more than any other watershed in Montana). Importantly, these efforts have been reached through a consensus-oriented, collaborative approach to decisionmaking and stewardship (http://www.blackfootchallenge.org/am/publish/).

The idea to create a community forest arose within the context of the recent Blackfoot Community Project, a joint effort of the Blackfoot Challenge, The Nature Conservancy, and Plum Creek to enable the latter to sell timberlands it intends to divest to the project instead of putting it on the open market. The goal of the project is to prevent further land fragmentation via land sales and residential development and to promote conservation of working forests, wildlife habitat, and a land-based, rural lifestyle. The project successfully produced an agreement for Plum Creek to sell approximately 89,000 acres of its former timberlands in the Blackfoot watershed to the project, with The Nature Conservancy serving as the bridge financier. The transaction involved years of quiet deliberation among the partners. The plan involved The Nature Conservancy owning the land until it can resell it to either adjacent landowners for consolidation of ranches, to private buyers with conservation easements, or to federal agencies for inclusion into public land holdings. Decisions regarding which lands are to be resold and under what arrangement are decided through a process of public involvement, led by the Blackfoot Challenge's land director. By late 2006, the partnership has been able to purchase 68,000 acres of former Plum Creek timberlands; nearly 25,000 acres have been resold to public agencies with money from the Federal Land and Water Conservation Fund and 160 acres have been resold to private buyers. To offset the loss of tax-exempt federal lands, the partnership is attempting to raise an endowment fund to pay payments in-lieu of taxes (PILTs) to the counties involved. PILTs provide funds to compensate for money lost when taxes are not charged, such as when property shifts from private to public ownership.

Approximately 5,600 acres of the project's acquired land located at the base of Ovando Mountain will be resold to the Blackfoot Challenge for the creation of the Blackfoot Community Conservation Area (BCCA). While these lands have been repeatedly logged and are of marginal timber value, they are located in an important transition zone between federally designated wilderness, national forest, and fertile valley bottomlands, rich in riparian and wetland vegetation and providing critical wildlife habitat. Furthermore, they are highly valued by valley residents and users from other communities (such as the city of Missoula located 45 miles away) for world-class recreation and hunting. With restoration, they also can be a future source of timber revenue. Thus, goals for the BCCA include restoring the 5,600 acres of the BCCA and coordinating its management to meet user as well as ecosystem needs and priorities of adjacent private and public lands (Blackfoot Challenge 2004).

From the project's inception, organizers of the BCCA have said that the specifics of who will own and manage the BCCA will be decided according to a "community-driven plan." Putting this mandate into action has posed many challenges. An initial challenge was identifying who constitutes the "community" for whom the BCCA shall be owned and managed by and for. The Blackfoot watershed consists of 1.5 million acres, including the 132 mile-long Blackfoot River, and lies within three counties containing seven towns with a total of approximately 2,500 households. Some households are part-time or seasonal residents. Much of the noncorporate private lands are large, working ranches. Prior to the Plum Creek sales, ownership was divided between public land (60%), corporate timber holdings (20%), and private landowners (20%), however, these statistics hide much of the complexity involved in the mosaics of land ownership and control associated with recent conservation transactions.

The leaders of the Blackfoot Community Project have pursued a definition of "community" based largely on the watershed's landowners. Public involvement practices initially involved meetings with landowners up and down the valley. The leaders of the project worked closely with town officials to organize and advertise public meetings, share information, and solicit feedback.

Additional activities involved maintaining websites and hanging posters and bulletins around town centers. Again, the focus was on the watershed's residents and landowners. According to press releases, meeting notes, and interviews with project organizers, participation at these public meetings was high, as was support for the conservation partnership to acquire former Plum Creek timberlands.

In an attempt to more systematically understand residents' views on the proposed community forest, a mail survey was sent to all landowners adjoining the BCCA; cost and logistics restricted the population to this sub-sample as an initial stage (Duvall and Belsky 2005). More than half of respondents defined the "community" for which the BCCA is to be owned and managed to involve the entire Blackfoot Valley rather than just nearby landowners in the town of Ovando, as well as users from other areas such as Missoula. Less than half said that the community should only refer to landowners near the proposed community forest. The survey also confirmed that residents supported acquisition of these lands to maintain undeveloped forest and grasslands for wildlife, to safeguard public access for hunting and recreation, and to more effectively manage grazing and invasive weeds.

A second set of challenges face all community forest regimes but present particular challenges for community forests established by community-based conservation organizations. These entail ownership and management institutions, rules, and objectives. Results from the landowner survey found that about half of respondents wanted more information before supporting the proposal that the Blackfoot Challenge becomes the legal owner and key manager of the BCCA. This finding is very important. It underscores the greater ambiguity regarding the terms and conditions of ownership in this third and evolving community forestry regime. Unlike in indigenous community forests and town forests, where local authority and jurisdiction is held by long-term and custom-established authorities, in community-based forests efforts, residents questioned the endurance of the sponsoring organization's authority, as well as its responsiveness to broad interests and to create institutions and rules for effective management (Duvall and Belsky 2005).

When asked if respondents supported the Blackfoot Challenge with community input to develop the BCCA management plan, approximately 21% did not answer and 16% wanted more information before deciding who exactly should develop the management plan (Duvall and Belsky 2005). Based on these results, in 2005 the Blackfoot Challenge leadership created a Blackfoot Community Conservation Area Advisory Council charged to solicit ideas and offer recommendations. Council membership was open to volunteers from across the valley. The council currently meets once a month to identify key issues and work toward developing a "community-driven" plan for owning and governing the BCCA.

Among the challenges facing the BCCA council is deciding what exactly it means for the community forest to be managed for the protection of the "rural lifestyle." The survey found that residents defined rural lifestyle as involving ranching and other natural resource-based livelihoods, as well as enjoying open space, low population density, close community interaction, and a variety of ecological amenities (Duvall and Belsky 2005). The challenge facing the BCCA management plan is to accommodate all of these values; trade offs and choices will be inevitable.

A third set of issues arise from the particulars of the Blackfoot experience. The Blackfoot Valley case suggests a winning mix of conditions that enabled a successful land sale and the promise of developing effective ownership and management institutions. The combination of factors that led to these successes are unlikely to exist elsewhere or even in this valley at a different point in time. The factors that were most important to their success include the following. First, there was a history of close personal relationships between leaders of the Blackfoot Challenge, The Nature Conservancy, Plum Creek, and local public natural resource management agencies. In reflecting about their experience, the partners emphasized the importance of their close and trusting relationships. Second, Plum Creek was a willing seller in the Blackfoot Valley. Plum Creek considers timberlands in the Blackfoot to be of comparatively marginal value to them—they are not particularly productive and are located far from the closest mill—and they are available in large parcels, which lowers transaction costs. Third, the market value of timberlands in the Blackfoot Valley is lower then elsewhere in the state. By way of comparison, Plum Creek has been more reluctant to sell "higher and better use" lands to a community conservation organization in the nearby Swan Valley, where timber is of higher quality and the company plans to remain in the timber business and where real estate prices are among the highest in Montana. They seem to be particularly unwilling to support land acquisition for the expressed purpose of developing a community forest, possibly because the latter could be perceived as competing with their corporate forest operations and demonstrating better forest stewardship practices. Lastly, finding a willing and able banker, or "bridge financier," is very difficult for most community-based conservation organizations. There are few organizations as capable and willing as The Nature Conservancy to take on a multimillion dollar debt. In fact, until The Nature Conservancy can resell the lands it has purchased in the Blackfoot Valley, it is not in a position to provide financing to other efforts, even if it desired to do so. A last site-specific factor underlying the success in the Blackfoot involves the high degree of support from Montana's former Senator Conrad Burns (himself a former farmer), who provided considerable influence to gain federal funds for the acquisition of public lands in the Blackfoot Valley.

Conclusion

Community forests have provided food, fuel wood, nontimber forest products, employment, and other forest values for nearby communities. In the past, community forests have been owned and governed by two types of communities: indigenous villages and towns and municipalities. Over the last few decades, a third type of community forest, spearheaded by community-based conservation organizations, has arisen to maintain local access to and control over forests for the goods mentioned above, to slow the advance of landscape fragmentation, and to conserve ecosystems and their ecological goods and services across landscapes with increasingly complex ownership arrangements. In this final section, I call attention to key lessons that both the literature and experience of the Blackfoot Challenge in western Montana suggest as particularly pertinent to this new experiment.

Ownership

Community forests are about ownership. As noted by Moote (Chapter 13 in this volume), collaboration in forest management in the United States has increased public involvement in forest management discussions on public lands but has not given them any more power over forest management decisionmaking, implementation, or stewardship over the long term. In the United States, that right and responsibility rests with forestland owners and, in the case of publicly owned forests, the land management agencies. Local residents compete with other stakeholders to influence public land policy, even when the lands under question adjoin their fields, homes, and communities. Involvement in collaborative forest management on public lands has produced recommendations and, sometimes, small forest management projects. But there is no guarantee that recommendations or the fruits of these collaborative efforts will persist into the future. Community-owned forests hold out the promise that local ownership will provide greater opportunities for local residents and community-based organizations to have authority and decisionmaking power over local forests and will allow them to control the future fruits of their collaborative decisionmaking, recommendations, and labor. Ownership is understood to be both materially and symbolically important. A long-term observer of the U.S. Intermountain West suggests that local ownership is critical to "a newly self-determining West" that can "begin claiming sovereignty over its own landscape" (Kemmis 2000, 3).

But there are limitations to ownership. We have seen above that changing ideas about property in the United States have been critical to the formation of new types of ownership arrangements and landscapes characterized by complex ownerships. The acceptance of property as a bundle of rights has facilitated the widespread use of easements as a conservation tool. Under these conditions, ownership no longer means total control over land, but claims of ownership also require persuasion in addition to a legal basis (Fairfax et al. 2005). Unpersuasive land ownership claims are common: governments often fail to protect their timber and land trusts may not be able to protect their agreements, especially as parcels change ownership. The most persuasive ownership claims are those with strong community support (Rose 1994). This observation underscores the growing popularity of community-based conservation. However, such organizations and efforts face many uncertainties regarding who they represent, how legitimate they are, and how capable they are of fulfilling their missions, including new attempts to acquire land and establish community forests.

Romancing the Commons

Conservation discourse worldwide has asserted a strong role for community support and governance, and there also has been a spate of calls to recreate, extend, or return to commons of many kinds (Bollier 2002; Donahue 1999; Klein 2001). Such invocations embrace a wide array of resources, domains, and scales but overlap in their desire to return to a local, community-centered scale defined by the culture and concerns of people at that scale rather than letting such things as food production and distribution, governance, and values be decided by market forces (McCarthy 2005). As people in places such as the Blackfoot Valley realize that markets are not responding to their own social and ecological concerns to maintain working forests, landscapes, and resource-based livelihoods, a window opens for alternatives that are outside the market to be considered. Community forests appeal to positive connotations of community, commons, and the good old days of rural, resource-based livelihoods. But community-based conservation organizations in the United States need to be wary of uncritically adopting community management and property models that co-evolved slowly over many generations under very site specific socio-ecological conditions. Indeed, when applied in the U.S. Intermountain West the concept can carry negative or even pejorative connotations for corporate timber companies or to rural communities who see communist features imbued in the term or fear that the "community" in charge of determining management priorities will not be their own.

While often trying to show themselves otherwise, community-forest supporters in the United States remain entrenched in interest group politics. A major goal of community forest efforts is to maintain the "rural lifestyle." Of course, the question becomes whose or which rural lifestyle? Even among small, rural communities there are various "rural lifestyles" to be recognized, respected, and accommodated in a community-based endeavor. A call to maintain rural lifestyles can be interpreted as an interest group strategy to privilege resource-based livelihoods and production landscapes over the recreation-amenity-consumption landscapes that are growing elsewhere. In the Blackfoot Valley, where land ownership and use involve large ranchers, easements have been widely established, growth is not as rapid as in other valleys, and there may be a larger consensus on the rural lifestyle most residents want to protect. Maintaining ranches and land-based livelihoods, as well as undeveloped landscapes and the activities they support, underlie the 30-year mission of the Blackfoot Challenge. In this situation, the call to maintain a particular lifestyle and land use may be widely supported and provides an effective defensive response to free market and development forces likely to spur development and sprawl. But even here it is important to remember that respondents to the survey administered in the Blackfoot Valley raised questions concerning the ability of the Blackfoot Challenge to represent broad interests in the valley. The reality is that most rural areas are internally differentiated and attention to public engagement rarely is sufficient to reach and resolve all differences. The opportunity for "misrepresenting" the interests of communities by communities themselves is high in places where there is greater heterogeneity. There is always the risk that conservation organizations (and the councils that so many rely upon as their chief governance units) can become strongly insulated and lose contact and legitimacy among the larger communities they claim to represent. Interest group politics are inevitable within and beyond rural communities and among so-called community-based organizations. The latter cannot and should not see themselves as above or outside politics.

Indeed, critics of community-based and collaborative conservation emphasize that such efforts are most definitely not above or outside politics. By definition, community forests privilege local residents and communities over others, including potential nonresident users of the community forests. As private forest owners, this may not concern those entrenched in the traditional Lockean property narrative. However, community-based land acquisitions and collective management regimes blur the lines between public and private transactions. Because of their goal to provide public goods on private lands, community forests are supported by private and public funds and involve public agencies, private nonprofit organizations, and private citizens. But critics remind us that the "public" they represent is local, not national. Furthermore, they are not legally obliged to follow standard protocols for public accountability. Organizers of the Blackfoot Community Project have said they considered years of relatively private negotiations to be imperative for sensitive land deals to be worked out and to raise the funds needed to make them happen. In the Blackfoot case, while no media coverage occurred during the early stages, meetings were held continually across the valley during negotiations and Blackfoot Valley residents were kept informed of the transactions and their input was solicited. These are delicate matters. Nonetheless, ethics of transparency, inclusion, and participation need to be recognized and addressed.

Coordinating Land Management Across Ownership Mosaics

By definition, community forests have a different mandate than federal or state forests and a narrower constituency. Those involved in creating community forests do so to maintain connections between intact and working forests and the rural communities and residents who live, work, and play nearby. Community forests are built upon the recognition that local residents represent the major stakeholders of these forest parcels and claim that they have stronger incentives for long-term management than distant owners and can offer long-term, experiential-based local knowledge to complement professional forest scientists in determining forest management objectives and procedures. As such, community groups and community forests may have greater potential (i.e., than the U.S. Forest Service) to be resilient and adaptive to change and to keep working forest landscapes intact and connected to the broader ecosystem.

But what is the capacity of community forests and community foresters to self-manage, let alone coordinate, management of their forest parcels with others across complex, mixed ownership landscapes? The reasons given for supporting cross-boundary stewardship are more highly documented than their challenges on-the-ground. It is well known that landscape-level conservation represents a formidable challenge in the Intermountain West, where land ownership reflects a complex, checkerboard pattern of alternating square-mile sections of federal, state, nonindustrial, and industrial private lands. Where the checkerboard pattern is pronounced, coordinating land management is difficult because individual landowners have different values, goals, and financial resources (Cestero and Belsky 2003). In landscapes such as in the Blackfoot Valley, where parcelization is not as extreme and relationships and partnerships effectively cross private, state, federal, and corporate landowners, cross-boundary conservation is possible.

But there are limits to the ecological benefits of community forests in landscape ecosystem management. Community forests strive to provide public goods on private lands, especially those in between more conventional public and private individual lands. Theoretically, they can enhance connectivity. But land acquisition generally and for community forests in particular is controlled largely by the priorities of the seller. In the Blackfoot case, the seller was willing to part with worked-over timber lands low on timber inventories but valuable to local residents and conservation organizations as important linkages between upland national forests, productive private valley bottoms, and productive grasslands, riparian, and wetland areas. Here, there is great ecological potential for the community forest to play an important role for scaling up community-based conservation to meet the goals of enhancing biological connectivity, ecosystem management, and biodiversity conservation. But as noted elsewhere (Fairfax et al. 2005), through their deference to willing sellers, local conservation organizations and the federal government itself reduce their ability to target ecologically important parcels for conservation. It is important, therefore, not to rely only on land acquisition as a conservation strategy but to utilize the full array of tools in the conservation toolbox, including measures such as zoning, regulation, and litigation (Doremus 2003).

Community forests clearly have captured the attention of community-based conservation organizations in the United States. They are showing great potential for exciting rural residents to not passively accept the increasing sale and subdivision of corporate timberlands and to work cooperatively for a common goal of conserving working forests. But land acquisition is extremely costly, requires a willing seller, and involves delicate deliberations. As such, community forests are likely to be possible in only a handful of places. Even where local acquisition is successful, there is no guarantee that ownership by a community-based conservation organization or affiliated entity will be able to produce inclusive, collective self-governance capable of meeting a wide array of local forest objectives coordinated further for ecosystem management across broad, mixed-ownership landscapes. Nonetheless, unlike in the case of collaborative, community-based forest management on public lands, creating community forests gives local communities real ownership and say in forest decisionmaking, management, and stewardship over the long term. Fruitful engagement between practitioners and academics can help to raise awareness of the promise and pitfalls of community forests and hopefully better enable them to be a progressive force for maintaining connections between working forests and an inclusive array of local people who desire access to and control of them.

Note

1. Definition from the Land Trust Alliance, the major coordinating and lobbying organization for the land-trust movement in the United States, founded in 1982. See the LTA web site: http://www.lta.org.

Acknowledgments

The author gratefully acknowledges the assistance of the Kellogg and Kelley Foundations, Swan Ecosystem Center, Blackfoot Challenge, Martin Nie, Maureen Hartmann, Ali Duvall, and especially the co-editors of this book, Ellen Donoghue and Vicky Sturtevant.

References

Agrawal, A., and C.C. Gibson. 1999. Enchantment and Disenchantment: The Role of Community in Natural Resource Conservation. *World Development* 27(4): 629–649.

Baker, M., and J. Kusel. 2003. *Community Forestry in the United States: Learning from the Past, Crafting the Future.* Washington, DC: Island Press.

———. 1999. Misrepresenting Communities: The Politics of Community-based Rural Ecotourism in Gales Point Manatee, Belize. *Rural Sociology* 64(4): 641–666.

Belsky, J.M. 2004. Results from the Swan Valley Land Use Survey. Upper Swan Valley Landscape Assessment, Appendix F—Trends and Issues Surveys. Swan Ecosystem Center, Condon, MT. http://www.swanecosystemcenter.com (accessed March 10, 2005).

Berkes, F. (ed.). 1989. *Common Property Resources: Ecology and Community-based Sustainable Development.* London: Belhaven Press.

Berkes, F., D. Feeney, B.J. McCay, and J.M. Acheson. 1989. The Benefits of the Commons. *Nature* 340: 91–93.

Best, C., and L.A. Wayburn. 2001. *America's Private Forests: Status and Stewardship.* Washington, DC: Island Press.

Blackfoot Challenge. 2004. The Blackfoot Community Conservation Area. Unpublished report.

Block, N.E., and V.A. Sample. 2001. Industrial Timberland Divestitures and Investments: Opportunities and Challenges in Forestland Conservation. Washington, DC: Pinchot Institute for Conservation.

Bollier, D. 2002. *Silent Theft: The Private Plunder of Our Common Wealth.* New York: Routledge.

Braxton-Little, J. 2006. Timberlands Up for Grabs. *High Country News*, pp. 9–13.

Bray, D., L. Merino-Pérez, P. Negreros-Castillo, G. Segura-Warnholtz, J.M.Torres-Rojo, and F.M. Henricus, 2003. Mexico's Community-managed Forests as a Global Model for Sustainable Landscapes. *Conservation Biology* 17: 672–677.

Brechin, S.R., P.R. Wilshusen, C.L. Fortwangler, and P.C. West. 2002. Beyond the Square Wheel: Toward a More Comprehensive Understanding of Biodiversity Conservation as Social and Political Process. *Society and Natural Resources* 15: 41–64.

Brick, P., and R.M. Cawley (eds.). 1996. *A Wolf in the Garden: The Land Rights Movement and the New Environmental Debate.* Lanham, MD: Rowman and Littlefield Publishers, Inc.

Brick, P., D. Snow, and S. Vand de Wetering (eds.). 2001. *Across the Great Divide.* Washington, DC: Island Press.

Bromley, D.W. 1991. *Environment and Economy: Property Rights and Public Policy.* Oxford: Blackwell.

Brosius, J.P., A.L. Tsing, and C. Zerner. 1998. Representing Communities: Histories and Politics of Community-based Natural Resource Management. *Society & Natural Resources* 11: 157–168.

Brown, B.A., D. Leal-Marion, K. McIllveen, A. Lee Tan with S.K. Loose. 2004 Contract Forest Laborers in Canada, the U.S., and Mexico. Land Tenure, Labor, Trade and Community Forestry: The Context for Restoration Forest Work in the NAFTA Region, Circulationg Draft. Jefferson Center for Education and Research. Olympia, WA. 83 pages.

Brown, N.C. 1941. Community Forests: Their Place in the American Forestry Program. *Journal of Forestry* 39(2): 171–179.

Cestero, B. 1999. *Beyond the Hundredth Meridian: A Field Guide to Collaborative Conservation on the West's Public Lands.* Tucson, AZ: The Sonoran Institute.

Cestero, B., and J.M. Belsky. 2003. Collaboration for Community and Forest Well-being in the Upper Swan Valley, Montana. In *Forest Communities, Community Forests*, edited by J. Kusel and E. Adler. Lanham, MD: Rowman and Littlefield, 149–169.

Coggins, G.C. 1996. Devolution in Federal Land Law: Abdication by Any Other Name. *Hastings West-Northwest Journal of Environmental Law Policy* 3(2): 211–218.

Conklin, H.C. 1957. Hanunoo Agriculture: A Report on an Integral System of Shifting Cultivation in the Philippines. Forestry Development Report No. 12. Rome: U.N. Food and Agriculture Organization.

Conley, A., and M.A. Moote. 2003. Evaluating Collaborative Natural Resource Management. *Society and Natural Resources* 16: 371–386.

Curtis, W. 2006. Mapled Crusaders: Community Forests Help Revitalize New England Towns. *Grist Magazine* February 28.

Donahue, B. 1999. *Reclaiming the Commons.* New Haven, CT: Yale University Press.

Doremus, H. 2003. A Policy Portfolio Approach to Biodiversity Protection on Private Lands. *Environmental Science and Policy* 6: 217–232.

Duvall, A., and J.M. Belsky. 2005. Blackfoot Community Conservation Area Survey: Your Views on Future Use, Ownership and Management. Preliminary Survey Results. January 26.

Fairfax, S., L. Gwin, M.A. King, L. Raymond, and L.A. Watt. 2005. *Buying Nature: The Limits of Land Acquisition as a Conservation Strategy, 1780-2004.* Cambridge, MA: MIT Press.

Ferroukhi, L. (ed.). 2003. Municipal Forest Management in Latin America. Bogor, Indonesia: CIFOR, IDRC.

Freyfogle, E.T. 1996. Ethics, Community and Private Land. *Ecology Law Quarterly* 23: 631–661.

———. 1998. Owning the Land: Four Contemporary Narratives. *Journal of Land Use and Environmental Law* 13(2): 279–307.

———. 2003. *The Land We Share: Private Property and the Common Good.* Washington, DC: Island Press.

Geisler, C.C., and Danker, G. 2000. *Property and Values: Alternatives to Public and Private Ownership.* Washington, DC: Island Press.

Global Caucus on Community-based Forest Management 2005. http://www.forestsand-communities.org (accessed June 25, 2005).

Gray, G.J., M.J. Enzer, and J. Kusel (eds.). 2001. *Understanding Community-based Ecosystem Management in the United States.* New York: Haworth Press.

Hartmann, M. 2004. Corporate Timberland Divestment: Community Options and Opportunities. Unpublished M.S. Professional Paper, University of Montana, Missoula, MT.

Ingerson, A. 2003. Communities and Private Forests. Issue Paper for the Communities Committee of the Seventh American Forests Congress. Private Lands Task Group.

Jeanrenaud, S. n.d. Communities and Forest Management in Western Europe. A Regional Profile of WG-CIFM, The Working Group on Community Involvement in Forest Management.

Kemmis, D. 1990. *Community and the Politics of Place.* Norman: University of Oklahoma Press.

———. 2000. Rethinking Public Land Governance for the New Century. Washington, DC: Pinchot Institute for Conservation.

Klein, N. 2001. Reclaiming the Commons. *New Left Review* 9: 81–89.

Kunstadter, P. 1978. *Farmers in the Forest.* Honolulu: University Press of Hawaii.

Li, T.M. 1996. Images of Community: Discourse and Strategy in Property Relations. *Development and Change* 27: 501–527.

———. 2002. Engaging Simplifications: Community-based Resource Management, Market Processes and State Agendas in Upland Southeast Asia. *World Development* 30(20): 265–283.

Lynch, O.J., and K. Talbott. 1995. *Balancing Acts: Community-based Forest Management and National Law in Asia and the Pacific.* Washington, DC: World Resources Institute.

Maine Forest Service. 2001. *Biennial Report on the State of the Forest and Progress Report on Forest Sustainability Standards.* Augusta, ME: Department of Conservation, Maine Forest Service, Forest Policy and Management Division.

McCarthy, J. 2005. Devolution in the Woods: Community Forestry as Hybrid Neoliberalism. *Environment and Planning* 37: 995–1014.

———. 2006. Neoliberalism and the Politics of Alternatives: Community Forestry in British Columbia and the United States. *Annals of the Association of American Geographers* 96(1): 86–104.

McCay, B.J. 2001. Community and the Commons: Romantic and Other Views. In *Communities and the Environment,* edited by A. Agrawal and C. C. Gibson. New Brunswick, NJ: Rutgers University Press, 180–191.

McCloskey, M. 1999. Local Communities and the Management of Public Forests. *Ecology Law Quarterly* 25(4): 624–629.

McCullough, R. 1995. *Landscape of Community: A History of Communal Forests in New England.* Hanover, NH: University Press of New England.

McKean, A. 2000. Common Property: What is it, What is it Good For, and What Makes it Work? In *People and Forests: Communities, Institutions, and Governance,* edited by C.C. Gibson, M.A. McKean, and E. Ostrom. Cambridge, MA: MIT Press, 27–56.

Montana Forest Owner's Association. 2002. Montana Forest Facts. http://www .forestsmontana.com/aboutus.html (accessed November 14, 2004).

Moote, A. 2002. Communities and Private Forest Lands. *Communities and Forests Newsletter* 6(2): 2.

Moote, A., and A. Bedel Loucks. 2003. Policy Challenges for Collaborative Forestry: A Summary of Previous Findings and Suggestions. Flagstaff, AZ: Ecological Restoration Institute.

Ostrom, E. 1999. *Self-governance and Forest Resources.* Occasional Paper No. 20. Bogor, Indonesia: Center for International Forestry Research.

Parker, M. 2005. Conservation and Community Forests in the Swan Valley. Presentation during the Swan Valley field trip at the conference "Community-owned forests in the United States: Possibilities, Experiences and Lessons Learned." June 16–19, Missoula, MT.

Peluso, N.L., P. Vandergeest, and L. Potter. 1995. Social Aspects of Forestry in Southeast Asia: A Review of Postwar Trends in the Scholarly Literature. *Journal of Southeast Asian Studies* 26(1): 196–218.

Poffenberger, M. (ed.). 1990. *Keepers of the Forest: Land Management Alternatives in Southeast Asia.* Bloomfield, CT: Kumarian Press.

Rasker, R., B. Alexander, J. van den Nooert, and R. Carter. 2004. *Prosperity in the 21st Century West: The Role of Protected Public Lands.* Tucson, AZ: Sonoran Institute.

Reynolds, H.A. 1939. Town Forests—A Neglected Opportunity. *Journal of Forestry* 37(5): 364–367.

Rose, C. 1994. *Property and Persuasions: Essays on the History, Theory, and Rhetoric of Property.* Boulder, CO: Westview Press.

Sayre, N. 2002. *Ranching, Endangered Species, and Urbanization in the Southwest: Species of Capital.* Tucson: University of Arizona Press.

Schlager, E., and Ostrom, E., 1992. Property-rights Regimes and Natural Resources: A Conceptual Analysis. *Land Economics* 68: 249–262.

Seeley-Swan *Pathfinder*. 2002. An Observation on Plum Creek Land Sales. September.

Stein, P. 2005. Presentation on "Changes in Timberland Ownership." Presented at the conference "Community-owned forests in the United States: Possibilities, Experiences and Lessons Learned." June 16–19, Missoula, MT.

Ward, S. 2006. Is the Sky Really the Limit? *Barron's* January 31.

Western, D., and R.M. Wright with S.C. Strum (eds.). 1994. *Perspectives in Community-based Conservation*. Washington, DC: Island Press.

Wood, A. 2004. Personal communication in Hartmann, M. 2004. Corporate Timberland Divestment: Community Options and Opportunities. Unpublished M.S. Professional Paper, University of Montana, Missoula, MT.

13

Collaborative Forest Management

Margaret Ann Moote

In 1992, Jack Shipley, an avid conservationist, and Jim Neal, a long-time logger, began talking about ways to overcome the gridlock over land management in the Applegate watershed in Oregon, where environmentalists, agencies, and the timber industry all were in conflict. Together, they wrote a short paper outlining basic tenets of their plan, such as responsible extraction, no clearcuts, and no pesticides. Shipley solicited comments from environmental groups and natural resource management agencies and Neal similarly approached industry interests. They found that everyone was concerned about maintaining the long-term health of the watershed and the stability of local economies. Encouraged by this apparent common ground, Shipley and Neal organized a meeting in October 1992 with neighbors, representatives from industry, community groups, land management agencies, and several local environmental organizations to discuss a plan to make the Applegate watershed a demonstration site for ecologically and financially responsible resource management; thus, the Applegate Partnership was born (Shipley 1995).

That same year, in Plumas County, California, a county supervisor, industry forester, and environmental attorney joined forces to work on alternative forest management in an effort to address conflicts between environmental protection and timber-production goals; their effort soon broadened to include other community members and became the Quincy Library Group (Anonymous 2001). In Montezuma County, Colorado, a Forest Service district ranger, a county commissioner, and the president of the Colorado Timber Industry Association were discussing their frustration over the negative effect of new ecosystem management policies on local ranching and timber economies (Richard and Burns 1999). Their discussions led to the development of the Ponderosa Pine Forest Partnership, which in 1993 penned the following mission statement:

"encourage sustainability by linking community, ecology, and economy." The partnership's goals were to "demonstrate that a healthy ecosystem and healthy economy are compatible goals" and "demonstrate a process of coupling scientific analysis with broad-based public input to inform management" (Preston and Garrison 1999, *12*).

As these examples illustrate, by 1990 many environmentalists, landowners, elected officials, industry leaders, and agency representatives were ready to start working together on forest management. Forest management had become polarized as federal land management agencies shifted their focus from commodity production to biodiversity and ecological sustainability; large private, industrial forests were being sold for development; timber harvests were down across the country; and there was a growing sentiment that the nation's forests were "unhealthy." Urbanites migrating to rural areas brought new perspectives on recreation, conservation, and resource management that often conflicted with the values of long-time residents. Many people in forest communities were frustrated by the changes affecting their access to both private and publicly owned forests and concerned about negative effects on both local economies and ecosystems. Forest management was increasingly contentious, conflicts were polarized and bogged down in litigation, and there were growing pleas from agencies and interest groups alike for alternative dispute resolution techniques that would help them reach some kind of accord that everyone could live with. New approaches to conflict management and public participation, such as alternative dispute resolution techniques and community-based resource management, offered appealing alternatives to contentiousness.

This chapter traces the roots and evolution of collaboration in resource management in the United States, then looks to recent experiences to determine how well early expectations of collaborative forest management have been met in practice. Although some expectations, such as mutual learning, have been met, others have not. Predominant power structures, including centralized land management agencies and the strong hand of judicial review in interpreting environmental policy, have limited the ability of collaborative efforts to achieve more integrated and adaptive forest management, shared decisionmaking, and local empowerment. Although these expectations arguably could be met by devolving decisionmaking authority to local actors, this is an unlikely option, and from many perspectives, an undesirable one. This chapter aims to help bridge the gap between expectations and outcomes of collaborative forest management by examining the aspects of power and authority that are posing problems. Equity, accountability, and legitimacy are critical aspects of this discussion. The final section of this chapter explores these issues and suggests ways they could be better addressed in collaborative forest management in the future.

Collaborative Forest Management in the United States

As noted above, across the country, nearly simultaneously and seemingly independently, collaborative, community-based groups began forming to address local environmental and natural resource management challenges. By the mid-1990s, hundreds of such efforts were underway in the United States, from watershed planning councils in the East to community-based farmland preservation task forces in the Midwest to forestry partnerships in the West. Community leaders were turning to collaborative processes to increase opportunities for local involvement in agency decisionmaking. Agencies were turning to collaboration as a way to move beyond conflict and gridlock. Collaboration was embraced as an opportunity to discard ineffective strategies, balance competing interests, and create more innovative management options.

Within 10 years, however, many of these groups were experiencing frustration and burnout. Long hours had been spent formulating common vision and mission statements, designing organizational structures and group rules, and listening to and learning from people with different backgrounds and perspectives. Yet there had been little tangible change in forest management practices on public lands. In September 2003, representatives of collaborative community-forestry groups from across the western United States gathered at Hart Prairie in northern Arizona to discuss why collaborative forest management groups were not achieving their land management goals at the rate and scale they had anticipated. These individuals—once wholehearted proponents of collaborative forest management as a new way of doing business—were now questioning the collaborative approach. Participants in the Hart Prairie workshop identified a number of social and political barriers to collaboration but focused in particular on "inconsistent and unrealistic expectations of collaboration, [which] lead to unfair criticisms of collaborative efforts [and] accusations of failure" (Moote and Becker 2003, 3).

Today, 15 years after collaborative forest management first surfaced in the United States, it has been embraced at the highest levels of government. Community leaders, natural resource management agencies, and forestry practitioners across the country can point to dozens of local examples. This chapter addresses the question of whether collaborative forest management is meeting the expectations that led to its emergence in the 1990s.

Although they have similar roots, collaborative forest management and community-based forestry are not the same thing. Collaboration in resource management is characterized by a diversity of participants and a discursive group process. Under twenty-first century conceptions of collaborative resource management, a collaborative group may consist of resource management professionals but no local community representatives. Community-based forestry, on the other hand, is characterized by the substantive involvement of local residents, particularly forest landowners and forest workers. A community-based forestry effort may or may not include people representing broader interests.

Expectations of Collaborative Forest Management

Collaborative forest management in the United States has roots in participatory government process, alternative dispute resolution, integrated and adaptive resource management, and international community forestry. Each influence is the basis for a slightly different set of expectations of collaboration, and understanding the promise of each helps explain these expectations.

Public demands for a greater voice in government, which had been growing since the first half of the twentieth century, took hold in forest management in the 1970s. The National Environmental Policy Act and other environmental and natural resource legislation passed in the 1970s explicitly required public involvement in resource management. Agencies responded by developing formal public input processes like hearings and comment periods, but by the late 1980s, there still were widespread complaints that scientific experts and policy elites—such as national interest groups—wielded too much power and that management decisions were being made behind closed doors. What the public wanted, social scientists explained, was to participate throughout the planning process and to help identify public policy needs, develop alternative ways to meet those needs, and select a mutually agreeable alternative (Shannon 1990; Wondolleck 1987; Blahna and Yonts-Shepard 1989). By the late 1990s, a variant of participatory democracy—discursive democracy, which further emphasizes dialogue and mutual learning among citizens—was being promoted as a new approach to resource management.

Another result of the broad-based dissatisfaction with administrative decisionmaking was an increase in appeals and lawsuits stalling or blocking agency projects. Appeals and litigation were costly and frequently resulted in decisions that were not favored by either party. By the 1980s, resource management agencies were turning to alternative dispute resolution (ADR) methods that had been developed for labor negotiations in the early to mid-1900s. As opposed to "zero-sum" management, which implies there always will be winners and losers, ADR is based on a "mutual gains" model, which calls for interest-based negotiation and consensus-based decisionmaking to develop management options that will benefit all parties. Interest-based negotiation means that instead of focusing on what they want (their demands or positions), participants share the underlying reasons, needs, or values that explain why they want these things. In the process, participants are said to gain a mutual respect for and an understanding of each others' viewpoints, enabling them to work together more effectively in the long term. Consensus decisionmaking means that every effort has been made to meet the interests of all stakeholders, and everyone agrees they can live with whatever is proposed. Advocates of ADR, such as Fisher and Ury, authors of the ADR classic *Getting to Yes*, claim that it allows disputing parties to jointly develop proposals and make innovative decisions that are more widely supported than those made through traditional government procedures (Fisher and Ury 1991).

Also during this period, boundaries were blurring between resource management disciplines and agencies. Federal land management laws passed in the 1960s and 1970s, including the National Environmental Policy Act, the Multiple Use-Sustained Yield Act, the National Forest Management Act, and the Federal Land Policy and Management Act, required agencies to consider multiple uses of the land and consult with other agencies and publics when developing management plans. The cumulative effect of these changes, combined with steadily decreasing funding for resource management, meant that by the 1990s, managers increasingly worked at larger scales and across jurisdictional boundaries.

As the politics became more complex, so did the science. Managers were charged with incorporating ecological science, which emphasized complex interrelationships among many environmental functions, into their management practices. Recognition of the constantly changing networks of interacting physical, chemical, and biological factors, which all are influenced by social, economic, and political systems, led to calls for more integrated and multidisciplinary resource management. By the late 1990s, the new concept in forestry was adaptive management, a process for managing ecosystems by applying principles of scientific experimentation, understanding that "surprises" are an expected element of the system. The advent of adaptive management, and more recently, adaptive *co*management, meant that resource management agencies, nongovernmental organizations, and local community groups now were expected to work closely to observe responses in ecological and social systems to management actions and adjust future management based on what they learned. Close coordination among professional resource managers and laypeople was a new paradigm in resource management. The need for legal and organizational flexibility to allow rapid responses to changing conditions also flew in the face of traditional resource management.

The collaborative forest management movement in the United States also has roots in new approaches to international development that gained popularity in the second half of the twentieth century, notably participatory development and community forestry. A core characteristic of participatory development theory is the empowerment of local residents and communities by treating them as engaged participants in resource management decisionmaking, rather than as the passive subjects of decisions made by others. This shift suggests the devolution of control and decisionmaking from national governments to local communities.

These different roots of collaborative forest management—participatory governance, ADR, adaptive ecosystem management, and international community forestry—led to four distinct sets of expectations of collaborative forest management in the United States. The first was that there would be new ways for multiple, diverse interests to share their knowledge and values regarding resource management, leaving everyone better informed. The second was that conflicts over resource management would be reduced because disputing parties would jointly craft innovative management options that met everyone's needs. The third was that land management agencies would become less hierarchical and bureaucratic, embrace innovation in resource management planning, and quickly adapt to new information and changing conditions. The fourth was that local residents and forest resource users would be empowered to bring their knowledge, opinions, and skills to the shared stewardship of the forests.

Collaborative Forest Management in Practice

Although it is common to think of collaborative forest management in terms of groups like the Applegate and the Ponderosa Pine Partnerships, a cursory survey of collaborative forest management underway in the United States makes it apparent that such "partnership groups" are only one form of collaboration in forestry. In practice, collaborative forest management may focus on a few hundred or millions of acres of public or private land; active participants may number fewer than 10 or more than 100, and they may include any combination of government agencies, nonprofit/interest groups, and others, including individual concerned citizens.

The most informal types of collaboration are networks—loosely defined groups of individuals and organizations with overlapping interests or responsibilities who occasionally share information or resources. Often, such networks facilitate interagency and intergovernmental cooperation but do not involve a broader array of stakeholders, such as local residents or the general public.

As collaboration has become increasingly mandated, some have pointed out that long-standing processes, such as advisory councils and planning commissions, could be considered a form of collaboration. These bodies typically have members appointed to represent specific interests because of their expertise or affiliation. Membership is limited, however, and the scope of work also is limited and defined by the appointing body.

Similarly, town halls, search conferences, and community visioning exercises could be considered collaborative. These are short-term, facilitated events in which participants share information and ideas, explore issues, and attempt to identify common values, but generally do not attempt to reach agreement or make decisions. They rarely attempt to empower locals, make bureaucracies less hierarchical, or explicitly address conflict.

Many proponents of collaboration consider only partnerships, councils, and comanagement agreements to be truly collaborative because they are the most open and give participants responsibility for setting their own goals and actions, whereas advisory councils and dialogue groups often are presented with a predetermined task and procedure. Some go further, suggesting that a process is not collaborative unless participants engage in joint decisionmaking and share responsibility for implementing those decisions. In 1999, the Food and Agriculture Organization of the United Nations published a guide to collaborative management of natural resources directed at government forestry officials around the globe. In it, the authors state, "collaborative management of natural resources refers to the process for sharing power among stakeholders to make decisions and exercise control over resource use" (Ingles et al. 1999). Based on a comprehensive review of research on collaboration, Mattessich, Murray-Close, and Monsey (2001) similarly conclude that collaboration "includes a commitment to ... a jointly developed structure and shared responsibility; mutual authority and accountability for success; and sharing of resources and rewards."

The following discussion looks primarily at partnership-type collaborative processes and asks how well collaborative forest management has met the expectations of more a more participatory process, conflict resolution, shared knowledge, and local empowerment.

Participatory Process

Several empirical evaluations of collaborative groups, such as Coughlin et al.'s 1999 systematic assessment of 10 collaborative resource management partnerships, demonstrate that participatory processes often do improve information exchange and mutual learning, giving participants a better understanding of issues and constraints and bringing better information and better problemsolving techniques into the decisionmaking process. In many cases, collaboration has facilitated participants' learning about local ecology, social values, and management constraints and has resulted in better informed or more innovative plans and projects that are expected to improve resource conditions. Yet the costs of participation in such forums have proven unexpectedly high in terms of participants' time and energy, and in most cases the ecological achievements of collaborative resource management efforts have been fewer and have taken longer than expected. As Su Rolle, the first interagency liaison for the Applegate Partnership, observed, an all-volunteer collaborative effort "creates a lot of work for a few folks, and burnout is real" (Rolle 2001). At least three studies comparing multiple cases of collaboration found that these groups rarely achieve measurable outcomes during their first three years and suggest that it is unrealistic to expect results any sooner (Born and Genskow 2000; Leach et al. 2002; White et al. 1994). The early years of collaborative group functioning are spent in learning, building mutual understanding, and ironing out collaborative processes.

The commitment required for successful collaboration is substantial. For example, a survey of Bureau of Land Management field offices found that national policy support for collaboration had not translated into material support in the form of time, budget flexibility, or training for staff to actually implement it (Laninga 2004). The time and resource demands of the collaborative effort may well be onerous enough that to fully meet the expectations of their fellow collaborators agency staff would have to neglect other commitments, including core agency missions. The same holds true for participants from other organizations—collaboration imposes a host of new responsibilities on top of their "day jobs." Some research, such as Johnson et al.'s interviews of 33 stakeholders from 12 agencies, has concluded that if upper management is not committed to the process and to implementing the outcomes of collaboration, collaborative efforts are more likely to fail (Johnson et al. 2003).

Conflict Resolution

Reduced conflict over forest management, leading to less gridlock and greater agreement over management decisions, is for some the primary objective of collaboration. In practice, many collaborative efforts have helped build new or improved relationships and social networks, reduced or resolved conflicts, and increased trust and common ground among participants. Collaboration has resulted in tangible products that are expected to improve resource conditions, including new plans, new policies, and on-the-ground projects. In the Dungeness River Watershed in Washington State, for example, 10 years of collaboration produced two new watershed management plans, several riparian habitat restoration projects, and a voluntary effort by agricultural water users to protect salmon runs by reducing withdrawals from the Dungeness River during lowflow periods (Born and Genskow 2000). Detailed case studies of collaborative resource management efforts have found that, in many cases, results would have been unattainable without the collaborative effort or that projects were more easily implemented because of broadened stakeholder support (Born and Genskow 2000; Doppelt et al. 2002; Coughlin et al. 1999).

As noted above, however, most collaborative groups spend years engaging in mutual learning and building trust before they are able to agree upon objectives or implement projects Resolving conflict can be an ongoing issue for collaboratives; there have even been reports of increased conflict. One study that interviewed hundreds of participants from 12 National Estuary Program collaboratives found that conflicts covering large geographic areas were less likely to be resolved (Lubell 2004). Another, based on interviews and surveys of 927 participants from 44 watershed partnerships, found that participants in one-third of these groups felt the partnership had aggravated economic, private property, and regulatory disputes (Leach et al. 2002). An unwillingness to negotiate and compromise and positional bargaining are commonly reported barriers to collaboration and reasons for failure (e.g., Johnson et al. 2003; Huntington and Sommerstrom 2000), perhaps because participants have determined that they can better meet their objectives through other processes, such as lobbying or litigation.

Shared Knowledge

Central to the collaborative process is mutual learning in which information from several sources is shared and used to inform planning and coordinate decisionmaking across land ownerships; in many cases this has contributed to effective group projects. A prominent example in the conservation literature is the Malpai Borderlands Group, which brought ranchers, scientists and key agencies together to create a series of programs and activities to conserve a million-acre landscape. Another is the Trinity River Program in which the Hoopa Tribe's knowledge was incorporated in a new river flow model used by the U.S. Fish and Wildlife Service to successfully restore salmon habitat (Barinaga 1996). Yet in other cases, translating information sharing into management actions has proven difficult. Engaging different land and resource management agencies in joint data management can be onerous: each agency has its own data collection and data management methods, making merging and manipulating information a daunting task that may undermine efforts for data consistency and sharing. The challenge of shared learning is further exacerbated by the centralized authority of natural resource agencies and managers unreceptive to forms of data and expertise provided by non-agency stakeholders in the collaborative project. Doppelt et al. (2002) documented many innovative approaches in their study of 14 U.S. Department of Agriculture (USDA) Forest Service collaborative watershed partnerships; however these operated on the "margins, or outside of, existing Forest Service structures, systems, and culture" (p. 12).

While federal and state natural resources management agencies are often blamed for difficulties in implementing adaptive management (the process of monitoring and evaluating management actions and applying lessons learned to future management), local governments and collaborative groups impose obstacles of their own or lack the capacity to "close the loop"–to apply shared learning to management, planning regulations, or decisionmaking. Lack of financial and human resources is cited as one reason (Born and Genskow 2000; Doppelt et al 2002; Lubell 2004); most collaborators are volunteers and ongoing funding for monitoring projects, even on public land, is uncertain. Another may be active or passive resistance to projects or proposals for policy change from landowners, environmental groups, or other resource users (Margerum 2001). And finally, collaborative groups can find it a challenge to report information or findings to the community, interest groups or land management agencies in a manner which accords with their goals or meets their scientific standards (Ballard et al 2008).

Local Empowerment

For many, particularly non-agency participants, the primary reason for engaging in collaboration is to increase the power of local voices in sustaining local communities and negotiating decisions regarding public land management goals, strategies, and practices. Recent mandates for local involvement in the Healthy Forests Restoration Act of 2003 and the 2005 National Forest Planning Rule suggest some political support for this goal. Yet even as these policies have opened the door for community members to engage more readily in forest management discussions, decisionmaking authority and implementation are fully retained in the hands of the landowner or land management agency. A review of two collaborative forest management projects initiated in the Flathead Valley in central Montana in the mid-1990s illustrates the frustration this can engender:

Through the lengthy process of meetings, deliberations, hard-won compromise, and at times passionate declamations, and always under skeptical surveillance, both of these groups managed nevertheless to develop detailed management plans for sensitive national forests. ... Neither plan, in its entirety, has been implemented. The will of the people to collaborate, as is the case in the [Flathead Forestry Project], and the capability of organizations with fixed organizational agendas to collaborate, as is the case in [Flathead Common Ground], is not sufficient to carry objectives to a successful conclusion. The Forest Service, as implementing agency, by law plays the decisive role. (Schwennesen 2001, 3) In the Flathead Common Ground case, the agency revised its decision under threat of lawsuits from environmental interests, one of whom considers collaboration "exclusionary, because it potentially gives a greater voice to people who live nearby and have the time to take part" (Schwennesen 2001, 27). Yet other environmental groups had engaged in the extensive give-and-take that led to the original agreement. The agency was left in the difficult position of choosing between defending the collaboratively crafted decision and demonstrating responsiveness to a stakeholder that had not participated in the collaborative process.

Expectations of shared decisionmaking remains a major issue for agency and non-agency participants in collaborative forest management. Participants who have embraced the concepts of discursive democracy have hopes that collaboration will redistribute power and authority. This poses a challenge for agency personnel who are constrained by legal responsibilities and jurisdictional limitations. Studies have shown that many agency employees view collaborative planning primarily to serve an advisory function, with the collaborative group making recommendations to the agency and the agency retaining full decisionmaking authority; non-agency participants, however, want their role to be more than sharing information or advising (Carr et al. 1998; Moote and Becker 2003; Sherlock et al. 2004). Part of this disconnect between agency participants and non-agency participants may stem from a difference in focus on ends versus means. To many resource managers, collaboration is a way to achieve a desired end, such as reduced conflict or better management of natural resources, while for others, particularly local communities, the means (shared decisionmaking) is an important dimension of the end (Cheng 2007). Yet as agency employees are only too aware, to fully engage in shared decisionmaking, agencies would have to change legally defined planning, management, and decisionmaking procedures, if not law.

Although collaboration in forest management often increases local community members' input to forest management discussions, in most cases, it has not given them more power over forest management decisionmaking or implementation. In the United States, that right and responsibility sits squarely on the shoulders of the forest land owners and, in the case of publicly owned forests, the land management agencies. Expectations of local empowerment are not likely to be met by through power devolution from centralized land management agencies.

Power in Collaborative Forest Management

As discussed above, collaborative forest management largely has failed to achieve more integrated and adaptive management or to provide a stronger local voice in decisionmaking. Three aspects of power in particular continue to frustrate place-based collaborative forest management planning efforts: legitimacy—the authority to make decisions; accountability—the assumption of responsibility for actions or inactions; and equity—fair distribution of costs and benefits resulting from those decisions.

Legitimacy

The first issue for collaborative forest management is a concern that collaborative processes are not legitimate governance forums. Legitimacy is commonly used to refer to a government's right to hold and use power, based on the consent of the governed. Collaborative processes can be considered illegitimate if they do not follow standard government procedures or are not representative of the citizenry. Collaborative forest management groups work to represent those unable or choosing not to participate, but they are not elected bodies representing the major interests involved (e.g., timber and environmental groups) or the community as a whole (KenCairn 1996). These groups can consist of only a few, highly engaged individuals who may or may not be well connected

to the broader communities of interest and place. Collaborative processes therefore are not always considered legitimate public participation forums, let alone
decisionmaking forums. How much weight anyone should give to projects and
proposals that come from collaborative processes remains an unresolved question. Yet this question may become less relevant if more attention is paid to procedural justice—particularly public access to and transparency of the process.
Research on justice and fairness in governance offers insights into what makes
a collaborative process legitimate in the eyes of both participants and nonparticipants. Studies have shown that procedural justice—the perceived fairness
of the decisionmaking process—positively affects people's reactions to agency
decisions (e.g., ACIR 1979; Blahna and Yonts-Shephard 1990; Smith and
McDonough 2001).

Since the late 1990s, Seth Tuler and Thomas Webler have conducted several
case studies across the United States that examine public involvement and collaboration in watershed planning, national park management, forestry, and
other environmental and resource management activities. In each study, they
asked participants to rank, in order of importance, critical aspects of the
process. In each case, they found a wide variety of perspectives on good process.
Yet the majority of participants agreed that public involvement and collaborative processes should

- ensure that all points of view have an opportunity to be expressed;
- have a clear process and goals;
- give participants an opportunity to make a difference by empowering
  them to influence the process and outcomes;
- provide equal access to information and enforce full disclosure of all available information;
- use the best available science; and
- result in a plan that ensures follow-through and accountability (Tuler and
  Webler 2003; Tuler,Webler, and Tanguay 2003; Tuler et al. 2003; Tuler and
  Webler 1999;Webler et al. 2004;Webler and Tuler 2001;Webler et al. 2001).

For most people, a "fair" process is open and inclusive, provides equal opportunities for meaningful input, and is rational and transparent. An open and
inclusive process is one that encourages participation from all interested parties and strives to involve all stakeholders. In addition to opportunities to contribute, participants want to know that their views and ideas are considered in
the decisionmaking process. This would include equal access to decisionmakers, opportunities for meaningful input, and assurance that no stakeholder
group is dominating the process. Interested publics in general ask to be integrally involved in the identification of problems and potential projects and the
development and analysis of alternatives. Participants expect to know what
information was used and how tradeoffs were made. Paying more attention to

procedural justice will help collaborative processes achieve perceived fairness for stakeholders while also maintaining agency authority. The challenge here is to adequately demonstrate access to and transparency in the decisionmaking process. One way to accomplish this could be through organizations that bridge the gaps between communities, national interests, and resource management agencies. In 1990, residents of Swan Valley, Montana, formed the Swan Citizens' Ad Hoc Committee to address conflict over forest degradation and diminishing employment in the valley. A core group of citizens had worked together for over a decade, building trust and broadening their understanding of both forest management and their community. But the ad hoc committee had struggled to broaden its participation, so many of these benefits were not realized beyond the committee membership. In 1996, they established the Swan Valley Ecosystem Center, whose staff now carry out projects initiated by the ad hoc committee and provide regular opportunities for public participation (Cestero and Belsky 2003). The Applegate Partnership described at the beginning of this chapter similarly found that years of discussion and debate helped overcome mistrust among participants, but this had not translated beyond the partnership to the rest of the community or stakeholders outside of the community. As in the Swan Valley, the creation of a more permanent and identifiable institution for collaboration—in this case the Applegate River Watershed Council—has broadened public participation and accelerated project implementation (Sturtevant and Lange 2003).

Accountability

In collaborative efforts addressing forest management on public lands, questions arise, particularly for land managers and national interest groups, as to the collaborative group's accountability to the broader public good and to the missions of resource management and regulatory agencies. Providing the flexibility for collaboration while also ensuring accountability is a critical challenge for the field of public administration in general and national forest management in particular. Yet experience suggests there is little reason to fear that collaboration will undermine government authority. In a study of collaborative planning in 200 cities, for example, Agranofff and McGuire (2003) found considerable collaboration and information sharing but also that the city governments retained ultimate decisionmaking authority. Federal land management agencies are legally accountable for any actions taken on land under their jurisdiction. Current federal, state, and local property laws make landowners accountable for any actions taken on private land. Similarly, land management agencies are accountable for actions on public lands. U.S. constitutional law stipulates that Congress may delegate authority to agencies to interpret and implement federal statutes, but agencies may not fully shift their administrative authority to collaborative groups (or anyone else). Other legislation, such

as the National Environmental Policy Act and state and federal open records
or "sunshine" laws, maintain opportunities for broad public input through
more traditional forums, including public comment periods, appeals, and litigation. A more serious concern for participants in collaborative forest management efforts is internal accountability—participants' responsibility to follow
through on agreements made within a collaborative group, such as obligations
to one another. In this sense, each partner may be said to be "accountable" to
the group for implementing a mutually agreed-upon project. Much attention
has been paid to the need to build relationships and improve trust among collaborative group participants. Interestingly, however, honesty and accountability (doing what one said one would do) may be more important predictors of
success than building trust and interpersonal relationships (Webler and Tuler
2001). In particular, there is a need for more predictability and less vulnerability within the process, with incentives for cooperative behavior and consequences for uncooperative behavior (Mandell 1999). Improving internal
accountability, for example by improving information sharing, can help collaborative groups better achieve integrated and adaptive resource management.
Here, one challenge for participants is having the authority to make a commitment to the group on behalf of one's employer or stakeholder group and, therefore, being able to provide assurance that a decision will not be overridden by
someone higher up in the organization. In addition to commitment from participants, internal accountability requires a commitment from decisionmakers
who oversee those participants. In some collaborative groups, agency decisionmakers have informally agreed to make every effort to adopt recommendations
or agreements that emerge from a collaborative process. In this way, although
decisionmaking authority clearly is retained by the land management agency,
participants in the collaborative process receive some assurance that their collective input will be used. Pooling finances also can encourage commitment to
a collaborative group's project and plan. Accountability within a group also
may be enforced formally, such as through legislated external oversight or joint
written agreements, or informally, for example through political and professional relationships and a shared understanding of agreements. The appropriate level of formal accountability rules is a function of the collaborative group's
goals and interpersonal dynamics, but some level of formality is likely necessary to help clarify roles and manage power differentials among partners.

Equity

Equity—the fair distribution of costs and benefits among stakeholders—may
seem a desirable precondition to participating in a collaborative effort. In surveys, interviews, and focus groups, participants in collaborative groups and other
participatory processes repeatedly report that they expect their input will be
reflected in a final decision and feel cheated when it is not (e.g., Blahna and

Yonts-Shepherd 1989; Webler and Tuler 2001; Smith and McDonough 2001).Yet the realities of landowner rights, decisionmaking authority, and preexisting power relationships make equity difficult to achieve and virtually impossible to enforce. As the Flathead Valley example above illustrates, federal land management agencies can and sometimes do decide against implementing a collaboratively designed plan, even one that they originally helped develop. Similarly, landowners who, for example, agree to change land practices to reduce nonpoint source pollution may later decide that implementing such a policy is not in their best interest. Individuals and organizations that fund collaborative efforts may have more influence over group decisions than those who only donate time and effort. And all participants retain their options to work individually with decisionmakers or to appeal or litigate a collaboratively developed plan. Expectations of equitable influence over decisionmaking may not be realistic, but they can be addressed to some extent when collaborative groups make a concerted effort to maintain broad representation and opportunities for input while at the same time implementing mechanisms for accountability within the collaborative process. In this way, it may be possible to achieve some degree of local empowerment without *dis*empowering stakeholders who are disinclined or unable to participate in the collaborative forest management.

The Future of Collaborative Forest Management

Fifteen years of experience with collaborative resource management in the United States have shown that in many cases, and particularly when it takes the form of partnerships and watershed councils, collaboration has achieved mutual learning, better decisions, reduced conflict, and improved social capital. Yet collaborative forest management largely has failed to meet expectations of local empowerment and integrated and adaptive resource management. With growing political support for collaboration, other forums, including informal networks, advisory councils, and short-term group events, are being endorsed. These forums expand opportunities for public input—and particularly local community leaders' input—into forest management. Yet such forums are likely to be eschewed by those seeking more meaningful involvement and more flexible, less procedural management practices.

To meet expectations of local empowerment and integrated, adaptive management, which are important goals for many community-based forestry groups, collaborative processes should be designed to ensure meaningful opportunities for input into planning and decisionmaking, with some level of internal accountability. In the best cases, collaboration marries fresh ideas with careful attention to legal and political constraints, allowing innovation and adaptation while maintaining accountability to nonparticipants. Formalizing collaborative practices in local or regional forestry institutions may help bridge local communities' desire for local input and resource stewardship with agencies' need to address national-level values and meet legal strictures.

References

Agranoff, R., and M. McGuire. 2003. Inside the Matrix: Integrating the Paradigms of Intergovernmental and Network Management. *International Journal of Public Administration* 26(12): 1401–1422.

Advisory Commission on Intergovernmental Relations (ACIR). 1979. *Citizen Participation in the American Federal System.* Washington, DC: U.S. Government Printing Office.

Anonymous. 2001. The Quincy Library Group. Case Study 6 prepared for the Liz Claiborne and Art Ortenberg Foundation. Workshop on Collaborative Resource Management in the Interior West, October 18–22, Red Lodge, MT.

Ballard, H.,L, V.E. Sturtevant and M.E. Fernandez-Gimenez. 2008. Improving Forest Management through Participatory Monitoring: A Comparative Case Study of Four Community-based Forestry Organizations in the Western United States. In *Taking Stock of Nature*, edited by A. Lawrence. Cambridge, U.K.: Cambridge University Press.

Barinaga, M. 1996. A Recipe for River Recovery. *Science* 273(5282):1648-1650.

Blahna, D.J., and S. Yonts-Shepard. 1989. Public Involvement in Resource Planning: Toward Bridging the Gap between Policy and Implementation. *Society and Natural Resources* 2(3): 209–227.

Born, S.M., and K.D. Genskow. 2000. The Watershed Approach: An Empirical Assessment of Innovation in Environmental Management. Learning from Innovations in Environmental Protection Project Paper. Washington, DC: National Academy of Public Administration.

Carr, D.S., S.W. Selin, and M.A. Schuett. 1998. Managing Public Forests: Understanding the Role of Collaborative Planning. *Environmental Management* 22(5): 767–776.

Cestero, B., and J.M. Belsky. 2003. Collaboration for Community and Forest Well-being in the Upper Swan Valley, Montana. In *Forest Communities, Community Forests*, edited by J. Kusel and E. Adler. Lanham, MD: Rowman and Littlefield, 149–169.

Cheng, A.S. 2007. Build It and They Will Come? Mandating Collaboration in Public Lands Planning and Management. *Natural Resources Journal* 46: 841-858.

Coughlin, C.W., M.L. Hoben, D. Manskopf, and S.W. Quesada. 1999. A Systematic Assessment of Collaborative Resource Management Partnerships. Master's Project, School of Natural Resources, University of Michigan. www.snre.umich.edu/emi/pubs/crmp.htm (accessed July 10, 2003).

Doppelt, B., C. Shinn, and D. John. 2002. Review of USDA Forest Service Community-based Watershed Restoration Partnerships. Portland, OR: Mark O. Hatfield School of Government, Portland State University.

Fisher, R., and W. Ury. 1991. *Getting to Yes: How to Negotiate Agreements Without Giving In* (2nd ed.). New York: Penguin.

Huntington, C.W., and S. Sommarstrom. *An Evaluation of Selected Watershed Councils in the Pacific Northwest and Northern California.* Report prepared for Trout

Unlimited and Pacific Rivers Council. http://www.pacrivers.org/ (accessed July 10, 2003).

Ingles, A.W., A. Musch, and H. Qwist-Hoffman. 1999. *The Participatory Process for Supporting Collaborative Management of Natural Resources: An Overview.* Rome: Food and Agriculture Organization of the United Nations.

Johnson, L.J., D. Zorn, B. Kai Yung Tam, M. Lamontagne, and S.A. Johnson. 2003. Stakeholders' Views of Factors that Impact Successful Interagency Collaboration. *Exceptional Children* 69(2): 195–209.

KenCairn, B. 1996. Peril on Common Ground: The Applegate Experiment. In *A Wolf in the Garden: The Land Rights Movement and the New Environmental Debate,* edited by P.D. Brick and R.M. Cawley Lanham, MD: Rowman and Littlefield Publishers, Inc., 261-277.

Laninga, T.J. 2004. *Collaborative Planning in BLM Field Offices: Where It's Happening and What It Looks Like.* Final Report to the Community Based Collaboratives Research Consortium. http://www.cbcrc.org/php-bin/grantsPublic.php?id=4 (accessed May 24, 2006).

Leach, W.D. 2004. *Is Devolution Democratic? Assessing Collaborative Environmental Management.* Sacramento, CA: Center for Collaborative Policy.

Leach, W.D., N.W. Pelkey, and P.A. Sabatier. 2002. Stakeholder Partnerships as Collaborative Policymaking: Evaluation Criteria Applied to Watershed Management in California and Washington. *Journal of Policy Analysis and Management* 21(4): 645–670.

Lubell, M. 2004. Resolving Conflict and Building Cooperation in the National Estuary Program. *Environmental Management* 33(5): 677–691.

Mandell, M. 1999. The Impact of Collaborative Efforts: Changing the Face of Public Policy through Networks and Network Structures. *Policy Studies Review* 16(1): 4–15.

Mattessich, P.W., M. Murray-Close, and B.R. Monsey. 2001. *Collaboration: What Makes It Work. A Review of Research Literature on Factors Influencing Successful Collaboration* (2nd ed.). Saint Paul, MN: Amherst H. Wilder Foundation.

Moote, A., and D. Becker (eds.). 2003. Exploring Barriers to Collaborative Forestry. Flagstaff, AZ: Ecological Restoration Institute.

Preston, M., and C. Garrison. 1999. The Ponderosa Pine Forest Partnership: Community Stewardship in Southwestern Colorado. Cortez, CO: Montezuma County Federal Lands Program.

Richard, T., and S. Burns. 1999. The Ponderosa Pine Forest Partnership: Forging New Relationships to Restore a Forest. Durango, CO: Fort Lewis College, Office of Community Services.

Rolle, S. 2001. The Applegate Partnership: What Makes It Work & What Are the Problems? Jacksonville, OR: Applegate Partnership.

Schwennesen, D. 2001. Flathead Common Ground and the Flathead Forestry Project. Case Study 1 prepared for the Liz Claiborne and Art Ortenberg Foundation. Workshop on Collaborative Resource Management in the Interior West, October 18–22, Red Lodge, MT.

Shannon, M.A. 1990. Building Trust: the Formation of a Social Contract. In *Community and Forestry,* edited by R.G. Lee, D.R. Field, and W. Burch, Jr. Boulder, CO: Westview Press, 229–240.

Sherlock, K.L., E.A. Kirk, and A.D. Reeves. 2004. Just the Usual Suspects? Partnerships and Environmental Regulation. *Environment and Planning C: Government and Policy* 22(5): 651–667.

Shipley, J. 1995. The Applegate Partnership. *Watershed Management Council Newsletter.* http://watershed.org/news/www_docs/sum_95.html (accessed May 24, 2006).

Smith, P.D., and M.H. McDonough. 2001. Beyond Public Participation: Fairness in Natural Resource Decision Making. *Society and Natural Resources* 14: 239–249.

Sturtevant, V.E., and J.I. Lange. 2003. From "Them" to "Us": the Applegate Partnership. In *Forest Communities, Community Forests*, edited by J. Kusel and E. Adler. Lanham, MD: Rowman and Littlefield, 117–133.

Susskind, L., S. McKearnan, and J. Thomas-Larmer (eds.). 1999. *The Consensus Building Handbook: A Comprehensive Guide to Reaching Agreement.* Thousand Oaks, CA: Sage Publications.

Tuler, S., and T. Webler. 1999. Voices from the Forest: What Participants Expect of a Public Participation Process. *Society and Natural Resources* 12: 437–453.

———. 2003. Perspectives on Public Participation in Forest Management Planning, Case Study: Forest Management in the Greater Flagstaff, Arizona Region. SERI Report 03-005. Greenfield, MA: Social and Environmental Research Institute.

Tuler, S., T. Webler, and J. Tanguay. 2003a. Perspectives on Public Participation at a Department of Energy Nuclear Weapons Facility, Case Study: Setting Clean Soil Standards at the Rocky Flats Environmental Technology Site. SERI Report 03-004. Greenfield, MA: Social and Environmental Research Institute.

Tuler, S., T. Webler, J. Tanguay, and R. Finson. 2003b. Perspectives on Public Participation in Forest Management Planning, Case Study: Forest Management in the Applegate Watershed. SERI Report 03-002. Greenfield, MA: Social and Environmental Research Institute.

Webler, T., and S. Tuler. 2001. Public Participation in Watershed Management Planning: Views on Process from People in the Field. *Human Ecology Review* 8(2): 29–39.

Webler, T., S. Tuler, and R. Krueger. 2001. What Is a Good Public Participation Process? Five Perspectives from the Public. *Environmental Management* 27(3): 435–450.

Webler, T., S. Tuler, and J. Tanguay. 2004. Competing Perspectives on Public Participation in National Park Service Planning: The Boston Harbor Islands National Park Area. *Journal of Park and Recreation Administration* 22(3): 91–113.

White, A., L. Zeitlin Hale, Y. Renard, and L. Cortesi. 1994. Lessons to Be Learned from Experience. In *Collaboration and Community-based Management of Coral Reefs: Lessons from Experience*, edited by A.T. White, L. Zeitlin Hale, Y. Renard, and L. Cortesi. West Hartford, CT: Kumarian Press, 107–120.

Wondolleck, J.M. 1987. *Public Lands: Conflict and Resolution.* New York: Plenum Press.

Conclusion

14

Taking Stock of Community and Forest Connections

ELLEN M. DONOGHUE AND VICTORIA E. STURTEVANT

Being remote, small, and economically dependent on timber extraction no longer typifies all forest communities in the United States and has not for decades. The relations that communities have to forests now are considered in terms of the variety of complex ways they are culturally, socially, and economically linked to nearby forestlands. Forest communities vary considerably, ranging from high-amenity commuter suburbs of urban areas to remote, economically depressed areas surrounded by public and industrial forests. The diversity of communities creates a number of different types of connections to forests. A key premise of this book is that the ability to achieve sustainable forests and sustainable communities depends on resilient, dynamic, and robust connections between communities and forests. What determines the nature of the connections that communities have to forests? Through an examination of a range of management issues, types of forest communities, and forest governance structures, the chapters illustrate how socioeconomic, political, and institutional structures and processes contribute to strong and resilient connections, as well as undermine them. We conclude this book by looking at some of the factors that influence how communities interact with forests and engage in forest management. Then we offer some considerations for social science research related to forest communities.

Determinants of Connections Between Communities and Forests

Of the many determinants of the strength and resiliency of connections between communities and forests we examine three. First, we consider the opportunities and challenges of integrating community development with forest management.

Second, we discuss how communities and governments deal with change and engage in adaptive management processes. Third, we consider how forest institutions shape community connections to forests and what role institutions play in sustaining communities and forests.

Is the Community Development Business Forest Managers' Business?

The chapters in this book raise a fundamental question: To what extent are forest management agencies in the community development business? The history of forest policy in the United States, as traced in several chapters, reveals that timber supply for local economies and associated timber-sector jobs long have been part of forest management strategies of the Forest Service and Bureau of Land Management. Management has shifted from an emphasis on sustained-yield timber production to a focus on forest health and restoration, habitat protection, and ecosystem functions. The four key threats to forests, as defined by the Forest Service, are fire and fuels, invasive species, loss of open space, and unmanaged recreation. Changing management direction and priorities contribute to the evolution of work in the woods, particularly on public forests in the West, where timber harvests have declined. Nonetheless, where public forests are designated to provide goods and services, some form of work in the woods likely will exist. Even designated wilderness areas or areas closed to public access to protect watersheds or sensitive habitats require monitoring or surveillance to ensure ecosystem health. Contract workers employed in restoration, fire, and other aspects of forest management are examples of how the well-being of a forest community is tied to the management of forests. Moseley (Chapter 9) shows that wages for forest restoration and fuel-reduction work fluctuate with changing values of products and services. The pay of contract workers employed to restore degraded ecosystems in the Pacific Northwest, for instance, currently is not commensurate with what loggers were paid when public forests were key contributors to the regional timber economy. And, the nascent restoration economy does not have the same type of institutional and political standing as did the timber economy. Moseley suggests that Forest Service processes of linking natural resource management targets with budgets, staffing, and promotions has kept the agency focused on natural resource objectives and thereby limited attention to the job quality of the contracted workforce. An important question raised by Moseley's chapter is why shouldn't resource management agencies play a more active role in ensuring quality jobs in the woods?

Employment is only one aspect of community development and well-being. Community development is also about access to information and resources that support existing community assets and create new ones. Development occurs when communities build and use assets to meet the needs of residents. Assets include leadership skills, civic capacity, financial capital, and physical infrastructure. Some community assets may not be owned by communities.

For example, forest management agencies have stewardship responsibilities for a host of natural assets important to the socioeconomic well-being of forest communities, such as water, air, scenic amenities, timber, nontimber forest products (NTFPs), and recreation. These comprise the natural assets of many forest communities. Despite these rather direct ways that management of public forests contributes to community well-being, specific roles and responsibilities of resource management agencies with respect to community development remain ambiguous.

Agencies' capacity for the social dimension of forest management is less than their capacity for the biophysical aspects of forest management. This discrepancy is the product of sociopolitical choices that have resulted in agency missions, budgets, programs, and, ultimately, capacity, that give priority to what might be considered "forest development"—the restoration and maintenance of healthy forest ecosystems to provide a diversity of goods and services to the public—with minimal regard for the opportunities and links to socioeconomic development. Some aspects of forest management, in particular fire suppression, demonstrate exemplary skills in communication, planning, and coordination and receive high levels of attention and expectations from the public. High-caliber performance in fire suppression on federal lands has come with investment in infrastructure, institutions, and training of personnel. Bringing that level of investment and commitment to agency engagement in community development in the context of forest management may seem a lofty goal. Evidence in this book of the profound interconnectedness of communities and forests suggests that forest community development may be a worthwhile pursuit for the mutual health of forests and forest communities.

Many public agencies, such as departments of health, education, and transportation, have mission-directed links to communities, where it is expected that these relationships are to contribute to the well-being of communities. The same sort of relationship is not established or necessarily expected between natural resource management agencies and communities. By law, federal forests in the United States are to be managed as much for a resident of New York City, who may only occasionally or symbolically visit a national forest, as for the person who looks out his window at the forested landscape serving as the source of his clean water, clean air, and perhaps his livelihood. Agencies are challenged by their dual responsibility to people in proximity of forests and the citizenry at large. Determining who is in proximity is complicated by the fact that the reach of forests is long. For example, forests in Plumas County, California, provide water to local communities as well as to the metropolitan population more than 100 miles to the south in the state's capital. Stewardship responsibilities and opportunities reside with all forest stakeholders near and far. Where forest communities connect to public forests through recreation, timber, fisheries, NTFPs, aesthetics, or ecosystem services (e.g., clean water), opportunities exist to contribute to the development of both forests and communities.

As Moote (Chapter 13) describes, over the past 15 years agencies have been increasingly partnering with organizations and groups to fulfill agency missions of providing goods and services to the public. Evidence of the reciprocal relationship, whereby agencies directly help community-based organizations achieve their goals of local capacity building and community socioeconomic development, is sparse. With agency downsizing and budget cuts in key rural development programs, such as the Forest Service's Economic Action Program and Rural Community Assistance (RCA) program, agency capacity to engage in community development is decreasing at a time when agencies are also relying on more and more communities to engage in forest management. Given these recent trends, what roles can forest management agencies play in community development?

Opportunities for reciprocated community development and forest development exist in an assortment of management scenarios. Small-diameter timber and biomass utilization are good examples of the possible convergence of economic development and forest management goals. For agencies, removing small-diameter timber may be a way to increase forest health and reduce hazardous fuel loads. For communities, a consistent supply of small-diameter timber may be critical for secondary wood production or biomass industries. Development of and access to markets is critical, and opportunities in remote communities may be constrained. Although a development strategy to revitalize the timber sector through utilization of small-diameter timber may be appropriate for one type of community, a strategy to develop infrastructure for recreation or tourism may be better suited in another. The range of forest communities is broad. Forest-oriented community development strategies, even within the jurisdiction of a single forest, will have to reflect a diversity of types of forest communities, particularly those associated with large, western public forests.

Amenity migration to forested areas affects the prospects for community development in a variety of ways. At one extreme are the forest communities that would welcome newcomers and their associated economic contributions. Some of these communities have not been able to attract people because they lack infrastructure or are too remote. The other extreme are those communities that have attracted so many amenity migrants that long-term residents feel alienated, their sense of place has been altered, or the cost of living has increased beyond their means. As Kruger et al. (Chapter 7) reveal, the types of communities in between these extremes are as numerous as the reasons amenity migrants are attracted to forest landscapes, making planning for change associated with amenity migration difficult. Some of their values and interests conflict with those of long-time residents, community leaders, and local resource managers. The roles agencies play in assisting forest communities to adapt to change, whether in response to amenity migration or other social or natural forces, are not well defined. Reinforcing connections between communities and forests by effectively integrating community development with forest management may provide a firmer foundation upon which progress toward sustainable communities and sustainable forests can be made.

Adapting to Change

The stewardship spectrum—the range of values, resources, and abilities that people and groups bring to stewarding forest lands—is shifting on public lands. On the one hand, decreased funding and agency staff mean fewer people doing more work and less agency contact with forest users and forest communities. On the other hand, as forest managers develop partnerships with groups and communities (e.g., watershed councils, hiking clubs, and homeowner associations) different people are participating in resource management. Increasingly, goods and services traditionally provided to the public by agency staff are being provided by contractors, partners, and volunteers. Collaborative approaches to forest management often are based on pooling mutual interests and resources to address resource management problems and are conducive to experimentation and a learning-process approach to problem solving.

Adaptive forest management is fundamentally about experimentation, exploration, and flexibility. It is often portrayed, however, as a somewhat formulaic process in which forest managers plan, then act on the plans, then monitor the results of the actions, then evaluate if changes to actions are needed to meet existing or new objectives, and then circle back to the planning process. Charnley (Chapter 3) and Moote (Chapter 13) indicate that although forest management agencies speak about adaptive management, it has yet to become an established approach to forest management. Part of the problem may be that approaches are in theory responsive to new information and changes in the system but in practice are constrained by existing institutions and processes. Also, agencies exert considerable effort to gather data and build databases to track performance and outcomes, but, as we suggest in Chapter 2 and Charnley echoes in Chapter 3, it is not clear how these types of data are used to inform policy development and change.

Yet natural resource management agencies, nongovernmental organizations, and forest communities are challenged to adapt to a host of changes brought on by shifts in policy, global markets, demographics, and other forces. Currently, the threat of wildfire is a predominant forest management issue, yet concerns about invasive species and water supply are mounting. Steelman (Chapter 6) suggests that agencies may have the capacity to manage the biophysical dimensions of forest health, but the more pressing issue is whether they have the capacity to manage the collaborative efforts necessary for successful wildfire policy. Can successful experiences in collaborative and adaptive approaches to forest management build capacity for diverse forms of forest stewardship across ownerships, and can doing so help managers and communities become more resilient to changing forest management issues?

Alignment of Forest Institutions with Goals of Sustainability

Forest institutions are the rules, procedures, processes, and norms that shape human action with respect to forest use and management. They are created by legislative processes, forest management agencies, the forest industry, and forest communities, as well as being artifacts of broader socioeconomic, cultural, and political forces. Institutions intended to achieve desired ecological outcomes are widespread in forest management. These include best management practices, forest certification procedures, contractual provisions, rules for access and use of forest resources, and agency and forest-user culture. In contrast, institutions supporting desired socioeconomic outcomes of forest management are less common. Those that exist tend to be more reactive rather than proactive in their consideration of the social dimensions of forest management. For instance, the Jobs-in-the-Woods program was largely a mitigation effort intended to retrain forest workers and thereby ease the transition of forest communities in the Pacific Northwest following the decline in federal timber harvests in the 1990s. An example of a more proactive institution was the Forest Service's RCA program, which provided technical and financial assistance to rural communities to help build their capacity to play meaningful roles in the management of natural resources.[1] The program began in 1992 but was cut in 2006 when federal dollars across executive branches were diverted to homeland security and Hurricane Katrina relief and reconstruction.

Several chapters stress how the lack of development and maintenance of institutions that support the social dimensions of forest management undermines the ability of community groups, nongovernmental support organizations, and resource management agencies to meet the simultaneous goals of healthy communities and healthy forests. Underdevelopment of these socially oriented forest institutions is an issue for many types of forest communities, several of which we will discuss here. For instance, harvesters of NTFPs are numerous, harvest across diverse forested landscapes, and contribute millions of dollars to regional economies. Although differences among harvesters exist, as a group they are considered an interest-based forest community. In general, institutions associated with harvesting focus on procedure and regulation, with little consideration of the actual and potential role that harvesters play as stewards of forest resources. Permits and procedures track who is harvesting how much and where in order to maintain and monitor the health of the forest. And yet, as Jones and Lynch (Chapter 8) explain, many NTFP gatherers have traditional and enduring relationships to forests, local knowledge about forests, stewardship ethics, and the desire to sustain cultural practices and to support the transitional economic needs of migrant or marginalized workers. These are important ingredients for long-term relationships to forests and long-term forest management. The challenge is reflecting these complex dimensions of the well-being of NTFP commercial harvesters in institutional mechanisms that administratively connect harvesters to forests. Arguably, acquiring merchantable products from a forest is an example of a socioeconomic benefit associated with a forest institution, in this case a NTFP commercial permit. But for many harvesters, harvesting NTFPs is a lifestyle as well as a way to make a living. Jones and Lynch caution that policies and management activities not based on local cultural, biological, or ecological realities can threaten stewardship and create tensions among stakeholders. One way to integrate local knowledge and improve harvester representation in discussions about NTFP management is for agencies to work with community-based forestry organizations and buyers and processors of NTFPs, who are usually more visible and accessible than harvesters.

Approximately 10 million acres of densely stocked stands are outside their historical fire regime class and are at risk of catastrophic wildfire. The threat of wildfire adjacent to forest communities and the need to restore fire-adapted ecosystems are critical issues for many forest managers and communities, particularly in the western part of the United States. Nechodom et al. (Chapter 5) indicate that the magnitude of this forest health issue for most forest communities is beyond the current capabilities of existing markets and institutions for small-diameter wood products. Despite these institutional constraints, forest managers are expecting businesses and communities to participate in the restoration of forest health. The authors suggest that reducing harvesting and processing costs or increasing the value of small-diameter and biomass products cannot be accomplished without some forms of market intervention. Administrative procedures, such as providing predictable flows of products, also are important. These and other forest institutions may have to be developed or modified in order for communities to feasibly and effectively deliver ecosystem benefits of public forests resulting from small-diameter wood and biomass utilization.

Although market incentives and policy reform may be needed to effectively engage the skills and capacities of forest communities in fuels reduction and forest restoration, some institutions are evolving in ways that meet forest management and community needs. Communities and groups are developing collaborative arrangements for wildfire preparedness and applying for grants and other development opportunities for the machinery and capital necessary for biomass and fuels-reduction industries. Other policy developments have begun to span the institutional gaps between community health and forest health. Stewardship contracting authorities allow federal forest managers to develop multi-year, goods-for-service-type contracts that bring together local community groups or businesses in collaboration with land managers on a broad range of forest restoration and biomass removal projects. A multi-party, multi-state collaborative effort in the Southwest called the Four Corners Sustainable Forest Partnership, for example, has invested in projects that reduce wildfire risks and develop community capacity.

A variety of governance structures link communities and forests. Some forms of forest governance have endured for hundreds of years, including family forests and rarer forms of community forests, such as town forests in New England. More recent governance structures have emerged in response to increased interest in collaborative stewardship of forests, resolving social conflict over resource management, and slowing the conversion of forestland. One of the primary goals of community-based forestry groups, for example, is to create convergent opportunities that increase and sustain both forest health and community health. As illustrated by Danks (Chapter 10), some community-based forestry groups are filling gaps in communities left by industry and agency downsizing. The groups are delivering services and building capacity without the intention of replacing government services or advocating local control of public resources. Instead, they want to ensure that forest communities participate in and contribute to fair and transparent processes of forest management.

Community-based forestry groups are helping to forge connections between communities and public and private forest managers that are otherwise separated by administrative, ideological, cultural, or sectoral boundaries and in doing so, contribute to the development of socially-oriented forest institutions. Some community-based forestry groups emerged to address the needs of forest communities that have had difficultly in making the transition from timber-based economies to other futures. Danks describes the programs of several of these groups, including the Flathead Forestry Project in Montana, the Partnership for Public Lands in Colorado, and Framing Our Community in Idaho. Currently, however, only a small portion of forest communities have the benefit of a resident community-based forestry group. What can be done for those communities that have connections to forestlands but lack the "bridging" capabilities to integrate community well-being with forest management? Danks suggests that as community-based forestry groups around the country work to realign and develop forest institutions in ways that integrate community health with forest health at the local level, broader institutional shifts may follow. With a solid foundation of both socially and ecologically oriented forest institutions beneath them, community and business leaders together with agency and nongovernmental partners will be empowered to effectively engage in forest protection and management. The ideal is to create sufficient community and agency capacity to "fill the gaps" such that community-based forestry groups will work themselves out of jobs.

Although collaborative arrangements between public resource management agencies and community groups are increasing in the United States, they often challenge the traditional norms, cultures, and procedures of agencies, communities, and industries. Many collaborative efforts promoted by community-based forestry groups and their partners emphasize decentralized power structures and mutually held interests. Groups such as the Watershed Research and Training Center in California and Wallowa Resources in Oregon often act as conveners of collaborative arrangements involving governments, industries, local businesses, and others, resulting in increased mutual learning about forest management and related community concerns. The ability of community-based forestry groups to function effectively in more rural places and across scales in the United States is hampered by what Moote (Chapter 13) describes as the absence of institutions in resource management agencies that support shared decisionmaking. She explains how some planning and management procedures lead to decisionmaking at regional and national levels, leaving few opportunities for local-level innovation and collaboratively developed programs. Community access to local decisionmakers is decreasing with the consolidation of forest management units and the increased centralization of decisionmaking and accountability at regional and national levels. The sense of disassociation of forest communities from decisionmaking processes that affect them is exacerbated by the fact that the legislated responsibility to manage public resources and the ultimate decisionmaking authority lie with the agencies. Moote indicates that to many resource managers, collaboration is a way to achieve a desired end, such as reduced conflict or better management of natural resources, whereas for others, particularly forest communities, the means (shared decisionmaking) is an important dimension of the end. Unresolved issues about decisionmaking authority and accountability threaten collaborative processes.

Family forest owners are a type of forest community that represent 42% of forestlands in the United States. Some family forest owners share a forest stewardship ethic passed down through generations. Others may be relatively new forestland owners who bring diverse values that have bearing on their lifestyles, their roles in the communities, and their relationships to forests. Bliss (Chapter 11) indicates that many of the institutional challenges typically associated with community-based forestry projects, such as establishing mutual objectives, communication, working across ownerships, and integrating local knowledge, are similar when working with groups of family forest owners. And yet discussions about the development of and advocacy for community-based forestry strategies rarely consider family forest owners. Improved sharing and integration of lessons, knowledge, and experiences associated with family foresters and community-based forestry practitioners will benefit both approaches to forest management.

Finally, we turn to an uncommon, though intriguing, form of forest governance in the United States: community forests. The prospects for community-owned forests in the United States are not without challenges. As Belsky (Chapter 12) explains, the people and groups involved in creating community forests do so to maintain connections between intact and working forests and the rural communities and residents who live, work, and recreate nearby. One premise is that local stakeholders have stronger incentives for long-term stewardship than distant owners and thus local knowledge can complement the knowledge of professional foresters in determining forest management objectives and procedures. As Belsky describes, even where local acquisition of forest land is successful, there is no guarantee that ownership by a community forestry organization will produce inclusive, collective self-governance capable of meeting a wide array of local forest objectives and coordinating broad management goals across mixed ownership landscapes. As echoed by Danks in her discussion about community-based forestry groups, factors such as community or group-leader burnout, new residents with potentially conflicting values, and the turnover of group membership challenge community forestry groups as well.

More progress is needed to develop institutions that better reflect the reciprocity of forests and communities if goals of sustainable forest management are to be achieved. Some institutions endure on the landscape, such as the culture and tradition of some family forest owners, NTFP harvests, and people who work in the woods. Other institutions are beginning to reorient forestry in the United States in ways that simultaneously support healthy forests and healthy communities, such as stewardship contracting mechanisms. These are signs that the integration of socially and ecologically oriented institutions is possible. However, if relationships between managers and some members of forest communities, including contractors, permitees, and other forest users, primarily are defined by permits or contractual mechanisms that have minimal consideration of local knowledge or cultural norms, then opportunities to expand stewardship of public lands may be missed. Investment in the development of institutions that build agency capacity and community capacity to engage in collaborative forest stewardship is necessary in an era when agencies increasingly lack the financial, physical, and human infrastructure to manage forests on their own.

Social Science Institutions and Forest Institutions

Social science approaches to better understanding the links between communities and forests are not uniformly suitable for all management issues or research questions. Some approaches such as participatory research require unique commitments on the part of researchers, communities, and often managers to meet their objectives and fully engage participants in collective problem-solving. Arnold and Fernandez-Gimenez (Chapter 4) describe their participatory curriculum development project as one in which they had to shift from data collectors and analyzers to facilitators of cooperative learning and applied problem-solving. Many common constraints to research, such as time, budgets, and administrative procedures, are exacerbated in participatory processes because building relationships and trust takes indefinable amounts of time and flexibility. Many resource managers are unfamiliar with the ways that participatory and civic science can build on existing knowledge to understand landscape or socio-demographic changes. Social scientists have a responsibility to inform and educate managers and community leaders of the opportunities of participatory methods.

Charnley (Chapter 3) identifies a number of reasons why socioeconomic monitoring, although part of an adaptive management process, is not well-integrated into forest management. She, together with Arnold and Fernandez-Gimenez, describe a general reluctance on the part of managers and stakeholders, and perhaps even some researchers, to acknowledge negative trends or negative findings resulting from monitoring, assessment, and participatory research, especially because such endeavors require high levels of coordination, time, trust building, and resources. In Chapter 2, we identify some of the challenges for social scientists participating in large-scale, interdisciplinary ecological assessments. These assessments, often commissioned to resolve ecological and social crises, have high expectations for scientists to develop constructs and compile data under time pressure and with unclear directives and competing stakeholder expectations. These examples emphasize the value of integrating decisionmakers and communities in the research design, implementation, and production process in some forms of social science research in order to ensure the relevancy and usefulness of end products.

Some social science methods challenge conventional ways of studying communities in the context of resource management. When complex relations are anticipated, participatory and qualitative research methods are well suited to illuminate the components of complexity. On the surface, some aspects of participatory research appear to threaten the validity and reliability of data. For example, some critics say that involving nonresearchers in data collection and analysis threatens the objectivity of the research. Finding irony in this type of criticism, Arnold and Fernandez-Gimenez (Chapter 4) counter that the social transformation that may occur because people affected by forest management activities influence the process of understanding those effects is in itself a source of validity of the approach. Heightened appreciation among managers, scientists, and the public for the complexity of forest management problems needs to be met with an appreciation for and familiarity with a range of scientific approaches to address problems.

Paths to Future Connections

Sustainable forestry often is described as the mutual consideration of the social, economic, and ecological aspects of forest management. Understanding and strengthening connections between communities and forests is important because they are the means through which actions toward sustainable forest management will take place. In contrast, unstable, unequal, or poorly understood connections likely undermine efforts to achieve sustainable forest management. For example, NTFP harvesters have important cultural and traditional ties to forests in addition to economic ones; therefore, a better understanding of these ties may help create opportunities for expanding harvester roles in forest stewardship. Many former timber-based communities have the capacity for emerging forest restoration work on public forests and, perhaps equally important, have local knowledge that may increase the effectiveness of projects designed to restore forest health. Connections to amenity-rich areas are diverse, and thus understanding the recreational, aesthetic, or health reasons that bring people to forest communities will contribute to the development of collaborative approaches to forest community development. Perhaps in the future, a core mission of natural resource agencies will be to assist forest communities in building assets for community development, such as leadership, civic capacity, and physical infrastructure, given the increasingly acknowledged notion, illustrated in many chapters of this book, that forest health is dependent on community engagement. Forest connections that can be developed or strengthened and combined with existing, resilient ones, provide avenues for engagement of forest communities in forest management.

This book asks whether key components of forest management as they currently exist in the United States—the rules, regulations, procedures, personnel, culture, and capacity—are properly aligned with the goals of sustainable forestry. Each forest institution that connects a person to a forest under private, industrial, or public ownership is an opportunity to cultivate a link in a chain of events and processes necessary for achieving sustainable forest management. Institutions reflecting the reciprocal nature of forest–communities connections simultaneously may contribute to community development and forest development. The perpetual scarcity of time, money, and human capacity will continue to constrain forest managers and forest communities in reaching these goals. To succeed, forest managers, communities, and researchers may need to critically evaluate forest institutions. Do institutions reflect the range of values and connections that communities have to forests? Are they adaptive and adjustable without need for undue procedure and prescription? Do they encourage participation of community leaders and engage local skills and knowledge? Do they simultaneously contribute to community development as they contribute to forest development? If we attend to the factors that determine the quality, durability, and meaningfulness of connections between communities and forests, we can make progress toward achieving goals of sustainable forest management.

Note

1. Personal communication with Ron Saranich, Forest Service, Regional Office (R6), Portland, Oregon, August 16, 2007.

Index